AF752205

Modern Applications to Group Work

MODERN APPLICATIONS TO GROUP WORK

KEVIN A. FALL
JUSTIN E. LEVITOV
(EDITORS)

Nova Science Publishers, Inc.
Huntington, New York

Senior Editors: Susan Boriotti and Donna Dennis
Office Manager: Annette Hellinger
Graphics: Wanda Serrano
Information Editor: Tatiana Shohov
Book Production: Latoya Clay, Cathy DeGregory and Lynette Van Helden
Circulation: Anna Cruz, Ave Maria Gonzalez, Ron Hedges, Andre Tillman

Library of Congress Cataloging-in-Publication Data

Modern Applications to Group Work / Kevin A. Fall and Justin E. Levitov, eds.
p. cm.
Includes bibliographical references and index.
ISBN 1-56072-857-4
1. Group counseling. 2. Group psychotherapy. I. Fall, Kevin A. II. Levitov, Justin E.

BF637.C6 M57 2000
158'.35 -- dc21 00-049002

Copyright 2001 by Nova Science Publishers, Inc.
227 Main Street, Suite 100
Huntington, New York 11743
Tele. 631-424-6682 Fax 631-424-4666
e-mail: Novascience@earthlink.net
Web Site: http://www.nexusworld.com/nova

All rights reserved. No part of this book may be reproduced, stored in a retrieval system or transmitted in any form or by any means: electronic, electrostatic, magnetic, tape, mechanical photocopying, recording or otherwise without permission from the publishers.

The authors and publisher have taken care in preparation of this book, but make no expressed or implied warranty of any kind and assume no responsibility for any errors or omissions. No liability is assumed for incidental or consequential damages in connection with or arising out of information contained in this book.

This publication is designed to provide accurate and authoritative information with regard to the subject matter covered herein. It is sold with the clear understanding that the publisher is not engaged in rendering legal or any other professional services. If legal or any other expert assistance is required, the services of a competent person should be sought. FROM A DECLARATION OF PARTICIPANTS JOINTLY ADOPTED BY A COMMITTEE OF THE AMERICAN BAR ASSOCIATION AND A COMMITTEE OF PUBLISHERS.

Printed in the United States of America

DEDICATION

Nothing can replace support and guidance shown by caring parents and the understanding and encouragement that comes from loving spouses and children. We dedicate this book to each of our families.

To my parents, my wife, Kim and my sons, Dylan and Blake. (KAF)

To my parents, my wife, Kathi and my daughters, Talya and Jana. (JEL)

CONTENTS

Section II: Adults

Section III: Theory and Training

CONTRIBUTORS

Robert M. Awalt, Psy.D., University of California, San Francisco and Veterans Affairs Medical Center, San Francisco, CA

Scott Baymiller, M.D., Brown University Medical Center

Robert J. Chapman, Ph.D., Associate Faculty, Clinical/Counseling Psychology, Center Coordinator-Alcohol and Drug Program, La Salle University, Philadelphia, PA

Lori Crutchfield, Ph.D., Associate Professor and Coordinator, School Counseling Program, Department of Counseling and Educational Leadership, Columbus State University Columbus, GA

Charlotte G. Dixon, Rh.D., Assistant Professor, University of South Florida, Tampa, FL

Diane Estrada, Ph.D., University of Colorado, Denver, Clinical Coordinator of the Counseling and Family Therapy Center and Student Counseling Center

Kevin A. Fall, Ph.D., Chair and Assistant Professor, Department of Education and Counseling, Loyola University, New Orleans, LA

Michael Tlanusta Garrett, Ph.D., Assistant Professor, Department of Human Services, Western Carolina University, Cullowhee, NC

Miller A. "Rocky" Garrison, Ph.D., Clinical psychologist in private practice, Portland, OR. He has served on the Board of Directors of North American Society of Adlerian Psychology and Oregon Society of Individual Psychology.

Joshua M. Gross, Ph.D., Professional Affairs Officer, Florida Psychological Association, Diplomate in Group Psychology

Richard L. Hayes, Ed.D., Professor and Department Head, Counseling and Human Development Services, University of Georgia, Athens, GA

Linda Homeyer, Ph.D., Associate Professor, Southwest Texas State University, San Marcos, TX

Susan Huss, Ph.D., Counselor Education program, Bowling Green State University, Bowling Green, KY

Lynda Dunn Johnson, Psy.D., Licensed Clinical Professional Counselor, Acadia Hospital, Bangor, ME

Helen Kim, Ph.D., Assistant Professor, Counselor Education Program, University of Virginia, Charlottesville, VA

Susanne Lapp, Ph.D., Assistant Professor, Department of Teacher Education, Florida Atlantic University, Boca Raton, FL

Keri Lemmond, M.D., Brown University Medical Center

Justin E. Levitov, Ph.D., Professor, Department of Education and Counseling, Loyola University, New Orleans, LA,

Lois N. Maroney, M.A., Rehabilitation Counselor, Friends of the Deaf Service Center, Inc., Seminole, FL, Regional Director, Association of Late-Deafened Adults, Inc.

George McMahon, M.S., School counselor, Trinity Episcopal School, New Orleans, LA

Deborah A. Miscoll, Psy.D., Public Health Institute, Berkeley, CA

Bogusia Molina, Ph.D., Assistant Professor, Department of Counselor Education, Florida Atlantic University, Boca Raton, FL

Angela Rhone, Ph.D., Assistant Professor, Florida Atlantic University, Boca Raton, FL Department of Teacher Education

James N. Sells, Ph.D., Assistant professor, Counselor Education program, Northern Illinois University, DeKalb, IL

Judith Simon, Ph.D., Private Practice, Los Altos, CA

Daniel Sweeney, Ph.D., Assistant Professor, George Fox, University, Portland OR

Marly Sweeney, MSW, BCSW, Private practice, New Orleans, LA

Kathleen F. Quinn, Ed.D., Ed.S., School psychologist, proprietor of Ed/Psych Associates, a counseling and consulting firm, Cheyenne, WY.

Rendueles Villalba, M.D., Brown University Medical Center

PREFACE

The idea for this book occurred, as many of our ideas do, while teaching, in this case, a graduate group counseling course. As the students eagerly read the required text and the recommended readings, they invariably asked for additional material on the use of specific types of groups. While the literature has many overview texts on group dynamics, in fact I (KAF) have co-authored one, we agree with our students that though general information provides a bedrock of knowledge, a book that addresses innovative applications would be a helpful addition to the literature.

As we explored the available material that would fulfill this need, we were surprised by the dearth of information. One book, George Gazda's (1968) *Innovations in group psychotherapy* was the perfect model we were searching for, but the book, clearly a classic, was quite dated. Most of the books that addressed specific group approaches were homogeneous with respect to the issue explored. Unable to find an existing book, we decided to edit one ourselves.

This book represents a culmination of over two years of work. We sought to produce a book that would capture the essence and flavor of various group approaches, practitioners, and mental health backgrounds. To accomplish this goal of diversity, we encouraged the contributors to write in their own style, using their own language to describe their view of group work. What we may lose in consistency we hope to gain in exposing the reader to an honest view of the wide variety of ways group practitioners facilitate groups, view group process, and consider member dynamics. We encourage you to attend to the differences in language, approach, and style, because growth occurs when we expand our horizons beyond our current frame of reference.

The book has three main sections: Children and Adolescents; Adults; and Theory and Training. Each section offers specific and practical examples of modern approaches to group work. In Children and Adolescents, the chapter *Unity circle: A model of group work with children* Crutchfield and Garrett applies Native American traditions to group work with children. Chapter Two: *Groups for bereaved children* by Huss informs the reader about many important issues concerning grief in children whose parents have died. The chapter also offers ways to address these difficult issues in a group setting. Chapter Three: *Engaging adolescent males: A group approach* by Fall and McMahon explores common problems associated with involving teenage boys in most forms therapy and details a group protocol for attracting adolescent males to the group process. Chapter Four: *The self image of adolescent females: A group exploration* by Sweeney, using a developmental task model, addresses several key developmental concerns of adolescent females and explains how the concerns can be explored in group. Lastly, Chapter Five: *Group play therapy* by Homeyer and Sweeney details the innovative use of the play therapy approach within a group setting to counsel a challenging client population.

The second section deals with the adult population, each chapter focuses on a unique type of group population. Chapter Six: *Restoring relationships: Forgiveness and reconciliation in marital group therapy* by Sells explores a unique application of group therapy to address couple's concerns. Conducting groups with multiple couples produces some interesting group dynamics that are not experienced in traditional group formats. Chapter Seven: *Women's empowerment and wellness group: An integration of solution-focused and relational models* by Quinn and Dunn-Johnson demonstrates the efficacy of theoretical integration as applied to the group treatment of women. Chapter Eight: *The inclusion of persons who are late-deafened into counseling groups* by Maroney and Dixon provides a rehabilitation counseling perspective on the application of group work. Chapter Nine: Community building through dialogue groups by Molina, Estrada, Rhone, Lapp, and Kim uses the group modality to explore multicultural concerns. Chapter Ten: *Involving the addicted client in group counseling* by Chapman outlines innovative group techniques for the addicted client. Chapter Eleven: *Anger Management for Substance Abusing Patients* by Awalt and Miscoll takes the information contained in the previous chapter by Chapman and illustrates how anger exists as a vital relapse issue that can be remediated in groups.

The Theory and Training section provides several chapters that address the structure and underlying constructs of a group approach. This section, like the others, is not meant to be comprehensive, but is instead designed to give an example of some of the most important issues related to developing a theoretical approach to group as well as some essential and thought provoking training and professional concerns. Chapter Twelve: *Individual psychology and group psychotherapy: Toward an Adlerian group psychotherapy orientation* by Gross and Garrison demonstrate the efficacy of Adler's approach to groups. Although largely considered an individual form of therapy, the chapter reasserts the notion that Adler was one of the first true group theorists. Chapter Thirteen: *Making meaning in groups: A constructivist developmental approach* by Hayes applies a cutting edge theoretical approach to group dynamics. Chapter Fourteen: *Therapist uses of self in group psychotherapy* by Simon is compelling because it demonstrates how a practitioner can conceptualize a universal dynamic through a theoretical base. While most of the chapters focus on the treatment approach or its impact on the client population, this chapter addresses the internal process of the group leader. Chapter Fifteen: *Addressing "group sclerosis" through fishbowl supervision* by psychiatrists Villalba, Lemmond, and Baymiller outlines a supervision model that can be used in a variety of settings. The approach provides a unique method for processing and supervising groups by using groups as the means of supervision.

We believe and hope that you will agree that the book fulfills the niche of developing a resource that demonstrates the broad application of group work. We also hope that this book will inspire new and creative applications for group. It is worth mentioning at this point that a work of this size could not have been completed without help. We would like to offer words of gratitude to the department's administrative assistant, Whewellene Fischer. Her tireless enthusiasm and careful eye for detail was greatly appreciated on this project. Additionally, we would like to thank all of the contributing authors. Without their vision and faith in the group process, this book would have been impossible.

INTRODUCTION: STAGES IN THE HISTORY OF GROUP COUNSELING

Justin E. Levitov and Kevin A. Fall

Group counseling is a valuable treatment modality that has gone through many changes during its nearly 100 year history. While the evolution of group leadership practices, group theory, ethical issues, clinical issues and the creation of new applications of group treatment for various social and psychological problems have been well documented, these changes have not been organized into in a meaningful and practical series of stages. In this chapter we develop the idea that one meaningful way of categorizing different periods in the history of group counseling is through the use of the same stages that a counseling group passes through during the course of its life. This historical review of group counseling also serves as an introduction to the 15 applications of group methods contained in the chapters that follow.

Unfortunately, in recent years, the need for a cost efficient method of providing counseling services to increasing numbers of people has often been cited as a major reason for using group counseling. This is unfortunate because we believe economy is the least important reason for selecting group treatment. Jack A. Duncan in a 1994 interview stated, "I am not a strong advocate or supporter of the fact that you can reach more people in a shorter period of time by putting a whole bunch of people in a group. You do reach more people, but I'm not sure that reaching more people is the purpose of group work." (Forester-Miller, 1993, p. 171). Group counseling is valuable because it offers clients a counseling setting that is more powerful and potentially more useful than individual counseling. The fact that many people can be treated simultaneously is a desirable added benefit, but clearly not the major advantage of group counseling.

Group is a unique counseling setting, where curative forces are multiplied through the membership of the group, where sharing emotional and psychological struggles with others is transformative, and where members can benefit both directly and vicariously from their involvement in the group. "In sum, a group approach can help people meet almost any need" (Corey, 2000, p. 4) principally because: (1) new skills can be learned and practiced with others, (2) the group setting generalizes better to real life social settings, and (3) group members provide diverse and enriched sources of insight, feedback, and modeling (Corey, 2000).

Studying the history of group counseling offers counselors a collection of valuable insights about the complexities of the human experience, and it chronicles the evolution of various approaches that theorists and practitioners have developed to take advantage of the curative forces that exist within group settings. Each recognized approach or group counseling theory represents a perspective that is based upon a set of basic assumptions. This book contains 15 different applications of group: five for children and adolescents, six for adults, and four that deal with theory or group-leadership training. Each application shares common assumptions about the value of group counseling and the importance of group dynamics, yet each one contains unique assumptions about the specific population the particular group is designed to help or the specific theory explored. Because basic assumptions play such an important role in the development of various group theories as well as the way in which the groups are conducted, and because a number of good histories of group counseling already exist, we chose to focus on the evolution of assumptions that underlie approaches to group counseling across time as a theme for introducing these 15 modern applications to group counseling. In our minds, this is desirable because the study of assumptions is a very practical way to explore group counseling from a holistic perspective – one that includes theoretical, clinical, ethical, multicultural, social, and group leadership concerns.

Assumptions

Our assumptions – what we believe about ourselves and the world around us – for better or worse, determine how we interpret events, how we act, and how we interpret the actions and reactions of ourselves and others. There are many varied explanations of how human beings develop, maintain and revise assumptions – all are interesting and informative. Because mental health professionals seek to help people make changes, they need to not only understand the processes that form assumptions but they must also be able to influence these processes in effective, efficient and ethical ways. Thus, as counselors, we are called upon to explore our client's assumptions – with one very important caveat in place – we always do so through the filters of our own assumptive world. We must therefore continuously grapple with the realization that our own assumptions not only influence the way we see ourselves, and the world around us, but the way we view our clients, how we make sense of their struggles, and what we eventually do to help them. When counselors have a sound understanding of their own assumptive world, they are in a better position to understand and help others.

Hermeneutics, or the theory of interpretation, offers a useful explanation of how our assumptive world influences our behavior, how experiences can affect our assumptions, and how we can influence our assumptions.

Originally a term applied by biblical scholars to the interpretation of texts, the word hermeneutics has more recently been applied to the interpretation of human experience. Individuals interpret their experience based upon a set of personally held assumptions with the result that interpretation of any kind is not possible without a knowledge of individual personal assumptions. These assumptions are not static, but are transformed as individuals act on their interpretations and as their actions are reacted to by others. Assumptions change as the interpretation continues. A cycle of assumptions, interpretations, actions, reactions, and new assumptions is posited by hermeneutical theory (for a more detailed explanation see Cowan, 1995, pp. 5-8). Counselors may attempt to influence clients at one or more of the stages within the cycle. This philosophical perspective is inextricably linked to counseling because it supports a phenomenological understanding of human beings and because it respects how individuals produce meaning in their own lives and reflects the truism that the meaning people develop is unique. (Cavanagh & Levitov, in press).

This philosophical perspective supports the ideas that (1) each individual client is unique because he or she holds a unique set of assumptions; (2) each approach to counseling is formed from a set of assumptions that were held by the theorist(s) responsible for the development of the theory, and (3) change is possible by intervening at any point in the cycle (assumptions, interpretations, actions, and reactions). Hermeneutics can also be used to describe how even very basic assumptions can change over time. For example if a particular deeply entrenched behavior is consistently greeted with negative reactions the individual may seek to not only change the behavior, but once having made the behavioral change, also modify the assumptions upon which the behavior is based.

Hermeneutics explains how an individual's assumptions and interpretations determine how they behave and think in a way that is particularly useful to counselors. It explains why behavior is resistant to change (people are not just changing behavior they are tampering with fundamental assumptions about themselves and the world around them), and it simultaneously locates points where change is possible. According to this model, counselors aid clients by cooperating with them in a process that is designed to help them change assumptions, interpretations, or behavior. Obviously, different theoretical approaches stress change in one or another of these three areas though it does not matter at which point in the circle of interpretation one intervenes; all elements are ultimately affected. For example, if someone takes steps to change their behavior, changes in the way they are perceived by others will ultimately affect the person's assumptions and, in turn, their interpretations. While space does not permit a deeper discussion of hermeneutics, the basic principles that were covered will provide enough of a foundation to understand references to the theory of interpretation that are found in the remaining sections of this chapter.

According to Hansen, Warner and Smith (1980, p. 3): "Much of what individuals believe about themselves comes from feedback garnered from interactions with other people." While Hansen, Warner and Smith poignantly began the first chapter of their book on group counseling with this sentence by identifying the power of social interaction, it also can be interpreted as a position in support of the application of hermeneutics to human behavior. We stress this point because we believe that group counseling and individual counseling are approaches that are based on two different sets of assumptions about human behavior. Since most counseling theorists originate from an individual approach to counseling, their view of group counseling is both aided and biased by their assumptive worlds. They understand group counseling differently than those who began by celebrating the interpersonal or social influences that form individuals instead of the individual, intrapsychic influences. The history of group counseling illustrates not only how group counseling evolved, but also how the assumptions held by many theorists, for better or for worse, shaped and molded its form.

Stages in the History of Group Counseling

There are many good histories of the development of group counseling (see, for example, Berg, Landreth, & Fall, 1998, or Gladding, 1995) that meticulously document: (1) the contributions of different counseling and personality theorists over the past 100 years, (2) the influence of other social science research on the field of counseling during the same time period, and (3) the evolution of the counseling profession itself as evidenced by the formation of professional associations, codes of ethics and standards for treatment. The thoughtful and reflective review of such histories is a valuable exercise for counselors because it helps them understand how the field has evolved. In this chapter we have opted to limit our discussion to the historical evolution of *assumptions* about group counseling. Also, each stage in the history of group counseling contains many more people and important contributions than space permits us to list in this chapter. As we suggested in the opening of this chapter, we see a similarity in the stages that the field of group counseling has moved through over the past 100 years and the stages that all groups move through from their formation through their termination. We selected Tuckman and Jensen's (1977) five basic stages: *forming*, *storming*, *norming*, *performing*, and *adjourning* to identify stages in the history of the development of group counseling. Clear lines of demarcation between stages do not exist, and moving from one stage to a more advanced stage does not guarantee that the group will not return to an earlier stage during the course of its life. The same is also true when the stages are applied to the history of groups. In this application, the stages offer a meaningful way of categorizing different periods in the history of group counseling.

Forming

According to Napier and Gershenfeld, the forming stage "incorporates all the discomfort found in any new situation in which one's ego is involved in new relationships" (1985, p. 467). This period in the development of group counseling is characterized by the discomfort that all people experience when they find themselves in novel situations where clearly defined, agreed upon, ways of interacting have not been defined. A profession in its infancy and competing theories or explanations of human behavior together formed significant levels of discomfort as the field of group counseling began to take its first steps. Just as the most talkative member of the group tends to set the tone during the earliest part of the forming stage, one well-published theorist had the same effect on the field of group counseling. Freud's pioneering work defined a point of origin that profoundly influenced all who followed him. Though some theorists advanced Freud's ideas, while others disputed them, all were tied to his early assumptions about personality and human behavior. While Freud appreciated the idea of groups, his work emphasized attention to intrapsychic issues and the exploration of these forces in an exclusively individual setting – one where the therapist and the reclining client were shielded from eye contact and where interaction on the part of the therapist was sharply limited. It is not surprising that by the 1920's, psychiatry's exclusive focus on intrapsychic issues and related preference for individual psychotherapy affected most, if not all, of the helping professions (Broderick & Schrader, 1981). An emphasis on the roles that instincts, developmental stages, and early childhood experiences play on the formation of an individual's personality (id, ego and superego) dictates how adherents to this approach view the causes of psychopathology and the methods that can be used to appropriately treat it. Such an approach locates the problem within the client and relies upon the individual's relationship (real and "transferential") to the therapist as a means to resolve the symptoms.

While Freud's influence, coupled with a Western cultural propensity toward *individualism*, mitigated against theories that emphasized social factors, some researchers succeeded in developing social, group oriented perspectives on human behavior and counseling. In the period between 1910 and 1920, J. L. Moreno, writing under the name J. M. Levy, authored a philosophical work on group methods (Milman & Goldman, 1974). From this very early beginning, Moreno would later develop Psychodrama, arguably the single, exclusively group-oriented, approach to counseling.

Neo-Freudians, including Adler, Horney, Erikson, Fromm, and Sullivan, to a greater or lesser extent, opposed some of Freud's more significant conclusions and successfully widened the theoretical lense to include the influence of social and cultural forces on the formation and maintenance of an individual's personality (Monte, 1980). This interpersonally expanded view of the determinants of human behavior relocates the problems people face and the source of their symptoms within a social fabric thereby extending the focus of treatment to not just the client, but to the client's family, and other important interpersonal influences in the client's life. "People are born in groups, live in groups, work in groups, become ill in groups, and so why not treat them in groups?" (Moreno & Elefthery, 1975, p. 71). Thus group counseling becomes more meaningful and a more efficacious treatment alternative under a set of assumptions that honor the interpersonal needs of the individual, the interpersonal source of difficulties in a person's life, and the recognized need for and appreciation of the power of a group.

The assumptions that underlie Adler's work beautifully illustrate the difference between an intrapsychic approach and an approach that stresses the importance of the individual's social and familial relationships. Hansen, Warner and Smith (1980, p. 60) summarized Adler's approach to counseling with four basic assumptions: "(1) people are social beings, primarily and exclusively; (2) all behavior is goal directed and purposeful;

(3) there exists within all humans a unity of behavior; and (4) behavior is lawfully organized." It is therefore not surprising that Adler was leading groups and meeting with families as early as 1922 (Gladding, 1995).

At about the same time, J. L. Moreno was continuing to develop his unique approach to counseling and psychotherapy. According to Gladding (1995, p. 7) "Some of the ideas stemming from psychodrama, such as role playing, taking of 'stage center,' the emphasis on here-and-now interaction, the promotion of catharsis, the focus on empathy, and the encouragement of group members helping each other are incorporated in many forms of group experiences today." While these group oriented principles and strategies are now commonplace, they represented a major shift in the 1920's and they are based upon a very different set of assumptions from what Freud postulated as the basis of personality. Moreno's assumptive world led him to recognize how important it was for people to communicate completely and empathically with one another (Moreno called this concept "Tele") even though this was a radically different way of conceptualizing why people experienced psychological problems and what could be done to help them. His principles and methods influenced many of the theories that followed.

Self-help groups began in the late 1930's with the formation of Alcoholics Anonymous. Such groups are based on the notion that individuals who share similar difficulties can be helpful to one another through various forms of sharing within the context of a group setting – the need for a specially trained mental health professional to lead the group is markedly diminished. Members contribute their own unique understanding of themselves and test their assumptions through contact with other members of the group. The approach capitalizes on many of the principles found in Moreno's and Adler's work while it demonstrates that well-meaning people, who do not have specialized mental health training, can be helpful to others, in this case other people who share a similar psychological problem.

The forming stage of group counseling was also aided by social science research conducted during the 1940's and 50's. According to Gladding (1995, p. 9), Lewin's *field theory*, "emphasizes the interaction between individuals and their environments. For Lewin, the group is a whole that is different from and greater than the parts that compose it." Lewin applied principles from Gestalt psychology to group behavior and in doing so illustrated that the group was a force more powerful than the individuals within it. Lewin's work coupled with Wilfred Bion's research exploring group cohesiveness advanced the study of group dynamics and demonstrated practical applications of group principles in varied settings. This social science research contributed to expanded group counseling applications and encouraged the use of group dynamics in other non-counseling settings. For example, Japanese industry began using W. Edward Demming's "quality groups" during the 1950's.

Briefly, the forming period is marked by individuals who, despite prevailing notions of human behavior that opposed them, offered theories and ideas that honored the social forces that influence human beings. Bolstered by social science research and successful applications of counseling in group, family, and school settings, pioneering group theorists developed ideas and counseling strategies that continue to this day to influence practice. Assumptions that group counselors hold about the importance of the *here and now*, the critical use of *feedback* in groups and the power of *group dynamics* all date back to the norming stage of development.

Storming

The transition from norming to storming occurs when group members, "react to the demands of what has to be done, question authority, and feel increasingly comfortable to be themselves (Napier & Gershenfeld, 1985, p. 467). Evidence of all three patterns of behavior can be found in this period of the history of group counseling.

In the 1960's and into the 1970's group counseling became more widely accepted as both a modality for treatment and as a route to personal growth. At the beginning of the of the 1960's the field was just beginning to emerge from the forming stage. According to Gladding (1995), "Some of the most creative leaders in the history of group work came into prominence during this time." Rogers, for example, applied basic principles found in his Person-centered approach to counseling and developed "encounter groups." The basic assumption that guided both types of counseling can be found in Roger's (1980, p. 115) quote:

> Individuals have within themselves vast resources for self-understanding and for altering their self-concepts, basic attitudes, and self-directed behavior; these resources can be tapped if a definable climate of facilitative psychological attitudes can be provided.

The encounter group is setting where people can interact with one another in a way that allows them to access the resources they need to produce healthy change. In Roger's terms the basic encounter group enhanced the actualizing tendency in human beings. Rogers also recognized that social conditions were producing deep personal needs that the basic encounter group could meet. He wrote, that the basic encounter group is, "one of our most successful modern inventions for dealing with the feeling of unreality, of impersonality, and of distance and separation that exists in so many people in our culture" (Rogers, 1970, p. 116).

Other theorists also developed group versions of their individual theories. Group forms of Gestalt Therapy, Transactional Analysis, Rational Emotive Therapy, Behavioral and Reality Therapy became popular during the 60's and 70's. While various theories emphasized different aspects of human behavior (cognitive, affective, behavioral, and spiritual) all of them successfully addressed group dynamics. However, the storming stage did not fully form until the work of these theorists found its way out of the mental health arena and into the popular culture.

The dramatic increase in popularity of groups also brought with it serious concerns. A growing number of psychological casualties, individual participants who for a variety of reasons were adversely effected by their involvement in groups, caused counselors, clients and the general public to raise questions about the proper way to conduct groups, the level of training necessary to qualify a person to lead groups, and the need for specific ethical guidelines for providing counseling services in a group setting. Such questions were propelled by growing concerns that groups of all kinds were being offered to the general public by poorly trained or untrained "group leaders," without properly screening potential group members, and with little or no follow-up for participants. Inexperienced people believed that they could lead their own counseling groups by simply imitating the group methods and techniques that they had themselves observed earlier as participants in groups. Such inexperienced and untrained people predictably harmed others and did much to tarnish the reputation of a very important counseling modality. Sufficient levels of concern on the part of the public and the profession eventually produced stricter regulation of groups, a collection of professional standards governing the training of group facilitators and the delivery of group services, that continue to evolve.

The fabric of society was also experiencing a storming phase that coincided with storming in field of group counseling. Groups offered estranged people a setting where they could interact with others on affective and cognitive levels, explore their feelings, and define themselves at a very complicated time in American history. Intense personal reactions to the Viet Nam War and the Civil Rights Movement isolated individuals from their families and friends. Conflict between political, social and economic trends and personal values further contributed to a growing sense of estrangement. The hunger for groups grew out of this isolation. In various types of groups, such people found and interacted with others who shared similar feelings and experiences. Their rejection of prevailing social, political and economic realities became a connecting point within the context of the group.

Norming

The norming stage is marked by the development of rules and a more orderly approach to the tasks of counseling (Napier & Gershenfield, 1985). Several important developments are associated with the norming stage of development including governance changes within the mental health profession and advances in counseling theory as it is applied to groups. While we recognize the subjective basis of this conclusion, we believe that the field of group counseling is currently in the norming stage of development.

In 1973 the Association for Specialists In Group Work (ASGW) was formed as a Division of the American Personnel and Guidance Association, now called the American Counseling Association. In 1980 the ASGW adopted *Ethical Guidelines for Group Counselors* and in 1983 the same organization adopted the *Professional Standards for Training of Group Counselors*. Nine years later, the ASGW adopted a revised and expanded version of the *Ethical Guidelines for Group Counselors*. These changes demonstrate the counseling profession's commitment to ensuring that the recipients of mental health services are properly protected and they illustrate the profession's ability to govern the actions of its members. By defining who could conduct groups and by specifying safe and ethical standards for treatment, mental health counselors combated the serious abuses of group that existed in the 1960's and took steps to restore the integrity of this treatment modality.

Irvin D. Yalom's work provides group counselors with a serviceable description of why group counseling works and how it should be used. In the Preface to *The Theory and Practice of Group Psychotherapy* 4th Edition, Yalom writes "One of the most important underlying assumptions in this text is that interpersonal interaction is crucial in group psychotherapy" (1995, p. xiv). With the importance of interpersonal relationships as a backdrop Yalom's eleven therapeutic factors illustrate the various routes of such interaction. They include:

1. Instillation of hope
2. Universality
3. Imparting information
4. Altruism
5. The corrective recapitulation of the primary family group
6. Development of socializing techniques
7. Imitative behavior
8. Interpersonal learning
9. Group cohesiveness
10. Catharsis
11. Existential factors. (Yalom, 1995, p.1).

While a more in depth discussion of each factor is beyond the scope of this chapter, the factors considered individually and collectively illustrate the basic assumptions that underlie Yalom's approach to group counseling. Jack Duncan commenting about Yalom in Forester-Miller's (1993, p. 171) interview stated, "I think Yalom has really captured the essence of what group work is all about and, in my opinion, universality is extremely effective in group work. Once group members understand this concept and internalize it, other concepts seem to fall into place pretty readily." We agree with Duncan; Yalom's factors offer a valuable guide to any approach to group counseling because he has identified the interpersonal dynamics that drive every successful group counseling experience. While different theorists may tend to emphasize certain theoretical assumptions (e.g., cognitive, behavioral, etc.) all would benefit by a reliance on the group dynamic that emerges from the 11 therapeutic factors. It is extremely important for people to know that others experience similar problems (universality) and that interacting with others has curative effects. Yalom's therapeutic factors additionally stress the importance of group cohesiveness while honoring the value of interpersonal learning.

The creation of professional associations, as well as professional standards for treatment and training propelled the field from the storming to the norming stage. Yalom's identification of the therapeutic factors associated with group counseling and his research on group leadership, continue to guide practitioners toward a more organized understanding of how group interventions work and offer clinicians direction on the formation, leadership and termination of various types of groups. While improved ethical and clinical guidelines coupled with a greater understanding of group process bring the next stage of group development closer, the field remains in what might be termed the *late phase* of the norming stage.

Performing

According to Napier and Gershenfield the performing stage occurs "when people are able to focus their energies on the task ... the group is now free to develop working alternatives to the problems confronting it, and a climate of support tends to remain from the norming stage" (1985, p. 467). In order for the field of group counseling to move from the norming stage to the performing stage certain advances will be needed including: (1) the creation of a unified theory of group dynamics, (2) group oriented theories that are derived directly from group dynamics research, (3) improved methods for assessing the effectiveness of group counseling, (3) a clearer understanding of how group counseling influences culture, and (4) the identification of situations and conditions where group counseling would not be appropriate (e.g., meeting affiliation needs in a counseling group instead of family, social, or spiritual settings).

Social science research offers one route to obtaining needed theoretical and clinical information. According to Janice L. DeLucia-Waack, (1998, p. 235), "It is essential that we begin to understand both the content and process of how groups work. We must know what kinds of groups are effective with what kinds of populations." In other words, clinicians need to know with some degree of certainty what is effective and why it is effective. While there have been important discoveries relative to group counseling effectiveness, more needs to be done. For example, according to Horne and Rosenthal (1997, p. 235) research over the past 90 years suggests that, "Group treatment efficacy seems to have less to do with specific theoretical persuasion than finding an optimum combination of pregroup training, patient characteristics, therapeutic factors, group structure, and group stage development." However, one question persists: Why does the influence of theoretical persuasion pale in comparison to the influence of factors related to group dynamics. As answers to important group dynamics questions surface, counselors will be better able to develop more effective problem specific approaches to group counseling and they will move closer to a unified theory of group dynamics. Both of these two outcomes would signal the field's entry into the performing stage of the history of group counseling.

The need for a serviceable and universally applicable model of group counseling is not driven solely by mental health concerns, or individual desires for personal growth experiences. While many of the social, political, technological, and economic issues of the 1960's that spawned such widespread interest in groups as settings for resolving feelings of isolation and alienation have changed, high levels of alienation and isolation persist and by some accounts are actually increasing principally because new, even more evocative issues have replaced the old ones. As Kottler and Forester-Miller (1998, pp. 347-348) concluded, "Regardless of what the future holds for us in our individual group practices, it clear that as our culture becomes more diverse, as the world becomes more closely interconnected through technology, fostering a sense of community will be far too large a job for politicians; it will be up to group leaders of various backgrounds and training to meet the increasing needs in every community for shared visions, cohesive functioning, and mutual support." It seems that technology and community exist in opposition to each other even though human beings seem to have deeply felt, though conflicted needs, for both.

Adjourning

Adjourning is the period in the development of a group where the tasks are brought to conclusion and membership in the group ends. The members no longer share a connection to each other through their involvement in the group; thus the way that they relate to one another changes significantly but they take with them experiences, insights, and models for behavior that can be applied in existing and novel situations.

The question of whether group counseling should advance to this stage of development is an interesting one. If we look at group counseling as a curative tool, then one would hope that advances in various fields may one day make psychotherapy groups unnecessary. On the other hand, if group counseling is seen as a valuable route to personal growth and development, its usefulness may appropriately persist indefinitely. Given the plethora of modern advances that seem to have the effect of reducing the amount of direct human contact people experience, forms of group counseling may become even more necessary as a method for combating social isolation and the myriad problems caused by this form of alienation, in the years to come.

Conclusions

The history of group counseling offers interesting insights into the varied ways that group counseling researchers and clinicians have explained social and psychological problems at different points during the past 100 or so years. By applying the stages of group counseling to specific periods in the history of group counseling, prevailing assumptions associated with those periods were identified and discussed. This categorization process also helped to show how existing social conditions directly influence the assumptions that different theorists held and how their assumptions influenced the approaches they took to group counseling.

While we recognize the expanding need for research into the effectiveness of groups and studies that determine why group counseling works, we believe that clinicians and researchers also advance the practice of group counseling by developing new approaches to group counseling that respond to particular types of problems, populations, or group leadership training concerns. The fifteen chapters that follow contain a diverse collection of group applications. Collectively they illustrate that groups can be designed to be very situation or problem specific yet they also illustrate that group dynamics underlie all effective group counseling efforts.

REFERENCES

Berg, R. C., Landreth, G., & Fall, K. A. (1998). *Group counseling: Concepts and procedures* (3rd ed.). Philadelphia, PA: Accelerated Development.

Borderick, C. B. & Schrader, S. S. (1981). The history of professional marriage and family therapy. In A. S. Gurman & D. P. Kniskern (Eds.), *Handbook of family therapy.* New York: Brunner/ Mazel.

Cavanagh, M. E. & Levitov, J. E. (in press). The counseling experience 2nd Ed. Prospect Heights, IL: Waveland Press.

Cowan, M. A. (1995). *Sociocultural context of ministry.* New Orleans, LA: Institute for Ministry, Loyola University.

DeLucia- Waack, J. L. (1998). What is the relationship between therapeutic factors and group work effectiveness really? *Journal for Specialists in Group Work, 23,* 235-236.

Forester-Miller, H. (1998). History of the association for specialist in group work. ASGW – Timeline of significant events. *Journal for Specialists in Group Work, 23,* 335-337.

Forester-Miller, H. (1993). Jack A. Duncan: Twenty years with ASGW. *Journal for Specialists in Group Work, 18,* 164-173.

Gladding, S. T. (1995). *Group work: A counseling specialty.* 2nd Ed. Englewood Cliffs, New Jersey: Prentice Hall, Inc.

Hansen, J. C., Warner, R. W., & Smith, E. J. (1980). *Group counseling: Theory and process. 2nd Ed.* Chicago: Rand McNally College Publishing.

Horne, A. M., & Rosenthal, R. (1997). Research in group work: How did we get where we are? *Journal for Specialists in Group Work, 22,* 228-240.

Kottler, J. A., & Forester-Miller, H. (1998). Personal and social change in the lives of group leaders. *Journal for Specialists in Group Work, 23,* 338-349.

Milman, D. S. & Goldman, G. D. (1974). Introduction. In D. S. Millman & G. D. Goldman (Eds.), *Group process today.* Springfield, IL: Charles C. Thomas.

Monte, C. F. (1980). *Beneath the mask: An introduction to theories of personality.* New York: Holt, Rinehart & Winston.

Moreno, J. L. & Elefthery, D. G. (1975). Introduction to group psychodrama. In G. M. Gazda (Ed.), *Basic approaches to group psychotherapy and group counseling* (2nd ed. pp. 69 - 100). Springfield, IL: Charles C. Thomas.

Napier, R. W. & Gershenfield, M. K. (1985). *Groups: Theory and experience.* Boston: Houghton Mifflin Co.

Rogers, C. R. (1970). *Carl Rogers on encounter groups*. New York: Harper and Row, Publishers.

Rogers, C. R. (1980). *A way of being.* Boston: Houghton Mifflin.

Roller, B. (1986) Group therapy marks fiftieth birthday. *Small Group Behavior, 17,* 472-474.

Yalom, I. D. (1995). *The theory and practice of group psychotherapy* (4th ed.). New York: Basic Books.

SECTION I:
CHILDREN AND ADOLESCENTS

Chapter One

UNITY CIRCLE: A MODEL OF GROUP WORK WITH CHILDREN

Lori B. Crutchfield and Michael Tlanusta Garrett

In a conversation with his aging grandfather, a young Indian man asked, "Grandfather, what is the purpose of life?" After a long time in thought, the old man looked up and said, "Grandson, children are the purpose of life. We were once children and someone cared for us, and now it is our time to care." (Brendtro, Brokenleg, & Van Bockern, 1990, p. 45).

Mental health professionals who work with children seek out the most effective and helpful interventions and attempt to offer these services in the most efficient ways. This chapter presents a "new" group work approach to serving the growing needs of children within our rapidly changing society. This approach represents a synthesis of contemporary counseling techniques and traditional wisdom (Garrett & Crutchfield, 1997).

Working with children in groups is recognized as an efficient and appropriate means of promoting wellness by helping them become healthier people (American School Counselor Association [ASCA], 1993; Ashby, Gilchrist, & Miramontez, 1987; Blum & Jones, 1993; Duncan, Beck, & Granum, 1988; Garrett & Osborne, 1995; Thompson & Rudolph, 1992; Thompson, 1987). Groups have been recommended as being effective in dealing with a variety of topics, including divorce (Burke & Van de Streek, 1989; Omizo & Omizo, 1988; Yauman, 1991), social skills (Mehaffey & Sandburg, 1992; Shechtman & Bar-El, 1994), low academic achievement (O'Dell, Rak, Chermonte, & Hamlin, 1994; Schnedeker, 1991), family alcoholism and chemical dependency (O'Rourke, 1990; Rohde & Stockton, 1993), parental military deployment (Mitchum, 1991), and school adjustment (Shechtman, 1993). Participation in such groups usually offers children the curative experience of discovering that they are not alone in their fears and concerns (Muro & Kottman, 1995; Yalom, 1995).

Group work with children, however, need not always be problem-oriented. Groups targeting personal growth and development may be ideal in helping young people get beyond society's imposed limitations and pressures (Gazda, 1989; Omizo, Omizo, & D'Andrea, 1992). Whether the emphasis is on problem areas or personal development, many counseling groups tend to focus on one specific personal dimension (e.g., cognitive, affective, behavioral). School counselors recognize, however, that a comprehensive approach should integrate many personal dimensions of functioning (ASCA, 1993) in order to seek an interactive inner balance. If children are encouraged to act, think, or feel in only one way, they may have difficulties in personal integration and harmonious functioning. Herein is described a group unit for children which will provide a balance of techniques and exercises aimed at exploring and integrating many different personal dimensions into a unified whole.

This approach is based firmly within Native American culture and tradition. However, this is not an approach specifically targeting groups of Native American children. Rather, this holistic, developmental approach to group work is presented as a model which can be useful with all children, regardless of race or ethnicity. The approach is presented in such a way as to emphasize certain universal characteristics, such as the need to feel a sense of belonging--"I belong somewhere," mastery--"I am good at something," independence--"I possess certain strengths and qualities," and generosity--"I have something special to contribute" (Brendtro et al., 1990), while encouraging group leaders to modify techniques and exercises to meet the needs for the population and specific age group with which they are working. As professionals in a multicultural society, we must look to all of the vast resources of our many differing and rich cultural traditions for valuable insight and methods for developing human potentials and promoting individual and group wellness. The holistic nature of the model complements the underlying philosophy of our profession by emphasizing the importance of facilitating the natural human processes of growth and development concerning how one feels about oneself, how one develops one's potentials, how one experiences one's physical presence, and how one sees/defines oneself.

THE UNITY MODEL

In Native American tradition, the whole is always greater than the sum of its parts, demonstrated, for example, in the essential belief concerning harmonious coexistence with everything in our natural environment. Wellness, as viewed from a traditional Native perspective, focuses on "relation" of a person with self, with other people and other living beings, with the surrounding environment, and with the "spirit world" (i.e., the Creator). If any one of these relationships is disrupted or not honored in the proper way, "dis-ease" of mind, body, spirit, or environment may ensue. Thus, harmony and balance of these many relationships are key, given that every individual affects and is affected by these many relationships by which he or she exists.

Many Native nations symbolize this concept of interrelationship through the Circle of Life, Medicine Wheel, or Web of Life, illustrating the way in which all aspects of life are interconnected. Each relation has energy referred to as "Medicine" as well as the unifying force that is created through the combined whole of these many relations. Therefore, in Native American tradition, one's inner dimensions (e.g., mind, body, spirit, "heart") are not separate parts like those found in machines, but rather, connected dimensions that flow from one another, and whose interrelation or flow may be disrupted by dissonance or discord. The challenge then becomes that of balancing the interrelation of all parts in context--not as parts, but as a unified whole (Garrett, 1996).

Native American tradition looks upon all things as having an important and necessary purpose in the greater scheme. This view also accentuates the idea of relationship and the powerful influence exerted by our relations in the individual growth process. All things are connected, all things have a purpose, and all things are worthy of respect and reverence in the Circle of Life. The Circle serves as a reminder of the cyclical nature of our world illustrated by the daily rising and setting of the Sun.

The Medicine Wheel is a traditional symbol for many Native American nations, emphasizing the cyclical nature of the world and the self, both of which are composed of four basic dimensions represented by the Four Directions--east, south, west, and north. Each direction represents one aspect of life or the living being. All of the directions together are necessary for a harmonious and functional way of life. The cyclical nature of world and self are only possible given harmony and balance among the Four Directions--"heart" or spirit, natural environment, body, and mind--symbolizing the four points on a circle or the four cardinal directions of east, south, west, and north, respectively. The Medicine Wheel shows the relationship of each aspect of life to the greater whole; it also demonstrates the interrelation of all dimensions within the living being (Garrett, 1991; Garrett & Garrett, 1994; Garrett & Garrett, 1996). The Unity Model, based in the principles of the Medicine Wheel, represents this interrelationship through a unity of the Four Directions (east, south, west, and north) and harmonious integration of inner dimensions:

East:	**Self-esteem** represented by how one feels about oneself and one's ability to grow and change.
South:	**Self-determination** represented in one's ability to use one's volition (will) to explore and develop potentials.
West:	**Body-awareness** represented in how one experience one's physical presence.
North:	**Self-concept** represented in what one thinks about oneself and one's potentials (Four Worlds Development Project, 1989, p. 17).

By viewing these four dimensions at each of the four cardinal points on the Circle (Medicine Wheel), we begin to focus our attention on seeking a harmonious functioning among each one as an extension of all the others.

The group format presented in this chapter utilizes Native American principles and techniques to seek harmony and balance among the four dimensions of self-esteem, self-determination, body awareness, and self-concept. The counselor, as group leader, functions as facilitator, mentor, educator, and support-giver (Corey, 1990). The emphasis of change in the Unity approach is placed on the powerful influence of group dynamics and the group setting in general. The Circle becomes an important context in which development of the four dimensions occurs within the participants.

THE PROCESS

Practical Considerations and Pregroup Planning

As with the establishment of any type of counseling group, practical guidelines must be followed (Cohn & Osborne, 1992; Corey, 1990; Morganette, 1990). When running this group with children, it should have no more than 5-6 members, should be conducted as a closed group, and defined as developmentally-centered. Recognizing the developmental needs of various age groups, a group of younger children should meet once a week for approximately 45 minutes, for a total of nine sessions--1 orientation session, 7 working sessions, and 1 follow-up session. For adolescents, the time per session could be moved up to one hour. The setting should be private and allow face-to-face interaction in the form of a circle. It is also especially important to obtain parental permission for their child's participation in the group. There are a number of important steps involved in pregroup planning to ensure that the group will be a good experience for participants and that group goals will be met. First of all, a pregroup interview with prospective members serves the purpose of assessing the individual's appropriateness for the group, level of commitment to the group, and allows the opportunity for obtaining informed consent (Corey, 1990).

During the pregroup interview, it is important to talk to the child about his or her expectations of the group and interest in participating. A brief orientation to the model is also provided in this pregroup interview, as well as during the first group session. Second, in selecting members for the group, it is recommended that counselors include children who: a) are no more than 2 years apart in age; b) have approximately the same social, emotional, intellectual, and physical maturity; c) work well in other group situations; d) are of different racial, cultural, ethnic, and socioeconomic backgrounds; and e) are of both genders (Morganette, 1990). Children who may not function well and benefit from the group experience include those who: a) are homicidal or suicidal; b) habitually lie or steal; c) are known or suspected to be survivors of abuse; d) who are extremely aggressive either physically or verbally (Morganette, 1990). Once members have been selected, have been prepared for the group experience, and permission has been secured for their participation in the group, the process is ready to begin.

The Talking Circle

The Circle is a reminder of the interrelationship that we all share with one another and with our world. In a traditional Cherokee "Don-ne-la-we-ga" or "coming-together," the Talking Circle fulfills an important purpose by ensuring that the interaction is conducted in a respectful manner. The Talking Circle serves as a forum for the expression of thoughts and feelings in a context of complete acceptance by group members; thus the Talking Circle may be utilized as the general format for implementing and processing various activities/exercises in the Unity Circle. The "talking stick"--a wooden stick embellished with carvings, paintings, or items from nature--is used as an object representing truth and understanding as powerful agents of learning, change, and growth. Possession of the talking stick signifies permission to speak (Garrett & Osborne, 1995). Thus, use of the talking stick gives each group member a chance to speak and encourages each member to listen more carefully without need for competition. Traditionally in many Native American tribes, people used the talking stick during council meetings to discuss issues or concerns peacefully by "speaking from the heart," and by listening intently to what others had to say.

The leader might introduce the purpose of the talking stick by saying, "We will use the talking stick here in our Circle because each person's feelings are important, each person has something important to say, and the stick reminds us whose turn it is to speak while the rest of us listen with our hearts." Ideally, the leader might want to have the group take a nature walk together in order to "let a stick find them" so that the group could fashion their own talking stick in a way that everyone feels is best. In this exercise, each group member contributes something to the stick (e.g., feathers, stones, acorns, yarn, ribbons, etc.), building trust, cooperation, and a sense of accomplishment and closeness among group members.

To begin the Talking Circle, participants form a circle together, leaving an opening in the direction of the east which is where the Sun rises, bringing with it clarity, honesty, warmth, and light. A song or music may be used for relaxation and settling as the children enter the circle (the group leader may wish to select a song or music that seems appropriate for the group, or have the group develop their own song together). When everyone has gathered, initial greetings are made.

The leader begins by picking up the talking stick to share feelings or concerns with the group. When the leader has spoken, the talking stick is passed clockwise (left) to the next person. Participants may be told that when they possess the stick, they have the choice of either speaking or remaining silent. During the circle, questions may be asked, but only by permission of whomever is holding the stick. Anyone else must wait his or her turn. The leader should feel free to ask questions or make clarifying statements by permission of the one who holds the stick (this is made clear and agreed upon from the beginning). The stick holder may not be interrupted or criticized. Statements directed to other members should, if possible, be framed as "I-statements" using feelings or ideas. In this way, an atmosphere of patience and respect is created. In dealing with potential situations of resistant behavior that can occur as a natural part of the group process, participants are reminded of the group rules that were agreed upon at the beginning. Responsibility for enforcing the rules is given to the group, and immediacy is used to deal with the situation at hand. In such situations, it is sometimes helpful to revisit the meaning and power of the group and how important practicing respect can be in contributing to the safe atmosphere and overall success of the group.

When the talking stick has made its way around the Circle, the leader can begin the group activity for that particular session. Likewise, the leader may wish to utilize the format of the Talking Circle in order to process the activity with participants during or following implementation. When everything is finished, the Talking Circle can be brought to a close with a song, music, or some kind of group-initiated ritual, such as a chant or poem. It is understood that what was said in the Circle remains in the Circle to demonstrate respect for all members.

The Format

The following seven-session group format is suggested, in conjunction with the Talking Circle, for use with children as a way of facilitating self-exploration, learning, development, and choice with the four dimensions of self-esteem, self-determination, body awareness, and self-concept. These exercises can easily be adapted for use with young people of different age levels and needs, but it is encouraged that the given session sequence be maintained for continuity of growth and identity development. Each session can be opened with and ended with the Talking Circle as "open talking time" in order to process what has been experienced in the current or previous sessions.

Session One: A Coming-Together

Begin by picking up the talking stick in order to relate the necessary information about the group, and share with the group any information about yourself including background, feelings, or ideas. At this point, an explanation of the talking stick and the Talking Circle can be made. For example, "When we come together here in the Circle, this is *our* Circle, to talk about some things that are important to us, and to do some fun things that help us understand ourselves better, etc. ..." This is also a good time to point out any guidelines that the group process may have. For example: "Now there are three major rules: (1) We are going to make sure that everything we say here in the Circle stays here in the Circle; (2) No one gets hurt (We are here to help each other); and (3) We all take part in our own way." When the orientation has been sufficiently made, the Time-perspective activity outlined next can be used as a way of having participants introduce themselves through story.

Time-Perspective (Self-Esteem, Self-Determination, Body Awareness, Self-Concept)

This activity provides a useful way of having participants introduce themselves through a description of a positive experience, thereby revealing the children's' sense of where they are (present), where they have come from (past), and where they are going (future). All three of these components work together to give each child a better sense of where he or she stands in relation to self. This is a first step in deepening a child's awareness of who he or she is. As always, the talking stick is passed clockwise to the next person, who may either choose to speak or remain silent. To facilitate an atmosphere of respect, participation should be encouraged but not demanded.

The following questions should be used for facilitation of the activity. As these questions are presented and discussed, group leaders might emphasize what members can learn from one another as they listen and provide feedback.

1. Can you describe a good experience that you have had, either recently or some time in the past? (Past)
2. Did you learn anything from that experience? What was it? (Present).
3. How do you see yourself now after having gone through that experience?
4. What kinds of things are working for you right now? Against you?
5. What is something you are looking forward to? What are you working toward? (Future)

When all those who want to speak are finished, the students are asked to bring something from nature in with them next time, to be attached to the Talking Stick so that it will belong to the entire group. (This natural item should hold some importance for each student.) Then the Talking Circle can be brought to a close with whatever ritual is appropriate. Again, reaffirm the idea that what was said in the Circle remains in the Circle. Subsequent sessions will be ended in a similar manner.

Session Two: A Personal "Way"

The Gift (Body Awareness)

After opening the session with a brief go-around with the Talking Stick, the group is taken on a walk outside. On this walk, the children are asked to search for "something special." This might be a rock, a leaf, anything that seems very special to the child and stands out for him or her in some way. The children are asked to bring it back with them to the Circle and are reminded that when they find something to thank Mother Earth for offering them this special gift. This is also a good point at which to talk about the importance of environmental awareness. At the completion of the walk, the group returns inside for the following activity.

Medicine Bag (Self-Esteem, Self-Concept)

Using the talking stick, each child is asked to show and talk about the special gift he or she received from Mother Earth. The leader may want to ask each child in what ways he or she is similar to the special gift. The children can be told that these special gifts are a part of their "personal way of life" (this is what is referred to as "Medicine" among Native Americans). These special gifts define a part of who the children are by representing something special about the child and should be kept in a special place (e.g., a special box, or maybe a cloth, or leather bag) to remind them of their personal strengths and the things that are important to them.

As an example of a group member's reaction to the above activities, consider the case of Shameeka. A small, quiet fourth grade girl, Shameeka spoke often of her family, especially of her mother. On our outside walk, Shameeka was very attentive to the group discussion but verbally contributed little. She seemed very intent on looking closely at the ground, seeking out her special gift from Mother Earth. When the walk was almost completed, Shameeka still had not found her "gift." Just as the group prepared to go back inside, she saw a medium-sized, milky white, quartz rock along the path and quickly picked it up.

During the discussion which followed when the group returned to the Circle, Shameeka volunteered early and seemed quite pleased and excited. She proudly passed her rock around and told us that this rock showed us her goodness and strength, two things that her mother consistently stressed to her. She planned to keep the rock in a box on her dresser at home and to share this experience with her mother. These activities were successful in helping to strengthen a connection between Shameeka and her family, as well as helping her become more connected with some of the strengths within herself.

SESSION THREE: "A PERSONAL WAY" CONTINUED

The Harmony Circle (Self-Esteem, Self-Determination, Body Awareness)

The activity can be introduced by noting that last time the group members learned things about themselves through a walk outside and that this time they will be able to achieve the same thing by listening to and playing music. The session is then opened by asking each child to select an instrument to play. The leader will provide a set of "musical instruments" such as wood blocks, bells, sticks, and plastic bottles, from which the children can choose. The children are told to familiarize themselves with their instruments and all the sounds that they can create. Next, the leader can begin the "song" by establishing a rhythm, with a rattle, for instance. Together, the group improvises a song. Afterwards, the ideas of cooperation and harmony can be discussed using the song as an illustration of how every person has an important purpose to fulfill in creating and maintaining the song. This is usually a very high-energy, often very loud, session. Ending the session with soothing music and quiet talk will usually bring members back to an appropriate level of stimulation and reflection.

Renaming (Self-Esteem, Self-Determination, Self-Concept)

We often let names dictate our worth. Everyone is given a name at birth. However, the worth of something or someone can easily change in spite of the names associated with it; true worth is independent of words. The exercise begins by having the members observe the names of animals, objects, anything in their familiar environment including themselves. Participants are then encouraged to generate names that are better fitting for the things mentioned. Participants are also encouraged to give themselves a name that is best-fitting, possibly based on a distinguishing characteristic (e.g., a very tall person might choose the name "Tree") or some personal achievement or experience.

Time is devoted in the Circle to a discussion of certain attributes represented by the new names and each person's reasons for choosing a particular name. This is also a good time for discussing the effects of calling people certain names, good or bad, and the overall power of words. The new names may be used, as a reminder of personal strengths and uniqueness, for the remainder of the sessions if the children so choose.

Questions for Facilitation:

1. If you could rename yourself with a word (any word) that best fits you as a person, what would it be?
2. What personal quality or experience makes you choose that name?

The following case briefly illustrates the power of this Renaming activity. A friendly, talkative fourth grader, Jackie took her time in considering what her new name should be. She passed when the talking stick came to her the first time, but when it returned to her, she was ready. She told the group that her new name should be "Cherokee Rose," which is the name of a lovely, pink-tinged white flower on a clinging wild vine. She indicated that she chose this name because it was her favorite flower and because she thought that most people liked her, just as most people liked this flower. Another member, with Jackie's permission to speak, pointed out that she was also pretty, just like the flower.

Session Four: The Inner Circle

The Four Directions (Self-Esteem, Self-Determination, Body Awareness, Self-Concept)

In an open space, have the children visualize a large circle (it may be helpful to make the circle by putting tape on the floor and labeling each of the Four Directions--East, South, West, and North). Begin by having all of the children move to the center of this Circle. The first child starts by moving to the direction of the East and answering the question for that direction. Each child follows the first, answering the question for the direction of the East. At this point, the first child then moves on to the direction of the South and answers the question for that direction. All of the children proceed around the Circle starting in the East (belonging), moving to the South (mastery), then to the West (independence), and finally to the North (generosity) answering the respective questions for each direction as they go.

Questions for Facilitation:

East: Belonging characterized by a sense of caring and connection with certain special others:

"Who or what are you a part of, where do you belong?"

South: Mastery characterized by a recognition of one's abilities and a meaningful sense of achievement in life:

"What do you enjoy doing or do well?"

West: Independence characterized by a belief in oneself through the presence of self-awareness, self-reliance, and self-discipline:

"What are your strengths, what's important to you?"

North: Generosity characterized by an openness to different experiences through the recognition of a (potential) unique personal contribution:

"What do you have to offer/contribute to others?"

As each child moves completely around the Circle, he or she returns first to the East and then back to the center of the Circle once again. Time should be given for discussion of differences and similarities among participants with an emphasis on each child's own answers to the four questions and ways of working on anything that he or she wishes to change (i.e., improving a particular direction or area of his or her life).

Session Five: Purpose and Direction

Twelve Statements Exercise (Self-Concept)

Each child is asked to generate a list of twelve statements about him- or herself by completing the sentence, "I am ___________." It may be best to have the children write these down for reference. Then, the children are asked to rank the twelve statements from most to least important.

By thinking about the various social roles and self-perceptions that comprise his or her identity, each child has the opportunity to understand and define important roles and the ways in which these shape who he or she is. Discrepancies among roles can readily be identified. In this way, a better understanding of strengths and limitations can be achieved within the context of choice.

Questions for Facilitation:

1. Fill in the statement, "I am ___________." (12 times)
2. Which of these is most important to you as a person? For what reason?
3. Which of these is least important to you as a person? For what reason?
4. Which of these takes up the most of your time?
5. Which of these would you like to spend more time on?

Storytelling (Self-Esteem, Self-Determination)

Storytelling is an important way of relating valuable ideas while allowing children the freedom to draw their own conclusions about the things that affect their lives. As such, the use of stories (e.g., animal stories) is encouraged in the group process. The group leader may want to choose stories that demonstrate a particular theme or lesson that he or she wishes to emphasize in the group or ask each child to either tell or read aloud one of his or her favorite stories. Traditional Native American animal stories are often appropriate to use here, as well as European fairy tales such as The Three Little Pigs, etc.

Session Six: Personal Space

Personal Distance (Body Awareness)

This is an exercise in body awareness, limit setting, and interpersonal respect. We all have our own preferences for personal distance, that is, the distance between ourselves and others which allows us to remain comfortable. We have all experienced the discomfort of having our personal space violated, for example, when someone bumps into us or stands too close to us.

The Personal Distance exercise demonstrates awareness of personal limits and respect for others. The leader asks for two volunteers. One person is asked to stand with his or her arms outstretched on both sides and instructed to say "Stop" when his or her personal space is beginning to be violated. The other person is asked to walk slowly toward the stationary person and stop when told to do so. The level of discomfort can be discussed using the stationary person's reactions to being in this awkward position. The moving person may also feel awkward by getting closer than his or her personal distance would normally permit.

Afterwards, the leader can repeat the process by assuming the role of the moving person and walking slowly toward the stationary person until being told to stop. Respect for others can be discussed with the group. The two volunteers can then switch positions and repeat the process to determine the other's personal distance. Everyone who wants to participate in the exercise should be allowed, each in turn. Comparisons can be made between the varying personal distances of group members, always stressing the importance of asking permission and not making too many assumptions about others. Often, during this discussion, children will note that they probably would have "said 'stop' earlier" if the person approaching them had been a stranger. This fact opens up a related discussion about relationships and safety.

The Special Path (Body Awareness)

The children are asked to find a spot in the room that feels good to them and sit or lie in a comfortable position. They are asked to take several deep breaths and relax. It may be helpful to play some soft, soothing music. The following can be read aloud:

"Close your eyes. Get comfortable. Picture where you live, and picture yourself there. Now, imagine yourself leaving the area where you live. Take all the feelings of stress and tension out of your body and leave them in a bag by the door. Imagine yourself going across a valley, moving closer and closer to a mountain range. Breathe in the fresh air and the smell of grass as you go. Feel the warmth of the sun on your skin ...

Imagine yourself walking in the mountains now. You are going up a winding road. Off to one side, you can see the misty mountains. Find a place on the winding road to stop. Listen to the rustling of leaves. Smell the cool mountain air. Feel the calmness all around you. Let yourself relax ...

Find a path leading away from the road, deeper into the forest. Start walking up the path. Take your time. Look at the animals as you go. Look at the trees ...

Listen to the birds singing. Feel the gentle breeze on your face. Nearby, you can hear the trickling waters of a stream. Keep walking up the path until you come to the stream ...

When you have come to the stream, find a comfortable place to stop. Listen to the water trickling slowly. Bend down and dip your hands in the cool water. Rub some of the water on your face and on your neck. Feel its coolness on your skin ...

Here, at this place, take some time to get rid of any stress and tension that is left in you. Take the stress and tension out and put it all down by edge of the stream. Listen to the water for a few moments before moving on ...

Now, continue walking up the path until you come to the top of the mountain. Walk through the deep woods, watching the sunlight flickering through the leaves as you move. When you come to the top, look out over the mountain at everything stretching out before you. What do you see? ...

Find an inviting, comfortable place and go there. Be aware of your surroundings. Be aware of the calm and the feeling of this place. Touch things if you want to. This is your special place. What is your special place like? Be aware of all that you see, all that you smell, all that you hear, all that you feel. Get settled and let yourself relax ...

You are now feeling completely relaxed. You are safe here. You are very relaxed ...

Look around at your special place once more. Remember that this is your special place, and you can come here anytime you want.

Slowly, come back to the room now. Keep the feeling of calm inside of you. Bring it with you. Slowly come back, and tell yourself that this is something you have created, and you can go to your special place whenever you want to feel calm. When you have come back, open your eyes."

At the conclusion of this relaxation exercise, group members should be allowed to describe their special places of calm, and discuss what they saw on their journeys. Invariably, children of all ages become very involved in this activity. They eagerly discuss the sights they saw and sounds they heard on the journey. It is not uncommon for some group members to become so relaxed during the exercise that they fall asleep; these children should be awakened gently and encouraged to join in the discussion afterwards. Group members usually enjoy this activity so much that they ask to go through the experience once more before the group meetings end.

Session Seven: Friendship and Reflection

The final session of Full Circle should be devoted to giving the children an opportunity to reflect upon and discuss what they have experienced in the group and learned about themselves. When this is done, it is time to have some fun and reaffirm the sense of support and connection in the group by closing with a Friendship Circle.

The Friendship Circle (Dance) (Self-Esteem, Body Awareness)

This is especially fun and effective with younger children. It evokes the image of children holding hands, laughing and going in circles. Its purpose is to reinforce friendship in the Circle. The tempo of the music can determine how quickly the Circle goes around while participants dance slowly together, holding hands. The Circle can go in either direction, but at a certain point, the leader or "Head person" drops hands with one person in the Circle and leads the group around like a snake while participants continue to dance. At some point, the Head person circles around and around until the Circle is bunched up tightly into the Friendship Circle. This can be repeated many times, as a way of reinforcing the connection established within the group. It ends the group process on an upbeat note, reminding the children in the group that they have become friends who can depend on each other.

Conclusion

The number and magnitude of contemporary issues facing children creates an added stress on an already difficult developmental process (Garbarino, 1994). Counselors working with children in a variety of settings are often forced into a role of remediation which can be both frustrating and tedious. Working with children in groups has long been recognized as an effective means of creating a therapeutic environment and promoting wellness, in addition to making use of opportunities for psychoeducational activities designed to improve basic skills and knowledge. By emphasizing the interaction of personal, social, and environmental aspects of development, the Unity Circle approach to group work offers a comprehensive approach to the integration of self-esteem, self-determination, body awareness, and self-concept.

The Unity Circle has been applied extensively with positive results by the authors and a number of other professional counselors working with children and adolescents in community settings and in schools. In addition, the Unity model has been presented in conference workshops and various presentations to counselors and educators across the country with the feedback received being quite favorable and enthusiastic.

A number of studies have indicated the importance of focusing individually on the dimensions of self-esteem, self-determination, body awareness, or self-concept without necessarily suggesting a unified approach which emphasizes integration of all these dimensions as equally important aspects of the same person. Although there is no direct empirical evidence supporting the effectiveness of such an approach, the authors are currently conducting studies in the public schools to examine the effectiveness of the Unity Model as a developmental approach to group counseling with children.

There are many other exercises that have been created for use within this Unity Model. Those activities presented in this chapter were chosen as a representative sample. Please see Garrett and Crutchfield (1997) for a more detailed description of additional group activities.

In summary, a Unity approach to group work with children promotes wellness by focusing on growth and learning in the context of the support, guidance, and creativity offered by other participants. Through participation in the Unity Circle, children are given the opportunity to acquire knowledge, awareness, and skills that come with experience and the continued development of each of the four dimensions: self-esteem, self-determination, body awareness, and self-concept. Children are given the opportunity through a unity of body, mind, heart, and natural environment to know who they are, where they stand in relation to the world around them, where they are, where they come from, and where they are going. Together, children can move "full circle" through a life filled with possibility, clarity, purpose, and the continuing process of self-discovery.

REFERENCES

American School Counselor Association (1993). *The school counselor and group counseling* (ASCA position statement). Alexandria, VA: Author.

Ashby, M. R., Gilchrist, L. D., & Miramontez, A. (1987). Group treatment for sexually abused American Indian adolescents. *Social Work with Groups, 10*(4), 21-32.

Blum, D. J. & Jones, L. A. (1993). Academic growth group and mentoring program for potential dropouts. *The School Counselor, 40*, 207-217.

Brendtro, L. K., Brokenleg, M., & Van Bockern, S. (1990). *Reclaiming youth at risk: Our hope for the future*. Bloomington, IN: National Education Service.

Burke, D. M., & Van de Streek, L. (1989). Children of divorce: An application of Hammond's group counseling for children. *Elementary School Guidance & Counseling, 24*, 112-118.

Cohn, B., & Osborne, W. L. (1992). *Group counseling: A practical self-concept approach for the helping professional*. Chappaqua, NY: L. S. Communications.

Corey, G. (1990). *Theory and practice of group counseling* (3rd ed.). Pacific Grove, CA: Brooks/Cole.

Duncan, K., Beck, D. L., & Granum, R. A. (1988). Project explore: An activity-based counseling group. *The School Counselor, 35*, 215-219.

Four Worlds Development Project (1989). *The sacred tree: Reflections on Native American spirituality*. Wilmot, WI: Lotus Light.

Garbarino, J. (1994, November). *Growing up in a socially toxic environment*. Plenary address at the annual meeting of the National Council on Family Relations, Minneapolis, MN.

Garrett, J. T. (1991). Where the medicine wheel meets medical science. In S. McFadden (Ed.), *Profiles in wisdom: Native elders speak about the earth* (pp. 167-179). Santa Fe, NM: Bear.

Garrett, J. T., & Garrett, M. T. (1994). The path of good medicine: Understanding and counseling Native Americans. *Journal of Multicultural Counseling and Development, 23*, 145-156.

Garrett, J. T., & Garrett, M. T. (1996). *Medicine of the Cherokee: The way of right relationship*. Santa Fe, NM: Bear.

Garrett, M. T. (1996). Reflection by the riverside: The traditional education of Native American children. *Journal of Humanistic Education and Development, 35*, 12-28.

Garrett, M. T., & Crutchfield, L. B. (1997). Moving full circle: A Unity Model of group work with children. *Journal for Specialists in Group Work, 22,* 175-188.

Garrett, M. T., & Osborne, W. L. (1995). The Native American sweat lodge as metaphor for group work. *Journal for Specialists in Group Work, 20*, 33-39.

Gazda, G. (1989). *Group counseling: A developmental approach* (4th ed.). Boston, MA: Allyn & Bacon.

Mehaffey, J. I. & Sandburg, S. K. (1992). Conducting social skills training groups with elementary school children. *The School Counselor, 40*, 61-67.

Mitchum, N. T. (1991). Group counseling for Navy children. *The School Counselor, 38*, 372-377.

Morganette, R. (1990). *Skills for living: Group counseling activities for young adolescents*. Champagne, IL: Research Press.

Muro, J., & Kottman, T. (1995). *Guidance and counseling in the elementary and middle schools: A practical approach*. Madison, WI: Brown & Benchmark.

O'Dell, F. L., Rak, C. F., Chermonte, J. P., & Hamlin, A. (1994). The boost club: A program for at-risk third- and fourth-grade students. *Journal for Specialists in Group Work, 19*, 227-231.

Omizo, M. M., & Omizo, S. A. (1988). The effects of participation in group counseling sessions on self-esteem and locus of control among adolescents from divorced families. *The School Counselor, 36*, 54-60.

Omizo, M. M., Omizo, S. A., D'Andrea, M. J. (1992). Promoting wellness among elementary school children. *Journal of Counseling and Development, 71*, 194-202.

O'Rourke, K. (1990). Recapturing hope: Elementary school support groups for children of alcoholics. *Elementary School Guidance & Counseling, 25*, 107-115.

Rohde, R. I., & Stockton, R. (1993). The group as an effective medium for working with children of chemically dependent families. *Journal for Specialists in Group Work, 18*, 182-188.

Schnedeker, J. A. (1991). Multistage group guidance and counseling for low-achieving students. *The School Counselor, 39*, 47-51.

Shechtman, Z. (1993). School adjustment and small group therapy: An Israeli study. *Journal of Counseling & Development, 72*, 77-81.

Shechtman, Z., & Bar-El, O. (1994). Group guidance and group counseling to foster social acceptability and self-esteem in adolescence. *Journal for Specialists in Group Work, 19*, 188-196.

Thompson, C. L., & Rudolph, L. B. (1992). *Counseling children*. Pacific Grove, CA: Brooks/Cole.

Thompson, E. C. III (1987). "Yagottawanna" group: Improving student self-perceptions through motivational teaching of study skills. *The School Counselor, 35*, 134-142.

Yalom, I. D. (1995). *The theory and practice of group psychotherapy* (3rd ed.). New York: Basic Books.

Yauman, B. E. (1991). School-based group counseling for children of divorce: A review of the literature. *Elementary School Guidance & Counseling, 26,* 130-138.

Chapter Two

GROUPS FOR BEREAVED CHILDREN

Susan Norris Huss

This chapter includes a brief description of the historical beliefs related to children and their ability to grieve. Also included is a discussion of the development of the current thinking about bereavement and young people and potential mental health issues related to unresolved childhood grief. This chapter explores the rationale for using the group model of intervention and offers a ten session outline for doing group work with bereaved children. For the purposes of this chapter, childhood is identified as the portion of the life span from birth to puberty (Corr, 1996). Adolescence brings its own uniqueness to the grieving process and is not addressed here.

HISTORICAL PERSPECTIVE

"Grief does not focus on one's ability to 'understand' but instead upon one's ability to 'feel.' Therefore, any child mature enough to love is mature enough to grieve" (Wolfert, 1983, p.20). This has not always been the accepted belief. Historically, mental health professionals erroneously espoused that children were incapable of grieving (Miller, 1971). While it is now generally agreed that children lack the maturity, emotional experience, autonomy, or previous experience with death to enable them to cope with the death in the same manner as adults, it is believed children do grieve.

Historical beliefs based on Freudian tenets stated that children were not capable of grieving because the ego of a child is so undeveloped that comprehension of loss and the ability to grieve were not present. Nagy (1948) challenged this belief in her landmark study that showed that children do have the ability to understand death and to grieve. Support for the belief that children do understand death and are able to grieve came from the work of Piaget and Erikson. These developmental psychologists focused on cognitive, social, and emotional development. Nagy (1948), Erikson (1968), and Piaget (1970) all believed that children develop in stages that are influenced by how an individual interprets and interacts with the world. All three believed that children are able to grieve and understand death in a manner consistent with their particular stage of development.

In 1961 Bowlby increased this new understanding of children's bereavement when he looked at the issues of attachment, separation, and loss. Bowlby's later work (1980) cited numerous studies contending that children grieve as painfully as adults. Current beliefs regarding children's response to death suggest that children are not only capable of perceiving and understanding death but are also capable of grieving (Pennells & Smith, 1995). The depth of this understanding, the intensity, and the characteristics of this grieving are dependent upon the cognitive level of development of the children and the amount of his or her previous experience with death.

Grief Characteristics

In working with children in bereavement, it is important to have a basic understanding of the grieving process. While this grief process is present in all losses, it will be described here in terms of grieving the loss of a close relative (i.e., mother, father, and sibling). There are general characteristics of the process that should be understood by anyone who works with bereavement. Unique issues related specifically to bereavement in children also must be addressed.

The stages of the grieving process established by the landmark work of Kubler-Ross (1969) have been rewritten in many forms, but the basic five responses identified can be found in nearly all models. Denial, the initial response, is a necessary defense that functions as a buffer to protect the person from an emotionally shocking reality. This is especially true for children who are not experienced in dealing with intense emotional experiences. They often go on playing because they don't know what else to do and adults often interpret this as a lack of caring or ability to grieve. In fact, it is a normal, age appropriate defense against the pain they are experiencing.

Once the death is acknowledged and the denial no longer provides protection, intense anger becomes the response. This assists in the externalization of the feelings that were too painful to experience directly but require release. This intense anger can be manifested in play as well as in relationships with the other people they love.

Expression and resolution of the anger leads to a period of bargaining. During this time there is a great deal of self-blame, guilt, and the game "if only" occurs. Bargaining manifests in children and young people who are not included in the reality of the death and/or who are being protected by well-meaning adults. The unknown is almost always worse than the known. Children are particularly vulnerable because they often create totally erroneous self-blame and guilt. For example, if a child has had an argument with a parent over homework and then the parent dies, the child may erroneously believe that "if only" I had done my homework, my dad would not have died.

When all efforts at bargaining have failed, a sense of resignation and discouragement often follows. Depression may be a part of this stage with feelings of victimization and sadness as the reality of the situation is accepted. This may be manifested as boredom, fatigue, difficulty concentrating, and aggression (Huss, 1997). For example, one child became totally disinterested in soccer, which had been his entire life before the death. Because of the difficulty in concentrating, academic work often suffers during this time.

Once the unfinished business of depression is resolved, the last stage, the acceptance of the death, occurs. Acceptance of the death brings the ability to talk about the death in a realistic manner and to comfortably talk about the person who died.

Kubler-Ross (1969) cautions that rarely are the stages of grieving passed through in a smooth, linear fashion. The process of resolution manifests itself as a back and forth movement between stages until acceptance of reality occurs. The process is further complicated by levels of cognitive, social, and emotional development that are unique to childhood. Worden (1996) believes that there are four tasks of mourning for children who have experienced the death of someone close to them. Although they are similar to those of Kubler-Ross (1969), he believes because children are unique, these tasks are more appropriate for consideration when working with bereaved children. The four tasks are to (1) accept the reality of the loss; (2) experience the pain or emotional aspects of the loss; (3) adjust to an environment in which the deceased is missing; and (4) relocate the dead person within one's life and find a way to memorialize the person.

Therefore, as children develop cognitively and emotionally during childhood and adolescence, the characteristics of the grieving process change. Although the stages of grief are the same for adults and children, each person grieves in a uniquely personal way. Though there are some identifiable characteristics of bereavement in children that are essential for a counselor to be aware of when working with bereaved children, whether individually, in families, or in groups, issues unique to each individual child need to be taken into consideration.

Unique Characteristics of Childhood Grief

Although children experience grief in basically the same manner as adults, there are some unique characteristics of childhood grief. If mental health professionals are going to counsel effectively with bereaved children, regardless of the setting, they should be aware of these characteristics. These uniquenesses emerge from children's level of cognitive development (depending on the age), lack of autonomy, limited experience with death itself, and inexperience in knowing they can survive without the more or less continuous presence of a parent attachment figure (Hawener & Phillips, 1975; Mishne, 1992). Webb (1993) identified the following considerations as differentiating the grief of children from adult grief:

1. Children's immature cognitive development interferes with understanding about the irreversibility, universality, and inevitability of death.
2. Children's limited capacity to tolerate emotional pain.
3. Children's limited ability to verbalize their feelings.
4. Children's sensitivity about 'being different' from their peers (p. 14).

The cyclical nature of the occurrence of grief is another distinct characteristic of childhood bereavement (McGlauflin, 1992). McGlauflin characterizes childhood bereavement as repetitive and cyclical in nature. It is repetitive because children often have to ask the same questions again and again before they clearly comprehend. As the level of cognitive development changes, there is renewed grieving at each level of cognitive understanding of the concept of death. A friend of mine died when her children were ages 2 and 3. Their father has observed over the years that as the children reached a different cognitive and/or emotional level, he needed to once again answer questions he had answered many times before. Examples of questions that are repeated include: "What did she die from?" "Why couldn't the doctors fix her?" "Tell me about the funeral.", and "Where is she now?"

Pennells and Smith (1995) describe the cycle as the resurfacing of grief in later years. As a child develops through the stages of cognitive and social/emotional development identified by Piaget and Erikson, the level of understanding changes and, as a result, questions need repeated answers. Adult grieving usually occurs within a period of time (maybe a year or two) immediately following the death with only some reoccurrence on anniversaries and special occasions. Childhood bereavement resurfaces in cycles as the child develops cognitively and emotionally. This maturational grieving (Johnson & Rosenblatt, 1981) frequently appears quite some time after the loss. It occurs often at milestones (i.e., graduation) and anniversaries (i.e., birthday), but just as often it occurs when the child's ability to understand reaches a new level.

Potential consequences of unresolved childhood grief, including the loss of self-esteem, behavior problems, depression, and other mental health illnesses, are found in the literature (Berlinksy & Biller, 1982; Furman, 1974; LeShane, 1976; Siegel, 1985; Worden, 1996). Fox (1985) suggests that there are "red flags" to be alert to when a child/adolescent has experienced the death of someone close to them. Taking into consideration the developmental and cyclical nature of childhood bereavement, these "red flags" can occur anytime in life. They include suicidal hints, psychosomatic problems, difficulties in schoolwork, nightmares or sleep disorders, changes in eating patterns, and temporary regressions.

Grollman (1995) strongly suggests the need to distinguish between normal and abnormal grief as well as what is simply developmentally appropriate behavior. Grollman indicates the need to look at the intensity of the symptoms of grief by watching for *continued* denial of reality, *prolonged* bodily distress, *persistent* panic, *extended* guilt, *unceasing* suicidal ideation, and *unceasing* hostile reaction to the deceased and others. The Diagnostic and Statistical Manual of Mental Disorders (DSM-IV) (1994) allows for depression to be attributed to bereavement unless it is persistent for more than two months or includes marked functional impairment. Needless to say, it is a very difficult task to determine if it is normal or abnormal grieving within the normal turmoil of childhood development.

GROUP INTERVENTION FOR BEREAVED CHILDREN

With the understanding that children can and do grieve and that unresolved grief could cause mental health difficulties later in life, developing effective interventions to assist children in the grieving process becomes very important. The literature offers various modalities for helping bereaved children including individual counseling, family counseling, and group counseling or support groups (Jacobs, Harvill, & Masson, 1994; Klass & Shinners, 1983; Pennells & Smith, 1995; Tonkins & Laubert, 1996; Webb, 1993; Yalom, 1995; Zimpfer, 1991).

The use of a group intervention for bereaved children is recommended as effective because it relieves the child's sense of isolation as it provides an opportunity for sharing common experiences with others. This sense of commonality (Jacobs, Harvill & Masson, 1994) and universality (Yalom, 1995) is therapeutic and provides a place where it is safe to practice skills such as expressing feelings as well as simply talking about the person who died.

Yalom (1995) describes eleven curative factors or helpful elements of group psychotherapy. Several relate specifically to groups for bereaved children. Yalom refers to groups providing an instillation of hope from the support of individual members of the group's experience as they learn that other members and the group's leader are willing to help them. This is demonstrated by the words of a 12-year-old boy on an end of the experience evaluation when he said, "... it makes you feel better and makes you go through your life easier."

The concept of universality, as suggested by Yalom, is especially helpful in bereavement groups as members learn that other people also experience some of the same conflicts and feelings as they do. After a bereavement group experience, a participant said she learned "that it is OK to talk about death because 21 other students in our school have had a parent die and they have the same feelings I felt when my parent died."

Another element of successful group intervention that is particularly apparent in bereavement groups is the catharsis that occurs as a member expresses his or her feeling within the safety of the group. Based on the work of Goldman (1996), Naierman (1997) suggests that grieving children need to acknowledge a parent or sibling who died by using his or her name or by sharing a memory; to tell their story over and over again, and to use tools such as drawing, writing, role-playing, and re-enactment to safely project feelings and thoughts about their loss. Fred, whose mother died when he was five, indicated that group was the only place he could talk about his mom without everyone getting upset. He said he enjoyed just being able to say, "my mom." With this understanding of the needs of bereaved children and the benefits of group intervention, one can begin planning the group experience for those children.

While planning my first bereavement group, I read and worried and fretted. I over planned and became overly sensitive to what I understood to be the delicacy of the situation. While I was metaphorically ready for the students to get their big toe wet, the children expressed a desire to dive right in. They were so anxious to talk about their own experience that I really need not have worried about how much or how deep to go the first session. Tom, whose father was killed in a gunshot accident, told his doctor that when he started talking in group, it felt like a dam had broken loose in his chest. This is not to say that one should not plan comprehensively, rather that many bereaved children are waiting for someone to open the door for them to begin to talk and process the feelings associated with the death.

When planning intervention groups for bereaved children, it is necessary to consider all the usual issues involved in planning groups (i.e., size, makeup, length, place, and recruitment). However, screening members is most important because each individual must be assessed to determine if a group approach is appropriate for them. It is imperative for group leaders to remain mindful of all the unique issues discussed in the first part of this chapter. This section of the chapter identifies the issues that should be addressed when forming a group for bereaved children, taking into consideration the unique circumstances involved with bereavement.

Normal or Distorted Grief

The first criterion is whether the grief being experienced by the child is normal or distorted grief. Normal grief is that which is expected after the loss of close loved one as identified in the literature (i.e., sadness, crying, lethargy, sleep difficulties) (Grollman, 1995; Webb, 1993). Distorted grief is prolonged or more intense than would be expected such as prolonged difficulties with nightmares or eating habits (Grollman, 1995; Webb, 1993). Distorted grief in children is sometimes called "unresolved grief" (Rando, 1991). Webb (1993) suggests that unsolved, absent or delayed grief may be the norm for children because of their age-appropriate inability to bear the pain of extended grief. There is no research to support having children with distorted grief in separate groups from children with normal grief, and it would seem that the same reasoning indicating the use of group intervention would also support heterogeneity of group types. The children with distorted grief could benefit from the universality and commonality aspects of the group experience. If the grief is so distorted that there is no semblance of day-to-day functioning, this would probably not be a child to include in a group, particularly in a school setting. Most importantly, it is the degree of intrusiveness into a child's life created by the grieving that should be evaluated to determine the disabling effect of the grief (Webb, 1993).

Age

The age of the child now and at the time of the death is an important screening factor. The current age of the children will determine the activities that will be used to meet the goals of the group. The activities must be developmentally appropriate. An example of age differences would be in the sessions about feelings. Drawing is an activity that is appropriate across ages but writing about feelings is less appropriate for younger children. Also, it is much easier for younger children to select feelings from a series of pictures than from words.

The age of child when the death occurred must also be considered when determining if the child has a real memory or an acquired memory of the death experience. Children who have only an acquired memory of the person who died may have difficulty with some of the activities (Huss, 1997). John, whose mother had died when he was six months old and who gained a stepmother shortly afterward, had trouble with some of the memory activities in the group because no one ever talked about his mother with him. Through the support of the other participants in the group, John found the courage to begin asking questions about his mother and was pleased to find out it was OK to talk about her at home. The group leader needs to be sensitive to this issue of memories or lack of memories as well as whether or not the person who died is discussed at home. The above case is contrasted with Jenny whose mother died when Jenny was almost three years old. Jenny's mother is discussed regularly in the home and Jenny has a photo album of pictures to help her remember her mother.

The age range within the group is also important. Too wide a range can negatively impact the success of the group because the levels of understanding and needs may differ too greatly. The recommended age range is three to four years (Huss, 1997), but cognitive levels of development also need to be considered. For example, there is a wide range of cognitive development between a typical 8-year-old and a 12-year-old, so just considering the number of years does not necessarily guarantee appropriate member placement.

Cause of Death

There has been some discussion about the cause of death being a determining factor in group participation. Some feel it would not be appropriate for children who have had someone close to them commit suicide participate in a group with people who experienced other types of death (Webb, 1993). Others indicate that if all members had experienced the suicide of someone close, it would create the bond of commonality that is beneficial (Huss, 1997). If children who have experienced the suicide of someone close to them are included in a group, it is necessary for the group leader to be aware of the unique issues involved in a suicide. Others believe that violent deaths bring a different perspective than accidental deaths or death from illness (Webb, 1993). It appears to this author that if the group leader is aware of these facts and gives them proper consideration when planning the group activities, the cause of death need not be a determining factor for group inclusion.

Relationship to Deceased

Webb (1993) suggests that the relationship to the deceased has an impact on the survivor. She indicates that the closer the relationship, the more profound the impact. Wolfert's Loss Inventory (1983) ranks the death of a parent or sibling as having the greatest impact, with the death of a close relative or friend lower in terms of impact. The intensity of the impact is also influenced by the amount of contact the survivor had with the deceased as well as the age of the survivor. Huss (1997) recommends that it is beneficial for the group to be made up of survivors with the same relationship to the deceased if at all possible (i.e., parents). Sometimes the setting for the group and the numbers limit this possibility. In most settings, there may not be a sufficient number of participants to keep the age span as narrow as would be optimum.

Time since Death

The recency of the loss has also been suggested as a possible determining factor for appropriateness for group participation. Webb (1993) suggests that a recently bereaved child may feel overwhelmed when exposed to the feelings of others. Counselors should use their skills and all the information available to determine the appropriateness of a group intervention for a bereaved child just as they do for any other child for any other type of group. Given what we know about the cyclical and developmental nature of children's grief, it would not appear to be a limiting consideration other than immediately following the death. One option might be to collaborate on the decision with the child.

Length of and Number of Sessions

A consideration of length of sessions and how many sessions the group should meet is also required when planning a support group for bereaved children. Obviously the age of the members of the group is a factor in deciding the session length (30-60 minutes). The younger the age, the shorter the attention span and, therefore, the shorter the time of the session.

Some recommendations of the group duration range from 4 weeks to 16 weeks. Based on experience, Huss (1997) recommended the use of at least 10 weekly sessions. Meeting weekly is important for continuity with children because of their short attention span. Since two of the benefits of the use of group are universality and a sense of community, it is imperative that the group is together enough to develop and to benefit from them.

Group Size

Another consideration is the size of the group. Generally, it is recommended that a bereavement group contain three to five participants (Corey, & Corey, 1992; Masterman & Reams, 1988). The group must be small enough to allow each participant time to share and benefit from the support of others in the group. The small size gives each member the opportunity to repeatedly share their own story as suggested by Goldman (1996). This author's experience is that a group of up to eight members can be effective as long as the number of participants with high levels of distorted grief is small. The larger the group, the less time each participant has to share. The age factor also affects group size. The younger the participants, the smaller the group because younger children do not have the attention span to listen to many others share.

Setting for the Group

The setting for the group is also important when planning a group for bereaved children. Huss (1997) strongly recommends that the school setting is a very appropriate place for effective bereavement support groups. The familiar school setting assists in normalizing the experience. If a child goes to a special place for group, the interpretation may be made that "there is something wrong with me." A mental health setting is probably more appropriate when there is distorted grief, but that could also be treated in a school setting.

All of the above issues require careful consideration when planning effective group intervention with bereaved children. Careful selection of children who will benefit from the group intervention is a necessary ingredient to a successful group intervention.

Session Content

After careful analysis of all the above issues, as well as the unique characteristics of bereaved children, the session planning can begin. All activities must be intentional in terms of the objectives established for each session as well as the overall goal(s) of the series of sessions. All activities must also be age-appropriate. Careful planning is imperative to having a successful group experience for everyone.

Group Goal

Goal establishment is crucial for a successful group experience. Is the goal to be a support group, an education group, or a therapy group? Or is it to be a combination of all three? All are appropriate goals alone or in combination, but the leader must determine the goal and plan the objectives and activities of each session accordingly. Although all bereavement groups may have an element of support, education, and therapy, it is important to know the intended focus of the group.

The setting for the group and the needs of the participants are two main issues to consider when determining whether the group is to be a support, educational, or therapeutic group. Generally a school setting would have more of an educational and support focus, and a community mental health facility might have therapy as a focus since children with distorted grief will probably be seen in that setting. However, it must be acknowledged that support groups and education groups have a therapeutic side effect (Corey & Corey, 1992).

Once the goal/purpose of the group is established, then the task of determining objectives for each session begins. Pennells and Smith (1995) suggest several general or universal goals for children's bereavement groups. They are:

- to assist the student in expressing the effect loss had on their lives.
- to increase the reality of the death.
- to provide an opportunity to voice fears and concerns.
- to provide opportunities to acquire new knowledge
- to encourage the withdrawal from the deceased.
- to have participants readjust and seek new relationships and to adapt to new family roles (p. 46).

Based on the literature cited previously, another goal should be the creation of a safe environment to share feelings, concerns, and hopes (Krementz, 1982; Pennells & Smith, 1995; Yalom, 1995; Zambelli & DeRosa, 1992). Other helpful goals include the creation of a sense of community and new social meaning from the death by having direct discussion of the death, the feelings associated with the death and the grieving process, and hearing others share their feelings (Zambelli & DeRosa, 1992). The sense of community also addresses the isolation experienced by bereaved children and assists in normalizing the situation for them (Krementz, 1982; Pennells & Smith, 1992). Another necessary objective is the inclusion of a discussion at the end of the group which provides an opportunity for participants to practice their newly acquired coping skills and knowledge to an anticipated loss experience (Moore & Herhily, 1993; Pennells & Smith, 1995).

Based on the discussion of all the issues cited, decisions must be made regarding each session. Obviously a great amount of time is spent during the first two sessions getting the participants acquainted with each other and feeling comfortable in the group setting. The last session should bring closure to the group but also focus on what has been gained so the participants realize what they are taking with them in terms of coping skills and new knowledge. The sessions in between can have objectives mentioned in the previous paragraph. The activities that can successfully accomplish the objectives are varied and can be drawn from many sources. The following outlines suggest activities to meet identified objectives of several sessions based on the overall goals listed earlier. These are just suggestions and should be altered to meet the needs of the specific group being serviced.

SESSION I

Introduction

Goal

To set the atmosphere for a productive group

Objectives

1. Participants will become acquainted with each other
2. Group rules will be established
3. Participants will be able to share who has died.

Materials

Magazines, glue, scissors, file folder (all colors), colored markers/pencils/crayons, and small ball or beanbag

Activity A

The counselor will explain the purpose of the group as being to assist anyone who has had a parent die. [Note: It is generally helpful for the normalizing of the experience to give statistics in the form the students understand such as "There are twenty students in this school who have had a parent die. That means that almost the number of students in one classroom have had the same experience you have had.] Then a discussion is held to establish group rules. Generally, the following come from that discussion with other added as the group deems needed.

1. One person speaks at a time.
2. Each person has the right to pass.
3. Each person is respected.
4. What is said in the group, stays in the group.
5. Others determined by the group.

These rules are displayed in picture form at each session.

Activity B

To learn names of all participants, a ball is tossed between participants saying, "I am Susie Smith and this is Johnny Jones" as the ball is tossed to Johnny. This is done several times until names are learned. This is not a contest and if someone has difficulty remembering, it is OK to help.

[NOTE: Any getting acquainted activity can be used. It simply must be age appropriate.]

Activity C

Each participant (counselor included) will create a folder that tells about themselves. In the center of the folder is a picture or word that relates the person who died. The rest of the folder is covered with pictures that tell about themselves.

Discussion is encouraged during this time.

Often this activity does not get finished during the first session, but before the group ends each participant is to share the picture in the middle of their folder that depicts the person who died and to relate how that person died.

Process the activities of the day by asking questions such as

1. What did you learn today?
2. Is this group what you expected?
3. What do we mean by "what is said in group, stays in the group"?

Closing Activity

Once more the ball is tossed to refresh names and Rule number 4 is re-emphasized.

SESSION II

Feelings

Goal

To continue getting acquainted and to provide information on the feelings associated with the grief process

Objectives

1. Participants become better acquainted
2. Provide opportunities for participants to begin to express their feelings about the death and to begin to normalize those feelings

Materials

Folders from first session, 4 x 6 cards, colored markers/pencils/crayons, group rules, small ball or bean bag, newsprint

Activity A

Twice around the group with ball to reinforce names [or a new getting acquainted activity could be used here]

Activity B

Review group rules. Have participants identify before putting them up for display

Activity C

Complete the creation of the folders. Share the folder information about themselves and about the person who died. Encourage each person to participate but do not force anyone.

Process this activity with questions such as

1. What did you think of this activity? Did you learn anything about yourself, the person who died or anyone in the group?
2. Was this activity difficult or easy for you and can you explain how it was difficult or easy?
3. Did you see any similarities between you and the person who died (i.e. both liked ice cream) or between you and someone else in the group (i.e. liked pizza or had a parent die of cancer)?

Activity D

Begin a discussion about feelings and generate a list of feelings on large pieces of newsprint. Point to each and have a show of hands to indicate they have felt that way at some time and record with checks by each word those numbers. Discuss how many of them had similar feelings.

Activity E

Final activity of day: Have students complete the sentence starter, "Today I learned …" on the back of their folder. Then have them verbally share what they have written.

Session III

Feelings II

Goal

To provide information on the feelings associated with the grief process

Objective

Opportunity for participants to begin to express their feelings about the death and to begin to normalize those feelings

Materials

Folders from first session, 4 x 6 cards, colored markers/pencils/crayons, group rules, small ball or bean bag, newsprint

Activity A

Twice around the group with ball to reinforce names. [Or a new getting acquainted activity could be used here.]

Activity B

Review group rules. Have participants identify each rule before putting them up for display

Activity C

Review the list of feelings the students generated in the last session. Ask if they have any they would like to add. Have students choose three feeling words they felt related to the death of their parent. Give each student three 3 x 5 cards and have them put that feeling (in words) on one side of a card. When complete, have them sort the cards so all like cards are together. Tabulate the results on the newsprint list.

Discuss the results in terms of similar feelings and the legitimacy of feelings. [NOTE: At this point a question about there being positive feelings related to death usually surfaces. This is an opportunity to discuss that all feelings are OK and ask those who wrote the positive feelings if they would like to share.].

Process this activity with questions such as

1. What did you think of this activity? Did you learn anything about yourself, the person who died or anyone in the group?
2. Was this activity difficult or easy for you and can you explain how it was difficult or easy?
3. Did you see any similarities between you and someone else in the group.
4. Did anyone have a feeling that no one else had? (Validate that this is OK).
5. Which of these feelings is most difficult to express? to recognize?
6. Did anyone in your family have similar feelings? How did you know?
7. Do you and your family talk about feelings? When? Is it easy or hard to have those talks?

Close this activity with a review of the importance of feelings in our lives and how feelings help to express our emotions as well as how healthy feelings are. Be sure to end on a positive note.

Activity E

Final activity of day: Have students complete the sentence starter "Today I learned ..." on the back of their folder. Then have them verbally share what they have written.

SESSION IV

Stages of Grief

Goal

To learn about the stages of grief/and to understand the grieving process.

Objective

Participants will learn about the stages of grief and feelings associated with each stage.

Materials

Feelings cards created in last session and tagboard showing each stage.

Activity A

Review group rules. Have participants identify before putting them up.

Activity B

Leader will teach the stages of grief. This will be done through conversation with participants. Once all have been identified and discussed in terms of characteristics and the roller coaster effect, participants will identify feelings associated with each stage using the cards created last week.

Activity C

Final activity of the session: Have student verbally share a completion to the sentence starter, "Today I learned ..." from back of folder.

Assignment

Each participant is to bring a "memory object" with them for the next session. This should be something that reminds the participant of his or her deceased parent. This could be a picture, keepsake, gift, food, or anything that shows the special significance of the relationship.

SESSION V

Memories

Goal

To offer participants a nonthreatening opportunity to share about their deceased parent.

Objectives

1. To explore the use of memories as a positive way in which to deal with grief.
2. Provide an atmosphere of trust for sharing about the deceased parent.

Materials

Items brought by students. Book: "The Tenth Good Thing About Barney" by Judy Viorst, magazines, one large piece of construction paper, scissors, colored markers, colored pencils and glue. Feelings cards created in Session II.

Activity A

Review group rules.

Activity B

Read the book, "The Tenth Good Thing About Barney" by Judy Viorst and discuss the importance of sharing memories during this session even though it may be painful.

Each participant who brought an item and wishes to, should share the item they brought and tell about it in terms of memories of the loved one. [NOTE: This activity needs to go over two sessions because students are often unsure of what to bring and so bring nothing but will the second session.]

Process Questions

1. How does it feel to talk about the person who died?
2. Did you find that you have similar memories to others in the group? What were they?

Closure Activity

Have participants select two feelings cards to describe their feelings today during the activities and share how they felt with the group.

SESSION VI

Memories II

Goal

To offer participants a nonthreatening opportunity to share about their deceased parent.

Objectives

1. To explore the use of memories as a positive way in which to deal with grief.
2. Provide an atmosphere of trust for sharing about the deceased parent.

Materials

Items brought by students, book: "The Tenth Good Thing About Barney" by Judy Viorst, magazines, one large piece of construction paper, scissors, colored markers, colored pencils and glue. Feelings cards created in Session II.

Activity A

Review group rules.

Activity B

Review the book, "The Tenth Good Thing About Barney" by Judy Viorst and discuss the importance of sharing memories during this session even though it may be painful.

Each participant who did not bring an item the session before but did today and wishes to, should share the item they brought and tell about it in terms of memories of the loved one.

Activity C

Place large piece of construction paper in middle of table. Ask participants to find pictures in magazines of things that serve as reminder of their deceased parent such as foods, hobbies, and interests. They should also be encouraged to draw pictures if none can be found. All are placed on the big collage and everyone shares at the end. [NOTE: This gives those students who have no memory object or are not permitted in the home to bring one to share memories.]

Process Questions

1. How does it feel to talk about the person who died?
2. Did you find that you have similar memories to others in the group? What were they?

Closure Activity

Have participants select two feelings cards to describe their feelings today during the activities and share how they felt with the group.

SESSION VII

Family

Goal

To encourage participants to discuss their feelings with their families.

Objectives

1. Participants to recognize changes in families since death both in terms of better and worse.
2. Participants identify ways to discuss feelings with their families.

Materials

Paper, colored markers, pencils, crayons.

Activity A

Review Group Rules

Activity B

Participants will first draw a picture of their family before the death occurred. On a second sheet, participants will draw a picture of family since the death.

Discussion of changes facilitated by questions such as the following:

Has anyone changed?
How have they changed?
Do you have more responsibility?
Can you talk with your living parent?
Could you before the death?
Who were you closest to before the death? Who are you closest to in the family now?
Participants should be able to identify some good changes and some not so good changes.

Activity C

Using the picture drawn in Activity B, ask participants to identify someone in their family they would like to be able to talk with about the person who died, their feelings, or just things in general.

Participants will brainstorm ways to approach these people to talk. After a generous list is created, each participant is to put on a card how he or she is going to try to approach the person during the next week.

Activity D

Participants will give encouragement to each other for their week's task with a barrage of encouraging statements to each other such as "Go for it", "Good luck", "You can do it", "We will all be pulling for you".

A brief discussion should be held about the final session. Begin to get the group talking about the end of the group meetings so they can be prepared for another loss situation. Suggest they think about ways they want to celebrate the group.

Closure Activity

Have student verbally share a completion to the sentence starter, "Today I learned ..." from back of folder.

SESSION VIII

Family II

Goals

To process the family conversations

To develop constructive ways to deal with grief.

Objectives

1. Students share experiences of attempting to talk with families.
2. Participants discover the wide range of ways to deal with grief and to validate each of them.

Materials

Writing paper, pencils or markers.

Activity A

Review Group Rules

Activity B

Each member shares how his or her planned conversation went. Group is encouraged to be very supportive of each other about the efforts. Often members have not been able to have the conversation for a variety of reasons beyond their control. Discuss what went well and how that happened and ways to improve those that did not go well. [NOTE: Include the entire group is these discussions. This time often slips into a dialogue between leader and one participant but is much more beneficial if all participate.]

Encourage members to try again before the next session and practice with role playing if needed.

Activity C

Begin discussion of coping skills related to bereavement. Ask them to share how they cope with their feelings and how others in their family cope with their feelings. List the ways on newsprint. Suggest they think about this between now and the next session and maybe include it is the discussion with the family member. Tell them they can add to the list the next time.

Discuss the last session and begin to generate ideas for celebration (i.e., ice cream, pizza, etc.).

Closure Activity

Have student verbally share a completion to the sentence starter, "Today I learned ..." from back of folder.

SESSION IX

Coping Skills

Goal

To develop constructive ways to deal with grief.

Objective

Participants discover the wide range of ways to deal with grief and to validate each of them.

Materials

Writing paper, pencils or markers.

Activity A

Review Group Rules

Activity B

Ask if there are any additions to the list of coping skills generated last session. Have participants brainstorm additional constructive ways of coping with grief. List on the newsprint in a new color so can see the difference. Leader may need to facilitate this by suggesting some ways of coping, or reminding them of ideas previously talked about with the group. Discussion can then take place about the specifics of each suggestion. Each participant will relate how he or she used one of these suggestions and then identify one they plan to use in the future.

A series of scenarios are presented and participants are asked to give suggestions for the person on how to cope with their grief. This may be done as a group or as a role-play situation.

Finalize plans for celebration at last session. This can take many forms. Some have created a collage of what they have learned, others have just wanted a party, others have opted to do nothing. The important thing is that they discuss the ending of the group.

Closure

Final activity of the session: Have student verbally share a completion to the sentence starter, "Today I learned ..." from back of folder.

SESSION X

Closure

Goals

To review the overall program and bring closure to the group.

To bring closure to the group.

Objectives

1. Participants review their new skills and knowledge and how they will use them in the future.
2. Participants will evaluate the group experience.

Materials

Writing paper, pencils or markers.

Activity A

Review Group Rules

Activity B

Each participant will write themselves a letter describing what was enjoyed most about the group, how the experience has helped, and how he or she feels differently about the loss. This can lead to a discussion of the benefits of journaling. The letters are collected and mailed to the participants approximately one month later with a personal note of thanks for participating in the group and an expression of appreciation for their openness and willingness to grow.

Activity C

Participants will fill out these questions and share with group ...

1. What I like most about this group is .... .
2. Three things I learned are .... .
3. I would recommend this group to another participant because .... .
4. One thing that is different because I participated in this group is .... .

Activity D

Here is where the celebration takes places. Whatever has been decided to do.

Activity E

Each participant is given a small stuffed animal as a reminder of the group, what was learned, and the support that is available.

SUMMARY

Groups for children who have experienced the death of someone close to them can be very effective. The key to effective bereavement groups for children lies in understanding their developmental uniquenesses and knowing specifically how they make sense of death. The grieving process is similar in children and adults, but it is more cyclical in nature for children because of developmental issues associated with the maturational process. Bereavement in children can, therefore, be repetitive and can resurface many times during childhood.

Peer group models of intervention for bereaved children can create a sense of community that relieve the child's sense of isolation, provide a sense of commonality with others who are parentally bereaved, and provide a safe place to practice newly acquired skills related to identifying, expressing, and communicating feelings. Peer group intervention instills a sense of hope as the bereaved child sees others "surviving" the intense pain of parental loss. Successful group leaders need to understand children's development needs as well as the uniquenesses of childhood grief, and select goals and activities to meet the needs of the participants.

Jenny was a 6th grader when her father committed suicide. She became part of my loss support group in her middle school setting, came to every session but never said a word. I was not at all certain she was gaining anything from the experience and thought maybe it was too soon after the death for her to be part of the group. Several years later when Jenny was in high school and her younger sister was in the middle school her mother came to see me to tell me that Jenny had told her to come and insist that her sister become part of my loss support group because she would never have gotten through that time without coming to that group. Jenny taught me never to doubt the effectiveness of a group experience for her children who have been touched by death. We as counselors never know the true effect of what we do.

REFERENCES

American Psychiatric Association. (1994). *Diagnostic and statistical manual of mental disorders* (4th ed.). Washington, DC: Author.

Berlinsky, E. B., & Biller, H. B. (1982). *Parental death and psychological development.* Lexington, MA: Lexington Books.

Bowlby, J. (1961). Childhood mourning and its implications for psychiatry. *The American Journal of Psychiatry,* (*Dec*), 481-498.

Bowlby, J. (1980). *Attachment and loss: Volume III. Loss: Sadness and depression.* New York: Basic.

Corey, M. S., & Corey, G. (1992). *Groups: Process and practice* (4th ed.). California: Brooks/Cole.

Corr, C. A. (1996). Children, development, and encounters with death and bereavement. In Corr, C. A., & Corr, D. M. (Eds.), *Handbook of Childhood Death and Bereavement* (pp 3-28). New York: Springer Publishing Company.

Erikson, E. H. (1968). *Identity, youth and crisis.* New York: W. W. Norton.

Fox, S. (1985). *Good grief: Helping groups of children when a friend dies.* Boston: Beacon Press.

Furman, E. (1974). *A child's parent dies: Studies in childhood bereavement.* London: Hogarth.

Goldman, L. (1996). *Breaking the silence: A guide to help children with complicated grief-suicide, homicide, AIDS, violence, and abuse.* Washington, D.C.: Accelerated Development.

Grollman, E. A. (Ed.). (1995). *Bereaved Children and Teens: A Support Guide for Parents and Professionals.* Boston: Beacon Press.

Hawener, R. M., & Phillips, W. (1975). The grieving child. *School Counselor, 22*, 347-358.

Huss, S. N. (1997). *The effect of peer bereavement support groups on the self-esteem, depression, and problem behavior of parentally bereaved children.* Ann Arbor, MI: UMI Dissertation Services.

Jacobs, E. E., Harvill, R. L., & Masson, R. L. (1994). *Group counseling: Strategies and skills.* Pacific Grove, CA: Brooks/Cole.

Johnson, P. A. & Rosenblatt, P. C. (1981). Grief following childhood loss of a parent. *American Journal of Psychotherapy, 35*, 419-424.

Klass, D., & Shinners, B. (1983). Professional roles in a self-help group for the bereaved. *OMEGA, 13,* 361-674.

Kubler-Ross, E. (1969). *On Death and Dying*. New York: MacMillan.

LeShane, E. (1976). *Learning to say good-bye.* New York: Avon.

Masterman, S. H., & Reams., R. (1988). Support groups for bereaved preschool and school-age children. *American Journal of Orthopsychiatry, 58*, 562-570.

McGlauflin, H. (1992). How children grieve: Implications for counseling. In Walz, G. R. & Bleuer. J. C. (Eds.), *Helping Students Cope with Fears and Crises.* (Report No. ISBN-1-56109-040-9). Ann Arbor, MI: Office of Educational Research and Improvement. (ERIC Document Reproduction Service No. ED 340987).

Miller, J. B. M. (1971). Children's reactions to the death of a parent: A review of the psychoanalytic literature. *Journal of the American Psychoanalytic Association, 19*, 697-719.

Mishne, J. (1992). The grieving child: Manifest and hidden losses in childhood and adolescence. *Child and Adolescent Social Work Journal, 9*, 471-490.

Moore, J., & Herlihy, B. (1993). Grief groups for students who have had a parent die. *School Counselor, 41*, 55-59.

Nagy, M. (1948). The child's theories concerning death. *The Journal of Genetic Psychology, 73,* 3-27.

Naierman, N. (1997). Reaching out to grieving children. *Educational Leadership,* 55-65.

Pennells, M., & Smith, S. C. (1995). *The forgotten mourners: Guidelines for working with bereaved children.* Bristol, PA: Jessica Kingsley Publications.

Piaget, J. (1970). *Genetic epistemology*. New York, NY: Columbia University Press.

Rando, T.A. (1991). *How to go on living when someone you love dies*. New York: Bantam.

Siegel. B. S. (1985). Helping children cope with death. *Family Physician,* March, 175-180.

Tonkins, S. A. M., & Laubert, M. J. (1996). A treatment outcome study of bereavement groups for children. *Child & Adolescent Social Work Journal, 13*, 3-21.

Webb, N. B, (1993). *Helping bereaved children: A handbook for practitioners.* New York: Guilford.

Wolfert, A. (1983). *Helping Children Cope With Grief.* Muncie, IN: Accelerated Development.

Worden, J. W. (1996). *Children and grief.* New York: Guilford Press.

Yalom, I. D. (1995). *Theory and practice of group psychotherapy* (4th ed.). New York: Praeger.

Zambelli. G. C., & DeRosa, A. P. (1992). Bereavement support groups for school-age children: Theory, intervention, and case example. *American Journal of Orthopsychiatry, 62*, 484-493.

Zimpfer, D. G. (1991). Groups for grief and survivorship after bereavement: A review. *Journal for Specialists in Group Work, 16*, 46-55.

Chapter Three

ENGAGING ADOLESCENT MALES: A GROUP APPROACH

Kevin A. Fall and H. George McMahon

Boys will be boys. That saying, which can mean so many things, usually refers to excusing a boy that has behaved in some aggressive or inappropriate manner. You will rarely hear that statement after a young man has performed well on an exam or treated someone with compassion. This chapter is written by a professor/private practitioner and a school counselor. We are both interested in the successes and perils that adolescent males face, but we are equally concerned about the perspective many professionals and citizens take when it comes to adolescent males. In one workshop given for mental health professionals, we asked the participants to define the term "adolescent male". The group came up with the following descriptors: "over-sexed, aggressive, rude, sometimes violent, apathetic, curious, hard on the outside but soft on the inside, athletic, strong, macho, egotistical, angry, confused". As we processed this seemingly negative definition, one member stated, "You know, how can we expect these guys to be anything but what we see them to be? I said a couple of those things, but I don't think that list applies to the adolescent boys I really know well. It fits those I don't know though (laughing)".

Sadly, this view seems to be common when it comes to adolescent boys. When I (KAF) tell people that I work with adolescent males I get one of two responses. The first one is the "better you than me" response and it usually sounds something like, "Oh, that population is so hard to work with. They are so resistant. I'm glad someone is willing to help them. They need it!" This response is aligned with the workshop definition and views adolescents as the pinnacle problem population. Gurian (1996) stated, "Those who fear masculinity have often let their fear turn to hatred rather than understanding, but they need not consume our cultural vision of boyhood" (p. xx). Resistant, apathetic, and surly, adolescent males are largely shunned by teachers, parents and mental health practitioners.

The second response is the "It's just a phase" response and sounds like, "Look, I was 15 once and you gotta give these guys some space. They don't need help. They need room to sow their wild oats". This perspective is similar to what is alluded to in the boys will be boys adage and has the tendency to ignore possible problems by turning pathology or cries for help into a "phase". Initially, adolescence was viewed as a period of storm and stress (Blos, 1962; Freud, 1946; Hall, 1904). However, research has shown that although adolescence does have trials, it is no more troubling than any other developmental phase (Douvan & Adelson, 1966; Esser, Schmidt & Woerner, 1990; Manning, 1983; Powers, Hauser & Kilner, 1989). Perhaps the negative connotation of adolescence constructs a negative filter through which the teen's behavior is filtered. The two most serious problems with this filter are: demonizing the adolescent male and failing to encourage appropriate behavior or rationalizing potentially serious issues and missing the cries for help. Both distortions can produce lethal consequences.

Recent violent incidents involving adolescent males have been catalysts for examining the issues of male adolescence. It is a shame it took such extreme behavior to provoke a closer look-- the evidence was there long before the infamous violence at Columbine, Springfield, or Jonesboro. According to a Centers for Disease Control Report (1997), drug and alcohol use among teenage boys is on the increase again (about 35% use); arrests have increased for violent acts over the past ten years, and child abuse is increasing. Garbarino (1999) asserts that all of these risk factors accumulate to form a very real and frightening foundation for adolescent male violence and even suicide. "Sometimes, only at the least minute does a boy choose between killing himself and killing others; sometimes he does both" (Garbarino, 1999, p.9). In light of the growing social problems faced by adolescent males, ways to address and remediate these risk factors are desperately needed.

The issue here is once again, not whether or not adolescent boys have problems. As a population, they have as many concerns as any other group. However, preconceived notions about teenage boys often block them from getting the help they need. Thus, for many, the lack of an outlet leads to enhanced feelings of isolation, hopelessness and depression. For many males the accepted way to handle these feelings is through withdrawal punctuated by moments of intense anger and lashing out at others. The task for parents, teachers and mental health professionals is not to try to assess whether this is a real issue or a phase, but instead, to treat each issue as important and to provide the adolescent with a setting to explore and process his experiences safely.

With this task in mind, this chapter discusses one way of using group counseling to provide a processing place for adolescent boys. In this chapter we will outline several key issues that are important in the life of the adolescent male and describe a session by session protocol for conducting a group that addresses these adolescent issues by using group process and experiential activities.

KEY ISSUES

Developing a list of key issues inherent within any population is a daunting task. In creating the list, one risks overgeneralizing and losing the experience of the individual within the given population. One could also potentially omit an important issue and thus miss a vital component in the process. We created our list through a careful survey of the literature and most importantly, by listening to our male clients. The issues that are discussed are by no means exhaustive in scope. As we learn more and are open to the experience of the adolescent male, existing issues will be expanded and new issues added.

Masculine Identity

Teenage boys are keenly aware of the experience of transitioning from boyhood into manhood. As the boy reaches adolescence, it is common to hear others say, "You are becoming a man, so it's time you started acting like one." Unfortunately, many teenage boys do not know what it means to be a "man", so they improvise, often adopting mannerisms, behaviors and values of men they know. Of course, this assimilation process is filtered through the mind of a thirteen year old, so some distortion is typical.

Pollack (1998) outlines what he calls the "Boy Code"; a set of rules that boys use to define masculinity. Along with this code of conduct are four primary injunctions that guide the boy's conduct. In the lives of many adolescent boys, the following rules are applied as they attempt to make sense of their metamorphosis into a man.

1. Be a "sturdy oak" (p.23): This rule requires males to be strong and stone-faced in the face of adversity and pain. Boys must always be sure of themselves, never wrong or confused, and must never be emotional. One 16 year-old boy tells the impact of this rule:

> I'll never forget when my dad lost his job. I could tell he was upset, but he just plainly told us about it and said everything would be fine. My sister and my mom busted out crying and stuff. I just sat there, stunned. I wanted to be upset too. I was scared and felt sorry for my dad, but I knew I had to be strong. That's what being a man is all about I guess.

2. "Give 'em hell" (p.24): Many boys we have worked with claim that they feel like they have something to prove. Going a step beyond just appearing tough, this rule compels boys to be abrasive and daring, often putting them at physical risk. James, a fifteen year old high school drop out portrays a classic example of the extreme expression of this rule:

> You have to be hard to get respect around here. People think I'm crazy and that's cool. I mean they give me lots of props and leave me alone. I remember this one time, my friends dared me to spend the night in this old abandoned bomb shelter. They were all scared, so I did it by myself. There were rats and the floor was covered in water, but I slept down there all night to prove I was tough as nails. That's me, man. I'll do anything.

3. The "big wheel" (p.24): Status, power and superiority are all things boys feel they must achieve to be men. Many boys watch their fathers work long hours to provide for the family. Although the job distances the father from the family, he, and often the son, see the job as a way to get power within the family and the world. Boys will often strive competitively instead of cooperatively, climbing over the backs of friends to be number one while also feeling the need to deny any feelings or experiences of failure. Tying feelings of self worth to being better than others can lead to problems in forming intimate relationships and at worst, has been linked to increased violence on the part of males (Miedzian, 1991). A father of a 13 year old boy discusses his familiarity with the big wheel.

> I feel like I do what I have to do. I'm an attorney. I'm a damn good one and I bring home a lot of money. That money pays for my son's school and whatever else he wants. I am respected all across this city. People know my name and yeah, I think they would rather be friends with me than my enemy. You sure don't want me to go against you. I have the reputation of being the best and that's important to me. I hope my son gets this quality. I mean, someone has to grab the brass ring and it might as well be me. I've thought about cutting back on my time at work. I usually work about 80 hours per week, but I would lose so much. There are a lot of lawyers just like me who are waiting to take my spot. He'll understand one day. To be the best, you have to put in the time.

4. "No sissy stuff" (p.24): This rule is less of a stand alone rule and more of an outcome produced by the cumulative effect of the other three. The result of this narrow, yet common, definition of masculinity results in boys fearing all that is feminine in an effort to be constantly strong, unfeeling, and powerful. This rule does imply the consequence of humiliation and ridicule for expressing anything other than stoic acceptance or macho acting out. We all know adolescent boys who rigidly adhere to these rules. They do so because they think they are doing what it takes to be a man. We also know boys that attempt to exist outside of these rules. Some do it very well, a testament to the fact that even the rule followers are uncertain about their way of doing things. Most however are called names like, "fag" and "queer" and are ostracized and bullied. The bullies often feel like they are proving their manhood by abusing the "sissies". Roger, a 17 year old tells of a time when he experienced the consequences of existing beyond the accepted definition of masculinity:

> My friend James was going through some tough times and I thought I would be there for him. You know, like a friend is supposed to be? He started crying and I was o.k. with that, but I could tell he was uncomfortable. Anyway, I guess he was embarrassed and so the next day he started making fun of me in front of all our friends. He called me a "homo" and stuff. I don't get it. I guess he was afraid that I would tell everyone about what happened and everyone would think he was a girl because he cried.

Pollack (1998) asserts that the "Boy Code" is something that every boy must contend with in some manner, but each individual boy determines how he will use the code. Because society's view of masculinity encourages the adoption of the tenets of the code, many boys adopt the injunctions to fit in, to be a man as defined by his environment

(Levant, 1995; Thompson & Pleck, 1987). Often it is the very nature of the code that prevents adolescent males from getting help when they need it, because counseling is viewed as violating the code. As one male client stated, "Counseling is stupid. It doesn't work. All you do is sit around and whine about your feelings. I don't need help. I can do it myself." Because the definition of masculinity restricts many adolescent males from counseling, the need for an acceptable venue where they feel comfortable working out their problems becomes essential.

An Emotional Life

The issues involving emotions are probably evident from the information in the preceding section, but the appropriate expression of emotions and the associated problems deserve considerably more attention. The most pronounced issue that parents often describe is the inability for their sons to show anything but anger. The rest of the emotional continuum seems to be absent from the repertoire of adolescent males. Two main factors, biology and culture, lead adolescent boys to restrict emotional expression. Biology, in the form of higher levels of testosterone and significant brain differences, produce gender variants in emotional processing and expression. Culture, as demonstrated in the preceding section, teaches boys to not feel sad or afraid. Parents tell their young sons, "Don't cry. You are not hurt." while they are more likely to comfort a female child who suffers the same injury (Pollack, 1998). The clashing of these two forces leads many adolescent males to constrict certain emotions. At the same time, others in his environment encourage this constriction of emotion and then ironically view the boy as unfeeling. This ensuing confusion often leads to a wide array of psychological and social problems.

The key to understanding the emotional lives of boys comes through the recognition of two interlocking principles. 1) boys are capable of all emotions, and 2) boys express and experience their emotions differently than girls. To further understand a boy's emotions, one must comprehend the mechanisms boys use to make sense of their emotional worlds. Gurian (1996, pp. 21-24) outlines several internal processing methods used by males to deal with emotions. Selected methods are discussed in terms of characteristics and implications.

1. The action-release method: In this method, boys will express and process emotions through an activity. This expression could be through an active means, such as stomping through the house or it could be seemingly passive, such as withdrawing to his room to read comic books. Although it may seem that the males are isolating or denying feelings, providing boys with space and acceptance helps them process their feelings at a safe pace and often leads to other more interpersonally connective ways of processing emotions.
2. The suppression-delayed reaction method: Often as the boy deals with emotions in action oriented ways, the true impact of the emotional issue is not felt or recognized until sometime later. Often counselors or parents attempt to force the

issue by wanting the adolescent to openly and honestly express the emotions in the present. This strategy drives the boy away, afraid of being judged and ridiculed for his feelings and uncertain about how or what to express. An atmosphere of trust, safety and patience must be formed to help the boy who uses the suppression-delayed reaction method to control feelings. Helpers can act as a beacon, letting the boy know where you will be when he is ready to talk.

3. The displacement-objectification method: This method refers to expression of feelings through projection onto objects, rather than personalizing the feelings. This strategy is misunderstood by helpers and leads to frustration on the part of both parties. For example, a boy when feeling sad might say, "The day sure is gloomy today. It just rains and rains. What an unhappy day." Gurian (1996) suggests that places or people that encourage the male to tell stories will often elicit more emotional information than direct questioning. What seems as indirect story-telling is actually emotional experiencing.
4. Physical expression method: Biology and culture instruct males to release emotions through physical means rather than verbal ones. Boys are well aware that physical venting is acceptable, even expected, but they often lack the training to differentiate between appropriate and inappropriate methods for physical expression. Adolescent males learn through experience and watching older males that physical expression not only works to release emotions, but also works to control other people. Boys who internalize physical aggression as an acceptable method of control may use physical force in inappropriate ways in later relationships (Fall, Howard, & Ford, 1999; Miedzian, 1991). The task for adolescents and helpers is to learn and teach appropriate ways of physically expressing emotions.

Each of these methods represent common and appropriate ways for boys to access and work through their emotions. When these strategies are respected, most boys feel safe enough to explore a wide range of emotions. However, the means of exploration are often tragically misinterpreted or circumvented by others. The need exists for a place where adolescent males feel their emotional process is respected. Parents can learn to recognize the specific ways their sons emote, and group counseling can provide a respectful setting for the adolescent boy to explore his feelings.

Fathers and Mothers

Parents play a vital role in the lives of adolescent males. As the teens transition from boyhood to manhood, the father/son and mother/son relationships change. This disequilibriation often leads to confusion and conflict between adolescent males and their parents. A chapter could be devoted to the discussion of these dynamics alone, but for our purposes, a more general overview of fundamental issues regarding both mothers, fathers and adolescent boys is offered.

The role of the father is vital to the well-being of any child, and is especially important in the lives of adolescent males. What is the role of the father? In the past five years, a heavy emphasis has been placed on encouraging fathers away from the traditional work role and toward a more involved role. Many fathers perceive that more involved means more time, but more time, while not necessarily a bad idea, seems less important than the quality of the time and the father and son's perception of the importance of the relationship (Lamb, 1997). In fact, many researchers have found that adolescents with highly involved fathers exhibit increased cognitive competence, increased empathy, less sex-stereotyped beliefs and a more internal locus of control (Pruett, 1987; Radin, 1994).

The impact of an uninvolved father can be devastating to both son and father. Many fathers were hobbled by the same constraining social forces that are crippling their adolescent sons. Working from what they learned from their fathers and society's expectations, fathers are unsure about how to relate to their adolescent sons. Larry, a 40 year-old father of a 16 year-old son captures the essence of this struggle.

> When Peter was young I took care of him all the time because his mother worked. We did everything together. It's like I wanted to be the father that my father never was to me and my brothers. When Peter turned 13, I thought, well it's time for him to let go of me and be on his own for awhile. To be honest, I didn't know what to do. He kept wanting to hang around me, but I would brush him off. I didn't want to baby him, but now, it's like we don't even know each other any more and I have no idea how to talk to him. It's like this wall is between us. I wish he was six again.

Now hear Peter's perspective of his relationship with his dad:

> It was so cool when I was a kid. Me and my dad would do everything together. I had my friends, but I knew my dad would always be there for me when I needed him. In a way I felt good, because it was like I was there for him too, like he somehow needed or wanted to be around me. I don't know. Anyway, when I got into junior high, he just bailed on me. I was scared, going to a new school and all, and he just started to ignore me. These past four years I have really been confused about that and it seems like those others years, the good years, never happened. Like they happened to someone else. The weird thing is, we never talk about what's going on, like he doesn't want it to get better. Every once in awhile he takes me to a football game or shows up at my practices, but our talk is awkward and most times, we drive home in silence.

This case poignantly illustrates the confusion many sons and fathers experience in their relationship. Both long for a re-connection, but neither possess the tools or insight to make it happen. Many fathers fail to realize that, in times of stress, they revert to the same strategies, regardless of effectiveness, that their fathers used with them. Even more common, are fathers who avoid the awkwardness of the relationship by putting in more hours at work (Levine & Pittinsky, 1997). Many sons, while observing their fathers, soak up the withdrawal and awkwardness as normal and will adopt the same methods with their sons. The legacy produces a cycle repeated from one generation of men to another.

An adolescent male's relationship with his mother also is in a state of transition. Like the father, mothers often feel a sense of safety when the boy is a young child. As the boy ages, the mom suddenly tumbles into a realm of relative inexperience and may feel confused or threatened by her son's need for independence and physical growth. Caron (1994) noted that many mothers will attempt to reuse childhood strategies with their teenage boys. These strategies are perceived as threats to his independence, and as such are judged by the boy as "nagging" and "babying me". The following case example demonstrates the common issues that surface between adolescent male and mother.

> I really don't know what to do with Kenny. He used to be such a good little boy, but I can't tell him anything these days. If I get too close to him, he seems to withdraw, like I have some form of communicable disease. If I stay away, he gets angry with me for ignoring him. I want him to do well in school and I want him to have friends so I do ask lots of questions. He hates that. He's doing fine, but I don't understand why he locks me out of his world. I wish he would share more with me. I wish he would let me know what's going on with him.

The son reported his view of the relationship.

> My mom won't leave me alone. It's like as soon as I get home from school, she is on top of me. "What did you do today?", "Did you make good grades?", "Do you have homework?", "Are your friends coming over?" It's like she never stops. I think if she could, she would follow me around all day long and hold my hand. I'm getting older and want to do stuff on my own. When she nags me I feel like she doesn't trust me. The weird thing is that I know she cares about me. She is always there for me. I just wish she would be more in the background. I want to do well and make her proud, but I want it to be me who is doing the work. Not her, If she has to nag me about it, then it's like I don't get credit for doing it.

The case example illustrates the dynamic that exists between many sons and their mothers. Sons are ambivalent about the love and caring shown by their moms. On one hand, they enjoy and desire the warmth and support. On the other hand, such support can often turn to "smothering". Boys often respond to the perceived smothering by withdrawing or by becoming angry--the two societally sanctioned emotional responses for males. Mothers often respond by being hurt and withdrawing or they turn up the emotional heat and try to force the boy to relate emotionally to close the rift. Both strategies are ineffective and often lead to more relationship strain.

Adolescent males rely heavily on their parents for guidance and support. When counseling parents of adolescents, sometimes the scariest idea they hear from the counselor is, "Your son is watching you. He is learning, from you, how to be a man, father, husband, wife, mother and woman. They are like sponges". As Lamb (1997) pointed out, "Parental warmth, nurturance, and closeness are associated with positive child outcomes whether the parent involved is a mother or father" (p.13). Thus, parents can model what they want their sons to learn, and sons need a place to process issues related to parental influences; a place to process feelings and thoughts about each of their parents.

Friendships

The relationships with peers plays an essential role in the development of adolescent boys. During the time of adolescence, romantic relationships begin to form, issues of sexual orientation emerge, and friendship relationships with other males become important elements in the boy's life. Although it is beyond the scope of this chapter to detail all the issues and implications of these relationships, each will be discussed in general terms.

Flirting, sexual exploration, and dating are topics that adolescent males enjoy discussing. While the anticipation of connecting with girls on a "more than friends" level is exciting, for many males, beneath the bravado lies a deep layer of insecurity and confusion. Most of this ambivalence is embedded in male stereotypes and societal norms and expectations. Adolescent males embrace these new experiences with all the clumsiness and sensitivity one would expect from a novice as they try out different ways of connecting and as they experience the pain of inevitable rejection. While the issues related to romantic relationships are many, adolescent males could benefit from a venue that allowed them to openly explore the issues of communication, intimacy, sexual behavior, sexually transmitted diseases, pregnancy, and sexual respect.

Many adolescent males do not fit into the heterosexual mold, but still need a place to process and feel accepted. For many, homosexuality is an issue that directly opposes society's view of manhood. Thus, adolescent males who are gay struggle with internal shame, humiliation, and confusion, while also bearing the teasing and ignorance of other males who may feel threatened by homosexuality. Homosexual and heterosexual males can learn respect from one another, as they process similarities and differences.

Male friendships take on a different feeling and meaning during adolescence. Transformed from the playground days, many males take the competitive lessons learned as children and apply them to the more serious tasks of academics, sports and girls. This need for competition is tempered by the equally strong need to feel safe in a group of peers. Thus, for many adolescent males, the task of friendship revolves around competing in certain areas, defeating your foes (who are sometimes your friends), and cultivating friendships with those same competitors outside the chosen arena of competition. It is here that boys learn how to respect those that are superior and learn the value of losing. Mark, a seventeen year-old sums up the dynamic of friendship experienced by so many boys.

> Lou and I are best friends. He is so cool. He's funny and smart and I tell him just about anything. We play football for different high schools and that gets rough, but when we are on the field, it's all business. Once the game is over, the game is over and we're just friends again. We play basketball every Sunday. Man, when we play, we play hard. I want to beat him bad, and if I lose I get pissed. It's not personal though. It's like we motivate each other. We are also there for each other. I want him to be the best he can be and I know he wants that for me too. I sure like winning though.

In summary, the issues covered are concepts common to most of our adolescent clients. Identity, emotions, parents and friends are important elements that are inter-related in the lives of adolescent boys. They are connected by the successes and failures in dealing with the tasks. It is unfortunate that one of the strongest messages society gives boys is that they must endure these struggles alone. Group counseling offers boys a safe place to address the need for re-learning and space to explore and try new strategies.

CONSTRUCTING A GROUP

Once the issues that the group is going to address are decided upon, the group must be assembled. Although we have conducted this group in a school setting only, the parameters of the group could be easily utilized in a private or agency setting.

Member Recruitment and Screening

Group member selection and screening are an important part of any group. For an adolescent male group one can expect that the population is going to be both curious and suspicious of the group opportunity. To construct the best possible group, the group leader must consider what group member characteristics are desired, size of the group, and screening format.

Group member characteristics considered for our groups were age and personality. When working with adolescent males, the group will already be homogeneous with respect to gender, so the group can either be homogeneous in age or the ages can be varied. We have found that 7th and 8th graders work well together as do 9th and 10th and 11th and 12th grades. With a two year spread, the group can cull the advantages of mentoring and varied experiences while not suffering the disadvantages of a wide developmental gap. The following case excerpt demonstrates the value of mixing older boys with younger ones:

> Billy (age 13): It was so cool hearing Argyle (age 14) talk about how he was intimidated by the high school guys. I mean, he is the toughest guy in school and he's scared? It helped me feel like less of a wienie for being afraid of going to high school. When I told him I felt the same way I thought he would laugh, but he didn't. He said I would make it. That felt good.

While two years might be optimum, occasionally a wider age spread might be acceptable depending on the personality of the members, the issues being discussed, and the available client population.

The issue of personality dynamics primarily addresses the need for some heterogeneity within the group. In a school setting, the group will live and die on the attractiveness (the "coolness") of the group. If the group is perceived as uncool, no one will be interested. The first time we selected members for the group, we specifically invited some popular boys to be in the group. One popular boy, Alex was having some difficulties with identity and his parents so not only was he a good fit based on the issues, he was also highly respected within the school. Once Alex joined the group, the group became “cool” and many boys were interested. Interestingly, the “cool” label lasted throughout the life of the group. Boys who initially opted not to be in the group started asking about how to get into the group. The next semester, interest was so high, two group were formed. In addition to the “cool” factor, the more varied the personalities of the members, the more learning can occur. As the males experience other males who are different from them, they begin to expand their personal definitions of maleness.

Group size is also an issue that must be carefully considered. A group that is too small may be perceived as too threatening (too intimate) for adolescent boys. A small group is also subject to failure due to drop outs and absences. A group that is too large may not give each member an opportunity to use the process and may allow group members to hide within the group. The groups we lead are psycho-educational in nature, but have a heavy emphasis on process as well. For this type of group, six to eight members seems to work best. Even when absences occur, the group will be large enough to not inspire the “I’m under the microscope” feeling, but small enough, even when everyone attends, for all members to have an opportunity to participate and be heard.

Methods of screening can be formal or informal. Without a screening procedure, the group members may not truly understand what is expected in the group and therefore, cannot give informed consent to participate. We invited students to participate by sending out a one page description of the group to all prospective members within the school. Information about the purpose of the group, time and place of meeting and duration of the experience were outlined. We also included open ended questions such as “What would you like to get out of the group”, “What could/would you contribute to the group” and “What do you think we will do in group” that the boys were expected to answer. Their answers to these questions shed some light on their expectations about group and aided us in selecting members that had expectations which were congruent with the purpose and format of the group. We also included a space for the parents’ signature as well as the prospective member’s.

In addition to the form letter, we also conducted a short individual meeting with potential members. This meeting gave the boys a chance to talk about their hopes and fears regarding the group, gave the leaders a chance to dispel any myths about the group process, and provided a setting for the members to meet the co-leaders of the group and ask any questions about the process. After all the members meet the leaders and discuss the group, leaders can then select appropriate participants for the group.

Scheduling and Physical Setting

In a school setting, scheduling is a vital concern. Fluctuating school schedules, different class schedules, exams, and extra-curricular activities are all obstacles to consistent group meetings. Collaborating with teachers, administrators, and the students help to identify the best possible time for all potential members to attend on a regular basis.

The literature is relatively silent on the issue of physical setting for group. The following guidelines from Berg, Landreth and Fall (1998) provide general considerations with some modifications specific to the adolescent population noted.

1. Comfortable setting: For this group, we tried many setting formats of various comfort: small rooms, large rooms, pillows, chairs, couches, etc. Based on our experiences, we recommend a medium sized room, one that is a little bit larger than the group, with comfortable, but independent chairs. The chairs need to be spaced apart enough so that the members do not feel cramped, but close enough to give the group a cohesive feel. Make sure the room temperature is comfortable; this seems to be a topic of concern/resistance for adolescent boys.
2. Limit outside distractions: The first time we conducted the group it was held in the computer classroom and the members had a predictably difficult time staying focused on the group activities. We were interrupted by students knocking on the door and the computers produced distracting noises and lights. The second group was in a pre-school cottage that contained many games, books and colorful pieces of art. Once again, the group had trouble focusing. We finally settled on a medium-sized room that was quite bare. Although not aesthetically pleasing, the lack of distractions helped the group focus of the process.
3. Keep the room consistent: Consistency aids in the cohesiveness of the process. The room becomes "our group room" and lends to a feeling of stability and comfort. So much of the group process is unexpected for the members, so it is nice for them to be able to rely on some aspects on the process.
4. Allow for circle seating format: This arrangement helps the members relate to one another and facilitates direct communication.

Group Structure, Role of Facilitators, and Overview of Sessions Group Structure

What follows is a basic structure for a twelve session psychoeducational group designed to help adolescent males gain a deeper insight into their perceptions about themselves and how those perceptions relate to the messages they receive from family, school, friends, and society as a whole about what it means to be a man. The group is designed to provide a basic framework for presenting important information and developing key skills while leaving a degree of flexibility to allow the overall structure to be adapted to meet particular needs. Our hope is that professionals will be able to take what follows and alter it in a variety of ways, whether it is condensing the group to ten sessions, stretching it out to fifteen or twenty sessions, or changing the skills presented in order to more closely reflect the needs of a particular constituency.

The group structure is divided into four stages: group introduction and identity exploration, examining father-son relationships, skill building, and generalization of skills/ closure. Although each stage has its own set of goals, the stages were sequenced so that each stage builds upon the skills and/or knowledge gained in the previous stages and, in some cases, introduce topics that will be discussed in more detail later in the group. Each stage consists of between two and four sessions.

Each session follows a basic framework. First, the group begins by reviewing significant topics or ideas from the previous session and facilitators offer to field any questions about the homework. Next, the facilitators introduce the topic of the day through a brief lecturette or group discussion. Following the topic introduction, the group members participate in a structured activity designed to help deepen the participants' understanding of the subject and help them begin to explore how the topic relates to their lives. The group will then process the activity through group discussion. This discussion consists primarily of questions to help the participants seek a deeper and more personally relevant meaning of the topic material. This is done by the facilitators asking group members how they would use their new information and skills in "here-and-now" examples from group interactions, or how they could apply their new knowledge to their friendships outside of the group. Then, as the session comes to a close, the facilitators introduce the homework assignment for the week.

Each group member is given a group journal which they are to use for their homework assignments. The homework assignments are usually in the form of questions the participants are to answer or brief assignments they are to complete on their own time. These assignments serve several purposes. First, they prompt participants to revisit important topics after the members have had some time to "digest" the information. The open-ended questions are meant to help the members to take the information out of the group setting and begin to generalize it to their lives, making the topics more personally relevant to each participant. In addition, the privacy of the journal provides each member with a safer vehicle for expressing any thoughts or concerns that he may not feel comfortable sharing with the larger group.

Although the sessions have a basic structure to help the group stay on task, the authors also believe it is important to keep the structure very flexible. Facilitators may want to think about telling group members in the past that although each week has its own topic, the group is also open to talking about any pressing issue in their lives related to their development and growth as a male. This helps to build trust between the group members and the facilitators and helps to ensure that the members find the group material to be relevant to their own lives. On the other hand, there is a chance that leaving this door open to the participants may provide them with an opportunity to spend group time talking about superficial topics instead of focusing on core issues. If this is a concern, facilitators may want to recommend that the group members turn their issues in written form so that the facilitators can find a way to weave them into the existing group material.

While developing the group structure, the authors decided to use a male co-facilitator model of leadership. We felt using co-facilitators held many advantages. First of all, each group facilitator brings his own strengths to the group, and having two leaders enables each leader to learn from the other. In addition, being able to consult with a peer after the group and hearing different perspectives on what has occurred and where the group might be going is an excellent opportunity for the group's development and for the professional development of the facilitators involved. Having co-facilitators also provides opportunities for the group leaders to model many of the skills that are important in adult relationships, including communication skills, managing emotions, giving and receiving encouragement, demonstrating mutual respect and trust, and empathic listening. Finally, if there are two facilitators, they can strategically place themselves between talkative pairs or next to daydreamers to help encourage the participants to remain focused as much as possible during the group.

The authors felt that having two males lead the group was the best model given the circumstances under which the group was originally conceived; specifically, the concern that seventh and eighth grade males did not have enough exposure to adult males at school. Utilizing two males proved to have other advantages as well. For instance, it gives group members the opportunity to see adult males model important social skills within the framework of a professional and respectful relationship. In addition, because the facilitators are friends, the participants witnessed friendly interaction and common joking around between two adult males. Perhaps most importantly, the group witnessed two males listening to each other, empathizing with each other, and encouraging each other--not the behaviors that adolescent males typically witness between men in movies or on television.

Although the authors choose two males to facilitate the group, having a male and a female co-facilitate the group would also have advantages. Having a female in the group might help the participants to check their generalizations and stereotypes regarding gender. It would also be a valuable experience for the young men to hear a woman's perspective on such important developmental and relationship issues, particularly in the safe, non-judgmental environment that group counseling provides. Furthermore, just as it would be beneficial for the participants to view two males in a mutually respectful working relationship, it would also be beneficial to see a man and a woman interact professionally and respectfully.

Group Facilitators' Role

The group facilitators have several roles. First, they must set the tone for the group by creating an environment that is relaxed and supportive while keeping the group on task. One of the most important ways the facilitators can accomplish this task is to focus on modeling the skills that will be addressed later in the group, including encouragement, appropriate communication, appropriate expression of emotion, being accountable for one's behaviors, and demonstrating trust for others. Not only will this help to create a therapeutic milieu, but the group members will be better able to understand these skills when they are presented later in the group if they have been effectively modeled by the facilitators throughout the first two stages of the group.

The group facilitators should also watch for the emergence of any common themes that may appear during the identity exploration stage. Many of the group activities and journal assignments during the first stage are designed to not only expose the participants to new ideas and concepts, but to provide information to the facilitators about what the key issues may be for each of the group members. Although most of the obvious themes and issues should be identified during the pre-group interviews, sometimes important information pops up unexpectedly in these introduction exercises. Once some common group themes are identified, facilitators may want to adjust the sequence of sessions, add or delete specific sessions, or alter the focus of a few of the sessions slightly in order to make the group more relevant to its participants and to give them specific skills and insights that they can use in the world outside of the group.

Finally, the facilitators need to have a feel for how closely the group is working together and where they are in terms of working within the group norms. Group facilitators need to be mindful of introducing activities at an appropriate risk-comfort level so that the group is able to get something out of the exercise without feeling discomfort to a degree where they would begin to shut down. A slowly norming group can take a few steps backward if confronted with a high risk activity too soon. Likewise, a well functioning group can get bored with exercises that do not challenge them enough. As with any group, helping the group find that balance between feeling anxious enough to be motivated to work and feeling safe enough to be able to work is an important component to the group's ultimate success.

Overview of Group Sessions

Stage 1: Introduction to Group/ Identity Exploration

The purpose of this stage is to introduce the group members to each other, the group facilitators, and the group process and to help them start examining different aspects of their identity as young men. By the end of this stage, the group members should be comfortable with each other and the facilitators, understand the group expectations, be able to work well within the group norms, and begin to develop an understanding of the different roles they play as young men and the different roles men are expected to play in our society.

Session 1: Group Introduction

Goals: The goal of the first session is to give the group members an opportunity to introduce themselves to each other, to the group facilitators, and to the group procedures as well as to help the group members begin exploring their identities as young men.

Group Introductions: The group facilitators begin by introducing themselves to the group members and asking the group to introduce themselves to each other and to the group leaders. The group facilitators give a brief overview of the group procedures including meeting times and frequencies, duration of the group, and group norms and expectations. The facilitators then give out the journals and explain the role that their journal assignments will play in the group.

Activity: The facilitators lead a quick introduction activity, such as asking each group member to pick a favorite animal, or to pick a "super hero" trait that he would like to possess. Their choices are discussed in an accepting, non-threatening manner so that the conversation flows well and sets the tone for open, non-judgmental discussion.

Homework: The first homework assignment is for each member to write down their first impressions of the group in their journal. Members are encouraged to write whatever positive or negative impressions they have about the group and its process and how their impressions compare with any expectations they had coming into the group.

Session 2: Who am I?

Goals: The goal of this group is for members to begin to identify some characteristics that describe their identity and make each member unique. Members are encouraged to consider deeper aspects of self, such as values, beliefs and interests and to share this information with the rest of the group.

Review: Facilitators ask the participants if they have any questions about or problems with the homework assignment and if anyone would like to share any thoughts regarding their first impressions of the group. The facilitators remind the group members that sharing of homework is voluntary. If the group leaders have constructed an atmosphere of acceptance and warmth, it is common for group members to validate the feelings of safety with disclosures such as, "This is a lot different than what I thought group was going to be. It's pretty laid back. I was worried it was going to be like a class or something". Group leaders can use the feedback to reinforce the aspects of openness and trust within the group.

Activity: The facilitators provide the group with large pieces of newsprint and several magazines. The facilitators tell the participants to find pictures in the magazines that say something about who they are and what they want, cut them out, and glue them on the newsprint.

Discussion: Group members show their collages to the group and discuss the significance of the pictures they chose for their collages. The group then discusses any similarities or differences they notice between the collages. This activity produces many informative processing issues. Some members will choose safe and universal symbols of masculinity such as females in swimsuits, athletes, and music or movie personalities. Although superficial, these choices represent the member's best attempt to try to fit into the group and the images can be used for later discussion about masculinity. It is common at the beginning of any group for the members to attempt to identify with one another, but what happens when a member risks and puts something on the collage that does not fit with the adolescent male ideal? In one group, a shy member sat off to the side of the group seemingly choosing nothing to put on his collage. At the end of group, the other boys shared images of self as defined by the before-mentioned masculine symbols. Finally it was his turn and he held his collage to his chest. The other members of the group encouraged him to show his work and reluctantly he held up his collage. He said, "This is all I could find of me"- a large white piece of paper, bare except for a tiny picture of a white kitten in the middle of the page. We, as group leaders held our breath, afraid of the possible laughter and degrading remarks that could follow. Instead, what happened next was awe inspiring, as each member carefully commented on the boy's disclosure with supportive words of, "That's cool", "I like cats too" and "Wow man, thanks for letting us see that." By sharing aspects of self, the group is offered the opportunity to risk and out of that risk, comes the need to be respectful of one another's offerings.

Homework: Group members write about common themes among the collages, and where they believe these common ideas may come from. For example, if most of the group had pictures of sports stars decorating their collages, members could write about why they believe sports appeal to so many young men. They are also encouraged to write about any image they thought represented them, but were cautious or afraid to put on their public collage.

Session 3: What am I?

Goals: The goal for this session is for group members to identify important characteristics of some of the roles that adult men often play, as well as identify inconsistencies between characteristics of the roles.

Review: Facilitators encourage those members who are willing to talk about their ideas to share excerpts from their homework.

Introduction of Topic: Group facilitators briefly discuss the idea of the different roles that men often play different roles in their lives. Facilitators explain what is meant by roles, and then ask the members to brainstorm different roles that they may play, such as son, student, friend, athlete, and brother.

Activity: The facilitators put up four large sheets of newsprint on the walls. Each one is labeled with a role males typically play in society, such as "Man", "Husband", "Father" and "Son". Group members then brainstorm characteristics they believe are consistent with performing each of the roles well.

NOTE: Because of the recurring role the father-son relationship plays throughout the group, this exercise is important not only to get the participants thinking about the roles they will play, but also to give specific examples of difficulties in male relationships that can be used later on in the group. However, if the group's issues merit it and time permits it, this activity can also be done looking at roles women typically play in society, such as "Women", "Wife", "Mother", and "Daughter". While the mother-son relationship may not become a recurring theme like the father-son relationship, it is still a worthwhile exercise for the young men to gain some insight into the confusion that young women experience as they grow up as well.

Discussion: Group facilitators ask the participants to look at the descriptions they came up with and discuss any common themes they see among the different roles. An example of the characteristics derived from one group appear below.

Man	*Father*	*Husband*
Hairy	Works a lot	Nice to wife
Drinks Beer	Mows lawn	Loving
Strong	Disciplines kids	Protects wife
Plays sports	Teaches kids	Works, makes money
Smart	Decision maker	His wife is his friend
Has a penis	Should spend time with kids	
Not scared- Be brave	*go to games, park, movies	
Lots of friends	His kids should be his friends	

After the lists are constructed, the leaders ask the participants to discuss any inconsistencies they see between the different roles. For example, are there characteristics that may help someone be a good man that are inconsistent with those characteristics that help men to be good husbands, good fathers, or good sons? What might the effect of trying to be so many different things to so many different people be? How do men begin to synthesize the different characteristics and expectations into their personal identity?

Homework: Group members interview three adult males, asking them to give their definitions of what it means to be a man. Participants write these definitions in their journals.

Session 4: How Others See Me

Goals: The goal for this group is for members to receive feedback concerning how they are viewed by other people, and see how this feedback fits with their view of themselves.

Review: Group members are encouraged to share some significant parts of their interviews. Any surprises? Any ideas that are particularly meaningful?

NOTE: Of all of the homework assignments we have given, this one seems to be the most thought provoking to those participants who put time and effort into it. It may be worthwhile to spend a little more time than usual reviewing and processing this homework assignment, especially if some of the group members do not seem to be involved yet.

Activity: Members fill out Part I and Part II of the "First Impression Sheets" (Peterson, 1993). Part I asks members how they believe they are viewed by certain people in their lives, such as parents, teachers and peers. In Part II, they are asked to provide a few adjectives that describe each member of the group. Members are encouraged to be as honest as possible, and are told that their comments will be read aloud but will remain anonymous.

Discussion: The facilitators collect the sheets. Processing this exercise may be done in a couple of ways depending on how much time is left and the group's comfort level with such a high-risk exercise. Facilitators may choose to process Part I of the worksheet by reading aloud each participant's responses of how he believes others see him and have the group guess which person it is. The facilitators may or may not choose to reveal the names; sometimes more interesting information comes when the feedback is not ascribed to a certain person.

If the facilitators wish to process Part II of the sheet, they may call one group member at a time and read all the adjectives that the other group members wrote about him without saying who wrote what. For instance, when it is Johnny's turn, a facilitator would read what each of the other group members wrote to describe Johnny. Afterwards, Johnny is asked for his reaction to hearing the feedback. Once Johnny has had a chance to respond, the next group member is picked and the facilitators read all the adjectives used to describe him.

This can be a high-risk activity, particularly if the group is not cohesive and/or supportive. By reading the adjectives without showing them to the group, the facilitators do have the option of deleting or ignoring any comments that are inappropriate or potentially damaging. However, we do not recommend that comments be deleted just because they are negative. The feedback is still important even if it is difficult for the member to hear—perhaps even more so. If negative feedback is not taken well by a group member, we recommend treating it as a group issue and using the opportunity to discuss the feedback process, the responsibility of giving honest feedback, and how each of us has the choice to accept or reject others' feedback.

Homework: Group members write about how the feedback they received fits with their perceptions of themselves. Examples of questions members might answer include: Does the feedback accurately describe who you are? Why or why not? To what do you attribute the differences between others' stated perceptions of you and your perceptions of yourself?

Stage Two: Examining Relationships with our Fathers

The goal of stage two is to enable members to look at their relationships with their fathers, share some common experiences with the group, and to begin to develop insight into how these relationships have affected their development as young men. The theme of father-son relationship will be revisited later in stage four.

Session 5: Fatherhood

Goal: The goal of this session is to give group members an opportunity to share stories about their fathers and have the opportunity to hear about other group members' relationship with their fathers.

Review: Each group member is asked about his reaction to the feedback from last week's group, as well as how it felt to hear feedback in such a direct manner. It may be important to briefly discuss how people usually receive feedback about themselves. Because the previous exercise was such a high risk activity, it is important that the group not move on until the facilitators feel that the exercise is properly processed.

Introduction of Topic: Group facilitators tell the group that the next section will focus on the members' relationships with their fathers. Members are asked why they think father-son relationships might be seen as such an important topic in a young men's group.

Activity: Each member is asked to tell about his relationship with his father. The guidelines for the discussion are left fairly general so that the members may talk about whatever seems important to them. Examples of what they may want to talk about include: what they like to do with their fathers, how much time they normally spend with their fathers, and how they would characterize their relationship. In order to give everyone sufficient time without feeling rushed, group facilitators inform the group members that this activity will be continued next week for those who do not get a chance to talk this session.

Discussion: As group members share stories, group leaders focus on linking stories, finding similarities between group members, and identifying unique aspects of members' relationships. Members are encouraged to empathize with each other.

Homework: Each group member outlines a story about his relationship with his father. Participants should write in the third person, and have the story only tell about their relationship so far (i.e., they should not write an ending).

Session 6: Fatherhood, continued

Goal: The goal of this session is for group members to continue sharing stories about their fathers and listening to each other's stories.

Review: Group facilitators ask members if they had any questions about or problems with their homework assignment. Facilitators then briefly review where the discussion left off last week, and ask the members who did not talk the previous week to talk about their relationship with their fathers.

Activity/Discussion: Group members continue telling stories about their fathers.

Homework: Each member writes an ending to the story of his relationship with his father as if things were to continue as they are now.

NOTE: When we first started the young men's group, we saved this topic until after the skill building stage. We found, however, that so much useful and important information came out of this stage that we decided to bring it up earlier in the group sequence so that we could use the information throughout the remainder of the group. Having the members discuss their relationships with their fathers provides a great opportunity to link group members who may otherwise see each other as different. In addition, the ability to use real father-son experiences as example situations during the skill building stage has proven particularly useful.

Stage Three: Skill Building

The goal of the third stage is to expose the group members to a variety of important interpersonal and coping skills, to provide a safe environment for the students to practice some of the skills, and to explore the possibility of using these skills in their lives outside of the group. Skills covered include becoming accountable, understanding and appropriately communicating emotions, giving and receiving encouragement, and building trust.

Session 7: Accountability

Goal: The goal of this session is for group members to develop a working definition of the term "personal accountability" and to be able to list specific ways in which they can become more accountable in their own lives. Members will understand common ways in which they keep themselves from being accountable, and identify which of these defenses they use in their own lives.

Review: Facilitators ask the group members if they encountered any difficulties in concluding their stories. Members are asked to think about how they would characterize their endings (i.e., sad, happy, or tragic). Similarly, members are asked how they felt as they completed the assignment (i.e., hopeful, anxious, or appreciative). Facilitators then remind the participants that the endings they wrote are supposed to reflect how things would end if everything proceeded as they are now, but that the endings may change if they are willing to look at things differently and try some new behaviors and skills. This serves as a segue into the section on skill building.

Introduction of Topic: Facilitators explain that the next few groups will focus on specific skills that the members will be able to use in their daily lives, especially in their relationships with the significant people. The first skill is the ability to be accountable for the choices they make. Members are asked to share their ideas of what it means to be accountable.

Activity: Each group member is given a copy of the "Defenses against Accountability" sheet (adapted from Fall, Howard, & Ford; 1999). The sheet lists three common blocks to personal accountability: minimization, denial, and blame. Beside each block is a series of lines meant to show the degree to which each item blocks accountability, with minimization being the least severe and blame being the most destructive.

Discussion: Using the defenses against accountability sheet as a reference, the group facilitators ask questions to help the members develop insight into what role accountability plays in people's lives and why people may choose to use defenses. Examples of questions facilitators can ask include: Why do these defenses exist? What purpose do they serve? How do they help us? From what do they protect us? How can they hurt us? What happens to someone who refuses to be accountable for his behavior?

Homework: Group members answer the following questions in their journals: In what areas of your life do you find you are accountable? In what areas of your life is it difficult for you to hold yourself accountable? Which of the blocks to accountability do you use most? Give an example of a situation in which you used one of the blocks to accountability.

Session 8: Emotions and Communication

Goal: Group members will expand their emotional vocabulary and develop some insights into their own emotions and how they communicate their emotions to others.

Review: Facilitators ask members to volunteer any insights they had regarding their use of blocks to accountability in their lives.

Introduction of Topic: Facilitators will present a brief discussion of emotion and communication. Facilitators ask the members why they believe "emotions" are an important topic in a young men's group.

Activity: The facilitators tape a large piece of newsprint to the wall. Members then brainstorm as many emotions as they can, with the facilitators writing each emotion on the newsprint. After the list is complete, facilitators then go back through the list and ask which of the emotions are okay for the members to express, and which ones are not okay to express.

The facilitators make a mark next to each emotion mentioned indicating whether it is an emotion that is okay or not okay to express. Using a pretty liberal definition of "emotions", many groups may be able to cite ten to twelve emotions without much prodding and can get the list to twenty or so with a little encouragement from the facilitators. When going back over the list, however, it is surprising to see how few of the emotions are deemed "safe" to express by the adolescents. In our experience, anger is the most common emotion that is seen as safe. Most other difficult emotions including, sadness, fear, frustration, loneliness, are said to be very risky. Yet even the emotions commonly seen as positive emotions—happiness, pride, joy—are judged to be risky to express under many circumstances.

Discussion: Facilitators ask group members to talk about the consequences associated with expressing those emotions which were deemed "not okay to express" and where these consequences come from. Finally, facilitators ask what happens when those risky emotions are experienced. For example, do we just keep them bottled inside or forget about them, or are they likely to be expressed eventually in another way?

Homework: Members complete an adaptation of the "dinner table" exercise (Trotzer, 1997). Members draw a picture of their dining room table and label where each member of the family typically sits. Each member then draws lines between the family members showing how they communicate with each other with different colors or types of lines representing different types of communication. Members should include a key of the different symbols they use.

Session 9: Encouragement

Goal: Group members will develop a working definition of encouragement and discouragement, discuss the role that encouragement plays in their lives, and begin to develop insight into how each of them gives and receives encouragement.

Review: Facilitators will ask the members who feel comfortable doing so to share their dining room table exercises. Often this exercise produces a wide range of emotional responses. As each member shares what it feels like to be in their family, through the symbol of the dining room table, feelings of pride, comfort, sadness, humiliation, anger, or abandonment may surface. The rich supply of content provides the group members an opportunity to experience safe/unsafe emotions within the context of the group's safety.

Introduction of Topic: Facilitators introduce encouragement as the topic of the day, and ask group participants to share any images that come to mind when they hear the word.

Activity: Facilitators hand each participant a copy of the "Encouragement and Discouragement" sheet (Peterson, 1993). The group may read parts of the sheet aloud or read the sheet silently to themselves.

Discussion: After the sheet is read, the facilitators ask the group members to summarize some of the important points on the sheet. Members then discuss how they see the information on encouragement and discouragement relating to the previous week's topic of communication and emotions. Examples of questions facilitators may want to ask include: is giving encouragement to someone else a risky thing to do? Is receiving encouragement risky? Under what conditions might giving or receiving encouragement be safe? Do we learn our personal patterns concerning giving and receiving encouragement from watching our male role models?

Homework: Members answer the following questions in their journal: From whom do you receive encouragement? How is that encouragement typically communicated? How is it received? From whom would you like to receive more encouragement?

Session 10: Trust

Goal: The goal for this session is for members to look at the role trust plays in relationships, develop insight into the dynamics of trust, and begin to see how they can be accountable for creating or enhancing the trust level in their significant relationships.

Review: Facilitators encourage group members to share any thoughts they had regarding their journal entries about last week's topic, encouragement.

Introduction of Topic: As members discuss encouragement, facilitators bring the conversation around to the issue of trust. Facilitators ask members whom they trust, how they figure out whom to trust, and how they can earn other's trust.

Activity: Facilitators hand out a copy of the "Trust Tube" Worksheet (Fall et al., 1999). After the participants fill out the worksheet, one of the facilitators draws a picture of a trust tube on the board, explaining that most relationships are like this tube and trust is like the liquid that fills the liquid. All relationships have different levels of trust, thus, some relationships are more "full" than others.

Discussion: Facilitators ask group members to think about how they would ordinarily fill up an empty tube. Do we tend to handle all relationships the same way? What sort of actions or behaviors can people do in order to help fill their tube? The following list is an example of answers found in group.

When I do trust, I	*When I don't trust, I ....*
Give gifts	Avoid people
Like to be around them	Am suspicious
Tell them secrets	Spread rumors
Am Honest	Lie
Share stuff with them	Feel angry
Listen to them	Ignore them
Respect their opinions	Think everything they say is wrong

The dynamic of the trust tube rests on a simple ironic fact: When we need trust the most (when we do not trust someone) is when we are most likely to participate in behaviors (lying, isolating, suspicion) that will actively sabotage the building of trust. The key to building trust is to behave in ways that facilitate trust, even when you feel hurt. Facilitators ask participants if there are any relationships in which they would like to increase the level of trust. Using the trust tube analogy, facilitators ask group members to think of specific things they could do to help increase the level of trust. Facilitators should ensure that members are focusing on things the individual participant can do, not what the other person can do.

This is also an important time to remind the group members that the group is nearing its end. Facilitators might want to encourage participants to think about bringing up any topic or issue that they would like to work on before the group ends.

Homework: In their journals, members write an alternate ending for their stories about their fathers. This time, they are to write how the story might end if the characters use some of the skills presented in the group, such as being accountable, effectively communicating emotions, giving and accepting encouragement, and building trust.

Stage Four: Generalizing Group Skills and Closure

The final stage of the group has two distinct goals. First, group members will identify specific ways in which they can generalize the skills and knowledge they acquired in the group to their relationships outside of the group. Secondly, members will be able to say goodbye to the group members and facilitators and appropriately express their emotions about the ending of the group.

Session 11: Getting what you want from your Relationship with your Father

Goal: The goal of this session is for group members to identify specific ways in which they can become accountable for getting more of what they want from their relationships with their fathers.

Review: The group facilitators will briefly review the skills presented in stage three of the group, including becoming accountable, managing and communicating emotions, giving and receiving encouragement, and building trust.

Introduction of Topic: After the brief review, facilitators will explain that one of the main goals of the group is for the members to be able to take the skills they discussed and practiced in the group setting and use them in their relationships outside of the group. Furthermore, the father-son relationship is a good one to use as an example because it is a very important and often difficult relationship.

Activity: Facilitators encourage group participants to share the alternate endings to their stories with the group.

Discussion: The group processes the alternate endings, with the facilitators making sure that each group member is able to identify specific actions he can take in order to become more accountable for any changes that take place. For instance, story endings that include magical transformations are challenged, and facilitators encourage the writers to find specific things they can do to help change the relationship instead. Those stories where change occurred through implementing new skills may be used as models.

Homework: Group members rewrite their endings so that they can increase their level of accountability. In addition, group members are reminded that the next meeting will be the last meeting, and are asked to think about how they would like to say goodbye.

Session 12: Closing

Goal: The goal of this session is to give members a safe environment to appropriately express their feelings about the group's ending, and to provide an effective closure experience for the group members.

Review: Members briefly discuss their rewritten alternate endings, highlighting the specific steps they have taken to increase their accountability.

Introduction of Topic: Facilitators remind the participants that this session is the final session, briefly discuss what termination is and how termination often brings up a wide range of emotions. If appropriate, the facilitators may want to remind the group about the work they did regarding their ability to express emotions, to trust each other, and to encourage each other, and suggest to the members that they use this termination group as an opportunity to demonstrate their new skills.

Activity: Each member is asked to express his emotions about the group's termination. In addition, each member is expected to listen respectfully as they express themselves. If time permits, facilitators may lead "pre-post" type, termination exercises. For instance, facilitators could hand back the collages that the participants made in session two and ask members what they would add or what they would take away form the collages to make them more accurately describe who they are as young men.

Discussion: Group members are asked to reflect on the group as a whole, and discuss any changes they have noticed in themselves through the course of the group. For instance, what skills have they developed? Do they have a new way of looking at certain situations? How has the group affected the way they see and feel about their fathers or any other male role models?

Homework: Facilitators ask group members to think about the changes they would like to see in their lives and specifics ways they can help make those changes occur. The facilitators then challenge the group members to make their positive endings happen. NOTE: As the group leaves for the final time, facilitators may stand at the door and model appropriate goodbyes by looking each group member in the eye, shaking his hand, and thanking him for being a member of the group.

CONCLUSION

Adolescent males in our society are pummeled by two seemingly contradictory forces: 1) the societal pressure to be strong and unemotional and 2) the internal need to be able to, at times, *not* be strong and unemotional. Our society also tends to view our adolescents as either going through a phase or as uncontrollable monsters. Each view risks ignoring real problems and issues as they surface. The group described in this chapter was designed to fulfill the need for a space for adolescent males to feel free to explore, not ignore, what was churning inside of them. The group provides a setting for boys to learn from boys while also learning new information, or exploring old information in new ways. While our feedback on the group has been positive, our hope is that other practitioners and researchers will continue to reach out and into the world of adolescent males.

REFERENCES

Berg, R.C., Landreth, G., & Fall, K. A. (1998). *Group counseling: Concepts and procedures* (3rd ed.). Philadelphia, PA: Accelerated Development.

Blos, P. (1962). *On adolescence: A psychoanalytic interpretation*. New York: Free Press of Glencoe.

Caron, A.F. (1994). *Strong mothers strong sons: Raising the next generation of men*. New York: Harper.

Centers for Disease Control (1998). *Youth risk behavior surveillance- United States, 1997*. Washington DC: U.S. Department of Health and Human Services.

Douvan, E., & Adelson, J. (1966). *The adolescent experience*. New York: Wiley.

Esser, G., Schmidt, M.H., & Woerner, W. (1990). Epidemiology and course of psychiatric disorders in school age children: Results of a longitudinal study. *Journal of Child Psychology and Psychiatry*, *31*, 243-263.

Fall, K.A., Howard, S., & Ford, J.E. (1999). *Alternatives to domestic violence*. Philadelphia, PA: Accelerated Development.

Freud, A. (1946). *The ego and the mechanisms of defence*. New York: International Universities.

Garbarino, J. (1999). *Lost boys: Why our sons turn violent and how we can save them*. New York: The Free Press.

Gurian, M. (1996). *The wonder of boys*. New York: Tarcher/Putnam.

Hall, G.S. (1904). *Adolescence: Its psychology and its relations to physiology, anthropology, sociology, sex, crime, religion, and education* (Vols. 1, 2). New York: D. Appelton.

Lamb, M. (1997). Fathers and child development: An introductory overview and guide. In M. Lamb (Ed.)., *The role of the father in child development* (pp.1-8). New York: Wiley.

Levant, R. F. (1995). Toward the reconstruction of masculinity. In R.F. Levant & W.S. Pollack (Eds.), *A new psychology of men* (pp. 229-251). New York: Harper Collins.

Levine, J.A. & Piitinsky, T.L. (1997). *Working fathers: New strategies for balancing work and family*. New York: Addison-Wesley.

Manning, M.L. (1983). Three myths concerning adolescence. *Adolescence, 18*, 823-829.

Miedzian, M. (1991). *Boys will be boys: Breaking the link between masculinity and violence*. New York: Doubleday.

Peterson, J.S. (1993). *Talk with Teens about self and stress*. Minneapolis, MN: Free Spirit.

Pollack, W. (1998). *Real boys: Rescuing our sons from the myths of boyhood*. New York: Random House.

Powers, S.I., Hauser, S.T., & Kilner, L.A. (1989). Adolescent mental health. *American Psychologist*, *44*, 200-208.

Pruett, K.D. (1987). *The nurturing father*. New York: Warner.

Radin, N. (1994). Primary caregiving fathers in intact families. In A.E. Gottfried and A.W. Gottfied (Eds.), *Redefining families: Implications for children's development* (pp. 11-54). New York: Plenum.

Thompson, E.H., & Pleck, J.H. (1987). The structure of male role norms. In M.S. Kimmel (Ed.), *Changing men: New directions in research on men and masculinity* (pp. 25-36).Newbury Park: Sage.

Trotzer, J. P. (1997). *Problem solving group counseling*. A presentation to the Association for Specialists in Group Work. Athens, GA.

Chapter Four

The Self Image of Adolescent Females: A Group Exploration

Marly L. Sweeney

Introduction

In 1990, the American Association of University Women (AAUW), published the results of a survey of adolescent girls that revealed, among other things, that girls' levels of self esteem in the United States drop dramatically as they enter adolescence. An abundance of research, several books, and various theories resulted from efforts to explain this reduction in self esteem. The search for a deeper understanding of why adolescent girls seem to be experiencing such severe difficulties and the pursuit of methods to help them become even more crucial when one considers the epidemic rise in internalized afflictions such as eating disorders and self-mutilating behaviors (e.g. cutting), and external forces such as sexual harassment and various forms of sexualized violence towards adolescent girls.

In a world of increased violence toward and sexual objectification of females, adolescent girls need help themselves by taking full advantage of affiliation, connection and relating skills. The ability to talk and express feelings are strengths that many teenage girls possess. Since friendships are essential positive forces in the lives of girls, relationship skills and abilities help girls manage increasing developmental and cultural demands as they mature (Apter & Josselson, 1998). By adolescence, these developmental demands, the need to talk, and the craving for peer friendship collide. Group therapy, because it stresses effective methods for dealing with these social forces, offers an ideal treatment modality.

The idea perpetuated in clinical circles that adolescents resist psychotherapy and counseling is probably false. The myth probably results from misinterpretations of adolescents' attempts to "save face" as acts of true resistance. A good example of this phenomenon occurred at a local Covenant House. Many of the female residents reacted cavalierly to the news that a psychotherapy group was planned for female residents. On the day and time of the first scheduled group, case managers, acting on what they perceived as resistance to becoming involved in the groups, were surprised to find the group room packed with adolescent girls. The participants were so motivated that the group leaders abandoned plans to use an "ice breaker" activity when the girls spontaneously began talking about themselves and their concerns. What the case managers perceived as evidence of resistance proved to be "face saving" comments. Of course, some youths are resistant, but many adolescent girls are asking, even clamoring to be in therapy.

While the broad tasks of adolescence as they were defined early in the 20th century remain similar for the girls of today, the contemporary context in which they are experienced and expressed have changed dramatically. History, economics, science, medicine, and other factors influencing culture alter the way adolescent girls demonstrate mastery of various developmental tasks. Culture changes the way internal conflicts and demands manifest themselves. While girls and women may revel in the new found freedoms of the 20th century, they must also contend with unanticipated emotional costs of these freedoms. The broader themes that have traditionally surfaced for adolescent girls persist; the radical changes exist not in the themes themselves, but in the way these themes are expressed today. Thus, helping professionals, if they are to be effective, must be willing to address age-old adolescent themes expressed in a contemporary context. In this chapter the age stage tasks as outlined by Havighurst in 1952 are used as a broad framework to explore modern challenges to adolescent female development.

A basic understanding of group theory and theories of human development (especially adolescent development) are presumed. While the chapter provides an overview of emerging issues related to girls in group psychotherapy, it does not include a review of the basic tenets of adolescent group psychotherapy. Group leaders will also need detailed information about common adolescent issues including the effect of divorce on children, healthy body image, sexual abuse, and self-esteem.

Discussion of Ideas

It would be impossible to successfully conduct a girls' group without being guided by the basic tasks of age-stage development in adolescence. Unfortunately, these important tasks of adolescence are frequently trivialized by adults. For example, adults are probably communicating hidden hurt, anger and disdain when they say: "you are just rebelling," "you are trying to be a grown up," "you are just going through a stage," "I can't wait until you start acting like a human being again," but they are also trivializing the adolescent's behavior. Thus the clinician helps by translating adolescent development into easily understood concepts and language for both the teenager and his or her parents. Adolescence is an essential developmental stage because it produces the transformation from child to adult. This section of the chapter describes a number of important themes associated with female adolescent development including: separation, aggression and anger, the power of the peer group, and puberty. Each of these tasks contributes to the individual's progression from child to adult.

Separation

Most contemporary clinicians understand psychological development from a perspective that honors male and female developmental issues. Historically, clinicians did not embrace such a balanced view of development. In an earlier time, clinicians studied theory that was predominately phallocentric, or male-oriented. This perspective distorted the way in which women were treated because female behavior was analyzed according to male models. Today, we understand that culturally, societally, and theoretically, we are heavily influenced by patriarchal models. Such models, together with the traditional "American spirit," compel us to believe that leaving, separation, independence, and freedom are goals for all young adults. Newer thought looks at female development quite differently. In brief, the newer models endorse the belief that the concepts of separation and autonomy (emotional and psychological components) have been confused. What is referred to in the literature of Gilligan (1982), Pipher (1995), DeBold et al. (1993) as "the lies of separation" refers to the fact that parents feel obligated to enforce the expectations of the culture, pushing girls to separate along the lines of traditional male models of separation. The female model of development suggests that you do not have to separate to be autonomous and that women arrive at adulthood through a different separation process than do men (Bloom, 1980). For girls, separation becomes one of redefinition of connection, rather than a severance of the relationship. Patriarchal culture and phallocentric theory combined, tell parents, clinicians and teenage girls that they must find ways to help adolescent girls leave their parents. Mothers, too, as agents of the culture, enforce the "lie of separation" (DeBold, et al., 1993) unintentionally and/or unconsciously betraying their daughters. DeBold et al. (1993) asserts transformation, rather than the perceived termination of the relationship, is the preferred goal for female adolescents.

We now know that girls stay connected to their families differently than boys throughout adolescence. Unlike the boy who can look at his mother or females and say, "look, I am clearly different than her," a girl looks at her mother/females and sees that she is in fact the same. "For healthy development, the girl must find safety in her differences from her mother, comfort in her sameness" (Benton et al., 1993, 134). Psychosexual theories relate the process of identity development to the difference in experience of one's body, sex and genitalia. Theorists such as Bernstein (1993) postulate that young women have a greater difficulty with the concept of separation due to the internal experience of one's sex and gender, while males are more externally focused, both in experience and anatomy. Overall, when working with adolescent girls, the emphasis should be on honoring the female way of individuating. Therapists are cautioned to avoid applying the male ideal of independence to female clients where the fit will be awkward.

Ethnicity and culture play an important role in the definition of separation and autonomy. The clinician must understand particular values in the African-American family, Chinese-American family, Hispanic family and others. While there are differences that require understanding in all aspects of adolescent development, it is most evident in regards to the role of separation and family. Many families believe in keeping their teenagers close to the family, and deny them some of the traditional "American" rites of adolescent passage that are expected. With pressures within the teen culture, at school especially, these minority girls may have even more influences and models to contend with that place her at greater risk for internal conflict. Or, she may find shelter from the storm in bypassing "American" adolescence. Now that we know that girls in particular may fare better if allowed to maintain more of an attachment, perhaps we can better allow for such differences. Groups may also be used to give her the added strength and support to explore and define a personal experience of separation.

Aggression and Anger

The issues of female aggression, anger and conflict must be understood to appropriately conceptualize them as they arise in development and group. Female aggression and anger are often uncomfortable, disturbing, and frightening to girls, their families, and society. The direct expression of anger by females continues to be poorly tolerated by both men and women. Mothers and fathers aid this problem as they attempt to raise a daughter to "be happy," "be feminine," and "be desirable." Often these attempts mean excluding feelings of anger.

While most adolescent females are inexperienced when it comes to appropriate ways to handle aggression, they also do not wish to emulate male models of aggression for it seems too hierarchical and power focused. She must create, find, learn, and master ways of experiencing and displaying aggression that are compatible with her own definition of femininity. Also there is much to override in terms of cultural and familial pressures. Most girls have learned early to send their anger and aggression underground which frequently leads to depression, manipulative handling of such emotions and vulnerability to myriad forms of danger (Parens, 1993). Girls fare better when they work in collaboration, aligned with others, to deal with anger openly and constructively. Power and resilience results when girls join forces and voices and when groups help girls find strength and growth together (Brown, 1998). Often, it is through this open sharing with other girls that anger becomes accepted and transformed into healthy experiences.

Peer Groups

Girls have the power to support one another, teach one another, be catalysts for growth, and provide strength against the hardships and the dangers inherent in life. Certainly negative peer pressure exists, and girls can and do enforce patriarchal culture. However, they can also provide valuable, positive peer pressure. Girls introduce and show each other how to be feminine, strong, smart, creative, powerful and aggressive in ways that they had never thought of or been exposed to before. They can also teach, promote and shape healthy values and beliefs. Positive peer pressure can be used within groups to enforce a healthy culture of femininity The power of the peer group often fills parents with apprehension. "Peer pressure" is commonly used in a pejorative sense although it can be viewed positively. Adolescents use their peers as a stepping stone to autonomy (Nowinski, 1990). While once conforming to the standards set forth by their families, adolescents now conform instead to the standards of their peers. Peers serve as a transitional object and as agents of the culture which implies that independence and separateness are desirable. They use peers, and their collective anger to help to propel them away from the family.

Keeping in mind the view of the power of the peer group, a whole new way of viewing female friendships is needed before attempting to run an adolescent female group. While other books are sure to emerge, *Best Friends; The Pleasures and Perils of Girls' Friendships* (1998) by Terri Apter and Ruthellen Josselson is a great place to start. While young girls want to model themselves after their mothers, as adolescents they transfer this passionate attachment to their girl friends. Adolescent girls' friendships take on the quality of a love affair or a romance. Throughout life, girls, then women, describe their love for girl friends as different from the love they have for males, yet it is a love they crave. The following excerpt is an example of the romantic like love between girlfriends:

> Every day my best friend Shawanda is the first person I talk to in the morning and the last person I talk to before I go to sleep. I sneak my phone under the covers when my momma thinks I am asleep. We are so close and I tell her everything and we share everything. She is more like family than my real family. She is coming to dinner this weekend and I made sure my momma is cooking Shawanda's favorite dish. She shows me how to dress and look good and she makes sure I do my homework every day.

These friendships are quite intense, providing close bonds and laboratories for experimentation. Girls go through an identification process. Sharing with girl friends becomes "the first real step out of childhood and out of their families" (Apter and Josselson, 1998). Group becomes a laboratory, too.

Girls use the peer group to test identity issues and try new ways of interacting with others (Levy-Warren, 1996). Girls are especially familiar with and comfortable with attachment, connection, agreement, assent, accommodation, pleasing, placating, conforming and being obedient. This helps them make friends, but harms them when they do not want to agree. Out of the fear of conflict, girls begin to demand that their peers conform to cultural standards of femininity. They become the enforcers of the culture. Many adolescent girls believe if they do not conform, then they will risk rejection, condemnation, being unliked, unloved and cast out. She risks being labeled nerdy, weird, brainy, stuck up, strange, pitiful or some other equally pejorative term. Not pleasing others is social suicide. There is a demand for cohesion, with scapegoating being the ultimate form of social control. Unlike boys, girls are not allowed to fight physically with their enemies. Instead girls express their anger and fear through words and the power to include and exclude. Girls have tremendous verbal strengths, quick understanding and a good grasp on psychology. Girls actually feel tremendous internal conflict about the cruelty they inflict on others, but even more, they fear being the object of the same ridicule and exclusion.

Apter and Josselson (1998) make the point that we have held a very unrealistic view of female friendships, romanticizing and idealizing what the perfect friendship should be. Of course that friendship has rules; always supportive, always consistent and reliable, never mean, conflictual, competitive nor envious. "Be sweet." This is impossible, yet it remains the standard. Instead it is important that female friendships be seen more realistically, particularly when it comes to the notions of aggression, anger, conflict and the positive power of peer pressure. It would be more realistic and healthier to teach that more mature forms of closeness require the management of tension. The practice of how to manage conflict and closeness in intimate relationships occurs here in these friendships, and by extension in groups too. Groups have the power to teach girls more realistic ideas and attitudes about living lives in relationship to others, and they can interpret each girl's unique experience.

Peers serve as "a bridge" (Nowinski, 1990) and as enforcers of the culture. They help each other to remain strong in the face of their pain and guilt, reinforcing the need to become increasingly emancipated from the dictums of family. Parents too, feel the pressure to force their children to separate, sometimes experienced consciously, sometimes unconsciously or as a collective unconscious. Group can serve both of these needs. It can serve as a vehicle for separation and it can mobilize the best of girls' strengths.

Role of Puberty and Physical Appearance

A brief discussion of puberty helps lay the foundation for a formal understanding of the issues of body image, sex, and violence in the lives of adolescent girls. Just prior to the onset of puberty, the technical definition of when adolescence begins, girls feel good about themselves and have very strong and definite voices. By the time girls reach adolescence, they run into "the wall." "The wall" is the obstacle of patriarchal culture. Girls realize that culture and its institutions value men and male models more than women and feminine models. To get through "the wall," girls must give up part of themselves (DeBold et al., 1993). Specifically, physical appearance overly determines identity in adolescent girls, leading to the forfeiture of a strong self and voice.

Everyone takes in and internalizes, consciously and unconsciously, what is feminine and what is masculine as they grow. By the time a girl is a teenager she has "internalized the contemporary imperative for a perfect body ... she knows that the power of her gender is tied to her looks and how sexy she is and not to her character or achievements"(Brumberg, 1997, p.195). The visual power of the media communicates to us all, and particularly to adolescent girls, that puberty is about getting her body under control, about hygiene and not fertility, about her outsides and not her insides, about perfecting each piece of her body, not about perfecting her mind (Brumberg, 1997). Many girls can intellectually understand they are overly obsessed with their appearance, yet they are at a loss as to where else they can focus their attentions. This is where groups can help her to reorient her thinking and attention. Groups, positive peer pressure and healthy adult role modeling can help girls to reorient themselves. Groups help girls to help each other to see and name the wall, and hopefully, healthy ways to resist it.

Some thoughtful and insightful people view adolescent girls from a feminine perspective. It is because of these people that there are movements afoot to combat every misconception mentioned. Education and even media concerns have begun to show girls how to be healthy instead of obsessed with appearance and thinness. Others are tackling the issues of sexual objectification, men's role in society, violence and self control. All of these issues, good and bad, infiltrate any girls' psychotherapy group. Groups help to buffer the forces that overwhelm her. They also give her a chance to think for herself and to be heard in a safe environment.

It should come as no surprise that psychotherapy and counseling groups are an effective treatment modality for adolescent girls, given what has been said about their psychological development in the context of today's world. Groups, like peers, can be used as a stepping stone to autonomy. Groups protect and nurture young people in ways that their families used to, or were supposed to (Lubin, Wilson, Petren, & Polk, 1996; Mishne, 1986; Rose, 1998; Sugar, 1975). Guidance, knowledge and practice can be offered in ways that are acceptable. Through the feminine styles of relating, girls make helpful connections and attachments. They talk with other girls, a process that allows them to feel relief and reassurance, and experiment with the first glimpses of their own sense of self. Within this separate peer group, girls have a survival network, a safety net, a support system, and a sense of belonging. All of these help a girl to find the strength to become what she was always meant to be.

Using Havighurst's Developmental Tasks as a Framework for Explaining Adolescent Girl Groups

Group issues will be discussed through the framework of the ten tasks of adolescence (Havighurst, 1952). One task has been added to the original ten in order to address the culture of violence in which girls now live. Noted author, Sandra Butler, when speaking in New Orleans in 1997 suggested that an addition needed to be made to the tasks of adolescence. She suggested something like "accepting that she lives in a predatory culture." The themes of adolescent girls' groups, like the tasks of adolescence, remain rather accurate. However, the actual ways these themes are discussed have dramatically changed to reflect the world of the modern the teenage girl. An outline of the tasks appear in Table 1.

Table 1: The Tasks of Adolescence (Havighurst, 1952)

1. Accepting one's physical self and using the body effectively.
2. Achieving a masculine or feminine social role.
3. Achieving new and mature relations with age mates of both sexes.
4. Achieving emotional independence of parents and other adults.
5. Achieving assurance of economic independence.
6. Selecting and preparing for an occupation.
7. Preparing for marriage and family life.
8. Developing intellectual skills and concepts necessary for civic competence.
9. Desiring and achieving socially responsible behavior.
10. Acquiring a set of values and an ethical system as a guide to behavior.
11. *Accepting that she lives in a predatory culture.*

Task #1 -"Accepting one's Physical Self and Using the Body Effectively" (Havighurst, 1952)

In girls' groups, a considerable amount of time is spent discussing virtually everything conceivably related to the body, and its inadequacy. Clinicians will find it tough and challenging to reorient the discussions towards healthy attitudes about the body's internal and external functioning. Adolescent girls today find it difficult to accept or like much, if anything, about their bodies, yet their task is to accept the body they have and to take care of it. The desire to please others predominates through the body. Adolescents compare themselves constantly to others in an attempt at self definition.
For example: "Jane" weekly paraded her tormented quest for the concave stomach. She would bring photo's from teen magazines of her role models, proving to the group just how inadequate her stomach was. Then one day, looking pale and weighing much less, she triumphantly demonstrated the bagginess of her jeans, and her beautiful (frightening) new concave stomach.

Unfortunately today girls compare themselves to cover girls, models, actresses, singers and other women whose full time job is to look beautiful and work out every day. Girls have become obsessed with their appearance, and, as Pipher (1994) emphasizes, appearance has come to overly determine identity. The culture communicates to girls that they are only as valuable as they look. Since girls must have a) beautiful shiny hair with body, perfectly cut and perfectly manageable, b) long beautiful hands with perfectly manicured long nails (pretty feet, too), c) a beautiful face with specific features (none of which she has to her satisfaction), d) breasts that are neither too small nor too big, e) a small waist, f) a flat, even, concave stomach, g) hips and butt that are neither too big nor too small, h) a very, very thin, yet toned and muscled, but not too muscular or masculine looking body, i) a quite tall, and j) just the right clothes for a certain "in" look. How could she possibly feel good about her real body?

Example: "Betty" sobbed in group because the boy she had a crush on liked her best friend. How can I compete or ever hope to be liked when I am half her size with a B cup and she wears a D cup?

While recent studies indicate that African American teenage girls have positive views and feelings about their bodies and their weight, they have paid other prices, as their survival has required them to stay out of mainstream avenues of power. While they have remained personally powerful, it has cost them economically (DeBold, Malave, & Wilson, 1993). When it comes to bodily self esteem however, Dickerson (1997), points out that if you look at feelings about hair and skin tone, the complexion changes. "At 200 pounds, a black woman may be perfectly happy with her body but spend $100.00 to $300.00 a pop on a hair weave, denying herself both exercise and sex to protect it. So while white women may express self-hatred by starving themselves, for black women, self-loathing centers around what grows out of their heads" (p.140).

When the stress becomes overwhelming, many teenage girls cut on their bodies (Miller, 1994). "Cutting" has traditionally been viewed by clinicians as related to the self hatred born of the dynamics of personality disorders, or has been strongly correlated with child sexual abuse. However this is changing. While there is still much "cutting" (seen in "average" girls) going on, what is called "self mutilation"(more serious) is also increasing (Conterio & Lader, 1998). These symptom behaviors reflect the violence of the culture and the self hatred for lack of bodily perfection played out on a girls body. Pipher (1994) references cutting as a behavior that is quite common, rather than related only to more serious problems. Clinicians and teenage girls report that cutting has become about as common as bulimia, which is quite common in the adolescent female population. Girls use various objects to cut or scrape themselves, usually on the arms or legs. It is most often done to vent feelings such as anger, rage, desperation, despair, hopelessness, and powerlessness. A clinician must carefully assess the particular behavior and clinical picture to determine the meaning of this act. Girls need group discussion about healthy ways to view and treat their bodies. They also need healthy strategies to replace these harmful pursuits and new methods of experiencing and managing negative feelings.

Adolescent girls will talk about every aspect of their bodies and physical selves in group therapy. Her entire external body becomes a project in and of itself. Since eating disorders are common, particularly bulimia, this is a common topic of discussion in many girls' groups. Group discussions can quickly bog down as girls share information about calories, fat grams and other details. The clinician must reorient the discussion to the feelings that underlie the content. Hopefully the "be healthy, not anorexic" movement will become successful and a part of groups.

In *Reviving Ophelia*, Pipher (1994) focuses on how the adolescent girl loses sight of the functional importance of her own body and how that translates into a loss of self confidence. Clinicians must help girls to think more deeply about her body's purpose. This relates to the importance of girls remaining involved in sports in adolescence. Findings suggest that girls who do sports fare better in terms of their positive feelings about their bodies and their self esteem. Since not every girl is athletically inclined, substitute the concept of involvement in something that requires commitment, passion, and caring that inspires self worth. Can her body be used in a functional, healthy way? Provocative, challenging, yet supportive and educational group discussion is vital and useful for change. Many clinicians develop their own exercises, yet there are numerous sources that assist clinicians in exercise preparation. *Reviving Ophelia* (Pipher, 1994) contains many techniques for accomplishing this goal.

In addition to obsessive talk about bodies, thinness, diets, fat, exercise, nutrition, attractiveness, body parts and so on, there are several other topics related to the physical self that often surface. Just about every girl or woman in this country can tell you about the day her menstrual period first began. Clinicians are advised to help girls talk about the meaning of their periods in an internal and life phase sense. For example, "What does it mean to be capable of reproduction?" Today the beginning of a girl's period is likely to be celebrated as an economic adventure, puberty means a shopping trip to the mall to buy supplies; lipsticks, bras, tampax, heels (Brumberg, 1997). The group might be encouraged to think about some additional ways that girls could celebrate the meaningfulness of their new biological functioning instead of "shopping."

Examples: a) the group of girlfriends who have coached one another from outside the stall or home bathroom on how to get a tampon in, and b) the girl whose mother invited her daughter's closest friends and her own for a party thrown in honor of her first menstruation.

The capacity to procreate produces many ramifications for girls. How a girl experiences the beginning of her period, emotionally, is vital to her positive attachment to her physical and sexual self esteem. Had she been educated or prepared for the onset? Does she understand what it is and what it means to her life? While parents and sometimes schools, are supposed to be the ones making sure that girls receive a fair and accurate sexual education, this usually does not happen. Girl friends are the primary source of sex education.

Example: The girls in one group described that they had a competition (betting money) about who would be first to start their period, and they had to have proof!

Depending on the practice setting, clinicians may or may not be allowed to encourage discussion that involves sex education. Newer clinicians will be amazed to discover the plethora of misinformation about bodies and their functioning shared by teenage clients. A particularly common misconception surfaces when girls are told that now that they have a period they can get pregnant is translated by some girls as "I can only get pregnant when I have my period." For this reason it is wise to know enough biology so that you can properly name body parts, genitalia, explain reproduction, STD's, pregnancy and so on. Diagrams, books and/or pamphlets are very helpful. Such literature can also be useful in helping girls to be able to accurately name their body parts, particularly their genitalia. To name and/or see (they can use a mirror at home) their parts is crucial to a more specific rather than diffuse sense of identity.

The pressure on girls to be sexual is so severe that it is very common to hear from very young teenage girls that they are just going to have sex to "get it over with." Although sexual pressure often begins in grade school and becomes increasingly intense in junior and high school, many parents and schools tend to begin to prepare girls in junior high. The average age at which girls become sexual is lower, with the average age of first sexual intercourse being close to 15 years old. Even though the world is filled with promise and more choices for girls than ever before, they are frequently having sex when their male relationships want it, not when they want it. As the media glorifies sex, teenagers receive the message that the personal expression of one's sexuality is the ultimate experience. It is a grown up experience that they should want ... and so they do.

The adolescent girl of today, even a 13 year-old, can look very mature. She has a vast expanse of advanced information about sex, without having acquired the maturity to manage what they know. Externally she looks as if she is ready to handle much more than she is really prepared for internally. Even the experienced clinician can become seduced into seeing her as mature despite the intellectual awareness that she in fact only possesses pseudo-maturity. Without being condescending or disrespectful to the adolescent, it is important for the clinician to retain an accurate assessment framework of the internal functioning of the adolescent. In terms of her age-stage development, just how old is she? Despite how she looks, what is it that she really needs to master next in order to progress?

It is not uncommon to hear strong, vocal adolescent girls who have developed the capacity for abstract thought, unable to say "NO." This difficulty exists even when they may feel discomfort, that they risk STD's, pregnancy, and when they do not believe that they are emotionally ready for sex. A girl's ability to assert herself, to say "No", and not place all blame and responsibility on males is a major problem in adolescent life that carries over into adulthood.

Body discussions are extremely common in adolescent girls' groups. The fact that girls need psychological understanding, education, practice/rehearsal and skill building to overcome these problems cannot be stressed enough. A young girl needs to practice saying "no" when it is difficult. She is also faced with the challenge of developing self imposed limits which spring from her belief system. The group milieu is an excellent avenue for this exploration through its use of peer encouragement, support, confrontation, challenge and guidance. Group exercises and homework assignments should be used. Opportunities for practice and rehearsal such as role-playing can occur in group extemporaneously or may be planned in advance.

In group, girls must be prepared for possible adverse reactions from others. As we know through systems theory, the system will resist change by a member, encouraging her to return to a previous role in the system. A group can prepare her for the potential of others' displeasure, yet help her know that she can manage the uncomfortable feelings that may accompany this situation. If reactions and responses from outside the group are not realistically addressed, the group, its leader and/or members may be seen as radical instigators of aggression (actually they still may be). Anticipating reactions and ways to respond can be helpful group topics.

Other concerns reflecting active or ongoing mastery of this task might include discussions related to the time needed in the bathroom, beauty products, hygiene, grooming, and feminine problems. Clothing, fads, (tattoos were once thought of as self mutilation amongst clinicians; today it is common and not thought of as pathological), body piercing, (extreme fads such as scarring and amputation, etc.), bra's, make-up, sexual characteristics, fashion, and other topics may also be discussed. Personal style relates to body, separation and autonomy, and consequently to struggles with parents. The clinician must be prepared to interpret the meaning of interests and struggles to both the adolescent and the parent in words they can understand. Group discussion can once again be used to peer below the surface literally and figuratively to the internal and emotional concerns evidenced by the external ones.

Task #2 - "Achieving, Accepting, and Learning one's Masculine or Feminine Sexual-Social Roles"

The clinician will have many opportunities to apply the concepts introduced earlier about "the wall" and girl's hopelessness in regards to who she is versus what she sees she must become. In an adolescent group, discussion inevitably focuses on one's sex and sexuality in a wide variety of ways. Again, the treatment setting, and the purpose of the groups will help to define and clarify at what level and how openly material will be introduced. The group leaders can help girls understand what they are trying to master by redefining the age-stage tasks in language comprehensible to them. Clinicians must learn to talk in everyday, uncomplicated language to model and facilitate and ensure communication. Do not assume that the girls have grasped the actual and proper definition of some words. Once again, there is a tremendous amount of misinformation that must be explored and corrected!

Social roles, sexual orientation, dating, sex, birth control and the values, beliefs, and teachings about these issues consistently surface as members struggle with defining gender roles in a world full of confusing messages. Family, school, mentors, and church all form the foundation of the belief systems for many adolescents. But it is now up to her to negotiate what she will keep and what she wishes to reject. How will she be like her family/teachers, and how may she choose to be different? In a world where the media wields such power to shape minds, and one in which girls are vulnerable to increased violence and sexual pressures, today's girl has even more to contend with than those who came before her. She is influenced by the women's movement, the men's movement and the movements against or in reaction to those movements. She is presented with conflicting messages. Messages that say: "Be beautiful, but beauty is only skin deep," "be sexy, not sexual," "be honest, but don't hurt anyone's feelings," "be smart, but don't let others know how smart you are," "be independent, but be nice," "be smart, but not so smart that you threaten boys," "girls who speak frankly are bitches," "girls who want to be sexual are sluts"(Pipher, 1994). Groups help girls to make sense out of these conflicting messages.

We ask girls to be strong and to be able to say "NO" and yet, in order for girls to be able to do so, they must have a fair amount of experience with conflict, that has been encouraged and well received in both female and male relationships. How can we expect girls to be successful in taking care of themselves when we do not equip them with the skills and the practice arenas for these skills of true assertion? Through group, clinicians can help girls see healthy aggression, conflict, anger and disagreement as part of healthy feminine sex role development. Group is the perfect arena for such experimentation. Her words, tone and inflection can be used to illustrate how she is indirect, how she defers and abdicates what she knows. Differences in male and female communication styles can be examined so unnecessary hurt occurs less often. Clinicians can remind girls that they are not supposed to have all of this worked out, or to be good at it, but that they can practice, allowing themselves to be awkward and to make mistakes. Taking responsibility and being accountable can be offered as avenues to increased feelings of power and self esteem. Group can be used to model, practice, rehearse, educate, and explore what a girl's healthy sex role might look like on her.

Certainly groups can be an extraordinarily meaningful and powerful way to provide girls with the experimentation, rehearsal, and practice needed to negotiate dating and sex in their world: in the hallways of their schools, the arenas in which they play and practice. Today, that world is more violent, not less. Even at school adolescent girls are more vulnerable to sexual harassment and rape. There are high percentages of both boys and girls who think coercive sex is acceptable if they have been dating for a while and/or the boy has spent a lot of money on the date (Curran, 1996). It is the clinician's job to guide the adolescent girl to a deeper understanding of her views and to challenge her thinking. Without education, examples, role-playing and rehearsal within a safe environment, the discussions are virtually useless.

> Example: "Cherie" laments that she will never know what it would be like to kiss a boy or have sex with a boy when she wanted to. Instead her fear of loss of love and relationship dictates her decisions to "let him do what he wants" … "I just want to get it over with" … "it's too much pressure to resist" ... "it's just not worth it".

While the term "assertiveness training" has become dated, groups that assist girls in realistic ways to negotiate their lives in an assertive manner remain helpful. Clinicians and group members can role-play based on the real situations they face everyday. Because group is a microcosm for life, using actual observable examples of their own group behavior is always preferable and the results more immediate. While this discussion focuses on adolescent girls, age 11-12 and up, it is likely that these girls have faced unexpected sexual situations. The girls will have no shortage of examples for group process.

Clinicians and other members help to sort out unique belief systems and what is the right way to be a girl or woman in the world today. Because experimentation is often necessary in order to determine what feels right, groups can help create and suggest ways for safe rehearsal and experimentation. While we continue to polarize masculine and feminine concepts, in today's world it is possible for girls to define themselves by encompassing a variety of masculine and feminine traits or abilities. Some think of this as androgyny, others may use the term He-Girl. Girls can come to know that their desire for relatedness is not wrong, in fact it is a feminine strength. Not all girls are, or want to be, feminine in the ways held out to them as desirable.

One example of reframing sex roles deals with the issue of emotion. Many girls have been led to believe that crying and emotionality makes them weak. Perhaps they were fed ideas suggesting feeling is feminine, therefore weak. Perhaps they have always been told to "quit crying," "quit being a baby," or to "get over it." Regardless of the reasons, girls need to see their ability to be in touch with and to express their feelings is, actually, a source of strength. Feeling, crying, releasing, emoting, expressing, yelling, are all routes to remaining healthy. Perhaps one of the group's most important functions is helping girls realize they can manage strong feelings, even the most profound, deep, intense, and difficult ones. Instead of "cutting" herself to vent feelings, binging to avoid anxieties, or attempting suicide to express pain and powerlessness, the clinician and the group can help each member identify better options for expressing such feelings and offer a setting to practice expression and gain support from others.

Homosexuality is also a frequent topic as group members struggle with sexual identity/ orientation/choice. Depending on the constitution of the group and the ages of the participants, such discussion may break down into homophobic opinions, disgust, fear, confusion, or openness. Sometimes a lesbian teenager is scapegoated by the group. As with most provocative subjects, the clinician must use skill, authority, and compassion to guide the group into a productive discussion relevant to their struggle with the identity task at hand. Whether experimentation takes place in real life or imagined, it is an important step in the definition of sexual self and roles. Homosexuality can be viewed (simplistically) in two ways here: as sexual orientation related to personal object choice or affectational preference, more than sex, or as one part of the sexual identity process for many individuals. Fair and ethical discussion on homosexuality does not require a homosexual clinician. However, an attitude of acceptance and willingness to help the group explore are important criteria.

Whether the discussion centers on sex roles, choice or homosexuality, the clinician is guided by a number of factors including the treatment setting and the purpose of the group. Additionally, parents/families/guardians are always pivotally important, whether they are involved, absent, alive, or dead. They are as much a part of the separation/identity process (symbolically present in group) as the teenager. Because the adolescent is returning to their home, foster home, hospital, group home or family home, it is important for the clinician to help the adolescent consider behavior and communication in light of that environment. For example, "coming out" can have a number of negative consequences with physical assault or being thrown out of the home being two of those possibilities. Both clinician and client must anticipate and discuss family reactions and make plans accordingly.

As with the other very difficult subjects, it is the clinician's responsibility to create and maintain an atmosphere of safety so opinions are respected or at least tolerated. Abuse or scapegoating of members must be redirected toward the underlying feelings that generate such attacks. Often it is fear, misinformation, powerlessness, helplessness, shame and/or inadequacy that facilitate such agendas. Getting below surface issues is always the key to gaining an understanding and obtaining resolution. At the very least, such difficult discussions provide excellent and real opportunities to practice the direct, responsible and appropriate expression of anger.

Task #3 -"Achieving New and More Mature Relations with Age Mates of Both Sexes"

The earlier discussion about adolescent females and their friendships becomes especially relevant for this particular task. Friendships and relationships are dominant themes in adolescent girls' groups. Initially, in early adolescence many long hours are spent on the telephone engaged in conversation about every topic mentioned in this chapter and others. Privacy and separation struggles manifest themselves through telephone use, writing, dramas and groupings. Important notes are written, guarded in purses and backpacks and special hiding places. Diaries and journals become safe hiding places for new and emerging emotions and experiences. These media help girls sort out their feelings. Friendship groups, cliques, and clubs are formed and reformed as membership frequently changes. There are horrible traumas and crises created as various members are targeted, ostracized, humiliated, rejected and subjected to great personal pain. Feminine traits of agreement and assent which discourage disagreement bump into envy, jealousy, aggression, and competition. All have the potential danger of leading to loss of love and group protection. Adolescent girls have a particularly difficult time with the direct and constructive expression of anger and aggression. Girls, realize at puberty that they have little power in a world which embraces a patriarchal model, "act out loss of power through competition and cruelty ... they duplicate the rivalry and competition they see underlying women's relationships within a male defined world ... act out their anger covertly through increasingly painful games of inclusion and exclusion. No way to authorize themselves as they enter a patriarchal society" (DeBold et al., 1993, p.43). Apter and Josselson (1998) see this differently, viewing the cruelty as the pressure for cultural enforcement that may save or protect the girl from being alone or on the outside. The clinician usually witnesses this behavior within the group and can comment on the various meanings and implied struggles as they pursue mastery.

For a long time it has been known that girl's/women's inability to directly express anger has been a major cause of rampant feminine depression and has contributed to the reputation (unfortunately often deserved) of feminine manipulativeness and deceptiveness. If anger is forced underground then it will come out in other ways. In group there is the opportunity to point these things out in ways that become enlightening, useful and constructive. It is helpful to teach girls the difference between taking care of someone (often unhealthy) and caring about someone (generally healthy). Modeling and role playing this distinction in group is critical to achieving a balance in empathy. The fear of hurting the others' feelings is the most common way for this discussion to emerge, and it will be encountered over and over again in any group with adolescent girls. In early adolescence, new ways of struggling with mastery of this task appear in discussions of "peer soap operas." Long, detailed, excruciatingly painful stories emerge, (about boyfriends and girlfriends and cliques) with much "he said," "she said," "and then." However, this process should not be trivialized for adolescent girls are developing a skill and strength that will serve them throughout life (Apter & Josselson, 1998). It is the clinicians job to listen beneath the story to the struggle for new observations, experiences, and feelings of love that become much less melodramatic as the girl becomes more sure of her identity and acting increasingly from a place of self knowledge.

The middle to late adolescent girl struggles less with the larger group and has often found a smaller, more select group of friends who share more in common with her. There are conflicts, but they are more about values and intimacy than those of the younger adolescent girl. The older girl spends less time on the phone and on note writing. Instead she may be more likely to spend time writing in her journal, more focused on defining herself more independently than through her peers. The importance of peers does not cease, but the quality of the relationship shifts. Because she is increasingly sure of whom she is, there is not the same need to reject parents to establish a sense of separate identity. More and more she is self-defined through experiences of her own choosing. She relates to friends, family and groups more maturely.

Clinicians have the opportunity to help girls sort out what they have been taught about friendship and relationships. Discussions focus on the realities of more mature relationships with their inevitable flaws and tensions. Since the group is a microcosm for their larger world, friendships and conflicts inevitably develop within the group. Within the safety of the group, clinicians can help girls express anger, discontent, frustration and criticism in responsible and constructive ways. Skillful clinical management is important here. Group members will likely feel scared and anxious about the conflict. It is important to keep the group under control and to process the material carefully. It is at this point that members gain experience managing their reactions to challenges and explore the feelings of the others.

Task #4 - "Achieving Emotional Independence from Parents and Other Adults"

In early adolescence the first strivings for emotional independence are manifested in their opposition or "rebellion" towards parents, other significant adults or authority figures. Frequently those adolescents who come to the clinician's attention are those whose rebellion is quite strong, those who are yelling the loudest. In these youth, their behavior occurs because there is much more going on in their homes besides a "normal" adolescence. Frequently these teens are rebelling because of abuse, drug addiction, and other serious problems which influence how they negotiate their identity process. However, the young teenager begins to disagree, talk back, take a different slant on things, and/or wants to stay home from events they had previously participated in with their families. Typical manifestations of early emotional independence and autonomy include increased amounts of time spent on the phone, in the bathroom or alone in their room. They may dress in an entirely different way than before. When commented upon, they may make statements such as: "what's the big deal?" "I can't go with you to grandma's; I'm meeting my friends at the mall; I don't want to go every Saturday anymore." "Twelve is not too young to date; all my friends parents let them do it." "It's not fair that _____________" (substitute almost anything that used to be OK). "No, I'm not going to church anymore; I no longer believe in God." "Mom, do you have to go out looking like that; it's embarrassing." Or, "My curfew is earlier that anyone else's; I need mine to be later."

It is also common for a young adolescent to showcase new attempts at emotional independence by sharing much less, by refusing to kiss or be kissed, and to accompany these behaviors with increased requests or demands for more money, more privileges, more freedoms, and fewer chores. Adolescents typically ask for more than they really ever expect to get as a way to test limits. These early struggles are frequently the ones that become trivialized. The adolescent is making a move towards a personal perception of adulthood while parents and other adults often misperceive such communication. Adults might not feel quite so abandoned, rejected and personally assaulted if they could reframe the communication as "I need space to define myself" and to "experiment with my emotional life differently and separately from yours."

Boys continue to be afforded more opportunities for autonomy in relation to girls. The thwarting of girls' autonomy is often experienced as a lack of trust on her parent's part whereas it is more accurately based on a mistrust of the outside world. At a time when the adolescent girl wants more freedom, when parents have a tendency to be less involved and where the world is a more dangerous place, it is challenging to help her grow and keep her safe. Through group, girls can teach each other how to think things through and how to stay safe in more mature, healthy and independent ways. Teenage girls are often afraid to tell their parents the real and often dangerous situations they encounter for fear their parents will immediately ground (punish) them by keeping them at home. There will be abundant examples and scenarios to work with. The clinician will have no trouble eliciting material. Ways to stay safe, plans of action, role-playing and information about real life all get talked about. The true nature of emotional independence and maturity relies on the ability to think things through. The group can be a catalyst, enabling each member to feel stronger and better able to make choices and choose healthy strategies that reflect more independent and mature thinking, such as choosing to stay home if the situation warranted.

For many adolescent girls, choosing to avoid social contact may be a way to keep herself safe. In the past, professionals would quickly recommend therapy if an adolescent girl was not interested in dating, wanted to spend time with her parents and family, and/or wanted to study all the time. The clinician needs to assess whether such behavior is actually a healthy solution for the adolescent girl in question. Some girls are finding creative ways to weather the adolescent years, waiting purposely to come into their own in early adulthood. Group may help to teach the adolescent girl that there are alternative ways to cope in addition to traditional or mainstream strategies. In today's world a non-traditional path may be healthy and safer given the pressures and demands she may face for which she is unprepared. Some examples from past group members include: developing high levels of involvement in sports or another passionate interest such as a volunteer job, a cause, club, or church; devoting all free time to studying; finding a way to be a nerd, or a misfit; sticking like glue to one best friend or one boyfriend; or being her own person, uninfluenced by the crowd, and going her own way, strong in conviction. Discussion of the range of possibilities can lead to greater insight on the part of the adolescent.

By mid-adolescence (14-16 or so), the push away from parents should be a less dramatic. However, continuous changes are ongoing which require constant flexibility in the family. The demands for more rights, privileges, freedom, responsibility and adult-like freedoms continue. While development towards emotional independence proceeds, it is never in a steady upward manner; rather it continues to oscillate. The adolescent that seemed remarkably mature one day may dissolve the next day into a regressed needy child. One day a girl wishes to confide her emotions and asks for help in sorting out her feelings and dilemmas; the next she tells parents to butt out, to quit being so intrusive, and that she's not a baby and can handle things on her own. This is to be expected as normal experimentation and rehearsal. It should be expected that, unless crises and situational traumas intercede, the periods of more mature behavior become more numerous and more prolonged. Clinicians can use group process to help girls and the adults who care for them to anticipate such behavior, or at least help them to understand and nurture the growth.

The book, *Substance Abuse in Adolescents* (Nowinski, 1990) focuses on the premise that relationships keep kids safe, not rules. Nowinski looks at the role of healthy familial dependency versus unfinished or inadequately met dependency needs as the roots for the capacity for an internalized sense of control. This internal state, when created, gives a teenager the strength and internal feeling of safety and security to handle difficult adolescent and adult situations without the presence of parents. Many of the girls in group may not have an adequate internal self in this regard; therefore group and clinician may become avenues for successful acquisition of such internal controls. Once again, the group may become the arena of mastery. Even where little impact or change can be made, due to irrevocable realities, the group and the clinician plant seeds which will germinate, inspiring hope, to be realized at a later age.

Clinicians must help the girl and her family accept that falling down, making mistakes, failures, and some breaches of trust are going to occur, and that they are normal, not signs of defects. In fact, this is how healthy, normal age-stage task identity development proceeds. Accepting mistakes does not mean consequences are not given or abusive behavior or language is tolerated. Recognizing setbacks means the girl needs to be reigned back in so she can consolidate before she is allowed to try again. But she should be allowed to try again. She can get it right with a more complete knowledge of the expectations placed upon her and parental guidance. The same is true in group, as a girl may come back without having been able to do what she and others had hoped for still she must experience the support needed for her to try again.

Discipline also needs constant readjustment depending on the abilities of the adolescent. There are six common problems the clinician must recognize to help parents employ the most meaningful form of discipline: 1) the inability to understand, recognize and accurately interpret the meaning of age-stage development, 2) the inability to enforce a reasonable consequence, 3) the enforcement of a reasonable restriction not too long and not too severe, inappropriate or unreasonable (creating an angry child), 4) the misunderstanding that discipline is punishment instead of teaching/learning, 5) the assumption that teenagers do not feel badly, remorseful and guilty when they do not show that face to their parents, and 6) the inability to follow through on discipline or to tolerate the anger/hatred of their adolescent is normal not harmful. The growth and abilities of the teenager require parental discipline that carefully balances consistent boundaries with enough space to allow the adolescent to prove success apart from parental supervision.

Example: A sixteen year old girl, Elena, who felt very special and proud to be working in an auto body shop, was having some discomfort in relating to the man she had to work with daily. It was disconcerting to her that she was much brighter and had to explain things to him, although not about body work. (She was working two other jobs as well for the summer.) This left her little time for friends and fun. (A bright capable girl, a high achiever, she had difficulty listening to what she actually wanted to do). Once she could hear her own voice, she had trouble with the idea of communicating it to the other body shop workers that she no longer wished to work there. It was more the inability to assert herself in a direct manner that gave her the most trouble. She expressed fear about hurting his feelings. While many adolescent themes which have been already mentioned appear in this example it is the resolution which exemplifies task #4. She appeared at the next group happy, bouncing, clearly looking resolved, and cheerfully announced that all was taken care of. She said no more. When asked how she had worked it out she said, "My mom told the auto body shop that I had taken on too much and she needed for me to be less stressed and, therefore, I would not be in for a few days. That's what mommies are for when we are still babies." Two weeks after that she came in and announced, "I know what I want and I know what I am going to do, and I am going to the body shop and give him notice that I am quitting, myself." And, she did.

As with Elena, through group the adolescent girl can be encouraged to "turn up the volume" on her own inner voice. The clinician can consistently inquire about the girls' feelings, ideas, and thoughts so as to encourage the task of emotional independence. "I know that's what your __________(mother, father, teacher, coach, etc.) said, but try to tell us, what you think?, yes but ... what do you feel? ... yes, but ... what is your opinion? ... what do you want? ... what do you think is right for you? ... what is your belief? ... but how do you think you should handle this? ... how are you stopping yourself?". The clinician has the opportunity to ask questions and use language to enhance and underscore the mastery of developmental tasks. Whatever the group content, the clinician can use vocabulary that highlights their individualism, independence, authority, and separateness; language implying the ability and capacity to know and master. This process allows practice in listening to, developing and making sense out of internal thoughts and feelings. It also empowers and encourages mastery versus helplessness, powerlessness and victimization.

Task #5 - "Achieving Economic Independence"

Many families experience incredible pressure resulting from increased demands for money, goods and activities requiring money. As girls pursue skills necessary for adult life, they increasingly wish to have money and be in charge of how they spend it. While, some girls have had the opportunities to manage money at early points in their lives, earned from chores, allowance, or special money earning jobs, etc., most girls today seem to know precious little about the value of money. They ultimately need to understand the value and the power of money so they can take care of themselves in the real world.

By adolescence, girls perceive a need for more material goods. Peers have become the enforcers of the culture, deciding what are the "things" that a teenager who wants to be cool must possess. Their concern about appearance and style produces increased requests for shoes, clothing, make up and other "beauty" products. Hair salon and dermatology appointments as well as, pocket money for transportation, food, movies, shopping, are all considered "necessary" activities. They are also confronted with the cost of jewelry, music, posters, tattoos, body piercing, beepers, cellular phones, and new fads.

Parents often feel this financial pressure and they usually feel guilty when they are unable to provide enough money to cover the cost of these so-called "necessities". Guilt frequently gets expressed as anger it fuels conflicts with their teenager. Effective methods to budget, spend, and save is what the young teenager and parents need. Realistic ideas about real life costs are also needed. Some families provide this and some schools provide a measure of this. Teenagers need the chance to practice so that when they are in fact out on their own, they will be ready but unfortunately, many girls are not properly prepared.

Discussions about of money and its uses regularly come up in group. Ways to earn money, how to get a job, budget and plan are topics girls help each other explore. There are just as many girls who expect to be taken care of by their boyfriend or husband as there are girls who do not believe in relying on others. It is important to allow for a wide variety of personal beliefs and styles, and yet the clinician must be on the alert to listen on several levels. Is this practice, experimentation, rehearsal or the real her? Clinicians help adolescents think through ideas and feelings related to money and to the larger issue of increasing independence. Themes of dependence and independence are common underlying issues that can provide a transition from concrete budget discussions to the underlying issues associated with money.

Focus on money raises underlying psychological concerns such as love, deprivation, tolerating frustration, and delaying gratification. The topic of money has emotional and psychological significance related to each individual's experience; the internal issues often surface after the concrete issues of money are explored. Through discussions on dependence and power, the theme of sexual violence and date rape are often revealed. Who spends what on whom may become an issue of sexual violence or coerced sex. Is she choosing a dependency model because she has inadequate belief in herself? Is her dependency healthy or unhealthy? Is she truly making a choice? Even when being taken care of does she see herself as having an equal voice? Does the person who controls the money have all the power? If so, how will she feel powerful if she is not the one who pays? The clinician who is working with a more heterogeneous versus homogenous group must guide the discussion so all girls have a right to their opinion and yet all must be challenged in their thinking in a respectful way. Interpretation, silence, and challenge all have the possibility of being experienced as criticism, anger, disapproval, and/or rejection. Since the stage of adolescence includes vulnerability, self-consciousness and narcissism, the clinician walks a careful line between respectful challenge and judgmental criticism.

Task #6 -" Selecting and Preparing for an Occupation"
Task #7 - "Preparing for Marriage and Family Life"

Both task #6 and task #7 are presented together, because for girls the pairing exemplifies the conflict apparent in trying to juggle these two roles. Whether a blessing or a curse, today's girl has the option to be a full-time mother, a full-time worker, or both. While a boy might think economically about having a family and the ramifications of teen pregnancy, he does not get pregnant. Understanding the issues related to occupation, marriage, parenting, and the interplay and balance of the these roles become vital issues in the lives of adolescent girls.

Certainly the younger adolescents will talk about this issue in a group setting, but it is more common in the middle and older adolescent girls' group. Younger adolescents typically relate to work superficially, in more of a wishful, fantasy-like manner. Girls in their mid to late adolescence are facing choices that directly relate to their future. Pregnancy for example, is a major issue that relates to occupation. For many girls, they see pregnancy as their only option for a source of hope, identity, value and worth. Being a mother is the only thing they think they can accomplish or succeed at in this world. Depending on the milieu in which they live, pregnancy can be viewed as immediately desirable and many girls may be actively trying to become pregnant. Pregnancy can also be used to help a girl to separate from her family, even though it often generates increased dependency. The Committee on Adolescence, Group for the Advancement of Psychiatry (1986) reported that early pregnancy has negative economic consequences and does make girls more vulnerable themselves. Many girls use pregnancy to get away from a situation that is or seems intolerable (sexual abuse, physical abuse, alcoholism, fighting, violence, etc.). These choices become acts of autonomy but emotional development and truer emotional separation are blockers.

Group can be a highly effective way to educate girls about the realities of pregnancy, child rearing, birth, health care, and the concrete and emotional costs. Group provides an ideal setting to help girls anticipate the emotional, psychological and monetary consequences to them, to their child, to their community, and to their future. Views about pregnancy are discussed openly, where girls can not only get vital information but also support for what they are experiencing. Within the group atmosphere, girls can find a workable solution that enhances their lives rather than terminating emotional tasks and development.

The world of work, money, benefits, and related costs are also commonly discussed. Sometimes the girls themselves are knowledgeable, and sometimes it is the clinician who must bring up points of reality to consider. Once again, the purpose of the group dictates the level of detail on these topics. If "Living Skills" or "Independent Living" is the purpose of the group, then budgeting, shopping, bill paying, the use of credit cards, saving, and taxes will be a larger part of the group discussion than say in an "Assertiveness Group."

Clinicians may need to be knowledgeable about community resources such as vocational rehabilitation, community college, apprenticeship programs, GED (high school equivalency exam), civil service, and the armed forces. Because negotiating the world of work is complex, exploring different options and resources is an essential element in the identity development of a young girl and the group. Open discussion and activities can aid in the mastery of this task.

In group, girls express a great deal of concern, confusion and conflict about work and motherhood. As children they have seen, the conflicts of their parents and have been the ones to experience a childhood with more working mothers. Within the same group, some girls may feel anger and resentment over being abandoned, while others may feel a deep sense of admiration and security. There are many opportunities to help girls differentiate between a reaction in opposition to their own experience because of their particular parents and choices made on the basis of their own voice and mind. Such ability to differentiate can be applied to many tasks.

Girls feel an internal collision between the desire to work, be independent, aggressive, and achieve and the desire to mother a child and nurture a man and family. There are also the girls that do not intend to marry, or to have children, or who plan to have a child and not to marry. Issues such as birth control/family planning, purposeful pregnancy, and intentions to live together out of wedlock are common themes though more common with older adolescents. Younger adolescent girls speak of marriage issues more as intangible future concepts, while the mid to late adolescent girl speaks of them as concepts closer to her reality and to her present life.

There are girls who have decided to love other girls. Girls need the safety and freedom to explore such ideas in group. They too, need to explore work and motherhood, but often need to feel that their concerns will be kept confidential by the group and that the group is safe where they will not be scapegoated or attacked. The ability to manage such discussion while allowing for healthy conflicts of self expression and ideas rests with the clinician. The concept of separation from family often surfaces because the member may fear coming out to her family and being rejected. Just as this fear is experienced and worked out within the group, other group members have an opportunity to express not only support, but also negative feelings that might surface regarding this issue. The resolution of these concerns in an open and honest manner is ideal for mastery of this task.

For the girl who hopes to go to college, concerns about grades, performance, SATs, ACTs and economic worries are common. Is she ready to go away? Even the girl who is emotionally ready to separate from her family may go through a period full of doubt and regret. Temporary regressions are expected and should be anticipated. College or community bound girls go through a phase of being afraid and feeling as if they are not ready for the challenges of being independent, away from parents. The fear often passes if they are allowed to ventilate and go through the phase, looking at both the emotional aspects and life skill aspects of their worries. Group provides an avenue for this exploration.

When the girl comes from a very autocratic family, one which has provided little room for self-determination, she may have had less opportunity to practice the necessary skills needed to handle her freedoms and the inherent choices. Yet at the other end of the spectrum, those girls who had too few limits and were allowed too much freedom may also be at risk, as they too may have little experience with self determination of limit setting to help them manage such an open environment. These extremes in family styles are also relevant to the other tasks.

The group setting can be most helpful to the girl who is preparing to go away or planning to leave home. Members can share ideas, help others to make plans, provide support, correct assumptions and misconceptions and suggest options. All of this support provides a structure that can repair and replace what these particular kinds of families have been unable to provide.

Task #8 - " Developing Intellectual Skills and Concepts Necessary for Civic Competence"
Task #9 - " Desiring and Achieving Socially Responsible Behavior"
Task #10 - Acquiring a Set of Values and Ethical System as a Guide to Behavior"

During the period of adolescence there is also a transition in terms of cognitive abilities. The adolescent moves from a concrete capacity for thought to abstract capabilities. Although vital to understanding of all tasks, it is particularly important in looking at tasks 8, 9 and 10. The youth who can think abstractly will more fully understand such concepts as morality, religion, remorse, and consequences (financial and emotional costs) to self and their family if caught doing something wrong. Groups can be challenging since it is not uncommon for members to be at different levels of cognitive development. Additionally, there may be a wide range in the level of intelligence among members. It is important for members to experience and understand that a higher IQ does not provide protection from any of the concerns discussed in this chapter. In fact the social skills of "gifted" girls may be less advanced than the skills of non-gifted girls (Frey, 1991).

An additional concern is the lack of ritual in our culture today. The onset of menstruation is the frequent formal demarcation of adolescence and in most non-European or U.S. cultures, it is celebrated in some formal ritual. Girls benefit from rituals celebrating adolescence because it delineates their internal, psychological, and emotional maturation. With adolescence trivialized and the lack of indoctrination traditions, the young person is uncertain about when they have achieved this level of development. The Jewish tradition provides a meaningful and important initiation rite, the Bar mitzvah (for boys) or Bat mitzvah (for girls). Unfortunately for many girls, the advent of puberty in Western society is heralded by little more than a shopping trip and the tasks of adolescent behavior are either trivialized or seen as irksome.

There are increasing attempts by some families and even groups of teenage girls to celebrate this coming of age. Even then, the tendency is to focus greater attention on sexual reproduction abilities than the rights and responsibilities that come with this phase of their development. There must be a parallel learning process that addresses internal capacities with external demands. Individual girls become obsessed with the external world's requirements for their external selves, focusing on body parts rather than attending to inner principals and values (Blumberg, 1997). For most, the important transition of adolescence happens without formal, sanctioned ritual, but adolescent girls with guidance and encouragement can and should create such rites within the context of their groups.

As girls make the transition into adolescence, they are rarely taught the formal and informal laws that are necessary for getting along as a member of a larger community. This culture reinforces "me'ism" rather than the good of the group. Considering one's impact on others is a key element of group. Group combats "me'ism" because skills for coexisting with others that are learned in group can be applied to a community setting. In setting rules and looking at the reasons for them, girls can look at the micro and macro impact of their own behavior. Through groups, girls confront accountability and responsibility in terms of group membership and citizenship. Who are their role models and what have they been taught? What is it that must grow internally to handle the external demands? All of these issues are viable group topics.

Task #11 - "Acceptance that We Live in a Violent and Predatory Culture (Specifically Girls) and Must Adapt Ourselves to Live with that"

Themes of violence are common in girls' groups because girls are exposed to violence at school, at home, in the neighborhood, and in the news. Violence and the threat of violence, which is equally powerful, interferes with all tasks related to age-stage development. "The adolescent who faces violence concentrates on survival, not on tasks and skills" and "violence makes it difficult to develop responsible adult relationships due to the lack of trust" (Strauss, 1994, p.17). If the exposure to violence is so pervasive, would not many young people enter adulthood without the trust and mastery necessary for true maturity?

Despite increased education about abuse, rape, anger, and violence, girls are at more risk not less (Strauss, 1994). Violence, especially sexual violence, can cause a negative identification with one's own body as victims may blame themselves for being physically weak and vulnerable. (Strauss, 1994). Being sexy and/or sexual is one way that girls learn to garner attention for themselves, to feel power over males, and/or to protect themselves from an untenable world. Even so, these solutions create their own dangers. In a group setting girls can be brutally honest, examining their conscious and unconscious use of sex and violence. They will talk about the many violent acts they have witnessed or experienced. If they honor the group by going into this material, clinicians would be wise to rely heavily on their clinical skills and exercise good clinical judgment about how deep exploration should go. Dismantling of defenses has serious consequences if the person is not prepared to deal with such vulnerability. And, time should always be provided help group members restore the emotional armor they need to properly shield them from threats found in the world that exists beyond the safety of the group.

Unfortunately sex sells, and violence has been made sexy. Boys are educated through movies, television programs, ads and so on that 1) girls really want it even if they say no, 2) they have a right to it, and 3) that they should always want it and go for it. Add to this the trouble that girls have in being direct, their confusion over being sexual, and their difficulty in saying no. Combine this with the male identity confusion and one quickly realizes that girls are in danger of great harm.

Other themes relate to the role of parent as protector. Conflict arises over imposing limits as teens press for more freedom than parents feel their adolescents can manage. Parents have been told they need to let go even in the face of traditional and contemporary threats to their daughters' safety. Their daughters' requests and demands for greater responsibility and freedom predictably frighten their parents. Girls often cry "double standard" when their brothers are allowed greater freedoms, and they are correct. Such parental fears and concerns produce many questions. Is this a double standard? Is this a case of overprotection? Is the double standard justified? Are the parents really in a bind?

For group, it is important to explore a wide variety of questions. Has the girl been prepared to think and act her way out of various risky situations? Once again group becomes a healthy modality as members can help the girl think through what to do when she is in danger. Does she have emotional, psychological, intellectual, and physical self-defense training? The group serves as a place where these questions are answered and re-asked as the members evolve and grow into their tasks.

Girls' groups inevitably focus on the full range of issues regarding sex and violence. They share experiences, and they share ideas about how to survive. Some are fond of saying that "rules do not keep girls safe, relationships do." For girls this is especially true. The girl who feels that she will not be abandoned or alone because she feels strongly supported by a family, a parent, a mentor, a friend, a church, or a group will be much more likely to have the courage to stand up for herself in a dangerous situation. Clinicians need to be able to help girls expand upon what they know by introducing both traditional and nontraditional techniques that can be used to keep girls safe. Examples of such coping strategies throughout the life of the group are found in Table 2.

Table 2: Coping with Violence (Strauss, 1994)

1. Develop a healthy degree of dissociation.
2. Find a place of sanctuary (e.g. group, school, job, etc.)
3. Make a plan to find a way out of the violent situation or environment.
4. Attach to someone trustworthy.
5. Find ways to excel.
6. Exercise.
7. Listen to music.
8. Talk with others.
9. Cry.
10. Express your anger.
11. Distancing from the violent experience:
    a. Learn and practice relaxation skills.
    b. Learn and practice communication skills.
    c. Utilize productive rationalization and minimization.
    d. Participate in self defense training.

CONCLUSIONS

This chapter has focused on some of the special considerations that clinicians need to be aware of when conducting groups with adolescent girls. Basic group counseling and psychotherapy theory remain relevant and should serve as the framework for the group. This chapter offers to augment the practitioner's knowledge of the specific adolescent issues and tasks that must be addressed if an adolescent girls' group is to be successful.

Havighurst's tasks (1952) for adolescents remain essentially the same; it is only the context that becomes transformed by history, culture and contemporary society. The overall task, to master a sense of identity in preparation to live as a responsible adult citizen remains vital especially in today's chaotic world. While today's girl has the capacity to step up to and meet such a challenge, there are mitigating factors making the road a difficult one. A group can become a powerful agent of change for girls of today. In her desire to balance the themes of separation and connection, anger and aggression, sexuality, and identity, the group provides her with a foundation for exploration. As she allows her peers to become a greater source of influence, she also permits the entrance of new ideas and ways of being. She looks to new role models for guidance and insight. In this, the group leader becomes a significant and powerful guide. Practitioners often wonder about what makes girls succeed. What made the difference? When I have asked that question to adult women, a common answer is, "It took just one person who really believed in me and was there to inspire me." The root of change is in the relationship. Groups provide such relationships and girls, due to the specific issues and tasks addressed, work especially well in groups.

To enter the clinical world and successfully understand today's girl, the clinician must be equipped with all of the following if they are to be effective a) a solid knowledge foundation in theories of human development and personality, b) a solid foundation in group theory, c) clinical assessment skills, d) communication skills, and e) the ability to honor cultural, racial, ethnic, environmental, and/or religious factors which influence clients' lives so that pathology is not misdiagnosed. Additionally, clinicians owe it to themselves and to their clients to be in the best mental health that they can be.

To this end, it is important that every clinician pursue psychotherapy of some nature, preferably before beginning to see clients in therapy. Transference and countertransference issues always surface, and this is particularly true when working with adolescents. The leaders unresolved separation and family issues are revived in work with adolescents and the risk of overidentification with the client is great. For this reason, it is vital that the clinician be able to accurately identify her/his own issues versus those of their clients and to be able to differentiate their own feelings from those of their clients. Supervision and/or peer consultation is also invaluable. They should always be used. This maximizes the possibility that the adolescent clients involved will receive the best possible clinical intervention.

REFERENCES

American Association of University Women. (1991). *Shortchanging girls, shortchanging America: A call to action.* Washington, DC: American Association of University Women.

Apter, T., & Josselson, R. (1998). *Best friends: The pleasures and perils of girls' friendships.* New York: Crown Publishers, Inc.

Benton, R., Czechanski, B., Pavy, H., & Sweeney, M. (1993). Breaking the law: a metaphor for female empowerment through aggression: Women in film. *Journal of the American Academy of Psychoanalysis, 21 (1),* 133-147.

Bernstein, D. (1993). *Female identity conflict in clinical practice.* Northvale, NJ: Jason Aronson, Inc.

Bloom, M. (1980). *Adolescent parental separation.* New York: Gardner Press.

Brown, L. (1998). *Raising their voices: The politics of girls' anger.* Cambridge, MA: Harvard University Press.

Brumberg, J. (1997). *The body project: An intimate history of American girls.* New York: Vintage Books.

Committee on Adolescence, Group for the Advancement of Psychiatry. (1986). *Crises of adolescence, teenage pregnancy: Impact on adolescent development.* New York: Brunner/Mazel.

Conterio, K. & Lader, W. (1998). *Bodily harm. The breakthrough treatment program for self injurers.* New York: Hyperion.

Curran, D. (1996). *Tyranny of the spirit; Domination and submission in Adolescent Relationships.* Northvale, NJ: Jason Aronson, Inc.

DeBold, E. Wilson, M. & Malave, A. (1993). *Mother-daughter revolution: From betrayal to power.* Reading, MA: Addison-Wesley.

Dickerson, D. (1997). Not so black and white. *Allure Magazine*, Sept. 1997.

Frey, D.E. (1991). Psychosocial needs of the gifted adolescent. In M. Bireley and J. Genshaft (Eds.), *Understanding the gifted adolescent: Educational, developmental, and multicultural issues.* New York: Teachers College Press.

Gilligan, C. (1982). *In a different voice: Psychological theory and women's development.* Cambridge, MA: Harvard University Press.

Havighurst, R. (1952). *Developmental tasks and education.* New York: Longman's Green and Co.

Levy-Warren, M. (1996). *The adolescent journey: development, identity formation, and psychotherapy.* Northvale, NJ: Jason Aronson, Inc.

Lubin. B., Wilson, C., Petren, S. & Polk, A. (1996). *Research on group treatment methods; A selectively annotated bibliography.* Westport, CT: Greenwood Press.

Miller, D. (1994). *Women who hurt themselves.* News York: Basic Books.

Mishne, J. (1986). *Clinical work with adolescents.* New York: The Free Press.

Nowinski, J. (1990). *Substance abuse in adolescents and young adults.* New York: W. W. Norton & Co.

Orenstein, P. (1994). *School girls.* New York: Anchor Books, Doubleday.

Parens, H. (1993). *Aggression in our children.* Northvale, NJ: Aronson.

Pipher, M. (1995). *Hunger pains: The modern women's tragic quest for thinness*. New York: Ballantine Books.

Pipher, M. (1994). *Reviving Ophelia: Saving the selves of adolescent girls*. New York: Ballantine Books.

Rose, S. (1998). *Group therapy with troubled youth.* Thousand Oaks: Sage Publications.

Strauss, M. (1994). *Violence in the lives of adolescents*. New York: W. W. Norton & Co.

Chapter Five

GROUP PLAY THERAPY

Linda E. Homeyer and Daniel S. Sweeney

OVERVIEW

When children experience interpersonal and intrapersonal difficulties, group play therapy can be a dynamic and highly effective intervention. Knowing how to integrate group play therapy into the ongoing work of the mental health practitioner is indispensable. To this end, this chapter will begin with an introduction to group play therapy, followed by a brief overview of four major counseling theory applications to group play therapy. Then, to set group play therapy into a broader perspective, Yalom's eleven therapeutic factors will be discussed as they are applied to group play therapy. General guidelines for putting a play therapy group together (screening, selection, size), setting and materials, and recommended length and frequency of sessions will be addressed next. Finally, case examples are provided that expose the reader to the inner workings of the group.

INTRODUCTION

The application of play therapy in a group modality is a growing trend among mental health professionals who work with children. In a recently published text on the subject, Sweeney and Homeyer (1999) provide the following summary observations:

> Group play therapy is a natural union of two effective therapeutic modalities. Play therapists and group therapists share several important traits. Both are committed to a therapeutic process that is creative and dynamic. Both are centered on the development and maintenance of safe and therapeutic relationships. Both are focused on facilitation of an unfolding process, as opposed to the application of an immediate solution. Both are engaged in efforts requiring prerequisite training and supervision. The marriage of play

> therapy and group process is a natural and intuitive response to the needs of emotionally hurting children. (p.3)

It is necessary to provide some fundamental information about play therapy in order to create a context for discussing group play therapy. Landreth (1991) provides a useful context in the following definition: "Play therapy is defined as a dynamic interpersonal relationship between a child and a therapist trained in play therapy procedures who provides selected play materials and facilitates the development of a safe relationship for the child to fully express and explore self (feelings, thoughts, experiences, and behaviors) through the child's natural medium of communication, play" (p. 14).

Therapists must understand the importance of play in the lives of children and realize that children naturally communicate through play. Therapists without this understanding will simply use traditional "adult" counseling with children, which is based on verbalization and abstract thinking and therefore reflects a misunderstanding of fundamental principles of child development. Landreth (1991) further suggests: "Children's play can be more fully appreciated when recognized as their natural medium of communication. Children express themselves more fully and more directly through self-initiated spontaneous play than they do verbally because they are more comfortable with play. For children to 'play out' their experiences and feelings is the most natural dynamic and self-healing process in which children can engage" (p. 10).

Children learn about themselves in group play therapy. They learn because they are permitted to communicate in their own language, play. They learn as they hear and observe the perceptions of the therapist and the other children. They learn that is not just acceptable to be unique, but it is valued. In any group cooperation is important, and compliance sometimes necessary. In therapeutic play groups, creativity and originality is also encouraged and honored. For some children, group play therapy may provide them with the closest experience they will have to the structure and acceptance of a functional family.

Group play therapy actively combines the benefits of the group process with the advantages of play therapy. Therapeutic play groups promote safety and foster growth through the combination of the natural medium of children's communication and the natural course of interaction with other children in the group experience. Children learn about themselves, others, and life.

Group Play Therapy Theory

Similarities exist between group play therapy and other forms of child, adolescent and adult group therapy. For example, all apply a variety of counseling theories: Child Centered (Person Centered), Adlerian (Individual Psychology), Jungian (Analytical Psychology), Cognitive-Behavioral, Gestalt, Ecosystemic, and others. Four of these theories will be described briefly below.

Child-Centered Play Therapy Groups

In Child-Centered Group Play Therapy an environment is established in which the children experience empathy, safety, acceptance, and permissiveness. Within this environment the group members and play therapist are able to develop the interpersonal relationships in which growth occurs. It is within these relationships, not the techniques and the structured activities, that the child is able to: (1) explore the self and self-in-relationship, (2) challenge and be challenged for incongruent behavior, and (3) develop a more positive self-concept.

The Child Centered play therapist trusts the children to direct the flow of the session. As a result the sessions are focused on the children, not their problems. The play therapist facilitates the group members' self-direction, self-evaluation and responsibility (Landreth & Sweeney, 1999).

Child Centered, or Person Centered, Play Therapy is not new, it was initially developed by Virginia Axline (1947) and further promoted by current leaders in the field (Guerney, 1964; Landreth, 1991; Landreth & Sweeney, 1997, 1999).

Adlerian Group Play Therapy

Given the importance of the Adlerian concepts of social embeddedness and social interest, it is no surprise that group play therapy is a natural modality for Adlerian play therapists. Adlerian play therapy has four phases: (1) building an egalitarian relationship, (2) exploring the child's lifestyle, (3) helping the child gain insight into that lifestyle, and (4) reorientation and re-educating the child (Kottman, 1995). Terry Kottman, the developer of Adlerian play therapy, indicates that group play therapy follows the same four phases (Kottman, 1993, 1994, 1995, 1997, 1998, 1999). Group play therapy has the advantage that the play therapist can observe the children interacting in the group setting. According to Kottman this is especially helpful in exploring the child's lifestyle, selecting techniques that can be used to help the child gain insight into his or her lifestyle, and learning new skills for relating to self, others and the world.

The concept of properly balancing group members is important to the Adlerian play therapist. The group leader will select children who are "experiencing higher levels of difficulty as well as children who are experiencing only minor difficulty. This provides the leader with potential members who are able and willing to provide encouragement and appropriate constructive feedback to other members. Children who exhibit positive behavior and attitudes can serve as models for the other children and as potential 'cotherapists'" (Kottman, 1999, p. 70). Other dimensions in which to balance are active with passive, outgoing with withdrawn, inhibited with impulsive, high social interest with low social interest, susceptible to peer pressure with resistant to contagion, and those children who strive toward positive goals of behavior with those who strive to negative goals of behavior (Kottman, 1999).

Parent and teacher consultations are important to the Adlerian play therapist. For the parents of children in group play therapy, the play therapist might provide group feedback and consultation, rotate one or two parents a week, periodic phone consultations, or invite the parents to participate in a parenting class. With teachers, the Adlerian play therapist advocates for the children by assisting in the development of skills to interact with the children in more effective ways. This goal is more readily achieved when the play therapist understands both the teacher's and child's lifestyles. Understanding lifestyles provides the play therapist with more effective ways to interact with the teacher and the opportunity to work together with the teacher to help the child understand his or her goals of misbehavior (Kottman, 1999).

Jungian Group Play Therapy

In group, as in individual Jungian play therapy, a primary role of the therapist is to provide a *temenos* or holding container in which growth occurs. The play therapist moves each session from the initial conscious level, to the working phase using the metaphor of the unconscious, and then ends the session by anchoring children in external reality. Through the metaphorical language of the unconscious, archetypal images are released through directed as well as nondirected activities such as play, drawing, sandtray, music, drama, journaling, puppets, etc. Together the therapist and the group members interpret the dynamics and create alternatives (Bertoia, 1999).

The play therapist must be able to work with both the transference from the individual child as well as that of the collective transference of the group, constantly negotiating between the conscious and the unconscious. Specifically, the play therapist gives "audible expression to psyche's language ... [mediating] the language of the unconscious, translating or interpreting the images so the entire group begins to grasp the invisible but certainly present archetypes" (p. 93).

Gestalt Group Play Therapy

Violet Oaklander has been the primary writer and trainer in Gestalt child therapy, an approach that includes play therapy and working with groups of children from a Gestalt perspective (1998, 1999).

Gestalt play therapists view group play therapy as a social microcosm of the outside world in which the individual child can find himself or herself. Initially, children take on roles in the group which reveal how they make contact with others in the outside world. The play therapist provides activities to bring these roles into the children's awareness. As the children feel safe and understood, they allow themselves to become vulnerable and receive support from and connection with the other children and the play therapist. This support strengthens the child's inner support and a stronger self develops (Oaklander, 1999).

Oaklander contends that groups of six to eight children are appropriate if the children are over eight years old, while a group of three to six children is a recommended size for children under eight. Believing it is sometimes necessary to give children individual attention within the group setting, she advocates for a co-therapist whenever possible.

These fairly structured groups meet for approximately one and one half to two hours. A typical group session format begins with "rounds," a time for individual children to share how their week has gone. Oaklander indicates that using a "talking stick" helps children to stay focused and wait their turn to speak. After the play therapist selected activity of the session ends, the children clean-up the room and re-take seats for closure. Again, the children share. This time the sharing is focused on what has happened in the session and the child's response to it. The Gestalt play therapist uses a wide range of activities, many of them are projective (e.g., clay, drawing, sandtray, collage, puppetry, music, body movement, creative dramatics, metaphorical stories, fantasy and imagery) (Oaklander, 1988, 1999).

THERAPEUTIC FACTORS

Yalom's (1995) eleven therapeutic factors have long been the standard for understanding the therapeutic effects of group therapy. These factors are important to group play therapy as well. However, given the developmental differences between children and adults, the factors may be enacted somewhat differently.

Instillation of Hope

Yalom (1995) indicates that this factor has two components. One, hope on the part of the client that group will be beneficial, and second, hope on the part of the group leaders based on a belief in their own skills and the efficacy of the group process. While Sweeney (1997) states that children benefit from the reciprocal encouragement which occurs in the group process, hope in group play therapy would be based primarily on the counselor's belief in this therapeutic modality. Children rarely have a choice about being in therapy. Thus, it is difficult for children to have a sense of hope that the play therapy process will benefit them. However, many children intuitively sense that play therapy is helpful. For example one child told her play therapist, "I wish there were enough play rooms so every kid could have one to go to ... but that they didn't have to."

Bertoia indicates that the therapists' belief in the process "must be absolute" (1999, p. 102). A Jungian play therapist, Bertoia states that the "wounded healer archetype is constellated, and the unconscious transference from the therapist activates the healer within the children" (p.102).

Additionally, because children are rarely self-referred and depend upon an adult, typically a parent, to get them to therapy, this hope needs to be instilled in the parents of the child-clients. Hopefulness on the part of the parents that group play therapy will be helpful to their child is one of the factors which engages parents in the therapeutic process. Engagement on the part of the parents is necessary to ensure their continued support of their child's therapy. This support is very often practical in nature, such as not missing sessions or reducing premature termination.

Universality

Discovering that you are not alone but that others share your experiences and how you think and feel is a powerful therapeutic element. This is a primary therapeutic benefit of group, as well as group play therapy. Children experience the therapeutic qualities of discovering that their peers have problems, too, thereby diminishing feelings of being all alone (Sweeney & Homeyer, 1999). Oaklander (1999) indicates that for most children it is a revelation that other children have similar thoughts, concerns, worries, fears, wonders, as well as experiences.

It is important to remember that in group play therapy this realization may occur in a variety of ways. This includes non-verbal expression, as children use the language of play as the primary form of communication.

Imparting Information

This variable is highly dependent upon which counseling theory the play therapist employs. Counselors who subscribe to more directive theories, such as cognitive-behavioral, would impart more direct advice and participate in didactic instruction. The more non-directive role of the counselor, the more likely that this factor would not be a focus of the work in the group play therapy process. Child-centered play therapists, for example, do not take this role with their child-clients. However, imparting information to the parents (or parent substitute) of the child-client would be a common, and very appropriate, activity. Parents may also participate in psycho-educational groups to complement their child's group play therapy. Or parent consultations can be used to help parents understand what is happening in group and obtain appropriate information regarding their child, parenting skills, and issues surrounding the reason for referral. Helping parents to understand their children is crucial, especially for those parents who are not participating in their own counseling.

One aspect of imparting information which would be done by even the most nondirective play therapist would be what Yalom (1995) refers to as the client's examination of misconceptions and self-defeating responses. The play therapist's facilitative responses to the children's play and interactions with each other put words to that which the children may not yet be able to express in words. Thus the play therapist provides the language, the cognitive rendition of what is occurring. This response may be termed enlarging-the-meaning or interpretation, depending on the theoretical orientation of the play therapist.

Altruism

In group play therapy, children develop a sensitivity to each other and increase their self-esteem when they are able to help each other (Landreth, 1990). Additionally, Yalom (1995) speaks of the group member experiencing a sense of being helpful and important to others. The client experiences this act as refreshing and as a boost to self-esteem.

Altruism readily occurs in group play therapy when the therapist uses frequent self-esteem building responses and comments on the positive interactions between children.

Corrective Recapitulation of the Primary Family Group

Play therapy groups serve as a microcosm of society in which children naturally play out their roles with peers. Children also play out their roles in their primary family groups. This comes easily to children, most of whom are still living in that family group. Consequently, the play therapist has the opportunity to gain substantial insight into the children's perception of their everyday lives (Sweeney, 1997).

The play therapist typically takes on the role of the parent/surrogate-parent in the group sessions. When this occurs the presence of other children is especially helpful for those children who have been abused or otherwise negatively impacted by adults. The other children are a source of comfort and safety. The children serve as a buffer between themselves and the play therapist/surrogate-parent (Homeyer, 1999). As Yalom (1995) indicates some groups are purposefully arranged with male and female co-leaders, just for this purpose. The same is true in group play therapy. Like all group counselors, the group play therapist has the task of providing an environment that allows for the recapitulation or reenactment of the family and the corrective emotional experiences. This occurs when the play therapist is able to establish a safe environment where trust is combined with permissiveness.

Development of Socialization Techniques

In the process of interacting in the group, children help each other assume responsibility in interpersonal relationships (Landreth, 1991). Play therapy groups provide opportunities for children to master new behaviors, offer and receive assistance, and experiment with alternative expressions of emotions and behavior (Sweeney, 1997). Feedback, both behavioral and verbal, helps children learn how others perceive them. The development of social skills is often the reason children in school are referred to the school counselor for treatment. Group play therapy very effectively meets this need.

Imitative Behavior

Vicarious therapy occurs in group play therapy as well. Through watching other children in the group, a child is able to gain enough courage to attempt changes he or she wishes to make (Landreth, 1991). Children observe the emotional and behavioral expressions of other group members and learn coping behaviors, problem-solving skills, and alternative avenues for self-expression from them (Sweeney, 1997). This fosters the development of sufficient courage to "try on" behaviors which may initiate Yalom's adaptive spiral (1995).

Interpersonal Learning

This therapeutic factor is likened to the primary family group, except that it deals with the social microcosm. In group play therapy children learn about themselves specifically through their interaction with each other. The group play therapist attends to the interaction between group members and interprets what he or she sees to the children in words. Again, children may be acting and reacting to each other in verbal and non-verbal ways. The play therapist must have a great deal of confidence and trust in the children's ability to work out issues between each other. Such trust and confidence allows children to assume responsibility for their relationships. Children gain the opportunity to reflect and achieve insights as they learn to evaluate and reevaluate themselves in light of peer feedback (Sweeney, 1997).

Group Cohesiveness

This is a crucial factor for both adolescent and adult group therapy. It's importance is equivalent to the therapeutic relationship in individual counseling. However, group cohesion is not essential to group play therapy with younger children (Landreth, 1991). Indeed it may not be developmentally possible. Often group play therapy may be more like providing concurrent individual sessions with parallel play occurring the majority of the time. Cooperative and associative play does occur from time to time.

Catharsis

Individual play therapy provides the setting for children to have cathartic experiences within the safety of a therapeutic relationship. The inclusion of additional children in the group play therapy setting promotes spontaneity. Catharsis relies upon spontaneity. Sibling play therapy will often provide a setting for children to begin dealing with their issues more rapidly.

The affective life of children is addressed at two levels: (1) the intrapsychic issues of individual group members and (2) the interpersonal issues between the therapist and group members. The group play setting may decrease a child's need or tendency to be repetitious and/or to retreat into fantasy play. While these behaviors may be necessary for some children in the processing of their issues, the group play therapy setting can bring those children "stuck" in repetition or fantasy into the here and now (Sweeney, 1997).

Existential Factors

Yalom (1995) identifies the existential factors as: (1) recognizing life at times is unfair, (2) there is no escape from life's pain, (3) eventual death, (4) facing of life alone, and (5) taking ultimate responsibility for ones own life. Work with dying children offers insights into the perceptiveness of even very young children's understanding of existential issues.

PUTTING THE GROUP TOGETHER

The success of a play therapy group begins with defining the purpose of the group. Purposes and goals are linked to the setting in which the play therapist is working. For example, play therapists working in public schools typically provide groups for increased social skills, anger control, and dealing with victims of loss and grief. Many agencies serve specific populations, such as family violence, sexual assault, or the homeless. Consequently, play therapists who work for these agencies will serve children with these issues. Those practitioners in private practice may be more likely to have mixed groups, or groups made up of children with a wider variety of presenting problems. Generally, heterogeneous groups are viewed as more therapeutic than homogenous groups. For example, it may be appropriate to avoid assembling a group of children who have experienced the same trauma. This may be necessary to prevent an escalation of traumatic behaviors or emotions. Conversely, if other factors are balanced, the universality factor of a homogenous group can be very powerful.

Additionally, the decision to have an open or closed group may also be determined by the needs of the play therapist's work setting. For example, schools, organized by marking periods and structured by holidays, tend to provide a setting for closed groups. Family violence shelters, with people literally moving in and out at a moment's notice, require open groups. However, the play therapist must be aware of the idiosyncratic needs of the client and be willing to advocate for those needs. Some children simply require more therapy so the artificial termination of a closed group leaves these children still needing more. Conversely, the more resilient child may be ready to terminate before the closed group concludes. It is important that the play therapist answers the issue of open vs. closed group in a purposeful and intentional manner.

Screening, Selection, and Size

Assembling the group is crucial to its success. Unfortunately, the screening, selection, and size concerns of group play therapy are often overlooked. These elements should be seen as the first phase of the treatment process. Children, who are developmentally egocentric, internalize beliefs about themselves. If group play therapy does not work for them, and they need to be removed from the group, the child internalizes another failure. For the child in need of therapy, this becomes another profound failure. Therefore it is incumbent upon the play therapist to make thoughtful and knowledgeable decisions while assembling the group.

Balance

The key goal for putting a group together is balance. As noted previously, heterogeneous groups are generally viewed as more therapeutic than homogenous groups. However, within each group, regardless of the heterogeneous/homogenous issue, balance is important. The following factors should be balanced: introverted with extroverted behavior; withdrawn with aggressive; serious levels of pathology with milder levels; and, active with passive (Ginott, 1961; Landreth, 1991; Sweeney & Homeyer, 1999).

Up until age nine, balancing gender works well. This means if a group has two girls, balance it with two boys. Psychosocial developmental tasks of children who are age nine and older favor treatment in single gender groups.

Although this varies with sibling group play therapy, the age range of children in group play therapy should generally not exceed twelve months. The developmental differences between a three-year-old and a five-year-old are simply too great. Unless developmental delays are an issue, this is an appropriate rule of thumb. Physical size of the children also needs to be taken into consideration. Given the range of growth patterns of individual children, a single larger or smaller child is not recommended.

Screening

During the screening process the play therapist seeks to identify children who have some ability to delay gratification because they can be a catalyst of change in others, and they will not monopolize the sessions (Ginott, 1975). Additionally, Ginott asserts that a basic requirement for placement into a group is the presence of and capacity for "social hunger" (1975). This refers to children's need to be accepted by their peers and a desire to attain and maintain a sense of belonging in the group.

Individual play therapy sessions are often used as an element of the screening process. A single play session can offer useful indications or contraindications for inclusion in the group. In some situations, a child may be moved from individual play therapy to group play therapy as part of an overall treatment plan. This may be particularly true with siblings. Each sibling may have a course of individual play therapy sessions and then shift to sibling-group play therapy. Or a child might participate in concurrent individual and sibling-group sessions, depending upon therapy issues.

Other screening methods may also be appropriate, including parent and/or teacher report, behavioral assessment, and child interviews.

Selection

Some children may not respond well to group play therapy. These children should generally be seen on an individual basis. O'Connor (1991), for example, states that children who have recently experienced a trauma are better served in individual play therapy. He feels that these children need more of one-on-one nurturing provided by group play therapy. Ginott (1961) suggested the following additional contraindications:

1. Siblings who exhibit intense rivalry
2. Extremely aggressive children
3. Sexually acting-out children
4. Children experiencing difficulty due to poor infant-mother attachment
5. Sociopathic children (intending to inflict harm or revenge without remorse)
6. Children with an extremely poor self-image.

Size

Another consideration in group work with children is the size of the group. Generally, the younger the children, the smaller the group. Very young children are just beginning to learn how to function in groups of any kind outside of their immediate family. An associated issue may be the level of structure that needs to be provided in the group. This will generally vary according to the group theory and the group population. It is important to remember that it is particularly challenging to lead large groups. Two children make a "group," and groups of two can be therapeutically beneficial. The typical size for group play therapy is 3 - 5 children. However, with co-therapists more children may be added.

Bertoia (1999) suggests that even groups of two provide sufficient intrapsychic images for group work from a Jungian perspective. She also indicates that groups of six to eight, within three years of age, function well when organized around specific therapeutic issues such as bereavement, divorce or social skills. On the other hand, Oaklander (1999) indicates that assembling groups around specific topics may tend to label children and further isolate them from other children.

Setting and Materials

The facility and the selection of materials to be used for the therapeutic play group are both important considerations. Though many group rooms are equipped with carpeting, chairs, and soft pillows, they do not work well for play therapy groups. Ideally, a group room that is set aside for play therapy groups is best, floored with tile and equipped with sturdy toys and furniture. An adequately sized room which is not devoted to play therapy will work, however, appropriate limits will have to be set. On the other hand, a regular counseling office may not be appropriate because of the necessity to set too many limits.

The room should not be too small or too large. A room that is at least 12 by 15 feet is recommended. A playroom that is too small can lead to frustration and aggression between group members. A room that is too large not only creates the possibility of uncontrolled behavior but also enables the withdrawn child to avoid interaction. The potential for high levels of noise and messiness should also be considered. The location of the group room in a counseling facility may, therefore, be important.

The play materials may vary according to theory and purpose. In general, play media should be selected that:

1. Facilitate a wide range of creative expression
2. Facilitate a wide range of emotional expression
3. Engage children's interests
4. Facilitate expressive and exploratory play
5. Allow exploration and expression without verbalization
6. Allow success without prescribed structure
7. Allow for noncommittal play (Landreth, 1991, p. 116).

It is not necessary to provide enough toys of any one type for each group member. Children lose the opportunity to learn to resolve conflict when provided with unlimited play materials.

With older children and adolescents an activity group setting of some kind is recommended. One of the primary benefits of activity groups is that group members enjoy the continued opportunity for nonverbal expression which play therapy provides, with the additional advantages of group activities and discussion.

Length and Frequency of Sessions

It is generally recommended to relate the length of the group session to the age of the child members. Simply stated, the younger the children are, generally, the shorter the session. Basically, the group facilitator must accommodate the attention span of the children. For preschool children and early elementary aged children, a play therapy group may run for 20 to 40 minutes. For children approaching middle or junior high school, the groups may run well over an hour.

The duration of the group will also vary. Gumaer (1984) noted that most research indicates that for group counseling to be effective with children, a minimum of 10 sessions is necessary. Again, this will vary for play groups meeting in different settings (schools, hospitals, etc.) and for different populations (sexually abused, grieving, etc.).

Frequency of group meetings is another important issue. Frequency is governed by the purpose of the group and the severity of the presenting problems. Intensive short-term groups, meeting two to five times per week can be very effective. Kot's (1995) research reported positive results on the efficacy of short-term, intensive, child-centered play therapy with children who had witnessed domestic violence and were temporarily residing in family shelters. Tyndall-Lind (1999) replicated Kot's research with the same population using group play therapy. She also found significant improvement in children using the intensive format, which in her research was 5 group sessions per week.

Case Example

In the following case example, three children [Randy, age 7; Judi, age 7; and Steve, age 8] are meeting for the first time in a play therapy group at an elementary school. They have all been referred because of "socialization problems." Randy has been described as an anxious child who does not have any friends; Judi as an introverted child who relates more to adults than to children; and Steve as a somewhat hyperactive child who tends to annoy his peers. The following is a brief transcript of some of the therapeutic interactions that occurred while the children were in the playroom.

Initial Session

Therapist: Randy, Judi, and Steve--this is our playroom, and you can play with the toys in a lot of the ways you would like to.

Steve: (rushing into the room towards the sandbox) I want to play in the sand!

Therapist: Steve, it looks like you've got something in mind. (Judi moves slowly into the room while looking at the toys) Judi, it looks like you're checking out the toys on that shelf.

Rationale:

The child-centered group play therapy approach is permission-giving. The therapist uses each child's name, which honors each child, and establishes the egalitarian status of each group member.

It is not unusual to have children of varying levels of emotional and sociable levels.

In group play therapy, it becomes very important to use the child's name, so that each group member is aware of who is being addressed. Steve has an intentional plan, and the therapist needs to acknowledge this. At the same time, the other children need to be responded to. It can be a temptation to respond primarily to the most active and vocal children, but therapeutic responses should be spread out equally among the group members.

Judi: Yeah, I guess so. (Judi has reached out tentatively to touch the cash register but has pulled her hand back. Randy is still standing next to the door, furtively glancing around).

Therapist: Judi, it seems like you're wondering if it's o.k. to play with that. In here, you can choose what to play with. Randy, it looks like you're wondering about this place.

Steve: (Grabs the rubber snake and runs across the room, poking the snake at Randy's face. Randy cringes and tries to fend off the snake.)

Rationale:

The initial session of group play therapy is often tentative and exploratory for the children. They are not just exploring the playroom but also checking out the therapist and the other children.

The therapist's voice tone should match the voice tone and activity level of the child. The response to Judi is warm and empathic but places the responsibility for making the choices onto her. It might be tempting for the therapist to give Randy a specific invitation to play, because of his tentativeness. He should be allowed to make this choice himself.

Therapist: Steve, it looks like you would like to scare Randy with that snake, but he is trying to tell you he doesn't like what you are doing. He wants you to stop.

Steve: (Leaves Randy and with great glee begins chasing Judi around the room as she screams: "Quit that!")

Therapist: Steve, you're having lots of fun chasing Judi; but Judi, you are telling him you don't like what he is doing

(Steve drops the snake on the floor and goes back to the sandbox. Judi picks up some puppets and begins to make a puppet show. Randy plays with a toy in the corner behind the easel stand, out of sight.)

Rationale:

Recognition of feelings is key to the child-centered approach. Verbalizing Randy's nonverbal message helps Steve to hear Randy's message and gives Randy needed support that he is understood.

Tracking of activity and responding to feelings is the same as in individual play therapy, just more so. It is important that both children be responded to equally. Both children need to know they have been heard and understood.

Therapist: So, Steve you decided to do something else; and Judi, you decided to play with the puppets.

Randy: (sits on the floor under the easel looking out at the group.)

Judi: (continues puppet story, saying to the therapist) Good morning. I'm the lion. (gives a loud roar)

Therapist: Good morning lion. That's a big roar.

(Other interactions occur as Judi develops the puppet story.)

Therapist: Randy, looks like you decided to sit right there.

Steve: (has been digging in the sand, burying toy soldiers and says to no one in particular) I'm going to bury all of these guys

Rationale:

Recognizing that children have made a decision affirms their strength. No response is made to Randy because he seems to need to be left alone at the moment. The therapist is keenly sensitive to where he is and what he is doing but respects his choice to hide. The therapist can interact without structuring. Nonevaluative recognition communicates acceptance of his decision to sit and look

Therapist: (to Steve) Yep, looks like you've buried a bunch of them
Randy: (emerges from under the easel, joins Steve and begins digging in the sand.)
Steve: (to Randy) Hey! Neat! You can dig the holes, and I'll bury these guys.
Therapist: Randy, you've decided to play in the sand with Steve--and Steve, sounds like you like that!
Steve: (grabs the sand pail and yells) This is going to be a bomb! (holds bucket up high and drops it on the floor as Randy protests.)

Rationale:

Toys are not labeled until the child identifies the item.

The activity of other children in group play therapy invites and entices shy, quiet children. Randy relaxes enough to begin playing. Steve's statement is encouraging to Randy and helps him feel included. A simple tracking of the play activity provides affirmation of the choices made by the children, particularly Randy.

Therapist: Steve, I know that was fun for you, but the sand is for staying in the sand box. You wanted the bucket--but Randy, you are telling Steve you want to play with it.
Randy: (picks up bucket and begins to fill it with sand again) I'm going to build a castle.

Rationale:

The therapist shows understanding of each child's behavioral and emotional message, and sets an appropriate limit. The limit setting follows the A.C.T. model, proposed by Landreth (1991). This highly effective models includes: (1) A - Acknowledging the child's feelings (it is important to begin the setting of limits by continuing reflection and acceptance); (2) C - Communicating the limit (in a neutral and nonpunitive manner); and (3) T - Targeting an acceptable alternative (which recognizes that the child still has a need to express self and can do so within acceptable boundaries). A limit that is set objectively, with acceptance, and without disapproval is most often received and responded to by children with compliance.

Steve: These soldiers can guard the castle.
Judi: (stands watching the boys) There needs to be a family living in the castle. (She retrieves the doll family from the doll house and adds them to the castle scene.)

Rationale:

Steve's aggression has subsided because he has been allowed to act it out, and he joins in the play activity in a helpful way.

Therapist You're all making that castle just the way you want it to be.
Judi, Randy, & Steve: (almost in unison) Yeah!

Rationale:

The therapist's comment empowers the children, recognizing their own decision making, effort, and creative ability. This comment also affirms their working together, while not providing praise and approval. The child-centered play therapist does not evaluate and focuses on the effort rather than the product. The difference between encouragement and praise is key in the child-centered group play therapy process. By focusing on the effort the therapist can make self-esteem building statements without creating the leading and approval-seeking dynamic that comes from statements of praise. It also models this important dynamic for the group members in their interaction with each other.

Each child in this case reacted differently to the therapist establishing basic rapport and a therapeutic relationship. Although this was an initial session, some of the previously noted benefits of group play therapy are already evident. Randy demonstrated movement from being generally anxious in the group to interacting with the other children. His physical movement from distance to closer proximity to the therapist and the other children was one example of the benefit of placing shy, anxious children in play therapy groups. Steve's aggressive behavior was ameliorated by the group, particularly by the therapist giving expression to the displeasure of the other children at some of his behaviors. He was given the opportunity to reevaluate his acting out behaviors in the presence of Randy and Judi, as well as the therapist. Judi begins by playing alone and seeking to engage the therapist, which is typical of her introverted behavior outside of the playroom where she attempts to relate primarily with adults. She, too, is drawn into the play process.

SUMMARY

Group play therapy is an effective mode of intervention for children. It provides many of the same benefits as adult group therapy. Screening and selection are important to the success of the group, because the therapist can properly balance the members' traits. Group size is dependent on factors such as age, presenting issue, and level of structure provided by the group leader. Research has indicated that providing children in crisis with intensive group experiences results in successful and expeditious treatment results. Group play therapy is an effective intervention for use in all settings in which children receive mental health services.

REFERENCES

Allan, J. (1988). *Inscapes of the child's world: Jungian counseling in schools and clinics*. Dallas, TX: Spring.

Allan, J., & Bertoia, J. (1992). *Written paths to healing: Education and Jungian child counseling*. Dallas, TX: Spring.

Axline, V. (1947). *Play therapy: The inner dynamics of childhood*. Boston: Houghton Mifflin.

Bertoia, J. (1993). *Drawings from a dying child*. New York: Rutledge.

Bertoia, J. (1999). The invisible village Jungian group play therapy. In D. Sweeney & L. Homeyer (Eds.), *The handbook of group play therapy*, (pp. 86-104). San Francisco: Jossey-Bass.

Ginott, H. (1961). *Group psychotherapy with children: The theory and practice of play therapy*. New York: McGraw-Hill.

Ginott, H. (1975). Group play therapy with children. In G. Gazda (Ed.), *Basic approaches to group psychotherapy and group counseling*. Springfield, IL: Charles C. Thomas.

Guerney, L. (1964). Filial therapy: Description and rationale. *Journal of Consulting Psychology, 28,* 304-310.

Gumaer, J. (1984). *Counseling and therapy for children*. New York: The Free Press.

Homeyer, L. (1999). *Group play therapy with sexually abused children*. In D. Sweeney & L. Homeyer (Eds.), *The handbook of group play therapy*, (pp. 299-318). San Francisco: Jossey-Bass.

Kot, S. (1995). *Intensive play therapy with child witnesses of domestic violence*. Unpublished doctoral dissertation, University of North Texas, Denton, TX.

Kottman, T. (1999). Group applications of Adlerian play therapy. In D. Sweeney & L. Homeyer (Eds.), *The handbook of group play therapy*, (pp. 65-85). San Francisco: Jossey-Bass.

Landreth, G. (1991). *Play therapy: The art of the relationship*. Muncie, IN: Accelerated Development Press.

Landreth, G., & Sweeney, D. (1997). Child-centered play therapy. In K. O'Connor & L. Braverman (Eds.), *Play therapy theory and applications: A comparative casebook*. New York: John Wiley & Sons.

Landreth, G., & Sweeney, D. (1999). The freedom to be: Child-Centered Group Play Therapy. In D. Sweeney & L. Homeyer (Eds.), *The handbook of group play therapy*, (pp. 39-64). San Francisco: Jossey-Bass.

O'Connor, K. (1999). Child, protector, confident: Structured group Ecosystemic play therapy. In D. Sweeney & L. Homeyer (Eds.), *The handbook of group play therapy*, (pp. 105-138). San Francisco: Jossey-Bass.

Oaklander, V. (1988). *Windows to our children*. New York: Gestalt Journal Press.

Oaklander, V. (1999). Group play therapy from a Gestalt therapy perspective. In D. Sweeney & L. Homeyer (Eds.), *The handbook of group play therapy*, (pp. 162 -175). San Francisco: Jossey-Bass.

Sweeney, D. (1997). *Counseling children through the world of play*. Wheaton, IL: Tyndale House Publishers.

Sweeney, D., & Homeyer, L. (Eds.) (1999). *The handbook of group play therapy*. San Francisco: Jossey-Bass.

Tyndall-Lind, A. (1999). *A comparative analysis of intensive individual play therapy and intensive sibling group play therapy with child witnesses of domestic violence*. Unpublished dissertation. University of North Texas, Denton, TX.

Yalom, I. (1995). *The theory and practice of group psychotherapy*. NY: Harper Collins.

SECTION II:
ADULTS

Chapter Six

RESTORING RELATIONSHIPS: FORGIVENESS AND RECONCILIATION IN MARITAL GROUP THERAPY

James N. Sells

INTRODUCTION

Marital Group Therapy (MGT) is the application of established group theory within the context of couples therapy. The presence of couples in a therapeutic group presents major alterations in the dynamics of group process. While individual group therapy can be viewed by clients as a respite from conflictual relationships, MGT brings the strained relationship to the session. The couple sub-group must interact with the whole group, the individual participants and the group leadership. Although MGT is a special form of group and marital therapy, it remains subject to much of the established knowledge applied to group therapy in more traditional settings. This chapter will focus on discriminating the unique aspects of MGT from those aspects which are shared with group and marital therapies.

This chapter has three goals. The first goal is to address the broad issues pertaining to the use of group therapy through an examination of the MGT professional literature. The second goal is to present my clinical work with marital group therapy. This approach is based on the interface between contextual family therapy, group therapy and forgiveness and reconciliation interventions. The third goal is to examine the unique technical and clinical issues which distinguish MGT from both traditional models of group and marital therapy. There are three specific distinctions. When compared to marital or group therapies, MGT has a unique client, focus, and process.

What follows is a review of the history of MGT, a presentation of my model of marital therapy within a small group context, and case studies which illustrate significant clinical issues.

MARITAL GROUP THERAPY: REVIEW OF PROFESSIONAL LITERATURE

Marital therapy and group therapy are two of the most highly regarded therapeutic modes. While data generated from process and outcome studies of marital and group therapies is extensive. Little attention has been given to the hybrid process of marital group therapy.

Significant attention was paid to marital group therapy during the 1960's. Most of the literature focused on MGT as a psychoanalytic intervention. Perelman (1960), Boas (1962), Flint and MacLennan (1962) and Gottlieb and Pattison (1966) all argue for the benefits of MGT within a psychoanalytic framework. At that time the prevailing analytic thought was that any real relationship occurring within a therapeutic context would block the more valuable transference relationship and thus obstruct the development of insight. At that time marital group therapy within the psychodynamic paradigm was considered an innovative intervention, challenging some of the most basic assumptions about the therapeutic change agent. Gurman (1971) observed that the later development of interpersonal, systematic and cognitive-behavioral marital interventions make the early psychoanalytic objections obsolete.

Gurman (1971) identified three themes which directed the focus of marital groups in the first 15 years of MGT (1955-1970). They are: 1) Using MGT as a mode to address individual pathology; 2) Using MGT to facilitate relational development through increased self understanding and insight; and 3) Using MGT as a learning tool to foster behavioral change. The later two themes have remained as significant foci within MGT.

The decade of the 1970's was characterized by continued interest in MGT as a therapeutic intervention. Alger (1976) suggested that the profession was integrating theory drawn from individual, family and group modalities. He believed that couples groups hold the common space shared by family therapy and group therapy. Shared factors include understanding of systems and communication theories, and the relationship of the individual with a community. Alger's work reflected the cultural change in the field of psychotherapy. The analytic tradition was being challenged by process and outcome research supporting the efficacy of short-term marital group interventions. These interventions focused on conflict management, communication skill formation, creating pleasureful experiences, and developing contingency-contracting skills (Lieberman, Wheeler, & Sanders, 1976).

Framo (1973), relying on the contributions from the psychoanalytic tradition, integrated the social influence of family of origin into marital therapy. He found that MGT was an ideal medium to develop his object relations family theory. To him, the group context facilitated a couple's ability to bring family of origin into the present marital relationship. Patterns exhibited by the couple in the presence of the group could be connected with patterns articulated by the individual group members recalling their family of origin. Framo believes that the observation of problematic behaviors by others is more powerful than the verbal explanation of the same behavior by the therapist in individual couples therapy.

Papp (1976) developed a marital group intervention based on brief strategic theory. She found that marital group therapy is particularly powerful because the multiple participants created opportunities to reconstruct the complexity of the marital conflicts. Language, being linear, restricts insight to marital conflict because one idea must follow another, and another, etc. In actuality, marital conflicts are occurring as multiple stresses/pressures exercise their effect on the couple. These, while exercising constant effect, are addressed one at a time in traditional couples therapy. In group therapy a psychodrama-like process, called group choreography, is used to accelerate the learning as the couples can partner with one another to create parallels to the life circumstance.
She divides the group by sexes early in the process so that men and women can serve as accountability sources for the individuals as they seek to implement changes to the relationship held in mystery by the spouse. Papp emphasizes the theatrical component of group therapy--everything that happens in a group happens before an audience.

Papp's model spawns 12 sessions with 4 couples to a group. The first session is devoted to choreographing their relationships. The couples only work together sporadically, in essence, to allow for the group to assess change and movement by the couples. The final session is a combined session to summarize their experiences and suggest direction. Hers is a strategic model which prompts couples to define a common metaphor to describe their current conflict. The couples separate and utilize same sex groups to strategize a change process which will hopefully encourage the alteration of patterns.

The past 15 years have seen a significant decline in the development of MGT. This reduction is noted by Marett (1988) in his review of the outcome research from the mid 1970's to the mid-1980's. Lieberman and Lieberman (1986), Neimeyer (1987), Coche and Coche (1990) and Coche (1995) are noteworthy because they have done the most recent work of substance over the past decade on MGT.

A model which provides a good example of the current trend, Coche (1995) uses an existential-humanistic model of group therapy, emphasizing the importance of personhood in the pursuit of intimacy. She believes that one's capacity for intimacy increases with each individual's development of personal meaning. Coche also emphasizes the assumption of responsibility as a foundation for intimacy. She holds that intimacy is maintained by responsibly making choices. She uses larger existential issues (e.g. life, death, loneliness, suffering) to elevate couples above common daily dilemmas. Finally, Coche emphasizes the communication skills developed in humanistic counselor training such as Truax and Carkhuff (1967) and Satir's (1967, 1988) marital communication model.

Coche conducts her groups in a 22-session package over 11 months. The group meets two times per month. Each session lasts 2-1/2 hours. The sessions are divided into halves, with the first half consisting of a spontaneous discussion of the couple's and the group's issues. The second half is didactic focusing on specific skills and exercises such as principles of communication, conflict resolution, or guided fantasy.

To summarize, MGT is an established therapeutic intervention for couples. It emerged from dynamic orientations in the 1960's and 1970's. Intervention models developed recently have emphasized existential-humanistic themes, psychodrama, and brief dynamic orientations.

FORGIVENESS AND RECONCILIATION MGT: THEORY AND PRACTICE

It could be said that the themes of forgiveness and reconciliation have both very long, and recent histories. Literature, history, philosophy and theology have for centuries addressed the topic of violation, conflict, and resolution. A fundamental requirement for a civil society has been the resolution of differences (Tournier, 1962). However, prior to 1995, the theme of forgiveness addressed in the professional mental health literature was almost entirely absent. On occasion when forgiveness is discussed in the professional literature, it often is a polarizing and incendiary idea (Bass & Davis, 1994, 1990).

In its most basic form forgiveness refers to relinquishing the right to retaliate for injuries experienced. Pingleton's (1989) definition is the most descriptive: "forgiveness recognizes, anticipates and attempts to mitigate against the *lex talionis*, or law of the talon--the human organism's universal, almost reflexive propensity for retaliation and retribution in the face of hurt and pain at the hand of another. Thus, forgiveness can be understood as comprising the antithesis of the individual's natural and predictable response to violation and victimization" (p. 27).

The most common understanding of forgiveness involves some aspect of release or letting go over time. The release may focus on the expression of anger (Davenport, 1991; Fitzgibbons, 1986), the seeking of revenge (Cloke, 1993), shame (Halling, 1994), the recording of wrongs (DiBlasio, 1992), and the outer and inner manifestations of resentment (Enright et. al, 1996; North, 1987). The component of time or forgiveness as an unfolding process taking months and possibly years to achieve is a fundamental component emphasized by most of the literature (Cunningham, 1985; Enright et. al, 1996; Fitzgibbons, 1996; Hope, 1987; Hargrave, 1994; Hunter, 1978; Kaufman, 1984; Kirkup, 1993). Reconciliation is seen as the process of two parties resolving differences. While forgiveness is held as a merciful action controlled by the injured, reconciliation is the means by which an injured person breaks the enmeshment of hate/resentment with the injurer (Benson, 1992).

Hargrave's (1994) work on integrating a forgiveness process in family therapy is the theoretical foundation for my work with couples in MGT. Using concepts from contextual family therapy (Boszormenyi-Nagy, 1987; Boszormenyi-Nagy & Spark, 1984), Hargrave developed a model to assist families in entering the process of relational repair. He focused on the contextual therapy dimension of relational ethics, which is the subjective balance of justice, trustworthiness and entitlement between family members. Relational ethics is the unwritten contract that can be used to establish fairness between individuals. It is the equitable balance of privilege and responsibility. This give and take process is the basis for family and marital interactions. The establishment of balanced entitlements and obligations over time builds trust, as the fundamental component of intimacy.

Figure 1 depicts a visual model of couples engaged in a cyclical conflict as they enter therapy. This cycle of perpetuating injury to each other is a necessary process to prevent injury. However, its ultimate effect is to stifle advances in the resolution of conflict and the formation of injury. The injury cycle is also exacerbated by unresolved pain from family of origin, previous relationships, or life events which is not or only minimally related to the current conflict.

Figure 1: Cyclical process of Relationship Obstruction

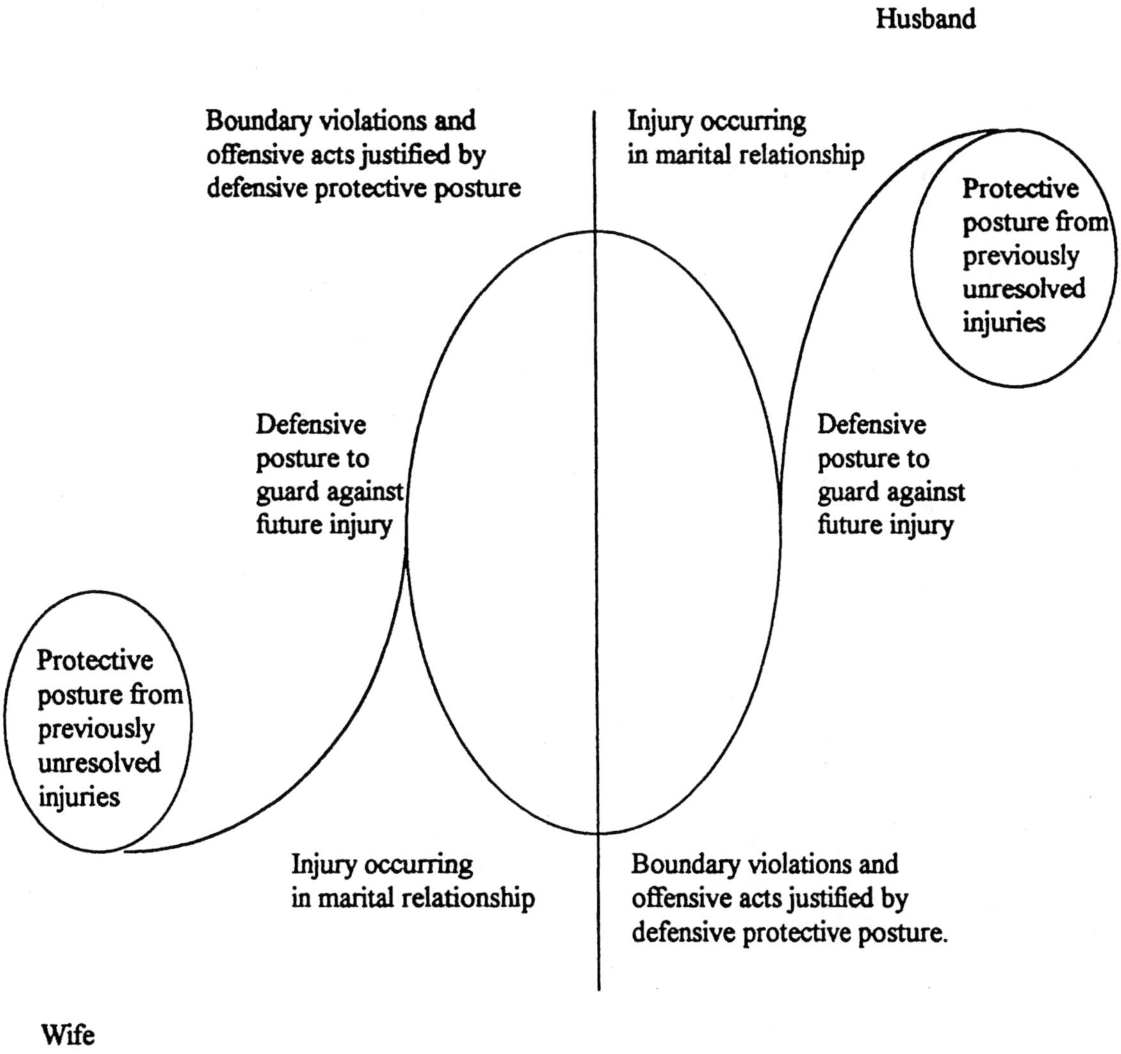

Given the condition that couples enter group, I have applied Hargrave's work on therapeutic forgiveness as a path to overcome the relational stalemate. The process of relational restoration occurs by movement through four stations: Insight, Understanding, Trust-building and Forgiveness.

Insight, depicted in Figure 2, focuses on the recognition and alteration of destructive patterns which perpetuate injustice or unfairness within the relationship. Within this system, insight is not a dynamic term to describe realized motives which were previously hidden. Rather, it is the ability for the couple to identify and stop the process which leads them toward conflict and relational injury. It is as if the couple can say with the formation of insight, we see how we get into problems, and we can stop the escalation of conflict early in the process.

Figure 2: Insight: The couple is able to see and block the behaviors which directly produce injury

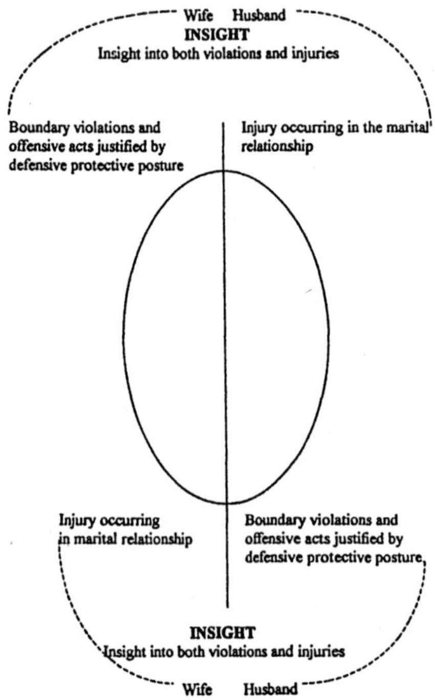

For example, Don and Mary can predict their fights. They disagree as to how to parent their two adolescent daughters. Both girls have had academic difficulty and both have been arrested for drug use. Mary thinks that Don is too harsh and that the girls need more nurturing from their father. Don thinks that Mary is too lenient and that the girls need more limits from their mother. They would fight at night when their daughters would ask/tell their parents about their social intents and automobile needs. To cease the last minute demand and the ensuing disagreement, Don was the decision maker for all even numbered days. Mary was to decide the odd numbered days. This solution was temporary. While it did not create a solution for their conflictual patterns, it was a cease fire.

Insight is a crucial construct when the themes of forgiveness and reconciliation become a focus of therapy. Bass and Davis'(1994) criticism of forgiveness intervention is that it could serve to perpetuate oppressive relationships--particularly toward women. This "forgive is to pretend like nothing happened" mentality is challenged in the beginning with the insight that injury did and is happening and that before the resolution of the injury there must be a cessation. Such an insight calls the couple to disarm and to recognize the fundamental necessity to stop the perpetuation of hurt.

The second station is developing understanding, which is depicted in Figure 3. Understanding calls for the marital partners to gain knowledge of the partners' mental and experiential processes that is influencing or directing their actions. In the example of Don and Mary, there are likely legitimate reasons for Don's harshness and Mary's leniency. Within the group Don and Mary are encouraged to identify childhood and marital issues which parallel the conflict being expressed. Both discover a reasonable motive for each other's behavior. Don, having had a drug history from college, is very much afraid of the problems, that he perceives his daughters are moving towards. Mary grew up with harshness and did not want to repeat the pain she experienced from childhood. They discover that both of them are expressing a portion of their own need through their actions. Understanding creates a place of mutual empathy and validation for each other's experiences while retaining responsibility for their own actions.

Figure 3: Understanding: The couple is able to comprehend and validate the logical process exhibited by the other to protect against future injury, and separate current injury from historical injury

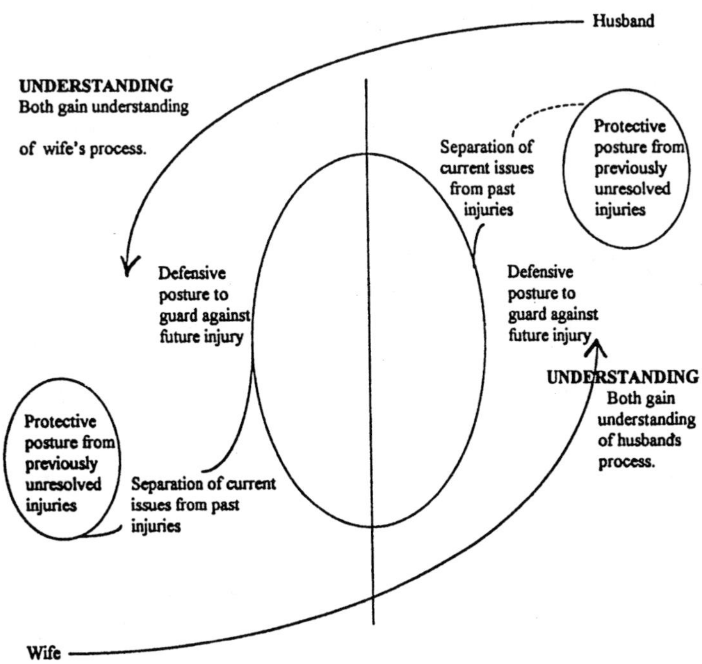

It should be noted here that though the assumption of responsibility is a necessary factor, it does not mean that all responsibility is equally shared. One spouse may be addressing responsibility for infidelity. The other may be addressing excessive criticism. Criticism and adultery are obviously not moral equivalents. Understanding calls the couple to see the complexity of the injury and to separate and account for the nature of the offense.

Trust building, illustrated in Figure 4, is creating overt opportunities to compensate for the injuries, which have occurred in the relationship. Having stopped the injury cycle and acquired an understanding of the complicated motives which influence the cycle, the couple now engages in the gradual reconstruction of the relationship. Hargrave believes that the individual has a "justified claim against their perpetrator. A victim who gives the opportunity for compensation must relinquish the claim to this injustice and be willing to accept the effort of the wrongdoer to make the situation right." (1994, p. 71) This process is conducted only in proportion to the development of insight and understanding. The stations therefore are oscillating constructs in which the couple moves as greater trust is developed.

Figure 4: Trust Building

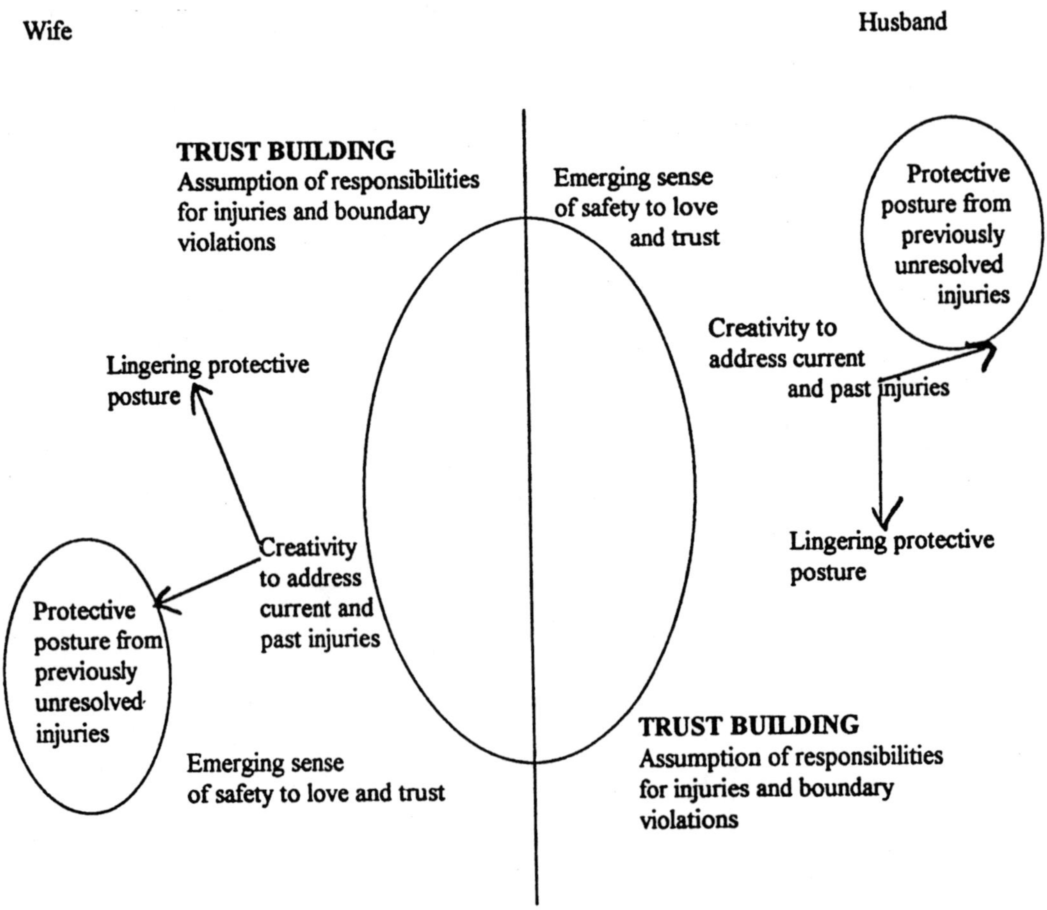

The final station, Overt Forgiveness, is the formal declaration that the relationship is restored. It is the validation of pain and injury and the exhibition of a new contract to engage in future interactions. Overt forgiveness requires that marital partners establish and respect boundaries which define how future painful events will be processed. Of particular importance is the commitment to engage in future injury in the present, without reintroducing previous hurts. In Contextual therapy thinking, justice has been accepted and delivered.

THE WORK OF RELATIONSHIP RESTORATION AND MARITAL GROUPS

My work with couples in MGT is conducted in a six month therapy experience. The therapy consists of 12 weekly meetings lasting for 1 hour and 45 minutes. In addition there are three follow-up sessions subsequent to the 12 week intervention. There are a maximum of 6 and a minimum of 4 couples in the group, with the ideal being 5 couples per group.

The sessions are semi-structured. There are 6 topical themes which form the structure of the 12 week intervention. They are communication skills, rules for conflict resolution, insight, understanding, trust-building and forgiveness. These topics form the basis for discussion and group interaction and weekly homework. After the 12 weekly meetings are completed, the group continues to meet one time per month for three months. The purpose of the monthly meetings is to extend the learning effect over time, offsetting the attrition effect.

I collect pre-group, post-group and 3 month follow-up information and data on each couple. Instruments which I have found useful are the Symptom Checklist 90-Revised (Derogatais, 1994), the State Trait Anger Inventory (Spielberger, 1991), the Dyadic Adjustment Scale (Spanier, 1976), and the Interpersonal Relationship Resolution Scale (Hargrave & Sells, 1997). These tools are used at pre-group to assess the nature and extent of the conflict and at post-test and follow-up to assess intervention effects. In addition, the sessions are taped and analyzed for group content, process and dynamics (Sells, Giordano, Valdez, King and Bucknam, 1998).

The first two topics, communication and rules for conflict resolution have a skill building emphasis and function as the prerequisite for the more substantial and threatening tasks of revealing personal experiences and injuries which prompted participation in the group. Establishing a skill-building focus early in the group process allows for the couples to negotiate the initial "normalization" stage of the group process.

Entry into the group occurs as couples are referred by therapists, ministers, or physicians who know of the group's existence. A screening session is always conducted to determine whether a couple represents a good fit for the group process. The couple must be committed to pursuing marital success. They must be in agreement to participate in the group process. They must exhibit a willingness and capacity to give and take in relational interaction. Finally, if there has been a traumatic assault to the relationship, such as an affair or abandonment, there must be the passage of sufficient time for the couple to have established an equilibrium and pattern of relational conflict. Severe Axis I or II disorders and active substance abuse limit the probability of successful group functioning.

Marital Group Therapy: Not Just "Group with Couples"

Marital group therapy is a unique therapeutic intervention from both traditional group therapy and marital therapy. Therefore, the assumptions established in traditional group and marital interventions have limited applicability. The variations from traditional group therapy procedures emerge from differences in the definition of the client, differences in the focus of therapy, and differences in the leadership process.

Marital Group Therapy: A Unique Client

In a couples group, each member enters therapy with a partner with whom there is a varying degree of conflict/cooperation. By definition, MGT consists of the multiple "subgroups" which would be viewed as detrimental to individual group therapy (Yalom, 1995). That the couples have failed to thrive as a functional and effective sub-group is a motive for seeking therapy, and assisting couples in their ability to develop a working sub-group, called a marriage, is the central goal in MGT. However, the presence of a marital partner means that there is a potential for group members to use their spouse or themselves as a protective device to guard against the threat of emotional vulnerability and exposure. I have observed numerous tactics exhibited within the marital group process which have potential for blocking therapeutic progress.

1) "I'll take the bullet": Protecting one's spouse from growth initiated by the group. I often observe individuals assuming full and complete responsibility for the difficulties in the marriage. The assumption of more blame than is merited usually creates passive agreement with the spouse who is protected from having to address their relational violations. This couple usually generates quick and easy confirmation by the group. It's as if the group collectively says to the couple: "You are right, the problem with your marriage is that you (focused on the relational martyr) are to blame. OK, we've solved that problem. Now let's move on to more difficult relationships".

This problem is often exhibited when there is a clear moral violator, such as an adulterer, a recovering alcoholic, or an absent parent. One way to redirect the focus is to ask the protected spouse about their sense of not often getting to have a turn to learn about their areas of growth, their imperfections, and "rough spots". "It's like you don't seem to get a turn to have needs and problems." By "turning down" the voice of the relational martyr and shifting the focus to the person deemed the victim, the balance of the relationship is altered in the giving and taking process. If, for example, the abandonment injury experienced by the victim has parallels to childhood pain, the injuring spouse is exposed to his/her spouse's pain as being much greater than the conflict associated with the current injury. The injuring spouse can be empowered to actively create experiences which enhance security.

2) I am married to a jerk: Excessive Blaming within the marriage. The individuals who manifest minimal insight into their own problems and unreasonably blame their spouse for the problems in the relationship tend to produce the same group dynamic as the protecting spouse just described. In this instance, the spouse's excessive blaming of the partner is so obvious that the group adopts the mission to convince the excessive blamer that he/she is actually being the insensitive person. The group tends to protect and console the spouse who has to live with such an unreasonable person. The excessive blamer tends to draw energy and attention from the group like bugs circling a light on a summer night. The group swarms around such energy and is easily tricked into thinking that the problem is so easily defined. Usually, the blamer is one who lives for a good fight and is merely inviting the challenge of the group.

An effective strategy to address the blamer is to use the current behavioral presentation as a window to observe the person relational patterns. This could be constructed as, "I notice how much opposition you are receiving from the group. I wonder if you often find yourself fighting with others who think that someone else's violation toward you is actually your fault". The purpose of such an intervention is to form an alliance with the client in their perception that they feel the need to be oppositional. Once that is established it is easier for the group to encourage separation of issues and to encourage the individual to assume responsibility for the issues pertaining to her/him.

3) "We have a good marriage (during the group session)": Being the saving couple. I often find a couple who has got it--the relational skills, the insight, the understanding, and the commitment to restore past injuries. The pull is toward relying on them as "non-commissioned therapists" for the group. This couple creates the impression to the group and, most unfortunately, to the group leaders, that they are the couple who has figured out their marital issues so they can instead help others. Early in the life of the group this couple usually conveys a level of competence and success, thus creating an impression that "we aren't in crisis, so we don't need the focus." This couple is particularly attractive to therapists who are in search of a success model for other struggling couples to emulate. If this presentation is allowed to occur, then later in the group's existence this couple will likely enter into a crisis which will shake the core of security the group has established. The group has conspired to make this couple the "good couple." When the "good couple" fails to exhibit their appointed goodness, other couples in the group experience increased doubt and hopelessness. It is as if they say, "If they can't make it, as good and together as they were, what chance do we have?"

Therefore, it is important to maintain a balance of vulnerability within the group--even if the leaders consider a couple as being more advanced, or able to exhibit higher functioning skills. While it is very advantageous to have couples model success, it is more important that they model truthfulness, openness, and integrity.

The Focus of Marital Group Therapy: Restoring and Building a Relationship

The second significant change in MGT from individual group therapy is the motive for participation and the focus of change. Typically, in traditional group, the members are present to change or recover some internal aspect of self (i.e., self image, survivors of sexual abuse, eating disorder, substance abuse, etc.). Though external social forces are typically used in these groups, the primary focus is the internal response and coping strategy to external social pressures. In marital group therapy, the mental frame of the members is to alter the external relationship. While there is some acknowledgment that to change the relationship requires change in the individual behavior, the relational focus uses the natural sub-groups as the therapeutic focus. I find clients who state, "I am here to work on us." Creating an "us" mentality becomes a crucial task. Consistently, individuals within the dyad see their spouses as oppositional forces rather than as collaborative influences.

The existence of a marital "us" implies a level of relational health in successful couples. It suggests the presence of trust, collaboration, compromise, and dedication to a greater good. The marital group becomes a culture constructing experience around the theme of a functioning dyadic team. I believe that the therapists shape a culture in which the most significant characteristic is a pro-active and empowered marital identity. This identity provides meaning for the sacrifices that each marital partner must make in forming intimacy.

Leading a Marital Group: The Power of Modeling

Finally, MGT is typically conducted by co-therapists, often by married or partnering co-therapists. Rutan and Stone (1984) believe that the limitation of co-leadership is that the complexity of power is less efficient and draws focus away from the group. However, I believe that the parallel process between co-therapists and couples demonstrates that a positive distribution of power, decision making, cooperation, team work and individuation can exist. Furthermore, because of the complexity of marital groups, the presence of a second leader is essential to observe and alter the group process. I try, working with my co-therapist, to make decisions public as we discuss the management of time and direction within the group session. In fact, we often sit opposite one another in the group, as the wives and husbands sit next to their spouses. We have found that sitting opposite diversifies the physical presence of the group leadership within the group. It allows us to more easily make eye contact and to communicate non-verbally. It broadens the scope of vision to observe the couple's behavior. Finally, it forces verbal communication between the leaders to be public. It is common for one of us to say, "I think that I am confronting the subtle criticisms and you are more inclined to let them slide in order to stay focused. I would like to shift roles and I take the supportive role for now." This shifting of roles provides a model of task and responsibility change within the relationship. The open vocalization of the leadership provides observation into the concept of teamwork and exemplifies an attitude of cooperation.

To illustrate the importance of this public thinking, while once working with Dr. Fran Giordano there was a leadership decision to be made regarding the use of the remaining time during a session. It was clear to the group that there was disagreement as to what we each believed should happen next. As we took a few minutes to determine a course of action one of the group member's interrupted and said with a humorous tone, "You two decide what ever you want, but just don't fight". His statement evoked within me the feeling similar to that of a small child who voiced insecurity over perceived parental conflict. His comment generated a third and most useful option, that of an immediate/process discussion of working as a team, of having differences without engaging in open or manipulative conflict in order to "win".

CONCLUSION

MGT is a powerful medium to assist couples in their efforts to restore and enhance intimacy. In contains the power of group therapy within the intimate context of marital therapy. It is an effective means for couples who seek to reconstruct their marital patterns. I have found that the therapeutic process is enhanced when couples have exposure to others who are addressing conflicts within their own relationship.

My application of MGT, drawn from contextual family theory and using Hargrave's (1994) model of forgiveness and relationship restoration, is one that was shown to be effective for couples who want to block previous cycles of relational conflict and to build successful patterns of intimacy. I believe that the therapeutic use of forgiveness and reconciliation is an essential skill for effective human interaction. I also believe that the marriage is the most appropriate format to develop those skills. Finally, I have found that group therapy is a powerful and efficient means for couples to develop the knowledge and skills necessary to exhibit on going qualities required for intimate functioning within a relationship.

The dirth of recent interventions and of scholarly examinations of the use of group as a means to treat couples warrants the creation of innovative methods to address relational issues through the group medium. Of particular use would be models generated from short-term cognitive and behavioral marital groups. In addition, the topics of forgiveness, reconciliation, and relationship restoration occurring within marriage have gained a level of validity within the professional community. Missing is a wide array of methods to be used by therapists with individuals, couples and families who are seeking to redress past injury and continuing conflict, while at the same time remain present in the lives of those with whom there has been pain, while not merely exercising simplistic denial or avoidance of injury.

REFERENCES

Alger, I. (1976). Multiple couple therapy. In P. J. Guerin, Ed. *Family Therapy* New York, Gardner Press. 364-387.

Bass, E. & Davis, L (1994*) The Courage to Heal*, New York: Harper Perennial.

Benson, C. K. (1992). Forgiveness and the psychotherapeutic process. *Journal of Psychology and Christianity, 11*, 76-81.

Boas, C. V. E. (1962). Intensive group psychotherapy with married couples. *International Journal of Group Psychotherapy, 12,* 142-153.

Boszormenyi-Nagy, I. (1987). *Foundations of contextual therapy: Collected papers of Ivan Boszormenyi-Nagy*. New York: Brunner/Mazel.

Cloke, K. (1993). Revenge, forgiveness, and the magic of mediation. *Mediation Quarterly, 11*, 67-78.

Coche, J. (1995). Group therapy with couples. In N. S. Jacobean & A. S. Grumman (Eds.), *Clinical handbook of couple therapy.* New York: Guilford Press.

Coche, J. & Coche, E. (1990) *Couples group psychotherapy: A clinical practice model.* New York: Burner/Mazel.

Cunningham, B. B. (1985) The will to forgive: A pastoral theological view of forgiving. *The Journal of Pastoral Care, 29,* 141-149.

Davenport, D. S. (1991). The functions of anger and forgiveness: Guidelines for psychotherapy with victims. *Psychotherapy, 28*, 140-133.

Derogatis, (1994). *Symptom Checklist-90-R.* Minneapolis, MN: National Computer Systems.

DiBlasio, F. A. (1992). Forgiveness in psychotherapy: Comparison of older and younger therapists. *Journal of Psychology and Christianity, 11,* 181-187.

Enright, R. D. & the Human Development Study Group, (1996). Counseling within the forgiveness triad: On forgiving, receiving forgiveness, and self-forgiveness. *Counseling and Values, 40*, 107-126.

Fittzgibbons, R. P. (1986). The cognitive and emotive uses of forgiveness in the treatment of anger. *Psychotherapy, 23*. 629-633.

Framo, J. L. (1972). *Family interaction: A dialogue between family researchers and family therapists*. New York: Springer.

Gottlieb, A. & Pattison, E. M. (1966). Married couples group psychotherapy. *Archives of General Psychiatry, 14,* 143-152.

Gurman, A. S. (1971). Group marital therapy: Clinical and empirical implications for outcome research. *International Journal of Group Psychotherapy, 21,* 174-189.

Flint, A. A. Jr., & MacLennan, B. W. (1962). Some dynamic factors in marital group psychotherapy, *International Journal of Group Psychotherapy, 12*, 255-361.

Halling, S. (1994). Shame and forgiveness. *The humanistic psychologist, 22*, 74-87.

Hargrave, T. G. (1994). *Families and forgiveness.* New York: Burner/Mazel.

Hargrave, T. G. & Sells, J. N., (1997). The development of a forgiveness scale. *Journal of Marital and Family Therapy, 23*, 41-62.

Hope, D. (1987). The healing paradox of forgiveness. *Psychotherapy, 24*, 240-244.

Hunter, R. C. A. (1978). Forgiveness, retaliation, and paranoid actions. *Canadian Psychiatric Association Journal, 23*, 167-173.

Kaufman, M. E. (1984). The courage to forgive. *Israel Journal of Psychiatry and Related Sciences, 21,(3)*, 177-187.

Kirkup. P. A. (1993). Some religious perspectives on forgiveness and settling differences, *Mediation Quarterly, 11,* 79-95.

Lieberman, E. J., & Lieberman, S. B. (1986). Couples group therapy. In N. S. Jacobson & A. S. Gurman (Eds.), *Clinical handbook of marital therapy,* New Your: Guilford Press.

Liberman, R. P., Wheeler, E., Sanders, N. (1976). Behavioral therapy for marital disharmony. An educational approach. *Journal of Marriage and Family Counseling, 2*, 383-395.

Marett, K. M. (1988). A substantive and methodological review of couples group therapy outcome research. *Group, 12*, 241-246.

Neimeyer, G. J. (1987). Marital role reconstruction through couples group therapy. In R. A. Neimeyer & G. J. Neimeyer (Eds.) *Personal construct therapy casebook.* New York: Springer.

North, J. (1987). Wrongdoing and forgiveness. *Philosophy, 62*, 499-508.

Papp, P. (1976). Brief therapy with couples groups, In P. J. Guerin, Ed. *Family Therapy* New York, Gardner Press. 350-363.

Perelman, J. (1960), Group treatment of married couples: A symposium. *International Journal of Group Psychotherapy, 10*, 136-142.

Pingleton, J. P. (1989). The role of forgiveness in the psychotherapeutic process. *Journal of Psychology and Theology, 17*, 27-35.

Rutan, J. S. & Stone, W. H. (1984). *Psychodynamic group psychotherapy,* New York: Macmillan.

Satir, V. (1967). *Conjoint family therapy.* (rev. ed.) Palo Alto, CA: Science and Behavior Books.

Satir, V. (1988). *The new people making.* Mountain View, CA: Science and Behavior Books.

Sells, J. N., Giordano, F., Valdez, M., King, L., & Bucknam, D. (1998). Forgiveness in marital group therapy: A process and outcome study. Manuscript submitted for publication.

Spanier, G. B. (1976). Measuring dyadic adjustment: New scales for assessing the quality of marriage and similar dyads. *Journal of Marriage and the Family, 38,* 15-28.

Spielberger, C. D. (1991). State Trait Anger Expression Inventory. Odessa, FL: Psychological Assessment Resources.

Tournier, P. (1962). *Guilt and grace.* New York: Harper & Row.

Truax, C. B. & Carkhuff, R. R. (1967). *Towards effective counseling and psychotherapy: Training and practice.* Chicago: Aldine.

Yalom, I. D. (1995). *The theory and practice of group psychotherapy, 4th edition.* New York: Basic Books.

Chapter Seven

WOMEN'S EMPOWERMENT AND WELLNESS GROUP: AN INTEGRATION OF SOLUTION-FOCUSED AND RELATIONAL MODELS

Kathleen Quinn and Lynda Dunn Johnson

On any college campus one can find a number of young women who are away from home for the first time, struggling to find themselves in relation to their new environment, new peers, partnerships, and career or life goals. This is a particularly confusing and vulnerable time for these women, who often seek differentiation from their families of origin, yet who remain connected to those families financially and emotionally. They are experiencing their first independence as women and strive to find a balance in their learning, friendships, life styles, and relationships with significant others such as family members or men they are dating. The concept of empowerment is often confusing for young women who may not have experienced connection in authentic relationships, or who may not have found a workable means of solving their own problems. This is the age of learning to be an adult, and the process of trial and error that many of our college students use on today's campuses can be overwhelming at best and dangerous at its worst. In our work in a university counseling center we dealt with young women who struggled with issues relating to abusive or demanding relationships, alcohol, sexual assault, sexually-transmitted diseases, family or origin issues, self-confidence, performance in school, and generally the overwhelming process of maturation into adulthood.

This chapter provides a theoretical overview of an integration of solution-focused and relational group therapy. As therapists we both worked within each of the models. We conducted family therapy in the Solution-Focused model, and began to integrate it more and more into our individual work with the college population. Our experience with the Relational model was grounded in individual work with our male and female clients and in a Non-traditional Women's Group, which consisted of older, mostly graduate students. Extensive discussion about an effective model of treatment led us to consider the integration of the beauty of Relational therapy and the efficacy of Solution-Focused work. We sensed an urgency in this population, a need for something concrete to use right away. We also sensed a great need for connection and resonance, a place for them to grow into relationships in an environment of support and empathy. These were young women who were unsure of how they looked, how others perceived them. They openly sought feedback and solutions from therapists, viewing us as the experts, in a more parental role than we wished to find ourselves. We sought to develop a group for these women that would give them a model of problem-solving that was grounded in their own empowerment and also a safe, authentic connection with trusted helping peers.

The application of these two collaborative and complimentary theories to the treatment of a group of young women working towards empowerment and wellness is demonstrated. A review of the course of treatment and intervention demonstrates the application of solution-focused therapy techniques, with specific emphasis on change amplification through the use of scaling and interactional questions.

A Theoretical Overview of Solution-Focused Therapy

Solution-focused therapy is embedded in a constructivist framework which draws on many of the principles of social constructionism. Similar to social constructionism, constructivism engages in a relativistic view of reality in which multiple realities are possible. Reality is understood as "a mental construction of the observer" (Nichols & Schwartz, 1991, p. 142) and is represented through language. "We believe that persons generally ascribe meaning to their lives by plotting their experience into stories, and that these stories shape their lives and relationships" (White & Epston, 1990, p. 79). By deconstructing and reconstructing problems and solutions it is possible to develop new views of reality that are no longer problem-saturated (Andersen & Goolishian, 1988). Constructivism approaches postmodernism with it's emphasis on definitions of problems; whereas the hermeneutic or social constructionist period, has become more interested in the societal influences that led one to these definitions (Anderson, 1993).

Solution-focused therapy presents new views of reality by shifting from emphasis on problems to becoming more concerned with solution-building and change. This is done through questions asked and expectations made evident in the use of language. For example, the therapist asks, "When the problem is solved what will you be doing differently?" Rather than, "If the problem were solved what would you be doing differently?" Problems are identified in terms of the client being stuck and unable to recognize the absence of the problem or prediction of success. This is different than asking about the cause of the problem, as traditional schools of thought might do. It is also different than asking about what maintains the problem, such as may be asked by systemic therapists that assume problems are maintained by the system (McFarland, 1995; Walter & Peller, 1992).

Solution construction presupposes a number of factors: there are solutions, there is more than one solution, solutions are constructable, the client and therapist can do the constructing, that solutions are constructed and not discovered, and that this process can be articulated through language (Walter & Peller, 1992). Consequently, "change is seen to happen within language: What we talk about and how we talk about it makes a difference, and it is these differences that can be used to make a difference" (Berg & de Shazer, 1993, p. 7). The negotiation of meaning that is arrived at within a specific context affects future interactions with others. "There is a ... circular relationship between how one defines a situation and what one does" (Walter & Peller, 1992, p. 30). With this in mind, any change within the description and interaction of a system changes further interaction (Walter & Peller, 1992). Therefore, change can be facilitated with any member of the system, because change with even one member affects the interaction between other members in the system (Walter & Peller, 1992). It is assumed that there is a ripple effect throughout the system so that one small change leads to further change.

The aim of solution-focused therapy is to co-construct a range of possibilities by highlighting what already works while uncovering the group members' resourcefulness and enhancing a sense of agency. Therefore, the therapeutic relationship is viewed as the co-creation of reality between client and therapist, as per the constructivist roots of the model. Through the use of the group process the therapist directs the therapy toward client strengths as they join in their efforts to build solutions.

Assumptions underlying solution-focused therapy include:

- Clients have resources and are already doing some things to solve their problems.
- Change is constant and inevitable.
- The therapist's job is to identify and amplify change.
- It is unnecessary to know the cause or function of the complaint in order to solve it.
- A small change in the system is all that is necessary to prompt other changes.
- Clients define the goals for therapy (McConkey, 1992, p. 6).
- Meaning and experience are interactionally constructed, and there is no right way to view things.
- Focusing on the positive, on the solution, and on the future facilitates change in the desired direction.
- The client is the expert (Walter & Peller, 1992).
- For every problem there is an exception
- Complex problems do not necessarily need complex solutions.

Equally important is the simplistic, yet effectively empowering philosophy of solution-focused therapy. First, if it works don't fix it (de Shazer, 1985; Walter & Peller, 1992). "In other words, if clients are already doing something that is working for them, stay out of the way. Do not-out of some desire to be helpful or sophisticated-suggest something more" (Walter & Peller, 1992, p. 37). Second, if everything you are doing is not working, do something different (de Shazer, 1985; Walter & Peller, 1992). Third, keep it simple. This perspective supports the notion that individuals are responsible for their actions; and more often than not, the solutions are already within the client's range of experience and often very simple to implement (Walter & Peller, 1992). Fourth, the therapist focuses on amplifying change with an eye towards empowering the client to feel on track to solving his or her problem (Walter & Peller, 1992).

The Solution-Focused model is distinguished by a very straight-forward manner of conceptualizing the commitment of clients to the change process. The therapists use their observation skills to identify three types of clients; Visitors, Complainants, and Customers. Given this observation, the course of a current session and the assignment of different homework tasks are assigned accordingly. Visitors are those who voice no pressing complaints. They usually describe their involvement in therapy as supportive of someone else; they are there because someone asked them to be there. Visitors are complimented for their interest and assigned no tasks. Complainants voice a concern or complaint and their expectation for a solution to the problem. They are given observational or thinking tasks. The therapist identifies the benefits they would receive from improvement in therapy and compliments their desire to improve. Finally, Customers are those clients who express the desire to do something about the complaint. They are given behavioral or doing tasks (Walsh and McGraw, 1996).

When employing the solution-focused therapy model, there are different phases or tasks throughout the therapy sessions. First, the general task is to ascertain the client's goal in coming to therapy. Often, the goals are developed through defining the problem. Once this is established, the clinician can quickly move into looking for exceptions to the problem, times when the problem is absent. One might elicit exceptions by asking, "How is the solution happening in some small ways now?" or "when is the problem not happening?" If the client has difficulty coming up with exceptions, the miracle question may be used to generate hypothetical solutions. "The miracle question" elicits what the client will be doing differently when the problem is solved. This allows the client to elaborate on what the solution would look like. Within a group therapy model, the clinician(s) use the resourcefulness of the group to elaborate on solution construction. Often times, we find that different perspectives provide a "richness to the process in that each person is contributing from his or her position in the conversation" (Walter & Peller, 1992, p. 113). Therefore, the group develops alternative, solution-based stories. The last stage of the session involves providing compliments to the group, a message, and possible task (Walter & Peller, 1992).

A Theoretical Overview of Relational Therapy

"Relational therapy suggests that mutual empathy and mutual empowerment in relationships are central to psychological growth" (Miller & Stiver, 1997, p. 42). A central tenet of this model is that empathy provides the foundation for human connection. Empathy suggests that one person can get a sense of how another person thinks or feels, also described as "one-way" empathy. Relational theory advocates for mutual empathy within the therapeutic interaction which creates a joining together in a shared experience that builds something new for both (or all) of the people involved (Miller & Stiver, 1997, p. 42).

The Basis assumptions of the relational model are:

1. Clients have the innate ability and resources to solve their problems, and as they establish authentic connection they will mobilize the resources necessary to take action.
2. Change occurs through authentic connection and relationships. Once one feels truly understood she will feel safe and positive enough about her true self to follow her own intuition, thus creating change.
3. The therapist's role is to create a safe place where the client feels understood and appreciated for her authentic self. This will be the foundation on which the client begins to explore her true self.
4. It is necessary to know the cause of disconnection and inauthenticity in past relationships. This insight leads to deeper self-understanding and motivates the client to seek authentic connections in the present and future.
5. Authentic relationships are all that is necessary to facilitate further changes in the client's life.
6. Clients define the goals for therapy.
7. The client's experience and the meaning that she attributes to her experience is honored. There is no right or wrong way to view things.
8. Focusing on what the client wants facilitates change in the desired direction.
9. The client is the expert of her experience. The therapist is the expert of authentic connection. Collaboratively they create a healing experience.
10. Every problem creates an opportunity for deeper self-understanding and healing through connection.

In the words of the relational authors: "Authenticity is not a static state that is achieved at a discrete moment in time; it is a person's ongoing ability to represent herself in a relationship with increasing truth and fullness" (Miller & Stiver 1997, p. 54). In risking to speak truthfully about oneself, further self and relational awareness is achieved.

"Participating in connections does not mean sacrificing the individual to the group or to "the team", nor does it mean being altruistic. On the contrary, it means that each individual has both the responsibility to respond to others. If we do not respond there is no flow, no movement. If, in fact, psychological development occurs only in interaction with other people, do we not all have the responsibility to be responsive to others? Who else will do this for us if not each other?" (Miller & Stiver 1997, p. 55).

The relational model provides, for our work, a means to enhance the connection that women need to achieve full development and resonance of self within the group. When individual development among group members is enhanced, the work of the group is also enhanced.

INTEGRATION OF THE TWO MODELS INTO A GROUP FORMAT

While developing the integration of the Empowerment and Wellness group model, we asked ourselves what we felt we as therapists needed to achieve our goal of a group that would empower women to achieve balance, self-care, and improve interpersonal relationships, while also providing a safe place for them to heal. "The role of emotion in solution-focused therapy has been neglected because the therapist pays attention primarily to cognitions and behaviors but because emotions are central in person's lives emotions are central in therapeutic work" (Kiser, Piercy, and Lipchik, 1993). Because of this need for authentic connection, the Relational Model was chosen. The goal was to work beyond emotions, while enabling women to be empowered and connected in relationships while maintaining a future-focus.

Miller (1986) describes five qualities of growth-enhancing relationships that can also be evident in therapy groups:

- Women together experience a high level of energy, or zestfulness.
- Women in a group who may have been stuck become empowered and get unstuck.
- Women begin to develop more clarity in their understanding of themselves and others.
- All the members develop greater authenticity and self-worth.

Because of the positive experience in a group, women experience a desire for more connection, both within and without the group (Miller, 1986 in Fedele, 1994). The authors had seen the same process occur in the integrated group setting.

Emotions and reality are based in relationships with others. The nature of group therapy heightens the need for addressing the relational and emotional issues of healing. We also feel that a part of living well is learning how to maintain connection and deal appropriately with emotions as well as behaviors. Working purely from a Solution-Focused Model, emotions may be viewed as resistance. One of the major tenets of Solution-Focused therapy is to connect the present to the future. Clients who are struggling to find feasible solutions often have difficulty imagining a future in which the problem has been resolved. Conversely, clients who can connect the present to the future buy into the process of constructing solutions whole-heartedly. With women it is important to address emotions and connections in a Solution-Focused format to avoid rumination and yet allow emotional growth. DeShazer (1985) believes that therapeutic interventions need to be tied to the context in which behaviors occur. Within this integrated view, living in this life is an emotional experience and therefore emotional experience is the context in which behaviors occur.

Working within the Relational Model, a need for more direction and focus arose, so clients could rapidly develop hope and empowerment. We overlooked the Solution-Focused tenet of connecting the present to the future. A future focus provides hope and a belief that one can change, using one's own expertise. We wanted them to have more direction, be able to develop more specific skills, and not become stuck in a problem-oriented focus.

Hudson (1996) suggested that there are four categories of solutions: action, dreaming, thinking and feeling. These solutions allow for acknowledgment of one's feelings and creation of "rituals to bring healing and comfort" (Hudson, 1996, p. 26). The Solutions model, with its emphasis on individual responsibility, allows group leaders to resolve any potential for misguided blaming that can occur within the attributional nature of the relational model. With this orientation, young women were still able to assign responsibility within societal context when appropriate. Part of learning to develop solutions for living is the ability to distinguish between appropriate attribution from blame and to be able to move forward into the future. Another part of our balance is helping clients to not blame themselves for their feelings. "Acknowledging your feelings doesn't mean wallowing in them. It means facing them straight on knowing that feelings are neither right nor wrong, they just are" (Hudson, 1996, p. 5).

Comparison of the Two Models

In comparing the Solution-focused and Relational models, we thought it would be appropriate to address the following: the process of change, the manner in which problems are addressed, the therapeutic relationship, conceptualization of pathology, the role of empathy, the role of the therapist and the client, the length of therapy, and session structure.

The Process of Change

In the Solution-Focused model change is paramount. Change is one of the main elements of this model, and most of the therapeutic focus addresses readiness for change and the means to achieve it. Change is the measure of client progress, with less emphasis on insight. In fact, change is measured regularly in session to determine how much change has occurred. It is assumed that the therapeutic process is powerful and that change is constant and inevitable. The treatment focus is limited to what is possible and changeable, not the impossible. It is possible for problems to be rapidly solved. A small change is all that is necessary so a change in one part of the system can affect change in another part of the system. This is known as the ripple effect. The methods of change are very simple "If it ain't broke, don't fix it; Once you know what works- Do more of it; and if it doesn't work, Don't do it again- do something different" (Berg & Miller, 1992). In fact, many sessions are opened with "Well, what's different?" In our groups, we often asked "What changes have you made?" or "What progress have you made?" as we opened group. Client-generated goals are essential to this model, because they cement the process of change.

Progress toward goals is scrutinized with scaling, adjustment of the goals to more effective or realistic ones. When goals are reached, the client is helped to identify the skills they used to make the changes occurred to allow them to succeed. For instance

"What did you do differently? How did you manage that? What kept you from sliding back and trying something new instead? Did you surprise yourself?" Achieving one's goals, even on a weekly basis is very empowering. When people identify their own expectations, set their own goals, and use their own hidden skills to reach their goals, they feel ownership and power in the process of change.

In the Relational model, change, empathy, and connection are essential to understanding one's authentic self. With this understanding of self comes the courage and power to change. Living a more authentic life is a means to achieving life goals. Therefore change occurs through the process of establishing more authentic relationships. In this model, it is easier for clients to be more accepting of themselves when they learn that people can be accepting of them, and vice versa. Unlike the Solution-Focused model, insight is paramount in the Relational model. Insight is geared around connection and disconnection. Thus the change process is oriented toward being more connected to others. The old ways of being and coping are the defenses that keep people disconnected from others. Change is the vehicle for learning new ways of interacting and thus connecting more authentically (Miller and Stiver, 1997).

Manner in which "Problems" are Addressed

In the Solution-focused model, problems are Complaints. They are presented in terms of outcome, identifying what is wanted, not what is wrong, In addressing the complaint we explore strengths and resources and design strategies for change. Some of those strategies are task assignment, exceptions, reframing, scaling, examining benefits, skeleton keys, and the miracle question. The therapist helps the client identify what is working and designs tasks to urge the client to do more of what's working. Exceptions are those times when the complaint does not happen. In examining exceptions, clients analyze how was it that the complaint did not happen (What did you do differently? How can you manage to do more of that?). Finding exceptions often provides a natural path to solutions. Reframing is changing the language that represents problems to a more positive, self-forgiving, and normalizing context. It is important that reframes promote optimism without minimizing difficulty (Friedman and Fanger, 1991). For example, a group member may describe her over-enmeshed relationship with her family. She receives a reframe from the group that she is "working very hard to remain in contact with her family" and then is encouraged, to identify comfortable exceptions in which she was able to feel more differentiated and yet remain somewhat connected with family members. Thus, she is encouraged to imagine a scenario in which she might gain more independence. It is also possible that this member plays out her over-involvement within the group as well. If so, she can receive similarly reframed feedback from the group members regarding her great concern for the group process and the member. Hopefully she will be able to reflect upon the amount of energy she is devoting to the group, at her own expense. Thus, her intentions are not questioned, only the manner in which she is expressing her concern.

In the Relational Model problems arise out of women feeling disconnected, deficient, and devalued by what is considered acceptable behavior through societal and cultural norms (Lawler, 1990). Emotionality and dependency are often devalued in Westernized cultures and as a consequence, women tend to marginalize and ignore their need for connection, leading to dissonance and disharmony, isolation, anxiety, and depression. The relational model promotes healing through relating and connection to others (Lawler, 1990). While in the Relational Model, lack of change is viewed as being stuck or disconnected and in need of more intense therapy; in Solutions lack of change is an indication that perhaps we were moving too fast or expecting too much. Slower progress is reframed from dependency into a state that simply suggests a need for a different solution.

The Therapeutic Relationship

A collaborative therapeutic relationship is crucial in both models. In the Solution-Focused Model, we believe in the client's innate ability to heal themselves and view our roles as consultant and facilitator. The group process focuses on solutions and change. DeJong and Berg, (1998), address the importance of trust development in the therapeutic relationship. Relationship-building enhances the trust the client feels, and also increases the probability that they will follow-through with change. The relationship-building and the emphasis on trust found in effective Solution-Focused therapy fits nicely with the Relational model. The Solution-focused therapist carefully chooses language which is called "change talk" or "solution talk". They are very active, (though directive only in the solutions process), and maintain a present and future focus. The therapist stance promotes optimism and an expectation for change without discounting difficulty. We imply positive regard for the client by believing that clients have the ability to be the expert in their own goals and change process. Another task of the therapist is to amplify, reinforce, and highlight change. As an example, our experience in group has been that clients often begin to use the term "Solutions" to describe the Solution-Focused group process. Readers will see in this chapter that we have adopted their term.

Relational therapy complements the Solution-Focused model by emphasizing the here-and-now in the therapeutic relationship. It utilizes the relationship as a vehicle for self-understanding but does not have a future-orientation. Relational therapists argue that relatedness enhances the self. These theorists perceive healthy connections as desirable, motivating, and empowering (Lawler, 1990, p.652). The therapeutic relationship provides a place for one to develop an identity in the context of relationships. "The ongoing process of connection, disconnection, and reconnection with the aim of enlarging relational possibilities is the very essence of group work" (Fedele, 1994, p.1). The therapists' role involves modeling and facilitating positive relationships.

Pathology

Discounted in both models as non productive at best and stigmatizing at worst, pathology is not an integral part of either model. In Solution-focused Therapy, people are not sick, they are stuck. This is a model of action toward wellness, not labeling and treating illness. In fact, pathology is so unimportant in Solution-Focused work that it was absent in the indices of all but one of the books we reviewed for this writing. Rather than "pathologize" our clients, we agree very strongly that as therapists we must assume that "people have all they need to solve their problems" (Walter & Peller, 1992 p. 23). Walter and Peller (1992) further note that models of pathological assessment assume that problems must result from a failure or dysfunction within the structure of the individual or family, leaving the therapist with the responsibility of unveiling the dysfunction. Solution-Focused therapists, on the other hand, proceed with finding the appropriate strengths within the individual or family to develop the solutions they need. Even resistance is not viewed as pathological. Rather, it is an indicator to the therapist that they are not on the right track, moving too fast, assuming the client wants to change something that they don't, or imposing a change that the client is not ready for or does not value.

In the Relational model, our perception is that pathology is occasionally viewed as a societal method of oppressing people of difference or people that are outside of the Westernized norm. For example, in traditional psychological theories independence, self-sufficiency, and decisiveness are highly valued while emotionality and dependency are sometimes viewed as pathological. The traditional values do not necessarily fit women's experience and thus, women are seen to lack something critical, a strong independent sense of self. Pathology, is also understood in this model when a person takes a characteristic to extreme (Lawler, 1990). For example, one can be too independent or too dependent. It is the excess that is the problem. Refreshingly, both models discount pathology as stigmatizing and an unproductive path in client assessment and the development of a treatment plan. The difference between the two is that in the Relational model, pathology is viewed as oppression while in Solutions work, pathology is a nonentity.

The Role of Empathy

Miller, Hubble and Duncan, 1996, term the empathic response in Solutions work as acknowledgment. Acknowledgment is often viewed as a "more purposeful activity than the traditional concept of empathy" (p. 244). However, they emphasize that perhaps there is no real difference between empathy and acknowledgment, as long as one's history is heard and understood in order to repeat the successes of the past. Critical in empathic acknowledgment is "the attitude of the therapist and the interchange between the client and the therapist" (Miller, Hubble & Duncan, 1996 p. 245). One of the reasons that the Solutions model is so versatile, would be the strong base of acceptance and client regard as well as an emphasis on action.

We find it important to note in this discussion of empathy that perhaps what sets one model apart from the other is the amount of time devoted to empathic reflection. It also seems that the focus of empathic reflections differs in the models. In the relational model the goal is to bring greater insight and understanding, hence more time is devoted to reflection. In Solutions, reflection is often concise, ongoing verbal tracking, aimed at joining the therapist and client as a solution-building team. It is our assumption that within any model therapists demonstrate individual differences in their work and there is certainly room for this same phenomenon in the Solution-Focused model. We agree that the amount of empathy, the time devoted to it, and the accuracy of the empathy will vary. The use of empathy is important in enhancing change, celebrating success, and building trust, but not the amplification of negative or non-productive feelings (Dejong and Berg, 1998). However, in a model which assumes that people have the ability to find their own solutions, respect and empathy will certainly be present.

To further the development of strong therapeutic relationships, DeJong and Berg, (1998) suggest the use of empathy, which entails "controlled emotional involvement, ... sensitivity to the client's feelings, understanding the meaning of these feelings, and responding appropriately" (p. 36). When expressing empathy, it is important that we are able to communicate with feelings as well as with thoughts.

Empathy is central in Relational therapy, because the nature of the therapeutic relationship is one of healing and accepting. Empathy is referred to as "a state of knowing and experiencing with the other to an over-arching sense of presence with and openness to the other person's experience and general point of view" (Jordan, 1987, p. 7). Through empathy, or another's responsiveness, one achieves a sense of self-acceptance and well-being. This self-acceptance often empowers people to move forward with their personal work. Because the therapeutic relationship emphasizes healing and accepting, Relational therapists are expected to have advanced empathy skills.

In our group, we found empathy between members to be very healing, so we used the solution-focused model to teach the use of empathy to participants. For instance, "She just shared something very sensitive. If you wanted to be more empathic in your response, so she could be sure you heard and understood her, what could you say?" In response, members often made comments like "I really felt heard the time you said ... Do you remember when you just took my hand that time, and she offered me a tissue? Sometimes you don't have to find the right words, just do something that shows you understand, or you care."

The Role of the Therapist

Solution-Focused therapists keep the pace of therapy quick and productive by being curious, respectful, humorous, and very active in the therapeutic process. They are directive only within the process of the model, they do not assume responsibility for direction of client change or prescription of methods of change. The client is the expert on themselves and their needs. Given what our expert clients tell us, we help direct change. Walsh and McGraw, (1996) concisely summarize the role of the therapist as:

> "To assist the family to uncover and amplify exceptions and solutions to the presenting complaint; to promote an atmosphere where change is expected and belief in the family is unequivocal; to present self as warm, caring, active, and directive; and to terminate therapy as quickly as is warranted clinically" (p.97).

We would add that one of the most important therapist roles in Solution-Focused work is to maintain an awareness of language. Not only do we need to chose our own language with great care to emphasize change and empowerment, we also need to be aware of the language our clients are using and help them to select words that are present and future oriented, more positive, and more goal-directed.

Relational therapists provide empathy and attunement. They also offer insight and most importantly provide a mutually empathic, mutually empowering relationship where the client feels safe to expose marginalized or hidden aspects of the self that have kept them out of connection and so minimizing their interactions with each other. One of the relational therapists' goals is to help the client move from a globally resistant stance to one of awareness of when resistance is actually healthy, in other words, assertiveness or appropriate boundaries (Giblin and Chan, 1995).

Basically, the therapist is aware of and open to the clients' processes. They model connection and healing within the therapeutic relationship and accept more responsibility for the process. Solution-Focused therapists, on the other hand, are scientists, consultants, and seek to provide a process where clients can find themselves, while emphasizing connection and insight less.

The Role of the Client

The client is clearly the expert in Solution-focused Therapy. It is assumed that because the clients are motivated and have the innate ability to identify solutions and implement change, that they are the party in the therapeutic relationship who makes the final decision about how to change, when to change, and how much to change. Belief in the client as the expert enables the therapist to assume that change is inevitable and lasting. The therapist respects the client in terms of knowing what is best and how soon it should occur.

Although Relational therapists do not identify clients as experts certainly the clients' experience is respected and viewed as valid. The therapeutic relationship is viewed as mutual and collaborative. The client is "in power with" or "empowered by" the therapist, using the relationship as a strengthening experience in either case. Acknowledgment that there is no one truth and that clients' behavior is an expression of their social context (Giblin & Chan, 1995). The models compliment each other by defining the client as one who is accepted without judgment and one who is capable of finding their own power for life change. The difference seems to lie in the elevation of the client to the status of expert in Solutions work, as opposed to the valued partner role of the Relational client.

Length of Therapy

Solution-Focused therapists strive to terminate therapy as quickly as possible, principally because they believe that the process of change, once learned, is lasting. Therapy may or may not occur on a weekly basis, though in our group, we met weekly. The therapist and the client determine together when it is time to terminate therapy, often with a tapering off of therapy to bi-weekly or monthly check-ins.

Relational therapists believe that healing occurs within the therapeutic relationship. The Relational model provides the client with a different experience than they have had with primary attachment figures in their life, which can require more time to develop. Relational therapy can run much longer than Solution-Focused work. Relational Women's groups can extend for well over a year, while Solution-Focused work traditionally ends within several months. Our group members were all ready for group termination within one semester.

Session Structure

Solutions Sessions are very structured: therapists join briefly with the clients, ask how they have progressed on last week's goals or assignments (What's different? What changes have occurred?), and new complaints and exceptions are examined using the techniques of the model. The therapists then take a consultation break and give compliments and clues or homework.

Relational sessions are not structured by the therapist in terms of the model, though the therapist is usually grounded in therapeutic goals and has a direction. Structure is more determined by the client presentation and need.

Use of the Integrated Model in the Group Setting

Our focus, both therapeutically and personally, is on healing and wellness, as well as the process of building skills for positive solutions and authentic connection. The relational model provides the environmental base for healing and growth, and the Solution-Focused model provides impetus for connection of the present to the future and the skills for change. We chose an integration of the two models for use with a university population because we wanted to provide a Relational group setting that would be safe and empathic for young women, while providing resonance, connection, and healing. We also wanted to instill hope and empowerment in the manner of Solutions. With hope, we expected that group members would be able to rapidly learn a change and problem-solving process which would serve them for the remainder of their lives. There were time constraints. The group was confined to one semester, a condition that fit with the Solution-Focused tenet of terminating therapy as soon as possible. We were optimistic about integrating the Solution-Focused and Relational models into the group setting because it offered the opportunity for authentic connection, and for interpersonal and relational learning. A group would also offer more opportunities for generating a wider range of solutions; solutions are more easily heard and integrated from peers, not therapists (remember—they are the experts, not us!). In group, clients who need help generating solutions can turn to peers and obtain a much wider array of options. We were aware that the Relational Model had been done in a group setting (Fedele, 1994) and had experience ourselves using Solution-Focused groups with younger children. We were anxious to bring the warmth of the relational model to a group with a strong emphasis on wellness and self-care, enriched by the change and empowerment found in the Solution-focused model.

THE INTEGRATIVE GROUP PROCESS

At this point we would like to outline our experience in developing and implementing our Young Women's group, as a starting place for others who may want to consider using this model with similar or even different populations. One of the foremost considerations when integrating models of therapy is the need to be firmly grounded in each of the models. We felt it important as therapists to be able to identify when we were using each of the models, and when we were deviating. We offered each other constructive feedback, and planned together before each group meeting. We shared materials, aired our differences, and felt that we knew each other as therapists and professionals as well as people.

Screening Considerations

As with all groups, screening is important in order to insure the maximum safety, functioning and connection of group members. We felt it particularly important because of the limited time for the group (less than one semester, after screening and orientation) and the specific focus of the group as Young Women's Empowerment and Wellness. We screened our members for age and selected 7 young women ages 19-23. To screen for adjustment, all prospective members were interviewed by both group therapists. Members who were assessed as unable to function autonomously in a group were referred back to individual therapy. We wanted a group that would be somewhat diverse, yet with some heterogeneity of age, presenting concerns; anger issues, process needs, gender, and an expressed interest in a need for connection with other women.

Getting Started

We feel that it is always important to use standard group guidelines regardless of the type of group. Thus, limits of confidentiality must be clearly defined, and commitment to the group is strongly encouraged. Though group is voluntary, members are encouraged to come three times before making a decision to terminate. We ask the group members to agree to come and say good-bye to the group if they choose not to continue. Safety is always addressed, and self disclosure is encouraged, though members are aware that the amount of their self-disclosure is voluntary. The importance of confidentiality from the group members is made very clear in our opening, and we emphasize that we have no way to guarantee that group members maintain the confidences of the group.

The use of co-therapists in groups is common practice. Given the relational nature of this group, the use of co-therapists was even more appropriate. We are able to work as a team in the Solutions model, gossiping as therapists ("Say, Lynda did you notice ... I wonder what she ...") and using circular questions between therapists as well as group members (Jane, did you notice what Sally just said to Sue?). In Relational work, we model authentic connections and effective communication, sharing our regard for each other as therapists, our minute-to-minute concerns about the group process, and general concern for each other. Group members often eavesdropped with interest and delight as our exchanges reflected our connection: "Glad you caught that one! I was going in a different direction and didn't read what you were doing with Jane". "Lynda, this reminds me of what you were telling me about ... can I share it with the group?". "Before I jump in, I want to be sure I understand you on this one ...". "Kathy, the way you did that reminds me so much of that way you. ...". "I love working with you, just because of times like this. I wonder if the rest of the group noticed how beautiful that summary was?".

What Does This Type of Group Look Like?

The main focus of the group is women's wellness and empowerment issues and their impact on the personal and academic/professional relationships of the group members. The initial stages of the group involve an orientation to Solutions work for the group members, teaching them about the change process and introducing them to the language of the model. During these sessions, the therapists are more didactic, using the black board, sharing examples, and setting an expectation for the development of individual and group weekly goals. Our first sessions were devoted to teaching the language of the model: reframes, solutions, etc. (see Appendix I - An Integrative Use of Solution-Focused Therapy: Solutions and Relational Model of Group Work). Rather than wait for clients to gradually grasp the concepts of finding solutions and connecting with each other, we taught them about feminist theory and the change model of solutions. We initially used the blackboard to introduce language, outline the process of solutions and use the Solution-Focused technique of "mapping hypothetical problems" devised by the therapists. We emphasized the language of the model, such as "try something different" or "let's reframe that so it's more forgiving". We emphasized that simple solutions can be just as effective, asking for their input and expertise as we worked through the model.

We presented one hypothetical "problem" in the following way: as one therapist at the blackboard, mapped and pointed to pertinent language, the other therapist, in the role of complainant, described her squabbling family members who called long distance each evening, disrupting her time with her spouse. Members mapped the problem, identified strategies that worked (not answering the phone, limiting phone time, etc.) and encouraged her to do more of what worked, and less of what only aggravated her and encouraged family to call more (empathic listening to family members, trying to help them resolve their squabbles). Members were encouraged to share empathic statements and similar experiences with the complainant, and offer solutions of their own. This exercise was particularly poignant when the therapists reminded the group members of their roles as expert in both models. We said, “Remember, you’re the ones with the wisdom. You’re the experts, not us.” Group members turned and looked at each other in surprise, then shared hearty laughter. They were ready to at least play at being the experts, in an authentic, supportive environment.

Because Solutions theorists agree that language is important, change is inevitable, and words are magic, we wanted our group members to have the language from the beginning and be able to listen for it, use it, even reinforce it in each other. They were thrilled to learn that they had “complaints,” and not “symptoms” or “problems,” or, as one member put it “mental illness!” They defined their own need for connection and the amount of time they would chose to devote to it. As they learned to incorporate the language of connection and change, we heard them challenge each other for “disconnecting” or “discounting” and compliment each other “Nice reframe!” They became more proactive with language like, “Since we are here for solutions, let’s focus on something more positive. How about change, remember?”

Solution-Focused therapists privately identify Visitors, Customers, and Complainants in order to plan appropriate interventions in the upcoming sessions. This information is observational in nature and a part of therapeutic planning; it is not to be shared overtly with the group members. Also during this time, the therapists are more active, using Solution-Focused Tools such as scaling, deconstructing, and identification of exceptions, while teaching the model to the group members. In order to enhance learning and set the ground work for more process, safety and the benefits of group work were emphasized. Therapists make a regular point of checking in with members to assess their comfort level. During this time, a lot of scaling was done on the blackboard to enhance the visual effect if there was a difference in opinion or growth from week to week. As the group progressed, members began to incorporate more change language, making statements like, “At first I thought it was about a 4, but the more I did it, it was definitely up to an 8 from last week” or “You might think 6 but I’d go higher. Look what you tried. That was risky, and you should give yourself more credit.”

When group members begin the working stage, therapists will notice a shift in the responsibility for change. Members will begin to rely more on each other and themselves, rather than on the therapists. We got an occasional compliment like “Nice catch!” when we were quick with a reflection or challenge, but generally, we became the consultants to their solution-seeking, and the enhancing partners to their relational connections. Solutions become more sophisticated and well-developed between members as they became more trusting and more connected with each other. Group members will also begin to demonstrate and use their understanding of the Solutions model, with statements like, “Well, as long as we’re looking for Solutions ...”or “OK, we need to focus on where you derailed.”

As in other groups, the working stage involves more interpersonal connection and affect between group members, safety issues are resolved and more member confrontation occurs. As this stage progresses, therapists become less vocal in the group process. Similar to the relational model, during this stage, women who are stuck become unstuck and begin to understand themselves with greater clarity. We also noticed a striking increase in metaphoric language, much of it related to travel. Members told metaphoric stories about travel, road blocks, flat tires, forks in the road, detours, etc. We viewed this as a deeper embrace of the process of rapid change, and less need for insight as they moved forward into empowerment. Our group developed the metaphor of a braided rug to demonstrate boundaries with people in their lives. They integrated this metaphor so fully that they would just point to the braided rug in the group room and comment, "You're in my inner circle" (the very center of the concentric circles of the rug) or, "I've moved him out to the blue circle."

We have also seen that members tend to use more solutions language in the working stage. They often use processes like scaling and mapping, without needing the therapist to prompt them. Further integrating the model, members began to compliment us as we did them, when we used the solution-focused model effectively, saying, "Nice reframe!", etc. We interpreted this as evidence of their understanding of our roles as helpers, rather than experts. Members began to use more humor in their group work, as their empathy and connection deepened. Often confrontations seem to have less emotionality and are resolved more quickly with less process and more productive problem-solving, or solution-finding. Members become more focused on identifying the possible benefits of trying something new and evaluating the new behaviors against old coping mechanisms. Solutions are often used in between-member group process as well as in out-side of group problems. The group developed a way to balance the relational context of group, with its unconditional support of members, the more business-like, forward motion of a Solutions approach. We have often been amazed at the natural integration of therapeutic language we heard in this setting; terms like "authentic connection" in the same sentence with "reframe" or "scaling." Members begin to say things like "it was an 8," or "I reframed it this way, so that worked better," and "I remembered the way you said that worked for you so I thought heck, I might as well try something different too." It rapidly became clear to us that in an environment of strong relational care, women can develop skills as well as relationships, and thrive with both.

Also in the working stage, therapist modifications may occur in the model. There may be a shift in focus from one model to the other, with more solutions, or more authentic connection emphasized at particular times. Once in group, we struggled with when to take our therapists' break, which is an integral part of the Solution-Focused model. During break, the therapists take approximately five minutes near the end of session/group to develop homework for the coming week. Therapists then reenter session, give compliments to members, and suggest homework. We decided to discuss our dilemma within the group, explaining the purpose of the therapists' break, which we felt modeled relational team work. We were given a workable solution by group members; take the break in the group, with them present. This window into our therapeutic process was almost like a reflecting team and had a similar effect. Reflecting teams are used in family systems work for families who are stuck. A team of therapists observe the session and at the end of session enter into therapy and give feedback and observations to family members and therapists. The reflecting team brings new perspective and new energy into the therapeutic setting. In our group, when we took the break within session, members listened carefully to our talk, and moved forward with it, or disagreed. It made for a nice closing of group each week and further enhanced our role as caring consultants.

As time to close the group approaches, it is important for both the therapists and the members to have a voice in when to terminate group. There are often pre-determining factors such as the end of the semester, summer vacation, attrition, etc. However, there can still be items pertaining to the termination that members and the therapeutic team need to discuss. At this stage, there is considerable emphasis on assessing the amount of healing that comes from authentic connection as well as client skill in the Solution-Focused process. There is also a place for humor. For example, clients complimenting therapists on their reframes; therapists gossiping with each other about the change process in motion. They might say: "did you notice that empathy/reframe, etc. ... they don't need us anymore!" During this time there is often a shift from the here and now of the relational model to the connection of the present to the future found in the Solutions Model. Members will likely begin predicting future change and anticipated successes through the use of newly acquired skills. Very likely they will begin to predict their own relapses, for the purpose of designing preventive measures. If this does not occur as a natural part of the group process, therapists are well-advised to initiate it.

The Joys of a Relational/Solution-Focused Group

We have been struck by the energy, or zest, produced in this type of group. Our excitement about wellness and healing has often felt minor when compared to the strength women have found through developing a process and a language of change within a healing relationship. This type of group provides an opportunity for what is often their first experience of authentic connection, besides the therapist-client relationship. Watching women develop and accurately express sincere empathy for one another is inspiring. As a result of their growth in group, many women reported healthier and more rewarding relationships with family, friends, spouses, and significant others. As their empowerment and relationships improved, they began to attend more to their physical selves. Group members made changes in their physical appearance first, coloring or cutting their hair, experimenting with dress, improving their grooming, and initiating exercise plans. All of these changes came spontaneously, without suggestion from the group. We viewed this new interest in health as an indication of more holistic healing and empowerment.

Our experience with this type of group suggests that clients tend to move more rapidly to the working stage. The task-oriented emphasis in the initial stages of the group allowed clients to externalize problems, consistent with solution-focused techniques. The initial externalization of problems or complaints allows members to safely express themselves early in the group. This early level of safety often leads to earlier expression of emotions and confrontation between members. During this time, members may typically complain about boyfriends, professors, families, etc., blaming rather than reframing, seeking exceptions and solutions. We were more involved in steering the group back to solutions, while allowing the natural process of confrontation to unfold. Much of the member to member confrontation took the form of typical relational work, challenging each other to be more empathic and authentic, and less discounting. Eventually, a new pattern in the way they confronted each other as well as the group leaders surfaced: it was a redirection to solutions, to reframes, to "something more productive". One member's comments beautifully illustrates the pattern: "Geez, if it isn't working, don't keep doing it - that would be stupid. Try something different!" Thus, empowerment combined, with the clear expectation that members are the experts on themselves and the group process mobilizes them to advance more quickly. When women have hope, trust, and support, they are free to try something different, and help their peers to try something different.

As members prepared to leave the group they asked for the materials that we used during the group. These same documents can be found in the Appendix at the end of this chapter. They also asked for reading references, a request that is typical of the university population. Suggested readings are also placed at the end of the chapter. As in the Solutions model, they wanted to be sure to remember to reframe, scale, and map. And as newly connected and empowered relational women, they wanted to share phone numbers and addresses, tears and acknowledgments as they left the group.

Potential Pitfalls

One of the risks we have identified in this type of group has been the early identification of the problem. There can be a tendency of members to use initial, less important problems/complaints to divert energy and attention away from more threatening problems. Initially, members may be aware that the Solutions Model will provide them the power they need to try new solutions, so they stay within the safety of more minor complaints.

Expectations from therapists' peers can be a challenge. Some colleagues may be critical or suspicious of a model that integrates these two models. The expectations that some people hold about a women's groups may bring the connotation of process rather than direction and length rather than brief therapy. To some, the two models may seem so different that they have difficulty imagining that integration is possible. The contradictions seem to fall within the belief that the Solution-Focused model minimizes the effect of societal and cultural influences on one's behavior, as well as the assumed stance of the therapist as very directive and dismissing of emotion versus empathy and process. Solution-Focused therapy is not always viewed as a very process-oriented model, because of the emphasis on goals and exceptions. The Relational model, on the other hand, is often viewed as having a focus on problems in current relationships and past patterns of connection. It may be difficult to imagine a brief examination of past patterns and then rapid movement into a solution-focused connection to present relationships and the future benefits of change. In actuality, our experience has been that this rapid movement from past to present skills and on to the future instills great hope and willingness for change, despite what critics may conjecture about this integrated model.

Challenges to the Therapist

Our main challenge has been finding a balance between affect and skill development. In any therapeutic work, we feel it is important to attend to client affect and cues regarding their comfort or process in group. At the same time, we find it important to orient clients to the Solutions nature of the model. Clients who come from a Relational or Psycho-dynamic therapist may expect more process and so therapists need to be aware of their need or desire for more insight and interpretive work, as well as a clear orientation to the Solutions model. We caution that both relational and typical approaches to group work put the therapist in the an expert position, which discounts the client. In this group we do not push people to process with each other as much. Interaction is more of a natural outgrowth of the integrated model. We found that members tend to give each other feedback as often as solutions.

Conversely, clients who come from a Cognitive-Behavioral or didactic therapist into this more affective and process-oriented group setting may miss the structure and direction that they previously experienced. There may be some insecurity in learning initially that they are the expert, not the therapist, or some frustration in perceived perceptions that they therapist is not "giving answers."

Cautions

It is our very strong belief that if one is considering facilitating a group in this integrative approach, it is important to be grounded in three models: general group work, Solution-Focused and Relational therapies. One also needs to be grounded in the developmental needs of the population of the group. Consider, too, that men also thrive and heal in relationships and consider using the model in a men's or a mixed group.

Be aware that this model is not appropriate for all clients, for example, clients with severely disordered thinking, or issues of safety may not be good conditions for such a group. As a therapist, you will be able to consider your level of readiness and that of your clients.

Our last caution would be more of an encouragement. Become grounded in each model and then use some of your own therapeutic creativity. You will find a balance between each model. Our note of caution in this area is not becoming too entrenched in either model. When working with a co-therapist, which we feel greatly enhances group work and this model, consider carefully the type of co-therapist that will fit with or compliment your work within this model.

SUMMARY

We heartily encourage readers to try their own integration of this type of group work. Moving from the problem frame to the possibility frame is invigorating. As therapists, we experienced empowerment in helping women to grow and thrive in an environment of great caring and change. Along with the group members, we too celebrated change. We learned new ways to identify solutions and exceptions. We experienced enhanced connection, within the group, and with each other as friends and professionals. Part of our process as cofacilitators involved examining our rhythm and pace and the synergistic nature of the group process between members and facilitators.

Overall, integrating two strong models of therapy gave us an opportunity to meet our needs in the therapeutic setting and so become happier and more confident as professionals. In giving power to others, we empowered ourselves.

REFERENCES

Andersen, H. (1993). On a roller coaster: A collaborative language systems approach to therapy. In S. Friedman (ed.:, *The new language of change* pp. 323-344.) New York: Guilford Press

Andersen, H., & Goolishian, H. (1988). Human systems as linguistic systems: Preliminary and evolving ideas about the implications for clinical theory. *Family Process, 27* (4), pp. 371-393.

Berg, I., Miller, S. (1992) *Working With The Problem Drinker.* New York: W.W. Norton & Company.

Berg, I., de Shazer, S. (1993) Making numbers talk; Language and therapy. In S. Friedman (Ed.), *The new language of change* (pp. 5-24), New York: The Guilford Press

DeJong, P., Berg, I. (1998) *Interviewing for solutions.* New York: Brooks/Cole Publishing Company.

de Shazer, S. (1985) *Keys to solution in brief therapy.* New York: W.W. Norton & Company.

Fedele, N. (1994). Relationships in groups: Connection, resonance and paradox. *Work in Progress, 69.* Wellesley, MA: Stone Center Working Paper Series.

Friedman, S., Fanger, M. (1991). *Expanding therapeutic possibilities: getting results in brief therapy.* Lexington Books. Lexington, Mass.

Hudson, P. (1996) *The solution-oriented woman: creating the life you want.* New York: W.W. Norton & Company.

Kiser, D., Piercy, F., Lipchik, E. (1993) The integration of emotion in solution-focused therapy. *Journal of Marital and Family Therapy, 19* (3), 233-242.

Lawler, A. C. (1990). The healthy self: Variations on a theme. *Counseling and Development, 68,* 652-654.

McConkey, N. (1992). Working with adults to overcome the effects of sexual abuse: integrating solution-focused therapy, systems thinking, and gender issues. *Journal of Strategic and Systemic Therapies, 11* (3), 4-19.

McFarland, B. (1995) *Brief therapy and eating disorders.* San Francisco: Jossey-Bass.

Miller, J. B. (1986). What do we mean by relationships? *Work in progress, 22* Wellesley, MA: Stone Center Working Paper Series.

Miller, J. B., Stiver, I. P., & Hooks, T. (1998) The healing connection. New York: Balentine.

Miller, S., Hubble, M., Duncan, B. (1996) *Handbook of solution-focused brief therapy.* San Francisco: Jossey-Bass.

Nichols, M. Schwartz, R. (1991) *Family therapy concepts and methods.* (second ed.). Boston: Allyn and Bacon.

Walsh, W., McGraw, J. (1996) *Essentials of Family Therapy: A Therapist's Guide to Eight Approaches.* Denver: Love Publishing Company.

Walter, J., Peller, J. (1992) *Becoming solution-focused in brief therapy.* New York: Brunner/Mazel Publishers

White, M. Epston, D. (1990). *Narrative means to therapeutic ends.* New York: W.W. Norton and Company.

APPENDIX

At our clients request, we developed a concise summary of the Solution-focused model, in the form of worksheets and a list of recommended readings. Both can be found in this appendix.

Suggested Readings

Besides the readings listed in the references of cited information in this chapter, there are several other readings which we feel might be helpful to prospective facilitators of groups which in this model. In fact, we encourage readers to find and develop materials for group members to read. Women especially enjoy Pat Hudson's book, *Solution-Oriented Woman,* listed in the references. Another book that women tend to purchase and read avidly is Harriet Lerner's *Dance of Anger*. Finally, Sue Bender's *Everyday Sacred; A Woman's Journey Home* offers women a nice opportunity to read another woman's reflections and solutions.

For therapists, we have included Barbara McFarland's book because eating disorders are such a common presenting problem with young women today. For clinicians who work in the school setting, the work of John Murphy and Linda Metcalf gives a nice perspective of how Solution-focused therapy can be used with children. Readers can easily adapt these works for use with groups of children. For therapists who wish to learn more about Relational work, Jean Baker Miller's *A New Psychology of Women* is a classic. We also highly recommend the writings of the researchers at the Stone Center are available from Stone Center Publications, Wellesley College, 106 Central Street, Wellesley, MA 02181-8259.

Finally, our favorite references in the area of group work are included as a basic reference for those who may be new to groups, but well-grounded in Solution-Focused or Relational Work. They include:

Corey, M., Corey, G. (1987) *Groups; process and practice (3rd ed.).* Brooks/Cole Publishing Company, California.

de Shazer, S. (1994) *Words Were Originally Magic.* New York: W.W. Norton & Company.

Furman, B., Ahola, T. (1992) *Solution Talk: Hosting Therapeutic Conversations.* New York: W. W. Norton & Company.

Kottler, J. (1994) *Advanced Group Leadership.* Brooks/Cole Publishing Company, California.

Lerner, H. (1985) *The Dance of Anger: A Woman's Guide to Changing the Patterns of Intimate Relationships.* Harper and Row, New York.

McFarland, B. (1995) *Brief Therapy and Eating Disorders: A Practical Guide to Solution-focused Work with Clients.* Jossey-Bass Publisher, San Francisco.

Miller, J. (1986) *Toward a New Psychology of Women.* Second Edition. Beacon Press, Boston.

Metcalf, L. (1995) *Counseling Toward Solutions: A Practical Solution-Focused Program for Working with Students, Teachers, and Parents.* The Center for Applied Research in Education.

Murphy, M. (1997) *Solution-Focused Counseling in Middle and High Schools.* American Counseling Association, Publisher.

Yalom, I. (1985) *The Theory and Practice of Group Psychotherapy.* Basic Books, A Division of Harper Collins Publishers.

An Integrative Use of Solution-Focused Therapy: Solutions and Relational Model of Group Work

Overview of the Model: Developed by Steve DeShazer at the Mental Research Institute, Milwaukee. Circa 1970's

- Brief Therapy Model, with emphasis on client as the expert and positive change.
- Words are Magic! (Language is very important!)
- Not problem-oriented. Not Past Oriented
- Change is inevitable, powerful and productive.
- A Change in any part of the system effects change in the other parts. (A snowball effect can occur when one person makes a change.)
- The presenting concern is the Complaint.
- People have complaints, not "symptoms." Complaints are problems to be solved.
- People do have the innate ability to find effective solutions to their problems.

- The "problem" is not what has happened, it is the solution that has been chosen.
- If one solution does not work, try another (do something different).
- If a solution does work, do more of that. There is usually more than one solution.
- Insight is nice, but not necessary.
- Complicated problems do not necessarily generate complicated solutions.
- Looking at problems in a different way can encourage their resolution.
- The therapist is not the expert. The therapist is curious, interested, keeps the change process in motion with carefully chosen questions.
- There is no such thing as "resistance" when we all cooperate to solve a problem.
- Focusing on the possible and changeable lessens frustrations.
- Going slowly with focus on realistic goals leads to success. People are motivated when they can define their own goals.
- This integration of Relational Therapy and Solution-Focused therapy does not discount emotions, but deals more with reality and facts.
- Women heal and thrive within authentic relationships.

The Role of the Therapist: Walsh, William and McGraw, James. (1996) *Essentials of Family Therapy*, Love Publishing Company

- To assist the family/(group) in uncovering and amplifying exceptions and solutions to the presenting complaint.
- To promote an atmosphere where change is expected and belief in the family/group is unequaled.
- To present self as warm, caring, active and directive.

A Different Way of Thinking

Problems: Using Solution-Focused rather than problem-Focused interactions allows problems to be viewed differently. A change in behaviors and perceptions does not allow the problem to remain a problem.

Goals: When goals are defined for a person in their own language, they are satisfied that they will be working on what they came in for, not what the therapist thinks they should work on. This is vital for all of us.

Discovery of Problem Maintenance: Discovering how one is maintaining a problem lessens the chance of blaming and encourages responsibility for one's actions. Identifying problem maintenance behaviors helps everyone move from a problem focus to a more future-oriented solutions focus. Blaming is thus not productive.

Exceptions: Exceptions to the problem offer clues for solutions. Exceptions empower students and offer them a different focus. We do not usually notice exceptions as much as the problems that occur each day. Empowerment comes from considering or examining how one encourages exceptions to occur. In de Shazer's words, doing more of what's working.

Task Development: Tasks that are collaboratively constructed by a family or a student through their examination of the exceptions they themselves described yield a higher degree of ownership and commitment.

Externalize Problems: Defeat Blaming: Externalizing problems gives people an opportunity to objectify them. The problem becomes something separate from ourselves, and so conquerable. When problems are externalized and personified, they become an entity in themselves which can either be maintained or dissolved. We then feel empowered and are able to eliminate the power of the problems over our lives.

Words are Magic: Some of the Language of Group:

- *Reframe*: Say or think about things in a more positive light.
- *Clues*: How will you know when changes are occurring?
- *Skeleton Key*: A key that opens any lock. I.E.: A solution that always works.
- *Solution*: An answer to a complain or "problem."
- *Connection*: Caring between two people, based upon understanding.
- *Authentic*: Honesty and empathy between people.

"Clue Card" for Group Members

Important Thoughts:

- For every problem there is an exception.
- Complicated problems don't need complicated solutions.
- If something IS NOT working, do something different.
- If something IS working, do more of that.

Language:

- *Reframe*: Turn it into a positive thought.
- *Exception*: Whenever it DOES NOT happen.
- *Master Key*: A Solution that works most of the time.

Techniques:

- What is Different?
- Circular Questions
- Scaling
- Mapping
- Clues
- Follow-through
- Curious Therapist
- Connecting present to the future
- How did you manage that?

- Why wasn't it worse? How did you manage that?
- Remember: Solutions, not Problem

"Clue Card" For Therapists

Opening:

- Change talk - what is different, what is improved/better? How did you accomplish that?
- Scale Change
- ID strategies, Skeleton Keys

Current Complaint:

- Observe: ID the Visitors, Customers, Complainants
- Find the exceptions (for every problem, there is an exception).
- When DIDN'T it happen? What were you doing?
- Mapping
- Deconstructing
- Go with the resistance
- Scaling
- Reframes
- Miracle Question
- What If, How, When and What ... NOT Why
- Circular questions - ask one person to comment upon another's beliefs, feelings or behavior
- Absence of advice/direction-giving
- Therapist gossiping

*Therapist Break**

Compliments

Homework and Clues (Do not say "Homework")

- What would you like to follow through with? What resources do you need to follow-through?
- What will be your first clue of success? How will you know you are starting to be successful? What will you be doing?
- Future Orientation (predicting)
- If you were almost ready to start trying, what would you be doing?
- Scale it. Where do you want to be next week? How can you get there?

Chapter Eight

THE INCLUSION OF PERSONS WHO ARE LATE-DEAFENED INTO COUNSELING GROUPS

Lois N. Maroney and Charlotte G. Dixon

The Americans with Disabilities Act of 1990 (ADA) mandates protection for the rights of individuals with differences in ability. The ADA challenges all members of society to eradicate discrimination against people who have different abilities. A counseling group represents a microcosm of our society and can serve as a model for the inclusion and accommodation of all individuals into the mainstream of society. Group counseling, because it can be used for many different purposes, has become a primary form of therapeutic intervention in a variety of settings. "One of the main reasons for this popularity is that the group approach is frequently more effective than the individual approach" (Corey, 1995, p. 4). Persons who are late-deafened represent one group of individuals with differences in ability that could benefit from greater inclusion into mainstream American life. This chapter addresses the implications of inclusion and accommodation of persons who are late-deafened into newly developing counseling groups with hearing members.

UNDERSTANDING LATE-DEAFNESS

Many individuals with profound hearing loss refer to themselves as deafened or late-deafened. The emphasis in using the past participle or adjective "late" is in the need to express that something they once had is now lost. Use of the word *deaf* may signify an awareness and/or acceptance that they depend more on their eyes than their ears for receptive communication. Persons who are late-deafened were not born deaf but rather became deaf. The causes of late- deafness may include, but are not limited to, heredity, accident, illness, ototoxic medications, or an unknown etiology. It may have occurred suddenly or as the result of gradual deterioration over the years.

The Rehabilitation Research and Training Center (RRTC) at the California School of Professional Psychology (CSPP) (1995) estimates that out of the 22 million individuals in the United States who have a hearing loss, 20 million are hard-of-hearing, 600,000-1,000,000 are prelingually or culturally deaf, and 800,000-1,500,000 are late-deafened. Whereas health care professionals tend to classify persons who are hard-of-hearing or late-deafened by decibel loss, this classification does not allow for personal choice. It is important to understand that many persons who experience a change in their hearing ability agonize over identification issues (i.e., identity as a person who is hearing, hard-of- hearing, or late-deafened). Individuals who have been hearing their whole life may deny or do not recognize that a hearing change has occurred and therefore do not refer to themselves as hard-of-hearing. Furthermore, persons who have a progressive hearing loss will likely experience identity issues at each stage of loss. Therefore, it is conceivable that two people within the same decibel range will refer to themselves differently in terms of hearing loss. It is important that the group counselor be aware of and sensitive to this issue of personal identification and avoid the tendency to label the individual as hard-of-hearing or late-deafened.

Becoming deaf later in life has an immense physical, psychological, social, vocational, and economical effect on a person's life. Depending on the age of onset, a person's life may be well-established as an individual who is hearing. Language skills, friends, spouse, and job may all revolve around the ability to hear. When deafness occurs it creates havoc in the life of a person who once had the ability to hear as late-deafness entails coping with the permanent deprivation of a primary faculty (hearing) upon which the individual once depended (Luey, 1980). Persons who are late-deafened lose their ability to communicate and interact freely and spontaneously with family, friends, co-workers, and the world in general. Because of these losses, late-deafness may be considered more traumatic than congenital deafness. Consequently, persons who are late-deafened may experience more difficulty adjusting to the isolation that accompanies a hearing loss than persons who are either born deaf or hard-of-hearing. Although each person's experiences are unique, each will go through a process of adjusting to deafness. Stages of adjustment and grief were first identified by Kubler-Ross (1969). More recently, Jacobs, Harvil, and Masson (1994) concurred in pointing out the following stages that an individual may go through: denial, anger, bargaining, depression, and acceptance. Group counseling is one type of mental health service that might help facilitate progression through the above stages.

STATUS OF MENTAL HEALTH SERVICES

Many individuals who are late-deafened encounter issues other than deafness that leads them to seek group counseling. The RRTC survey indicated that persons who are either late-deafened or hard-of-hearing sought mental health services for the same reasons reported by the general population, such as marital problems, self-esteem, death, and grieving. Most respondents reported that hearing loss was not the reason they sought help (Stika, 1997). How has the mental health profession responded to the challenges of providing counseling services to persons who have become deaf?

The RRTC conducted a survey of persons with hearing loss to determine their experiences with the mental health care system (Stika, 1997). Surveys were distributed among members of Self Help for Hard-of-Hearing People, Inc. (SHHH) and the Association of Late-Deafened Adults, Inc. (ALDA). Of the 970 persons responding to the survey, 69% had severe to profound hearing loss. Nearly half of the respondents indicated difficulty obtaining a counselor or therapist who understood or was sensitive to hearing loss issues. Many respondents noted frustration at having to spend time educating their counselor about hearing loss. Educating the counselor took valuable time (in terms of money and emotions expended on discussing deafness) away from addressing the issue at hand. The author summarized that the counselors did not know how to utilize assistive devices to enhance communication and lacked a basic understanding of the psychosocial impact of deafness. The results are not surprising since the majority of the literature that examines the mental health needs of individuals with hearing loss focuses on those persons who are prelingually deaf and use manual communication (Stika, 1997). Clearly, mental health professionals could benefit from learning more about the needs of persons who have become deaf.

The personal attitudes, biases, and beliefs of counselors toward hearing loss may influence their willingness to interact with or learn about people who are late-deafened. Counselors may hold some of the same prejudices, biases, stereotypes, and values found among the general population. American society values those persons who are considered strong, powerful, physically fit, independent, and "normal." Persons who deviate from this description have been ascribed a lower or inferior social status which is often reflected in such terms as de-formed, dis-eased, ab-normal, in-valid, and dis-abled (Rubin & Roessler, 1995). Consequently, it is important that group leaders confront their personal feelings regarding persons who are late-deafened prior to initiating any group counseling procedures.

According to Patterson, Mckenzie and Jenkins (1995) people are frequently unaware of the assumptions or myths they hold towards individuals who are deaf. This lack of self-awareness can hinder the effectiveness of the group leader and diminish the overall value of the group counseling process. It is pivotal that leaders possess an awareness of: (a) their own values, beliefs, attitudes, and feelings of how they are likely to affect the member who is late-deafened; and (b) their limitations relevant to helping. Second, group leaders must possess (or be willing to obtain) an appropriate level of knowledge relevant to: (a) the psychosocial impact of late-deafness; (b) the availability of community resources for persons who are late-deafened; and (c) environmental and institutional barriers that prevent persons who are late-deafened from making full use of community resources. Lastly, group leaders must possess (or be willing to obtain) the skills necessary for an effective group experience: (a) be able to use counseling methods and goals consistent with the life experiences of all group members, and, (b) be able to modify and adapt conventional approaches to counseling in order to accommodate individuals who are late-deafened. Awareness, knowledge, and skills have been identified as characteristics of a culturally skilled counselor (Sue & Sue, 1990). Viewing adults who are late-deafened as a culture or subculture may help counselors to better understand and help their clients.

Attitudes surface in many different ways. A counselor's choice of words can either empower or create feelings of worthlessness. Although terms such as hearing-impaired are commonly used, counselors are encouraged to examine whether or not other terminology could be used which has no chance of being construed to mean "I am impaired." Behaviors may also surface via body language; for example, a deep breath taken when a counselor is asked to repeat him/herself. Are people who have differences in ability a burden to society or do they bring to society a special gift (Vanier, 1991)? If so, what could that gift be?

Hulnick and Hulnick (1991) recognized that each individual is faced with challenges and gifts, and a functional limitation should not be confused with a person's intrinsic worth. "We all have our challenges. Some of us wear them on the outside and some on the inside. Down deep, we're all whole and complete, and thank God, we're all worthy" (p. 259). Quite often individuals who are faced with the challenges that differences in ability bring into their lives develop a profound sense of value of themselves, others, and life (Hulnick &Hulnick, 1991). Such individuals often inspire others by their courage and resourcefulness and ultimately impugn the validity of the values imposed by society.

SETTING UP THE GROUP

The group leader has many considerations and challenges to address in order to ensure that the group experience is positive for all members. A necessary first step is the establishment of the group's purpose (i.e., psychosocial group, care-giver's group, etc.). The group's purpose will dictate its membership (Card & Schmider, 1995); therefore, once the purpose has been clearly articulated, selection of group members can begin.
Group leaders employ rules for selecting members. "The group leader should interview the prospective group member in the same way other prospective members are interviewed" (Patterson, et al., 1995, p. 80). Generally, group leaders select individuals who will be able to interact with each other. When considering the member who is late-deafened, a working knowledge of alternative communication modes and available technology is necessary in order to dispel concerns about the individual's ability to interact with other group members. A variety of assistive listening devices (ALDs) are available that can enhance the capacity of the individual who is late-deafened to interact with other members. To exclude the individual for fear of his/her inability to communicate with other group members reflects a lack of knowledge and/or an unwillingness to accommodate the individual who is late-deafened. The initial interview can be used to determine the individual's preferred mode of communication. The counselor should be prepared to provide written text of what will be discussed during the initial interview and not make the assumption that the individual will be able to speechread or make use of residual hearing. The initial interview also is an opportune time for the group leader to discuss telephone communications. Many individuals who

have become deaf have not set up their homes for outgoing or incoming telephone calls. It is important for the counselor to establish how telecommunications will take place in both emergency and non-emergency situations. Providing information about teletypewriters (TTY), amplified phones, ring signalers, and relay services can help the individual achieve independence in telecommunications. Information about the rights of adults who are late-deafened could also be discussed during the initial interview (Brown, 1995).

Additionally, it is important that consideration be given to determine which stage of adjustment the prospective member is experiencing relevant to dealing with hearing loss. Because of the intense anger, depression, and anxiety that may be experienced during the initial stages of adjustment, certain types of groups may not be appropriate. This assessment must be made early in the screening process. A clearly articulated purpose will help to determine the appropriateness of the group relevant to the member's needs. Other factors to consider when setting up the group include determining the number of leaders, size of group, and the use of dyads. Card & Schmider (1995) listed the benefits of co-leaders when one group member has a hearing loss. The advantages include increased eye contact, modeling interaction, conservation of energy as different modes of communicating can be tiring, and reducing the chance of isolation by shifting the focus among members. Smaller groups (4-6 members) tend to be more effective for communication purposes. Dyads and one-on-one communication work very well with individuals who have a hearing loss.

Communication Issues

Results of the RRTC survey as reported by Stika (1997) indicated that respondents felt counselors were willing to speak up, face the person, and to reduce background noise; however, very few of the counselors were willing to use ALDs. The group leader must attend to the individual's needs for equal access to communication. Individuals who are late-deafened may depend on any one, or a combination, of the following modes of communication: sign language, residual hearing, hearing aids, ALDs, cochlear implants, speechreading, and written text. Not all individuals who are late-deafened become fluent in sign language or are able to speechread. Counselors may be able to draw on their past experiences regarding the difficulty of learning or becoming fluent in a second language. For those individuals who have become fluent in sign, sign interpreters will be required during the group sessions. Additionally, individuals who speechread may prefer an oral interpreter who is trained to rephrase words that are less visible on the lips.

Quite often people who are late-deafened require written text for total (100%) comprehension. One of the best ways to accommodate this need is through Computer Assisted Real-Time Captioning (CART). CART can be used to caption group counseling sessions and is similar to live captioning used on television. A CART provider transcribes the session using a specialized shorthand system, typing at 200 words a minute (Preminger, 1997). The words appear on a computer screen in front of the member who is late-deafened. It is also possible for remote transcription services to be arranged using a conference telephone system. The benefit of this system is that the CART provider may be at a different location and listen to the group session via a speaker phone. The typed text would be transmitted on a second telephone line to the computer screen in the counseling room (Preminger, 1997).

The group leader may find comfort in knowing that interpreters and CART providers have their own Code of Ethics (COE) that governs their behavior. Their COE provides guidance regarding confidentiality that is extended to all group members, not just the member who is late-deafened. Furthermore, the COE provides guidance regarding these professionals' responsibility to remain in their respective roles. For example, interpreters and CART providers are not allowed to step out of these roles and engage in any conversation directed at the person with a hearing loss. Consequently, group leaders should not ask the interpreter or CART provider to give any personal input, as doing so would conflict with their COE. Additionally, these professionals know where to stand and how to set up their equipment so that it does not obstruct group members' view of each other. In this capacity, interpreters and CART providers may offer assistance to the group leader in setting up the group.

Environmental Challenges

A number of factors must be addressed when preparing to set up the counseling room. Primary among them is lighting. "Even though a dimly lighted room tends to be more relaxing, it creates a difficulty for most individuals who rely on the visual dimension to communicate" (Card & Schmider, 1995, p. 87). Consequently, lighting should be as bright as necessary to accommodate the needs of the group member who relies on vision to communicate (e.g., speechreading, sign language). Secondly, background noise (i.e., air-conditioning, music, window to outside, etc.) may present a problem for those individuals relying on residual hearing, cochlear implants, or amplification. Efforts may need to be taken to reduce background noise when selecting the location and time of day of the group meeting. Third, for speechreading purposes, the group leader should be prepared to provide strategic seating of group members so that all group members may be seen.

Attending to the Group Process

Once group members have been identified and the proper set-ups are in place, attention should be given to the group process. It is important to avoid starting the group session with a lecture on how to accommodate the member with hearing loss. Group rules can be introduced in a way that does not single out the member who is late-deafened and can be presented in a manner that has universal appeal. For example, instead of saying "please raise your hand before speaking so that our member who is late-deafened will know who is speaking," the group leader might say "it would be helpful for all members to raise a hand before speaking in order to recognize who would like to talk and to maintain order." Stating rules in such a way avoids bringing unwanted and unnecessary attention to the member who has a difference in hearing ability. This also allows the member with a hearing loss to know who is speaking, and at the same time prevents that member from speaking over another's voice. By lessening the attention given to the member who is late-deafened, group leaders can better ensure that the rest of the group does not become jealous or begin to view the group member who is late-deafened as the favorite child (Hittner & Bornstein, 1990).

There are several communication issues specific to the group process that warrants attention. Communication is always delayed when a third person relays information. Because of this delay, it is usually difficult for the person who is late-deafened and who uses an interpreter or CART provider to jump into a conversation or to respond to group questions before the topic has been switched. For example, a group leader may ask for a show of hands and then move on to a different subject before the member who is late-deafened has had a chance to raise a hand. Consequently, it is very important to provide ample time for communication to be relayed in order to increase group interactions for the member who is late-deafened. Group leaders should speak directly to the member who is late-deafened regardless of the third person facilitating communication. Also, when scanning the group and establishing eye contact, leaders should look at the member who is late-deafened even though he/she may be looking at an interpreter or reading captions. To avoid doing so may reinforce feelings of isolation.

When considering the utilization of group activities or exercises, it is important to give thought ahead of time to how the member who is deafened will be included. "Any technique that is designed for all group members should not exclude or set apart a group member who has a *disability* [italics added]" (Patterson, et al., 1995, p. 81). Caution should be given before putting any group member on the spot, particularly the member who has a difference in hearing ability. Asking for immediate suggestions on ways to include him/her into the group activity may bring painful feelings of being different. Contacting the member prior to the session to discuss the activity or exercise and any necessary accommodations will lessen the likelihood of the member experiencing unnecessary group attention. An activity that requires group members to close their eyes may be modified to instruct members to fix their eyes on one object in the room. Another alternative may be to explain the activity before eyes are closed and to give no further instructions until eyes are open. A chain reaction of touching each other's shoulder (started by the group leader) may be a signal to open eyes. This would allow members who are late-deafened to use their eyes for receptive communication but still close their eyes and participate in the group exercise. Group leaders are challenged to be resourceful and creative in planning activities and exercises that all members can enjoy.

The mode of communication should be evaluated continuously throughout the group experience as the initial method of communicating may have been selected for the wrong reasons. Some communication modes are more economical (speechreading, residual hearing) than others (CART, interpreters). The individual with hearing loss may have felt pressure (internally/ externally) to settle for a method of communicating that is not appropriate. Alternatively, a person who is late-deafened may not be comfortable admitting a dependence on a third person to facilitate communication. This person may therefore, choose to speechread and make use of residual hearing and not fully comprehend group communication. If this occurs, it may present problems for the overall group process. For example, the group member who is late-deafened may either monopolize the conversation, fake comprehension, or withdraw from discussion.

A second way it may appear is when the group member asks for constant repetitions or clarifications. As Hittner and Bornstein (1990) stated, "Although repetition, increased loudness, and clearer enunciation may help the *hearing impaired* [italics added] person understand other group members better, this technique could inhibit open and spontaneous communication" (p. 339). Both examples indicate that the communication mode may need to be re-evaluated.

Conclusion

Counseling groups represent one type of therapeutic intervention which can be beneficial to persons who are late-deafened. The inclusion of members who are late-deafened into counseling groups offers unique opportunities for group leaders to accommodate and promote individual differences. We have identified barriers to inclusion, as well as provided a number of alternative ways in which members who are late-deafened may be successfully included in counseling groups. The process of inclusion outlined herein can be used in most counseling groups and would be a significant step in the right direction toward complying with the mandates of the Americans with Disabilities Act.

References

Brown, B.M. (1995). A bill of rights for people with disabilities in group work. *The Journal for Specialists in Group Work, 20* (2), 71-75.

Card, K. J., & Schmider, L. (1995). Group work with members who have hearing impairments. *The Journal for Specialists in Group Work, 20* (2), 83-90.

Cory, G. (1995). *Theory and Practice of group counseling* (4th edition). Pacific Grove, CA: Brooks/Cole.

Hittner, A. & Bornstein, H. (1990). Group counseling with older adults: Coping with late-onset hearing impairment. *Journal of Mental Health Counseling, 12* (3), 332-341.

Hulnick, M. R., & Hulnick, H. R. (1991). Life's challenges: Curse or opportunity? Counseling families of persons with disabilities. In R.P. Marinelli, & A.E. Dell Orto, (Eds.), *The psychological and social impact of disability: Third edition* (pp. 258-268). New York: Springer.

Jacobs, E. E., Harvil, R. L. & Masson, R. L. (1994). *Group counseling. (2nd edition).* Pacific Grove, CA: Brooks/Cole.

Kubler-Ross, E. (1969). *On death and dying*. New York: MacMillan.

Luey, H. S. (1980). Between worlds: The problems of deafened adults. *Social Work in Health Care, 5*, 253-265.

Patterson, J. B., Mckenzie, B., & Jenkins, J. (1995). Creating accessible groups for individuals with disabilities. *The Journal for Specialists in Group Work, 20* (2), 76-81.

Preminger, J. (1997, Spring). Remote transcript services. *LexAcess, 2*, 5.

Rubin, S. E., & Roessler, R. T. (1995). *Foundations of the vocational rehabilitation process* (4th edition). Austin, TX: Pro-Ed.

Stika, C. (1997, May/June). Mental health services for persons with hearing loss: The rehabilitation research and training survey. *Hearing Loss*, 20-25.

Sue, D. W., & Sue, D. (1990). *Counseling the culturally different: Theory and practice* (2nd ed.). New York: Wiley.

Vanier, J. (1991). The contribution of the physically and mentally handicapped to development. In R. P. Marinelli, & A. E. Dell Orto (Eds.), *The psychological and social impact of disability: Third edition* (pp. 3-8). New York: Springer.

RESOURCES

ADA Title III: Public Accommodations
Department of Justice
Disability Rights Section
Civil Rights Division
P.O. Box 66738
Washington, DC 20035-6738
(800) 514-0301 Voice
(800) 514-0383 TTY

ADA Title IV: Telecommunications Relay Services
Federal Communications Commission
1919 M Street, NW
Washington, DC 20544
(202) 632-7553 Voice
(202) 418-0485 TTY

Association of Late-Deafened Adults, Inc. (ALDA)
1145 Westgate Street
Suite 206
Oak Park, IL 60301
(708) 358-0135 TTY
(877) 348-7537 Fax/Voice
http://www.alda.org

Disability and Business Technical Assistance Centers (DBTACs)
(800) 949-4232 (V/TTY)
Call the toll-free number above for information, materials, technical assistance, or training on the ADA. This number will automatically route your call to the DBTAC in your region.
http://www.adata.org

National Association of the Deaf, Inc.
814 Thayer Avenue
Silver Springs, MD 20910-450
(301) 587-1788 Voice
(301) 587-1789 TTY
(301) 587-1791 Fax
http://www.nad.org

National Court Reporters Association
8224 Old Courthouse Road
Vienna, VA 22182-3808
(703) 556-6285

Registry of Interpreters for the Deaf, Inc.
8630 Fenton Street #324
Silver Springs, MD 20814
(301) 654-2245

Self Help for Hard of Hearing People, Inc.
7910 Woodmont Avenue
Suite 1200
Bethesda, MD 20814
(301) 657-2248 Voice
(301) 657-2249 TTY
(301) 913-9413 Fax
E-mail: national@shhh.org
http://www.shhh.org

Chapter Nine

COMMUNITY BUILDING THROUGH DIALOGUE GROUPS

Bogusia Molina, Diane Estrada, Angela Rhone, Susanne Lapp and Helen Kim

"Is this really what I have strived for in my life? What do they think of me? How can I be surrounded by so many people and yet feel so lonely? I wonder if others feel that way ... but maybe I should not say anything."- Gabriela, new faculty.

"What a strange environment. On one hand there are so many friendly individuals, yet we do not seem to be connected. My family and friends are so far away. Part of me is scared to show my heritage. Will they think I am one of those Nazi descendants who destroyed their people? Maybe I should join the reading group that is being formed. Then again, maybe I should lay low. After all, I just arrived here and I have a long way to go before I get tenured here."- Helga, new faculty.

"How am I going to embrace the challenges of teaching here? Once again, I was cursed out by students when I confronted them about smoking. One of them, for the third time witnessed his mother getting arrested for prostitution. He does not know his father and the rest of his relatives live far away. I feel so overwhelmed and lonely."- Orlando, new teacher at a local school.

"Do they think I am here because they needed to fill in the gap as there were no Asians hired before me? Yet it seems like there are so many other people here from diverse backgrounds who seem so fascinating. It sure would be nice to get to know them."- Lee, fiscal officer.

"Wow, one of the students was surprised that I am punctual and precise. He said, 'that is not how I viewed black people.' Chances are other people think so, too. This one was just outspoken. I feel like I have to constantly prove myself and apologize for being here."- Jamal, new faculty.

The previous statements are examples of stories shared by individuals who feel isolated due to issues of ethnicity, gender, hierarchy, power, race, sexual orientation, socioeconomic status, and spirituality. These stories reveal how the experience of isolation can lead to a lack of community bonding experienced by individuals in our society. As practitioners and researchers, we believe that in an environment where isolation has created chaos, confusion, and emotional distress, there is a great need for individuals to reconnect with others so that the community once lost can be experienced again.

The consequences of not having community bonding are menacing. Research conducted over the past three decades has identified disorganization, isolation, low community attachment, and transitions and mobility as variables that hinder healthy human development and lead to a lack of community bonding (Bandura, 1977). Lack of community bonding correlates highly with delinquency, drug abuse, and major mental health problems (Hawkins & Catelano, 1992). Simultaneously, variables that promote healthy human development and increase resiliency against risk factors were recognized by researchers. Bonding has been identified as a significant factor in fostering resistance to risk factors. Hawkins and Catelano (1992) described three major components of strong bonds: 1) attachment - the ability to develop and maintain positive relationships with others; 2) commitment - an investment in the future; and 3) belief - in self and others, with an orientation towards positive behavior.

The lack of community bonding is widespread and prudent. Mobility rates continue to increase (Hawkins & Catelano, 1992). Alienation, high levels of stress, and isolation are rampant (Robins & Przybeck, 1985). Living, working, and learning in an environment where one experiences bonding can help adults successfully progress through developmental adult issues. Among these developmental issues are: adjusting to new transitions, coping with age and gender discrimination, identity clarification, intimacy exploration, learning to work effectively in a diverse environment, searching for belonging, and striving for competence (Santrock, 1997). Numerous individuals in our society share this lack of community bonding. We believe individuals need to focus on decreasing the lack of community bonding by creating opportunities where a sense of attachment, community bonding, can emerge and grow.

One may wonder why we should focus on facilitating groups for community bonding. Groups are a microcosm of our society (Yalom, 1995). It is within the context of small group interactions that members can create long lasting friendships, exchange ideas, learn from each other, and experience the feeling of "familyhood." As group members weave their ideas, a safe web is created where a synergistic experience of community bonding evolves. Then, the group members can not only voice their thoughts and feelings but they can also experiment with unchallenged assumptions.

In response to the lack of community bonding experienced by individuals, we developed a psychoeducational/support diversity dialogue group design which uses story telling as a vehicle for increasing community interaction in settings where members feel isolated and stressed. Psychoeducational groups facilitate shared learning experiences where individuals recreate new meaning and, in the process, experience interconnectedness and community bonding. The use of structured exercises such as storytelling accompanied by processing is consistent with research based recommendations regarding effective group practices (Conyne & Wilson, 1997, DeLucia-Waack 1997, Gladding 1999, Jacobs 1994). It is the personal storytelling and the sharing of each other's experiences in response to the stories read that helps individuals ensure their voices are heard, acknowledged, and validated. Throughout this process, a sense of community bonding evolves.

While describing the psychoeducational/support diversity dialogue groups, three variables will be addressed. First, an overview of dialogue groups will be presented as an instrument for community building. The following four variables will be addressed: 1) history of diversity dialogue groups; 2) the focus of diversity dialogue groups; 3) the fundamental elements of dialogue groups and; 4) a case example. Second, the process of starting and maintaining the groups will be explained. Member recruitment, norms, group processes and dynamics, as well as rituals will be shared. Third, the language arts selection in light of diversity issues of race, class, gender, sexual orientation, spirituality, ethnicity, power, and hierarchy will be presented. The literature that was selected for story sharing depicts individuals whose life stories are embedded in diverse issues. Special attention will be given to the use of psychodrama for self-disclosure and the use of childhood recollections as tools for reflecting on our multicultural roots. Finally, a review of how communities were, are, and will be defined is presented.

DIALOGUE GROUPS: THE INSTRUMENT OF COMMUNITY BUILDING

History of Diversity Dialogue Groups

> Most of us learn best, from our own experience-not simply from having things happen to us but from reflecting on what happens, both alone and in exchanges with others, so that the meaning of our experience becomes clear and we can make choices on growing awareness rather than unchallenged assumptions ... Very often such learning is enhanced and deepened when we work with a supportive group- a group where we can do more than discuss ideas objectively. We need a chance to work experimentally with the ideas, as scientists experiment in a laboratory, and then apply the finding to our lives. (Peck, 1998, p. 3)

Utilizing small groups as an instrument for community building is not new. During the 1800's Jane Adams initiated what one may now call psychoeducational/support groups for immigrants (Gladding, 1999). The purpose of the groups was not only to provide information but also to support individuals who were new and/or felt alienated from the majority culture. Several decades later, Lewin (1944) initiated groups focusing on tension reduction and improvement of racial attitudes so that diverse individuals could work together in harmony. Lewin was one of the pioneers of T- (training) groups. These groups focused on the leaders' skill development in light of diversity. The movement, initiated by Lewin, seems to have reached moratorium after his death. Yet during the past decade, interests in community building, diversity issues, and group work have been rejuvenated. For example, Merta (1995) described multicultural perspectives in group work and stressed the importance of learning about the differences within multicultural groups. DeLucia-Waack (1992, 1996a, 1996b) identified the need for facilitating diverse groups in response to the increased diversity in our society. In addition, she described the multicultural group goals and identified the myths regarding multicultural groups. One of the myths, "groups can be truly homogenous" (p.220), seems to be especially crucial to dispute because such overgeneralizations can hinder the group's ability to experience cohesion. Johnson, Torres, Coleman, and Smith (1995) identified issues and strategies pertaining to facilitating diverse groups. Bohm (1990, 1985) dedicated two books to learning about the unfolding of the meaning and dialoguing.

Issues of diversity have been addressed throughout the history of groups. The development of community building dialogue groups adds to the previous gifts of group work, the social component of community building through the use of storytelling. Within the process of storytelling, group members facilitate dialogues about the experience of diversity. The use of stories has an abundance of research support (Sedney, Baker, & Gross, 1994; Becvar & Becvar, 1993; Schnitzer, 1993). In community building through dialogue groups, stories selected by the group members provide some level of structure and focus which is essential for the group to accomplish its goal. As group members dialogue about the story, they are encouraged to focus on the following six areas: 1) describe the events of the story and characters' feelings; 2) describe differences between story characters and yourself; 3) identify similarities between stories read and your "real-life" experiences; 4) what do I want to learn?; 5) with whom and from whom do I want to learn?; and 6) what have I learned?

The Focus of Diversity Dialogue Groups

This process of community building takes place only when individuals interact with each other. For example, Yalom (1995) theorized that when a group member is "fully aware of his [sic] responsibility for his interpersonal world, he may then begin to grapple with the corollary of this discovery: since he created his world, it is only he who can alter it" (p. 138). Small group interactions can help in gaining awareness of one's constructs and the impact they have on others. Consistent with Dewey's (1944) notion of democratic groups, "democracy begins in conversations because in conversations one must take the other into account" (p.87), the goal of the diversity dialogue groups is to take into account each others' experiences and respect differences while simultaneously recognizing the interconnectedness of the members. Hayes (1994) pointed out from a constructivist view that "truth and knowledge are constructions within the mind of the individual and the meaning making and valuing are based on those constructions" (p.9). Diversity dialogue groups provide individuals with an opportunity to learn about others' meaning making as well as how their constructions influence the group members and the group as a whole.

Centering on differences can be a highly emotional experience. Consistent with Walker's (1994) recommendations, the nucleus of diversity dialogue group dynamics is embedded in safety. Safety in the group context can only be established and maintained when all of the individuals "hang in there," focus on diversity, feel included, have equal air time, and participate in dialogue by taking responsibility for their thoughts, feelings, and actions.

As Yalom (1995) described, groups are a microcosm of our society. Thus, small groups provide individuals with opportunities to examine their interactions embedded in their personal constructions regarding diversity. Recognizing that other members also experience stress and lack of bonding instills hope in the group members who, by sharing their thoughts and feelings, start to weave a supportive web of interactions. The group members recognize that they are not "crazy, sick, or weak." What is happening around them might be. The group members' recognition that they can relate to others and others can relate to them is consistent with Yalom's therapeutic factors of instillation of hope and universality (Yalom, 1995).

For example, during one of the group meetings, a group member expressed her struggles with adjustment to a new career and a new geographic region. Another member stated she, too, experienced mixed feelings of excitement and fear of the faculty role along with dislike of the new geographic region. Another group member, who had lived in the area much longer, shared her initial struggles with adjustments to career and a new location. The group members discussed how helpful it was to know that others can relate to their feelings.

Fundamental Elements of Dialogue Groups: A Look at Symbolic Interactions

Our community building dialogue groups adopted Huang-Nissen's (1994) fundamental elements of dialogue groups in order to create an atmosphere of equality and mutual understanding. Huang-Nissen (1994) identified seven objectives of dialogue groups which were conceptualized in order to create a work atmosphere conducive to learning and working effectively. These identified objectives are:

1. To develop trust and become comfortable with differences
2. To learn different perspectives from other participants
3. To remove barriers and fears about differences
4. To learn about and find value in diversity
5. To enhance communication skills
6. To become effective in multicultural workplace, and
7. To bring about positive impact on the organization

Trust and comfort are prerequisites for dealing with and discussing differences. As each member trusts himself or herself in the group and becomes comfortable with his or her own differences, levels of safety increase and differing or even contradicting views on issues that arise from stories and narratives read can be discussed. As trust and ease are established, the members become open to learn from other members' varying perspectives. Each member contributes unique, personal viewpoints and reactions where other members can expand and challenge their own way of thinking. In trusting and processing different perspectives, the group members also learn to lower their barriers and fears about the inevitable diversity in the group. As the group develops, differences become less threatening. At this point, the group not only shares differences; the members discover the true value of differences and how heterogeneity shapes a community.

An example of experimenting with ideas can be found in the story of two women, who were very different, but who were able to connect with their shared experience of dealing with divorce. Although one lived on a farm in the Midwest and the other in Jamaica, they both felt the loneliness and emptiness that transcended their different backgrounds. Their relatives could not understand why they were not happy. The Midwestern woman was challenged by her family because, in their view, she had everything a woman "should be" happy with: a "white collar" husband, a nice house, and she did not "have to" work. The Jamaican woman also had a "white collar" husband, drove a Mercedes Benz automobile, and did not "have to" work. Although both women had financial wealth, their life was like a cage, perhaps a velvet one, but a cage nonetheless. By voicing their experiences, they could relate to each other and express their feelings, emotions which before were not heard and/or acknowledged.

As the dialogue about losses continued, one of the women shared that in her European culture, poppyseed flowers were a symbol of mourning. A Jamaican member looked up with excitement and shared that in her culture, the same flower had a similar meaning. So the two, seemingly different group members were able to interconnect through shared symbolic meaning. A German American was very actively listening to the two group members and shared her feeling of connection to them as a result of this symbolic connection.

Buoyed by the sense of community, the members developed and enhanced trusting communication skills in the midst of their differences. This lends itself to another related objective, to become effective in a multicultural workplace. The transferable skills and attitudes that were cultivated in the dialogue group will be actuated in the professional arena where members become change agents.

Thus objectives start from the individual, then to the group, and connect both to the communities outside the group such as the workplace and its organization. Members convey their genuine learning and teaching that transpire in the dialogue group about diversity to their professional community.

Group members build authentic relationships as they establish norms and focus on sharing their interpretations of stories read. Group members concentrate on learning to identify and strip away stereotypes. The breaking down of stereotypes is evident in group members' ability to carefully reevaluate their own perspectives, a process quite consistent with the fundamental elements of dialogue groups (Walker, 1994).

In our diversity dialogue, members decided to use literature, specifically novels, as a unifying force. During story sharing dialogues, members gradually began to share stories and relate events in the literature to their own lives. In an effort to make greater strides in cultural awareness, participants often found themselves carefully revealing information which they normally would not disclose to others. Thus, they were willing to take risks due to creation of a "safety zone." The group became a community. Using literature as a vehicle for cross cultural dialogue, participants learned that they could confide in one another, share and reflect on various aspects of the literature and how it directly affected their lives without the fear of ridicule and retribution (Wolfson & Pearse, 1983). The behavior manifested by the group members closely parallels the social-psychological philosophy known as symbolic interaction (Mead, 1934). Symbolic interaction emphasizes the importance of common, negotiated definitions which emerge as people interact and communicate (Blumer, 1969). This notion is further supported by the group members' ability to develop/maintain a positive view of self as well as individuals from other cultures. In the process members demonstrate listening, social, and encouraging skills, all of which help to reduce the experience of isolation and stress. This is consistent with the last stage of minority development leading to a synergetic articulation and awareness (Atkinson, Marten, & Sue, 1993).

As members relate their social context or "social ecology" directly and indirectly, they influence one another (Gladding, 1999). This influence also affects individuals outside of the group, and it actuates productivity in the workplace. In the process of community building, it is necessary to honor fundamental criteria for membership (Huang-Nissen, 1994). Underlying all criteria is trust, a basic component in any group or community building. These criteria include a serious consideration and respect for anonymity. Trust promotes another criterion, sharing and learning from each other without judgment. Eventually, each member becomes secure enough to take risks in exploring their own personal, social, and political stereotypes and "-isms". The group becomes a safe place to challenge one's own beliefs and develop self awareness. Similarly, the group is used to focus on personal growth.

Fundamental Elements in Action: A Case Example

What follows is a case example containing group interactions that illustrate show how the objectives identified by Huang-Nissen (1994) work in our group.

In one of the community building groups, interracial relationship issues were stimulated from a story read. An African American group member was opposed to her son dating a Chinese American woman. In essence, she was uncomfortable with the situation because it surfaced her personal and social ambivalence and distaste. She feared what these interracial differences would mean to her, her son, their family and his girlfriend. She talked about the victimization of African Americans and discussed how often Asians are perceived as the "model" culture. She felt safe enough in a group to discuss her fears.

As the dialogue continued, a Jamaican member shared a similar fear, but from a different perspective: she shared her strong feelings about dating only Jamaicans. As these views were exchanged, ethnocentric attitudes were echoed throughout the group. A Jewish American woman shared the feelings of pain she experienced when she married a non Jewish man. A Slavic person married to a Latino shared experiences of her family of origin's fear of the loss of their culture and thus perpetuating the victimization process that Slavic people have experienced for centuries. A universal theme evolved: feeling abandoned from one's primary family while not being accepted by the members of other cultures. The Slavic woman shared how she did not realize how different and deeply embedded her cultural values were until she experienced living with someone from a different culture. She stated, "I didn't know who I was until I learned also who I was not. And I did not experience the richness of my culture until I'd experienced the richness of another culture." Through the dialogue, a deeper even more universal theme emerged: the richness of diverse couplehood.

In the process, another group member, a German American, stated, "Isn't it ironic that when a white family would reject a non white individual, that behavior would be considered racist." At this point the African American stated that until she had heard the views of other members, she did not realize that she, too, was not immune to racism. She added that she could relate to the fear of repeated victimization that Slavic families experience. She stated, "All this time I've feared that the Asian girl would put herself in a one-up position and deny my child his culture, so it was easier to reject her first. I've got to do some talking with my son. He may have felt as abandoned by me as you folks have by your people." Several of the group members applauded for her for the courage to learn from her dialogue with them.

Making it Happen: The Process of Starting and Maintaining the Group

Group Goal

The purpose of community building groups is to provide individuals with an opportunity to create a supportive community for one another, an extended kinship, where they can learn from each other about how diversity issues touch their lives and the lives of those around them. Thus, the group becomes a community for the members. The group's goal is to build genuine relationships with people whom they perceive as different by emphasizing their common need for community belonging. Through a series of structured activities such as reading stories about diverse experiences and sharing meals, the group members reflect on their assumptions and cultural attitudes and examine the efficacy of their assumptions. In the process, members identify similarities which interconnect them. Larson, (1982) pointed out that in order to understand the concept "different" we must understand "same." Similarly, Bernard and Goodyear (1992) suggested that one of the many contributing factors in the complexity of appreciating differences and sameness is that "each is partially true" (p. 195). Thus, to be effective group members must dialogue about differences as well as similarities.

The community building group follows the guidelines for psychoeducational group with the Association for Specialists in Group Work (1991). Ample research evidence supports the use of structured exercises accompanied with processing (Conyne & Wilson,

1997, DeLucia-Waack 1997, Gladding, 1999, Jacobs, 1994). This group design also includes processes and goals associated with counseling/interpersonal problem solving groups.

Group Composition

Initially, two of the authors decided to form a club named The Story Sharing Club. Adults who were interested in community building through diversity awareness, sensitivity, and respect were encouraged to join. The authors designed invitations that contained information about the purpose of the club, along with the time and place of the first meeting. Invitations were disseminated, and colleagues interested in joining were also encouraged to invite other community members. Criteria for membership focused on bringing together individuals who were willing and able to form a safe place where dialogues regarding diverse experiences could take place. Potential group members were informed of the emphasis on learning. Groups were open ended and new members were welcome to join. The group consisted of 17 members of whom 10-12 attended the group meetings on regular basis. Four men and 13 women comprised the group membership. The groups's diversity reflected the diversity of the state's population. The group consisted of African Americans, Caribbean-Americans, Eastern-Europeans, Western Europeans, and Latinos. They represented a broad range of spiritual beliefs and family structures. While the age range in the group was from 30 to 60, individuals from 18-80+ would be invited to join.

In terms of screening issues, potential members are informed that the primary focus of the group is to learn to value all diversity via dialogue. Potential members are told that the focus is on learning, not teaching, and they are encouraged to think about what it is that they want to learn. Leaders also emphasize to all new members and remind the "regular" members that keeping the group safe and sharing responsibility for readings and dialoguing about each other is a norm. No one is excluded unless they voice harmful statements regarding diversity.

Group Setting and Timing

This group has been implemented in an urban area on the South-East Coast of the United States. Group members hold 4-5 hour meetings once a month. It is an open ended group, and meetings are held in one of the members' home. The groups rotate the meeting place since many of the members live a distance from each other. Sharing one's home with others creates a sense of community belonging. Since each group meeting consists of sharing a meal prior to discussing the stories and each others' experiences, 4-5 hour sessions are necessary. Due to group members' busy schedules and the rigors of urban living, members could not commit to meeting more frequently. The group activity takes place in settings where members can gather around a circle, share a meal and have opportunity to dialogue with one another.

Group Procedures

The group experience consists of three stages: sharing of the meal, discussing the story, and reflecting personally on what the story means to each member. Each person brings a dish for the pot luck meal. This in itself is a diverse experience since group members often share their favorite ethnic food. Frequently, group members discuss the meaning behind the dishes and the rituals associate with meals. From a collection of stories which contain examples of diversity, group members decide on the story that all will read before the group meeting. The stories are diverse in content. After sharing the meal, group members discuss their interpretations of the story as well as their personal meanings. Frequently group members discuss who in the story they relate to, what events in the story were very different from their own experiences and what events were similar to their experiences. They reflect and work experimentally with ideas. As Peck (1998) mentioned in *The Road Less Traveled*, "learning is enhanced and deepened when we work with a supportive group--a group where we can do more than discuss ideas objectively. We need a chance to work experimentally with ideas, as scientists experiment in a laboratory, and then apply our finding to our lives" (p. 3). We can make choices on growing awareness rather than unchallenged assumptions. The techniques associated with psychodrama are frequently used. It gives group members an opportunity to be heard and validated. Unexpressed emotions regarding the self, others, and societal ecosystems are explored.

Story Processing

After group members share the meal, usually 1-1 ½ hrs. into the group time, the focus of the group process shifts to dialoguing about the events in the story and exploring the personal meaning members attach to these events. Although the group does not have an official leader or co-leaders who facilitate the group on a regular basis, the person at whose home the group is held takes the responsibility for starting dialogue by generating a list of processing questions. The focus of the processing is growth oriented. Honesty, exploration, self-disclosure, confrontation, and emotional expression are all valued. The members share in the leadership role and emphasize expression of care and meaning attribution. Emotional stimulation and executive functions are kept at moderate levels, consistent with the research findings pertaining to group leadership (Liberman, Yalom, & Miles, 1973). Some examples of processing include: (a) what did it mean for the story character to be a Black male teacher? (b) what does it mean today in our communities to be a Black teacher? (c) what does it mean to you to be a professional in your career, in light of your gender and cultural backgrounds? (d) which story character could you related to? (e) what did it mean to be a child of bi-racial family? (f) what does it mean to children today to be biracial? (g) which story characters and events could you relate to? (h) what does it mean for your children to have the cultural make up that they have? and (i) what are your feelings about your children's meaning regarding their cultural make up? When all the group members have an opportunity to share their thoughts and feelings, they process the experience by focusing on what it is like to be in the group and then brain storm to produce a list of potential readings for the next group time. Once the list is generated, they vote on a story that all members will read within the next month, prior to the next group meeting. They decide as a group at whose home the next meeting will be held and say goodbye.

Using literature as a vehicle for cross cultural dialogues, participants learn that they can confide in each other, share and reflect on various aspects of the literature and how it directly affected their lives without the fear of ridicule and retribution. They courageously experience all the group stages, conflict and the harmony. As new group members join, the whole group revisits the group norms. Respect for diversity and use of I statements to convey one's feelings are reemphasized. These are the lessons that all the group members learn, and through various routes each person will have another chance to reach in successive approximation the ultimate goal of interconnecting.

Connecting Through the Use of Psychodrama

The main focus of community building groups is to decrease the sense of isolation in individuals. The techniques of psychodrama allow for a connection to be created by identifying the common challenges in our interactions with others, institutions, and ourselves. The acting out of internal interpretations and dialogues frees the individual to examine the process of interpersonal interactions and allows the expression of feelings in a safe manner by detaching the self and incorporating roles to play out past, present, or future life situations in order to gain a better understanding of self and others (Corey, 1995).

"Does art imitate life or life imitate art?" In the community building groups, group members are encouraged to use literature as a way to explore their own experiences. In a very real sense, the literature portrays scenes from the groups members' lives. While not every group member can relate to all the characters in the literature, those who do, find it easier to express their own life events and feelings around those experiences which contribute to their sense of grief and isolation.

For example, when one of the Jamaican women shared her interconnectedness with a story character who was struggling with parenting challenges, she acted out a scene from her own life experience where she had to rush washing diapers so that the sun would dry them, while her child was crying for her attention. "I was not weak, crazy ... the system was harsh," she voiced as other members reached out to comfort her. The cathartic experiences of the members who closely link themselves to the characters in the books provide a deeper understanding and a sense of empathy for those members who are distant from a particular book experience. The creation of an empathic experience contributes to the enhancement of connection between group members.

Empathic experiences in psychodrama groups provide the conditions for *tele*, "a two way flow of feelings between people, or therapeutic love" (Corey, 1995). Tele is described as the ultimate aspect of empathy, transference, and countertransference (Corey, 1995). Tele allows individuals to create bonds that are experienced as primary family group. Positive tele facilitates group cohesion and continuity. Group cohesion and continuity contribute to group members sense of safety, a necessary ingredient for exploring of emotions and processing interpersonal and intrapersonal conflict resolution.

According to Moreno, founder of psychodrama, participants not only explore "reality" but also what they remember which may not have actually happened but may have been constructed by their own imagination or fantasy. During the groups, participants are able to vent their hopes, fears, projections, resentments, and judgments. In the process of venting their emotions they cathart which allows individuals to let go. Catharsis opens up the sense of self on four levels: (1) abrasion, (2) an awareness of disowned feelings, (3) experiencing a sense of being part of social network, and (4) participating meaningfully in the universe (Corey, 1995).

Insight is often gained from the unobstructed expression of emotion. Insight may be provided through the shared story with the characters in the literature or through an emotionally triggered memory. Reality based on memories holds not only our true experiences but our fantasies as well. The shared dialogue of our memories allows group members to participate in reality testing. The process of reality testing continues to enhance group members' insight into the scripts of their life stories. The knowledge of their reality offers group members the opportunity to rewrite their stories and empower themselves to search for alternative endings. The power to change their life scripts is enhanced through the group cohesion and their sense of community and connection. As we have mentioned in the examples of literary works, it is the use of psychodrama techniques and processing of the personal meaning attached to the stories that are read that gives group members an opportunity to examine their constructs and apply their findings to life situations.

THE DIVERSITY ISSUE

"Prejudice is a burden which confuses the past, threatens the future, and renders the present inaccessible" - Maya Angelou, 1986, p.155

Race, ethnicity, gender, sexual orientation, socioeconomic class, and spirituality are the sociopolitical organizing principles which shape an individual's experiences of the world. The personal is political (White, 1990). Various mental health associations--American Counseling Association (ACA), American Psychological Association (APA), American Association of Marriage and Family Therapists (AAMFT)--have acknowledged the influence of the sociopolitical organizing principles in people's lives. Issues of oppression and discrimination are difficult to speak about in a nonthreatening way. The literature selection used for the community building groups is a tool which facilitates this process for members.

In hierarchical institutions where issues of power are prevalent, diversity issues become pronounced as evidenced through various studies on faculty stress (Bartlett, 1994; Fontes, Piercy, Thomas, Sprenkle, 1998; Gainen, 1993; Sorcinelli, 1994). Numerous studies (Ashraf, 1995; Conroy, 1994; and Wilson, Tienda, & Wu, 1995) point out that workplace discrimination is still experienced by minority members. For example,

Ashraf, (1995) reported that African Americans earn approximately 54% less than whites in the South and about 33% less that whites in other parts of the country. Other work by Wilson, Tienda, and Wu (1995), revealed that African American males with a college degree have higher unemployment rates than their white counterparts. Minority group members and individuals with low income have higher rates of lead poisoning and are more likely to live near toxic waste sites (Wilson, Tienda, & Wu, 1995). Conroy (1994) provided a detailed review of the challenges faced by minority groups in his book "Faded Dreams: The Politics and Economics of Race in America." From the economic perspective women's wages are much lower than their male counterparts, ranging from 66% to 50 % less than what men make. (U.S. Department of Labor, Employment and Earnings, 1994). Sharf (1997) identified organizational culture as one of the core issues for discrimination. According to him, "patriarchal views toward women, unequal promotion practices, and evaluating jobs in terms of gender" are examples of organizational culture which promote discriminatory practices. Yet, Witkowski and Leicht (1995) in the same year reported that men who have families benefit economically yet as women assume family roles their earnings are reduced. One may conclude that gender bias is embedded in our society. As a result, individuals are likely to experience a lack of bonding with the workplace as well as their community in general. Dialogue groups provide an arena for those issues to be discussed in a safe personal manner.

Race/Ethnicity

"I never knew I was Black until I came to the United States." - Jamaican woman

This statement prompts the following question: Did the question of race not come up in the writer's country because the writer had no consciousness of race or was it because she was in a predominantly black country where the significance of race appeared to be unimportant? One of the dangers for individuals who come from predominantly black countries and who enter a predominantly white country is that their "sense of dislocation" becomes skewed because they maintain that racism was absent in their country. Thus they incorrectly conclude that it is only their new country that suffers from the "illness of racism." Many people deal with this through alienation from the dominant culture, keeping company only with those who belong to their "in" group. On the other hand, some may create a diverse community that includes not only people from their country, but individuals from other cultural groups. This healthy attempt to maintain a sense of their own identity while concurrently living and working within the dominant culture has been one of the most difficult tasks for new black immigrants, especially those working within the academic communities. A sense of belonging, a sense of "peoplehood" based on a combination of race, religion, and cultural history" (McGoldrick, Giordano & Pearce, 1995, p.1) prevails among those who have successfully transcended cultural differences. The components of peoplehood provide a conscious identity and connection to group members. This sense of connection is often missing in the majority group.

Extended kinship groups have been the survival mechanism for many minority groups in this country (McGoldrick, Giordano, & Pearce, 1995). Kinship groups create communities which provide the necessary support in times of adversity and change. In this case, the Jamaican woman was able to connect with other immigrants because they could relate to each others' acculturation struggles, many of which were shared by Black Americans. Most importantly, because of the transcendence of race and culture she was also able to understand not only the oppression of African Americans, and even herself as an immigrant to this country, but also she was able to understand the oppression of white immigrant groups who attempted to make their stay in the United States. This "pedagogy of connection" comes out of a deep understanding of the history of American education and its connection to very important issues that have affected all of us as a nation. The understanding of the "pedagogy of connection" facilitates the teaching of diversity issues in a more holistic manner than previously experienced.

The Voicing of Race Experiences Through Literature: A Case Sample

A Lesson Before Dying (1994) by Earnest Gaines, one of the books discussed in group, addresses the issues of race/ethnicity. Questions related to the text such as a) what is the role of a Black man in this society, b) what is the role of a Black teacher in this society, c) how do we come to grips with the oppression of Blacks in this society were posed during the group meeting. The discussion of this book produced one of the most painful dialogues that the group members experienced. Present at the meeting were two white women, three Black Jamaican women, and one Black Jamaican man. Because the book had not been completely read by all members, the important issue of race and its profound ramifications on American society became highly charged instead of being dialogued about as group members initially agreed to do. What really took place in the story became secondary while confusion and chaos emerged. There were no African Americans at this meeting. The Jamaicans saw the African Americans as victims who have failed to live up to what it is to be an American in this society. As immigrants, three of the Jamaicans felt that they had done well because of hard work. One Jamaican woman, who understood the Black history after teaching African American history for several years, challenged these beliefs without success. The three white women remained silent, except for one who stated "but the Jews made it, so why can't Blacks?" The woman who understood the historical perspective continued to share with the group how different it is to be a Black American because of the sociopolitical factors that have shaped the Black individuals in this society. It is profoundly important to realize that just as most of the Jamaican members, including the group member herself at one time, were not aware of the oppression which they experienced by being black in their own country, they can become immune to the oppression experienced by Black Americans in this country. This lack of connection to their own Africaness, their own blackness, their own oppression, prevented them from deeply understanding the plight of the African Americans.

The processing question which seemed to be a critical incident in the group was posed by the Jamaican woman who understood the African American history. She asked others the following provocative questions: a) what is the role of the Black teacher in the Black community and b) are their roles different from white teachers in that community. Many responded by arguing that the roles were the same. Nothing that the group leader said seemed to matter. The next important question that drew much criticism was: can individuals who teach and have no historical knowledge of their students' culture understand the struggles experienced by them? The knowledge of the history of African American oppression seemed minimal. Neither did they have a well rounded historical understanding of the suffering experienced by other groups. Therefore, although the book told a story of a young man who was being put to death for being at the wrong place and at the wrong time, the group members did not seem to want to look at the historical theme of black people being placed in jail for crimes which they did not commit. The idea of being lynched just because one was black was not an issue that anyone wanted to deal with. Ultimately, the "pedagogy of connection" which the group leader attempted to make between the historical context and Gain's fictional work was completely lost.

The group became a social microcosm experiencing dynamics present in our society. For example, according to Brice-Baker (1994), Jamaicans have been frequently placed on pedestals by white society as examples of "the good and industrious Black" whereas American Blacks have been stereotyped as "lazy, criminal, and willing to live on public assistance" (p. 87).

The end the meeting was tumultuous. One Jamaican woman said that she would not return, and the sole Jamaican man echoed these sentiments. He stated, "I have no problems in America because I can pass as white". It was not until months later that one of the women who initially could not relate to Black Americans, stated that she was finally able to recognize, at least to a limited extent, the pain and suffering experienced by Black Americans. The group leader's response to this was, "Not until we as teachers understand our own personal culture and understand other cultures can we become able and centered to teach in a 'pedagogy of connection' and liberation to our students." Although the community once lost has been regained, this inability to study the history and openly dialogue about the differences now has hindered the process of interconnecting and talking about issues of race and gender. Critical topics which must be openly, honestly, and ethically discussed here and now as we move toward the there and then in the 21st century.

The community building groups attempt to create an extended kinship to address the issues faced by faculty, teachers, staff, and other members of hierarchical systems. Fontes et al. (1998) spoke of the importance of feeling less isolated and more supported in her workplace. Fontes and her colleagues created a group in which they were allowed to release their creative energies in a protected space, naming the problems, and working toward solutions.

Sexual Orientation

"If you really knew me, would you still accept me?"- a lesbian woman asked. Issues of sexual orientation and discrimination cross gender, race, ethnicity, religion, and social class. Society at large and its subcultures exhibit heterosexism and homophobia throughout different social institutions from families to government agencies. Heterosexism is "a world-view, a value system that prizes heterosexuality, assumes it is the only appropriate manifestation of love and sexuality, and devalues homosexuality and all that is not heterosexual" (Herek, 1986, p. 925). Homophobia is "the prejudice, discrimination, and hostility directed at gay men and lesbian women because of their sexual orientation" (Ellis & Murphy, 1994).

Discrimination and hostility towards gays and lesbians has historically lead to issues of violence from verbal harassment to murder. Gay and Lesbian civil rights have been under constant threat in this country. The issue of "coming out" in work settings has been a painful experience for gays and lesbians. Hostile environments in the workplace and a lack of protection from the law create a sense of isolation and fear.

Even within the counseling field, we struggle to understand the complex issue of sexual orientation. Therapists often find themselves stereotyping and exhibiting subtle biases. In classes when students are asked to report on the sexual orientation of their clients, they often state "heterosexual because they are married or have a child." Society and our training programs have created a secretiveness around issues of sexual orientation which prevent an honest and comfortable discussion of sexual orientation for ourselves as well as our clients. If the field of human understanding and mental health has a difficult time speaking about issues of sexual orientation in a respectful and open manner, how are these issues addressed in other less sensitive institutions?

Silence and isolation once again surface as coping mechanisms. Issues of sexual orientation have begun to be addressed in some of the community building groups' literature. Gay relationships are silently alluded to even though few stories depict the challenges faced by gay couples. The oppression experienced by gays and lesbians is evident by the almost silent presence of stories depicting gays/lesbians as story characters. The group members, however, frequently discussed the challenges of gay relationships by wondering what it would be like if the characters of the stories were gay. They provide an end to the silence and begin to whisper about issues which traditionally go unspoken.

Gender Issues

> "... the ghost I was fighting was an assumption: That men and women see the world in the same way" (Turpin, 1993/1994).

It is not until recently that women outnumbered men in the workforce. As a society we have lagged in our ability to create an environment and levels of support necessary for women and men to feel comfortable with each other in the workplace. Most work settings have been managed by men who have traditionally related to other men, but exclude or ignore women to some degree (Kaufman, 1995). In the world of work, women face societal constraints, e.g., child care alternatives, sex role stereotyping, inequitable compensation, and a lack of career development models for women working outside of traditional careers (Wolfe, 1995). Many women in academia, as well as in the workforce in general, may identify with Fontes' (1998) statement, "I was the only one who is marked by my gender, so my opinions may be viewed as women's opinions, whereas my colleagues' opinions appear ungendered" (Fontes, Piercy, Thomas & Sprenkle, 1998, p.316). Stories read and discussed by the group members created a shielded space for this politically charged topic to be discussed. It appears less threatening to first share one's views about the story characters and then share which story characters group members relate to. The members' creative energies are released as they share stories, food, laughter, tears, and anger. In other words, the extended community created in this group allows the group members to lighten the load. This is particularly important because struggles experienced by women are embedded in historical settings where democracy and wholeness of women are not valued.

The Parallel Story: Gender and Ecology

One book which was discussed in the dialogue group is Jane Smiley's *A Thousand Acres*. This book deals with a story of three sisters who were vying for a thousand acres of farmland in rural America. This land was poisoned physically and emotionally. It was a toxic waste dump site and a place where the psychological trauma of incest, rape, and abuse of women by family members was common. All the women who lived there had cancer. The total destruction of the land was interrelated to the total destruction of a woman's body. Yet the silence about the victimization of both women's bodies and the land, over the years, was what eventually tore the families apart in the end.

The silence was broken in the group when discussions between group members emerged. As group members dialogued about the experiences of the story characters, some took risks and shared the pain experienced among their own family members due to various types of abuse. Being able to discuss, without constraints, one's thoughts and feelings seemed very therapeutic for the group members. For example, one of the women talked about anger toward a relative who attempted to violate her daughter. Another woman shared her struggles of raising a child in very tough economic conditions with no support from others. Those women connected with each other by allowing themselves to honestly share their experiences, without worrying about having to meet expectations placed on them by male expectations of what it means to be a woman. It was at this meeting that the group experienced cohesion and sharing far beyond the focus of the story characters.

In addition, group members were able to identify hardships experienced as women, even though they came from many different cultural traditions. For example, one of the women with German background shared a story about struggles experienced by white, poor immigrants from the Midwest whose land was also used as dump sites for toxic waste. The Black Jamaican group member was surprised to hear stories of oppression experienced by “white folks.” One of the Jamaican group members summarized the dialogue by saying “ unless the silence is stopped--unless the violence against women’s and children’s bodies is stopped--we can not stop the abuse of the land.” The only man present in the group stated he was aware of the abuse of women and that it must be very hard to be a woman. He seemed to be listening to others, yet he was the silent member who refrained from interjecting ideas. As the dialogue about this book drew to a close, each of the group members became empowered in their knowledge not only though their connection as people but also through their interconnectedness to one another, easily transcending different cultural backgrounds. Thus, the sense of community building was experienced.

Social Issues

Issues of race, gender, and class intersect (Kliman, 1994; McGoldrick, Giordano,& Pearce, 1995). It is difficult to talk about issues of social class and not mention the struggles of women, ethnic minorities, and economically disadvantaged individuals. Social class speaks to struggles within institutions such as academia. Many women and minority members begin their career without “having experienced the advantages of rich graduate school mentoring experiences equivalent to those of their colleagues” (Gainen, 1993, p. 91). The added socioeconomic status stress contributes to the feeling of not belonging and isolation. The lack of resources and the stigma attached to obtaining resources creates an added barrier to connection. Within academic settings there exists a hierarchy of social class based on titles and positions. The hierarchy is evident in the use of first names of support staff and the use of titles for faculty and administrators. Names and titles contribute to the identity of power and self. The explicit and implicit group membership is created by having a separate category for the outsiders and insiders. This process is parallel to the societal norms of having separate settings of social interactions for the ones who “have” and the ones who “have not.” Thus, the walls which prevent human connections are maintained.

Diverse Relationships/Spiritual Beliefs: A Group Experience

> “Later he wondered if he was different, too, and asked his mother if he was black or white. ‘You are a human being, she snapped.’ And when James asked what color was God, she said, ‘God is the color of water.’” James McBride (1997).

As important as it is to openly address “obvious” diversities, it is equally important to convey respect for the not so obvious differences. Unlike the other books, *The Color of Water* by James McBride (1997) deals with two very important issues in our culture; 1) the dislocation of immigrants; 2) the intermarriage of two individuals coming from seemingly bi-polar groups: one Black and Baptist, the other White and Jewish. We as a society have not come to accept intercultural marriage, especially when the marriage is between white and black persons. Throughout the book, the protagonist experienced the isolation from both communities: the black and the white. In order to cope, she associated herself with the black community and raised her children similarly, despite the difficulties, in order to maintain their father's black heritage. The profound injury to this approach is that one cannot, as an interracial child, be deprived of the other culture because that too can lead to the dislocation of the human spirit. In a society that subjugates one on the basis of skin, how can parents of interracial unions prepare the child for a healthy life in the American society? The protagonist decided to cut her children off from the Jewish heritage as her relatives performed "shiva," mourning ritual associated with a death of a family member, as their critical response to her marriage.

The social and political ramifications as were discussed in the group centered on children of intercultural relationships. The society's relationship to these children was discussed in the educational context. Furthermore, the group members reflected on the meaning of interracial relationships in their own life. For example, one of the Jamaican women, despite having taught both culture and history courses, stated that she could not see herself in a relationship with a non Jamaican man. Her Polish friend, married to a Latino, challenged her on this point and asked can love transcend cultural boundaries--can we say that couples from the same cultural background experience love that others would not? A Jewish man who was present at the group shared his experiences of being married to an Italian American woman. Even though they both experienced tension from their families of origin, he stated he has not regretted it because of the strength of their relationship.

Reflecting on the stories of the book's characters, group members started to share their personal beliefs, fears and joys about relationships, marriage, and friendship. One of the black women, who attended this group, shared that not until she started to listen to others' experiences of joy and sadness, did she realized that she too expressed opposing views to biracial relationships although she did not consider herself to be racist. She stated that if she would hear that a white girl was not allowed to see a black boy, her family would be considered racist, but she did not realize she was doing the same by telling her son that his Asian friend is not welcome in their house.

One of the issues that came out of the discussion was the fear of losing one's own cultural identity. Most group members recognized that while hoping to be inclusive of others, they too have excluded others from their life. It was when they recognized how harmful this can be that the members started to rethink some of their beliefs. It was evidenced in the Jamaican woman saying that she no longer thinks she would reject someone because of their cultural difference and the African American woman who stated that she felt guilty about not accepting her sons's Asian girlfriend. In this effort of openness that is so painful to discuss, group members concluded this discussion with new insights into the pains and joys of intercultural relationships as well as the greater understanding of the offshoots of these relationships.

Community building groups are a microcosm of our society. The richness of the community building is provided by the equal exchange of ideas and equalitarian interactions. In the group process, individuals share the meaning they attach to stories read and focus on their personal experiences and feelings of joy, isolation, connection, pain, pride, and shame, and not the hierarchical experience. They move beyond the limits imposed by the hierarchy.

Community Redefined-Future Applications

Communities have been defined as (a) a group of people living in the same locality under the same government; (b) a social group or class; (c) similarity; (d) Society as a whole; the public (The American Heritage Dictionary). Lewis and Lewis (1989) defined community as a "system of interdependent persons, groups, and organizations that (a) meets the individual primary needs, (b) affects the individual's daily life, and (c) mediates between the individual and society as a whole" (p. 7). The Community Building Groups defined community as power, connections, integration of different people, and arena for discussion of socialization issues through literature and the development of a sense of self. The reading club defined itself as a community which guaranteed unconditional support of new ideas as well as opposing views. Participants disclosed personal information which helped other members reevaluate and create new, more open attitudes (Cohen, 1985). Norkunas (1987) defined those characteristics as customs and habits of the community. Participants in the reading community willingly shared and discussed ideas and perspectives which became the identifiable symbols of the community.

In response to the lack of community connectedness in our society, numerous communities are likely to benefit from such experiences. The business sector is starting to acknowledge dialogue groups' role in enhancing productivity and has started to implement dialogue groups. If we really believe that prisons are centers of rehabilitation for the inmates (most of whom have not experienced community bonding), then they would also benefit from such experiences, along with inner city communities where connectedness has been shattered by numerous risk factors.

A workplace and even a family group does not necessarily guarantee the opportunity for having a safe refuge where individuals can freely be who they are, where they can share what they feel. The diversity dialogue group creates such environment which in itself becomes the synergistic web where the experience of the whole is greater than the sum of the individuals working separately.

References

Angelou, M. (1986). *All God's children need traveling shoes*. New York: Vintage.

Ashraf, J. (1995). The effect of race on earnings in the United States. *Applied Economics Letters 2 72-75.*

Association for specialist in group work. (1991) *Professional standards for training of group work generalist and of group work specialists*. (Revised. Alexandria, VA author.)

Atkinson, D. R., Morten, G. & Sue, D. W. (1993). *Counseling American Minorities: A cross-cultural perspective* (4th ed). Dubuque, IA: Brown and Benchmark.

Bandura, A. (1977). *Social learning theory*. Englewood Cliffs, NJ: Prentice-Hall.

Bartlett, S. J. (1994). The psychology of faculty demoralization in liberal arts: Burnout, acedia, and the disintegration of idealism. *New Ideas in Psychology, 12*, 277-289.

Becvar, D. S. & Becvar, R. J. (1993). Storytelling and family therapy. *American Journal of Family Therapy, 21*, 145-160.

Bernard, J. & Goodyear, R. (1992). *Fundamentals of clinical supervision*. Boston: Allyn & Bacon.

Blumer, H. (1969). *Symbolic interactionism*. Englewood Cliffs, NJ: Prentice Hall

Bohm, D. (1985). *Unfolding Meaning*. London: ARK Paperbacks.

Bohm, D. (1990). *On Dialogue*. Ojai, CA: David Bohm Seminars.

Brice-Baker, J. (1994). West Indian Women: The Jamaican women. In L. Comas-Diaz & B. Green. (Eds.), *Women of color: Integrating ethnic and gender identities in psychotherapy* (pp. 139-160). New York: Guilford.

Cohen, A. P. (1985). *The symbolic construction of communication*. Chichester, UK: Ellis Horwood, Ltd.

Conroy, M. (1994). *Faded dreams: The politics and economics of race in America*. New York: Cambridge University Press.

Corey, G. (1995). *Theory and practice of group counseling* (4th ed.). Pacific Grove, CA: Brooks-Cole.

Conyne, R. K. and Wilson, F.R. (1997). *Comprehensive group work: What it is and how to teach it.* Alexandria, VA: American Counseling Association.

DeLucia, J., Coleman, B., and Jensen-Scott, R. (Eds.) (1992). Cultural diversity in group counseling: *Journal for Specialists in Group Work, 17*, 194-195.

DeLucia-Waack, J. L. (1996a). Multicultural group counseling - Addressing diversity to facilitate universality and self-understanding. In J. L. DeLucia-Waack (Ed.) *Multicultural counseling competencies: Implications for training and practice.* pp. 157-195. Alexandria, VA: American Counseling Association.

DeLucia-Waack, J. L. (1996b). Multiculturalism is inherent in all group work (Editorial). *Journal for Specialists in Group Work,21*, 218-223.

DeLucia-Waack, J. L. (1997). The importance of processing activities, exercises, and events to group work practitioners. *The Journal for Specialists in Group Work, 22.* 82-84.

Dewey, J. (1994). *Democracy and Education*. New York: Free Press.

Fontes, L.A., Piercy, F., Thomas, V., and Sprenkle, D. (1998). Self issues for family therapy educators. *Journal of Marital and Family Therapy, 24*, 305-320.

Gainen, J. (1993). A writing support program for junior women faculty. *New Directions for Teaching and Learning, 53*, 91-100.

Gaines, E. (1994). *A Lesson Before Dying*. Westminster, MD: Random House.

Gladding, S.T. (1999). *Group Work: A counseling specialty* (3rd ed.). Upper Saddle River, NJ: Merrill

Hawkins, K. J., & Catalano, R. F. (1992). *Communities that care: Action for drug abuse prevention.* San Francisco: Jossey-Bass Publishers.

Hayes, R. (1994). Counseling in the post-modern world: Origins and implications of a constructivist developmental approach. *Journal of Counseling and Human Development, 26.* 1-10.

Herek, G. M. (1986). The social psychology of homophobia: Toward a practical theory. *Review of Law and Social Change, 14*, 923-934.

Huang-Nissen, S. (1994). Learning about differences through the group process. *Association for Specialists in Group Work Conference Presentation*. Athens, GA.

Jacobs, E. E., Harvill, R. L., & Masson, R. L. (1994). *Group counseling: Strategies and skills*. (2nd ed.). Pacific Grove, CA: Brooks/Cole.

Johnson, I. H., Torres, J. S., Coleman, V. P., & Smith, M. C. (1995). Issues and strategies in leading culturally diverse counseling groups. *Journal for Specialists in Group Work.* 20. 143-150.

Kaufman, D. B. (1995). Professional Women: How real are the recent Gains?. In J. Freeman, *Women: A feminist perspective* (p.287-305). Mountainview, CA: Mayfield Publishing Co.

Kliman, J. (1994). The interweaving of gender, class, and race in family therapy. In M. P. Mirkin, (Eds). *Women in Context: Toward a feminist reconstruction of psychotherapy* (pp. 25-47). New York: Guilford.

Larson, P.C. (1982). Counseling special populations. *Professional Psychology, 13.* 843-858.

Lewis, J. A. & Lewis, M. D. (1989). *Community counseling*. Pacific Grove, CA: Brooks/ Cole Publishing Co.

Lieberman, M., Yalom, I. & Miles, M. (1973). *Encounter groups: First facts*. New York: Basic Books.

Lewin, K. (1994). The dynamics of group action. *Educational Leadership, 1.* 195-200.

McBride, J. (1997). *The color of water: A black man's tribute to his white mother*. New York: Riverhead Books.

McGoldrick, M., Giordano, J. & Pearce, J. K. (1995). *Ethnicity & family therapy* (2nd ed.). New York: Guildford.

Mead, G. H. (1934). *Mind, self, and society*. Chicago: University of Chicago Press.

Merta, R. J. (1995). Group work: Multicultural perspectives. In J. G. Pinterotto, J. M. Casas, L.A. Suzuki, & Alexander, C. M. (Eds.). *Handbook of Multicultural Counseling* (pp. 567-585). Thousand Oaks, CA: Sage.

Norkunas, J. K. (1987). Women, work and ethnic identity, personal narratives and the ethnic enclave in the textile city of Lowell, MA. *The Journal of Ethnic Study, 15*, 27-48.

Peck, M. S. (1998). *The road less traveled.* (2nd ed.). New York: Touchstone Books.

Santrock, J. W. (1997). *Life-span development* (6th ed.). Madison, WI: Brown and Benchmark.

Schnitzer, P. K. (1993). Tales of the absent father: Applying the "story" metaphor in family therapy. *Family Process, 32*, 441-458.

Sedney, M. A., Baker, J. E., & Gross, E. (1994). "The Story" of a death: Therapeutic considerations with bereaved families. *Journal of Marital and Family Therapy, 20*, 287-296.

Sharf, Richard, S. (1997). *Applying career development theory to counseling* (2nd ed.). Pacific Grove, CA: Brooks-Cole Publishers.

Smiley, J. (1992). *A thousand acres*. New York: Fawcett Books.

Sorcinelli, M. D. (1994). Effective approaches to new faculty development. *Journal of Counseling and Development*, *72*, 474-479.

Turpin, B. (1993/1994). Then she'll fly away. *Perspectives* (Winter), 77-79

Walker, Barbara. (1994, January/February). *Diversity 101: A guide to the multicultural experience.* Northridge, C. A. Wolfe & Company.

Wilson, F.D., Tienda, M., & Wu, L. (1995). Race and unemployment: Labor market experiences of black and white men, 1968 - 1988. *Work and Occupations 22*, 245-270.

Witkowski, K. M. & Leicht, K. T. (1995). The effects of gender segregation, labor force participation, and family roles in the earnings of young adult workers. *Work and Occupations. 22.* 48-72.

Wolfe, H. B., (1995). Women entering or reentering the workforce. In N.A. Vacc, S.B. DeVaney, & Wittmer, J. (Eds.). *Experiencing and counseling multicultural and diverse populations* (3rd ed., pp. 317-338). Bristol, PA: Taylor & Francis.

Wolfson, K., and Pearce, B. (1983, Summer). Implications of self disclosure on conservational logics. *Communication Quarterly*. pp. 249-256.

Yalom, I.D. (1995) *The theory and practice of group psychotherapy*. (4th ed.) New York: Basic Books.

Chapter Ten

INVOLVING THE ADDICTED CLIENT IN GROUP COUNSELING

Robert Chapman

INTRODUCTION

Addictive disorders may be one of the most pressing issues in professional counseling today. While this is primarily the personal observation of this author, the need to possess cursory knowledge regarding alcohol and other drug problems in counseling can be summarized by two significant realities faced by all professional counselors: 1) the preponderance of substance abuse issues in all clients presenting for counseling (Lawson, Lawson, & Rivers, 1996) and 2) the treatment challenges presented by the substance-abusing client which include resistance to change and the difficulty in committing to treatment create unique treatment problems for mental health professionals in any setting.

Efforts to address the problems of engaging substance abusing clients in treatment have been many over the years (White, 1998), but two in particular have shown great promise in the professional treatment of addictive disorders, group counseling and an appreciation for the process by which individuals change. When employed in tandem, the combination enables the practitioner to conceptualize the developmental stages of change found in substance abuse clients (Prochaska & DiClemente, & Norcross, 1992).

While all counselors have or will develop their own style of conducting groups with clients who have addictive disorders, the particular approach to delivering counseling or therapy plays an important role in the practitioner's ability to effectively reach members of the group. Specific group techniques can help create an environment that is energizing for counselors as well as therapeutic for clients. Since the hallmark of an addiction is the client's initial difficulty, if not inability, to recognize the symptoms of the disorder, effective group techniques are particularly important with this population. Inherent in the addiction process, clients learn to deflect the consequences of their substance abuse, often projecting onto others or situations external to themselves. This propensity to rationalize the result of the decision to drink/drug becomes a survival skill for the addicted individual lest she/he be forced to admit that the source of the recognized problems is a personal decision to engage in the pursuit of the addiction. The treatment of an addictive disorder in the context of a supportive group, composed of individuals who share common symptoms, provides the client with the opportunity to consider problems as resulting from the personal choice to use substances. Such an approach to counseling presents the therapist with a valuable tool to help the addicted client realize that change to one's life necessitates change in one's decisions about alcohol and other drugs (Lawson, Lawson, & Rivers 1996).

This chapter presents a number of easily employed techniques that can become part of an effective group counseling experience for clients diagnosed as having an addictive disorder. The strategies will be cross-referenced according to their ability to help clients contemplate the need to implement change in their lives using Prochaska and DiClemente's transtheoretical model (Prochaska & DiClemente, 1984; Prochaska, DiClemente, & Norcross, 1992). Specifically, each technique will be tied to one or more of the five specific stages of preparedness to change that an individual must pass through as outlined in the transtheoretical model, e.g., precontemplation, contemplation, preparation, action, and maintenance.

The suggestions proffered in this chapter fall into one of two broad group categories: 1) didactic or psycho-educational groups, and 2) counseling groups. As with the use of any technique, none of these suggestions should be employed without first carefully considering the objective of its use. Once a clinical objective for a client or group has been identified, an approach can be selected based on its likely positive impact in motivating the group to enter the next stage in the process of changing addictive behaviors.

Group Treatment of Addiction

For individuals unfamiliar with counseling, a group approach to treatment is apt to be viewed as little more than individual counseling done en masse or with an audience. While experienced professional counselors recognize this view as naïve and overly simplistic, it is easy to understand how individuals unfamiliar with professional counseling may assume that group counseling involves the same activities as individual counseling, only "done in a group." Knowing this, the counselor can increase the likelihood that group counseling will be a meaningful occurrence for an addicted client by designing the experience to create an environment in which clients can consider their own behavior in the context of a homogeneous group. By experiencing the dynamics of working on personal issues as a member of a group composed of individuals addressing similar problems, clients are presented with the opportunity to test self perceptions against the feedback from other individuals wise to the pitfalls of addiction.

The effectiveness of using groups in the education and treatment of addicted clients has been debated for some time. Group counseling allows the counselor to interact with multiple individuals simultaneously. It affords the opportunity for vicarious learning and modeling, which shapes individual member's behaviors, by presenting a "family-type" approach to problem solving (Yalom, 1995). Group settings provide the opportunity for individual members to receive feedback from multiple sources rather than just from the counselor as is the case in individual counseling. Consequently, group has become the standard approach for providing treatment to addicted clients (Doweiko, 1996; George, 1990).

Levy (1997) speaks of the advantages of group therapy with dually diagnosed clients. In particular, the social and interpersonal aspects of group counseling are outlined, with psychoeducational and therapeutic groups singled out as particularly effective in the professional treatment of clients in this population. Straussner (1997) echoes this argument, stating that group therapy is the treatment of choice for counselors working with alcohol or other drug abusing or dependent clients.

Group approaches to providing education about and treatment for addictive disorders are the preferred approach of treating individuals with addictive disorders (Doweiko, 1996; George, 1990). However, this preference does not seem to be supported by outcome studies (Holder, Longabaugh, Miller, & Rubonis, 1991). So what options are available to the counselor to increase the likelihood of successful group work with addicted clients? It seems logical that if individuals pass through recognizable stages of change (Prochaska, DiClemente, & Norcross, 1992) then targeting clients in particular stages with effective stage-specific therapeutic interventions proven to be effective in that stage of change, would increase the likelihood of moving a client to the next stage. By repeating this process, i.e., recognizing that change occurs in stages, identifying a client's readiness to change, and using techniques proven to be effective in that stage, it stands to reason that group treatment will be more effective.

Prochaska & DiClemente (1984) suggest that individuals are often unable to recognize the need to change their personal behavior because they are blind to the indications that their behavior is in need of change. They refer to this as one stage in a series of five that represents the process by which individuals make change in their lives. Thus, the first stage is called "precontemplation" because it even predates an awareness, of any indication, that problems in an individual's life might be related to a personal pattern of behavior (cf. Prochaska, DiClemente, & Norcross, 1992).

Most counselors who work with addicted clients and their families encounter this pre-awareness of a problem as resistance to "seeing" the problem as their own. Labeling this as denial and approaching it as something that must be confronted and broken down rather than viewed as a recognizable stage in the process of change, enters the counselor and client into an adversarial relationship where one party's success occurs at the expense of the other's failure. Historically, individual or group treatment of addictions has been predicated on this need to eliminate the client's denial of the problem before treatment can begin. To accomplish this, a very direct and all too often aggressive approach to confrontation has been the addiction counselor's treatment approach of choice (Miller, Genefield, & Tonigan, 1993).

While it is true that the other clients in a group can offer the confronted individual the support necessary to process the confrontation being mounted by the counselor, it is equally true that the others in the group will model the counselor's confrontational style. This combative approach to counseling generally results in the confronted client assuming either a stance of compliance or internalization (Kelman, 1971). In compliance, the client says what is expected and mouths the words, but this results from the client's acceptance of the counselor's and the group's position of authority and power more than an acceptance of the client's specific problem. When internalization is the assumed posture, the client realizes a more genuine acceptance of the existence of a problem, or at least the possibility that a problem exists. This is what Prochaska & DiClemente (1984) refer to as contemplation or the second stage of change.

This chapter is designed to offer specific group techniques or strategies that can be employed in counseling with addicted clients who have historically been viewed as "in denial" of their problems with alcohol or other drugs. Clients exposed to these techniques while in the "precontemplative, contemplative, or preparatory" stages of change will likely be more effectively engaged in the group counseling process. Consequently, the use of these techniques will enable clients to increase the likelihood of moving from a current stage of preparedness to change to the next stage in the Prochaska & DiClemente (1984) hierarchy of change.

Two distinct types of group strategies will now be presented; didactic or psychoeducational techniques and counseling or applied techniques.

DIDACTIC AND PSYCHOEDUCATIONAL GROUP TECHNIQUES

In their consideration of how individuals make changes in their behavior, Prochaska, DiClemente, & Norcross (1992) suggest that consciousness raising and awareness-type interventions are particularly effective when counseling individuals in a precontemplative or contemplative stage of change. The direct and educational nature of didactic of the psychoeducational groups is one approach to accomplish the objective of increasing awareness about a particular problem or issue. These groups can be used for either prearranged instruction of important concepts associated with recognizing an addiction or as an educational component of the traditional counseling group. In either case, the ultimate objective of the group is to impart information and to do so in such a way as to supplant the misinformation individual members of the group may hold. This often has the result of helping individual group members better understand addiction in general and contemplate their personal need for treatment. This change from rigid denial of a personal addiction (precontemplation) to accepting that a disorder may exist (contemplation), can be facilitated by the group's pursuit of accurate information. In addition, these techniques are useful in enhancing a sense of self-efficacy in individual group members while at the same time enabling the group to see itself as an effective agent of change in the pursuit of specific treatment goals for the group.

When conducting such a group, experiential activities and/or humor can be highly effective ways of inviting clients to substitute the new information for old myths. The following represent two examples of techniques that can be used within a psycho-educational modality to facilitate movement from the pre-contemplative to the contemplative stage.

Client Generated Definitions

A classic example of correcting client "misinformation" can be seen in this simple group technique. Let's assume that it is the counselor's intent to confront the common belief of those new to alcoholism treatment that the term "sobriety," as used in addictions treatment and 12-step oriented self-help groups, simply refers to a blood alcohol level below the legal limit of intoxication. This particular group technique is designed to involve the entire group in the educational process of accurately identifying a more comprehensive, and therefore more precise, definition of the term. Clients are allowed to discover the more comprehensive meaning of the term or concept rather than simply have it presented to them as fact.

The addiction counselor introduces the exercise as a group "Think Tank". Individual members of the group are invited to collaborate on forming a comprehensive definition of the word "sobriety." In the process, they will also develop an action plan to achieve sobriety and review the possible benefits to be derived from sobriety. A blackboard or large pad and easel are required to record individual responses. The counselor entitles the discussion "Sobriety" and then solicits five to seven one-word or short phrase synonyms for sobriety. These synonyms, e.g., 'abstinence,' 'peace of mind,' 'honesty,' 'responsibility,' are then placed on a chalk board or large piece of newsprint under the title in horizontal fashion as headings for columns.

Next the counselor solicits specific steps that can be taken to accomplish/demonstrate that particular heading. For example, listed under 'abstinence' might be, "don't drink and go to meetings," "avoid drinking/drugging places," "take a new way home from work," etc. For 'peace of mind,' examples might include "morning meditations," "find and talk with a sponsor," "keep a journal of daily accomplishments," or "do an anonymous good deed each day." This is then done for each of the remaining segments of the definition in turn. Of particular importance is the verbatim recording of the suggestions. This becomes important as the compilation of group suggestions will become a final plan for pursuing sobriety. The suggestions as they exist on the blackboard serve as proof that the group already has an idea of what to do to get sober. The group can now work on identifying the support needed to follow through with the suggestions and a framework for accomplishing the goals.

After defining sobriety and recording behavioral steps to realize each part of the definition, it then becomes important to identify indications of success. In other words, how will the individuals know they are getting sober? For example: Evidence of abstinence might include, "not drinking/using," "willing to talk about wanting to drink/use," or "changes in personal schedule to avoid use". For peace of mind, "smiling," "sharing positive thinking," or "feeling human". It is important to record any reasonable suggestion or activity mentioned by a member of the group. Should a client proffer an unreasonable comment, a response intended simply to disrupt the group or intended to allow the client to show off, find some redeeming quality, however slight, in the comment and thank the client for the contribution. The significance of recording all client comments on the board, even if requiring the counselor's efforts as a "spin doctor", will become evident when the result of this exercise is outlined at its end.

The final aspect of this technique is to draw the apparently disparate sections of the exercise together by asking the group to identify specific and tangible rewards or incentives that are likely to result from attempting the suggested steps to becoming sober. To suggest that few individuals, if any, are likely to do something difficult and/or uncomfortable, at least in the beginning, if they can see no reward in the change, provides a nice segue to inviting the group to brainstorm the rewards of sobriety. If the group does not include such benefits as financial solvency, sexual satisfaction and performance, or physical well being, then it is suggested that the counselor suggest these as well.

This exercise takes about 45-60 minutes, depending on the detail sought, and can be used with other addictions related terms besides sobriety, e.g., recovery, serenity, Higher Power, etc. The key to this exercise's success is its ability to challenge members of the group to explore some aspect of addiction without feeling as if they are being confronted. This increases the likelihood that clients will recognize the product of this group as "their" work, further inviting them to contemplate behavioral change as an objective that is in their best interest to pursue. The utility of this exercise can be seen in its ability to involve the group in a collaborative effort to increase awareness of the need to change. This collaborative effort is demonstrated, in part, in several ways including 1) all suggestions come from the group. This allows the counselor to congratulate the group for its communal work as well as demonstrate the extent to which the group is already on its way to realizing the identified objectives of counseling; 2) The group is encouraged to adopt an internal rather than external locus of control regarding the identified topic. This furthers the groups sense of cohesiveness by empowering its individual members with a sense of self-efficacy, and; 3) client's are provided with a practical demonstration that individual hard work does result in positive pay-off.

The Cultural Researcher

Another group technique that can increase awareness about issues related to addictive disorders, especially their impact on family and significant others, is the "Cultural Researcher" group. This technique, adapted from the cross-cultural counseling training exercise, "Outside Expert" developed by Pedersen (1994), enables clients to better understand the concepts of their addiction as seen through the eyes of family and friends. Participants are presented with the opportunity to witness how one's own attitudes, values, and beliefs can represent a very distinct set of lenses through which to view the world. This individual "world view" can have significant impact on interpersonal interactions. Not realizing that the family has remained essentially unchanged while the client has been in treatment, the client will expect to return home and find the same insight and understanding about addictive disorders displayed during treatment. Clients often fail to realize that their increased understanding and acceptance of a personal addictive disorder does not automatically translate into a similar degree of familial understanding and forgiveness for past aberrant behaviors. Consequently, clients are often surprised when their declaration that they are "changed people" is greeted with suspicion, if not outright contempt, by family and friends who see the same person returning who entered treatment earlier.

In this group, clients are provided with the opportunity to explore how the specific attitudes, values, and beliefs of significant others can lead to biases and skew one's perceptions of reality. The "cultural researcher group" is an experiential group designed to help addicted individuals appreciate the subtle but significant role stereotypes play in the way others conceptualize reality. This is a particularly useful group for preparing clients for the family's all to often continued resentment of or continued lack of trust in the newly recovering individual. If unprepared for such familial reactions upon returning from treatment, clients may begin to question the utility of the recovery process and become vulnerable to relapse. Consequently, therapeutic interventions such as groups that focus on awareness and consciousness raising have been found to be useful in facilitation movement from a precontemplative stage of readiness to change to a contemplative if not preparatory stage (Prochaska, DiClemente, & Norcross, 1992).

To employ this technique with a group, request the assistance of four to six volunteers. Assure the group that no one will be placed at risk of harm and announce that volunteers have the tendency to learn just a bit more from the experience than the rest of the group. If this group of volunteers is not diverse by gender (all male or all female), internally note something that denotes diversity within the group - some wear glasses, some do not; some are wearing earrings, some are not; some have facial hair, some do not. Ask this small group of volunteers to leave the room and wait for you in an area where they will not be able to hear what you say to the rest of the group.

Once the "researchers" have left the group room, inform the remainder that they represent a heretofore-undiscovered tribe of people and you are getting ready to study their culture. In preparation, you have asked the "cultural researchers" to come and do some preliminary investigations by asking "yes/no" question of them. As these clients represent a very simple culture, there are but three rules in the entire culture 1) men only talk to men - or glasses to glasses, etc.; 2) women only talk to women - or earrings to earrings, etc., and; 3) no matter the true answer to the yes/no question asked, if the person asking is smiling it means a "yes" is the desired answer and they are to respond accordingly. Likewise, if the "researcher" is frowning or has neutral facial expression, a "no" is the expected answer, and the tribal member accommodates.

Then leave the group and join the "researchers" outside the group room in order to instruct them regarding their task. Inform them of their task, but do not say anything about the three rules of the culture they are investigating. Tell them they will have ten minutes to ask "yes/no" questions in order to make a preliminary report to you about these people and their culture. Recommend they work independently in order to poll more individuals in the culture, but let them decide whether to work as teams or not (a dual gender team can make for an interesting experience and results). Lead the research team back into the room and allow them to begin their task.

After ten minutes, thank the researchers and then give them two to three minutes to compare notes outside the group room. While the researchers are conferring outside the group, process with the tribe the experience of having been interviewed and having to abide by the rules of the culture. Almost always, the group will talk about "feeling uncomfortable" or "being frustrated and confused about how to act." This becomes a convenient opportunity to invite the group to think about how this has happened in their lives or to put themselves in the position of their families when having to read a client's mood or degree of intoxication.

When the researchers have had time to consult with each other, invite them back into the group room. Interview the research team about 1) the facts they learned. Note that these facts will vary from group to group as you do this over time, and rarely serve a useful purpose in the exercise, other than the frequent laughter that erupts in the group as the facts are recorded on a blackboard or newsprint. 2) Ask the research team for its collective recommendations about what to expect/how to behave when interacting with members of this culture.

Invariably, the subjective recommendations of those on the research team will be steeped in their individual value judgments about the culture. These recommendations are taken from the facts individual researchers have teased out of the "culture" and then processed as a group when conferring after the data collection phase of the exercise. Make sure you record these facts and recommendations on a blackboard or newsprint pad so the whole group can see. Dismiss the research team and then begin to turn to the board. Interrupting yourself, apologize to the team for having neglected to share some preparatory information with them, but assure them it could not possibly have influenced their powers of observation and interpretation. Then inform them of the three rules of the culture. This always results in chuckles and "oh yeahs…" from the researchers as they rejoin the group.

Now, turn the group's attention to the board containing the facts and recorded recommendations. Dismiss the facts as unimportant to the exercise by explaining that these will always be different and that they change with different groups of researchers and tribes. Then direct the group's attention to the recommendations offered by the researchers and based on the facts they collected. Often, the recommendations include statements like, "You can't trust these people…" or "you might as well not even bother trying to understand these people ..." As you review each recommendation proffered by the researchers, ask the entire group if what they are reading/hearing is similar to what family and friends have said/done with regards to them or other addicted individuals. This will often open the door to discussions of not being trusted or expected to always lie when asked about a situation. From this point, it is relatively easy for the counselor to direct the group's attention to the question of familial expectations of the client when s/he returns home. The group will usually come to the realization on its own that because an individual with an addictive disorder has received treatment and accepted the need to change, family and significant others are not going to automatically know that the individual has changed. This can also become an excellent point for the counselor to mention the importance of family members participating in their own course of treatment, or perhaps introducing the importance of viewing the family as a client (Lawson, Lawson, & Rivers, 1996) and recommending family therapy.

The counseling as well as the pedagogical point of this group exercise is to create an opportunity for the clients to experience how judgments based on incomplete or erroneous facts can result in myth and stereotype. The stage is then set for the counselor to invite clients to consider how such attribution errors result in discriminatory and condescending behavior. This exercise works very well in preparing clients for the resistance of families to change or reject the invitation to participate in treatment. As stated earlier, such an experience is helpful in raising client awareness of the problems associated with their addictions. This increased awareness, in turn, increases the client's preparedness to address change as a reasonable objective (Prochaska et al, 1992) and serves to inoculate the client against relapse.

COUNSELING GROUPS: INTRODUCTIONS

If the groups outlined above are intended to educate clients, what follow are techniques designed to stimulate group discussion and facilitate openness. Different groups will present with their own distinct personalities. One problem counselors may encounter when conducting groups with addictive disordered individuals is the unresponsive or so called resistant group. Usually indicative of clients in a precontemplative stage of change, the following techniques are designed to present the group with stimuli to which individual members can react, thereby opening the group by circumventing obstacles that preclude participation.

The Bottle Gang

Before group, plant a beer bottle or some other specific drug-related paraphernalia, in a paper bag, in the site where the group will be conducted, e.g., wine bottle if appropriate, or bong, crack pipe, etc. Place the bag under your chair or some less conspicuous spot in the group room. After your routine opening activities, and only if there are no spontaneous opening comments by clients (none of the techniques in this chapter should be used to stifle a group's spontaneity), introduce the concept of cues and their ability to trigger cravings. As this technique results in a rather intense group experience, it requires that the counselor adequately prepare the group. This should include, but is not limited to, informing the clients that you intend to expose them to certain drug paraphernalia, which can trigger strong reactions, and talking about how they react to these stimuli is the purpose of the group. It is advised that this technique only be used with in-patient groups in order to assure adequate time to process the experiences this groups is likely to generate. Depending on the nature of the program in which this group is conducted, e.g., minimum security where individuals can easily "walk off" the premises, it may be advisable to obtain a consent to participate in the group. The consent itself can underscore the power of the symbols of addiction that paraphernalia represent and set the stage for this group experience.

As you conclude your introductory comments, reach under your chair and retrieve the paper bag. Mention how first impressions and former people, places, and things can trigger the craving to use. While mentioning that this experience is normal and to be expected, (Beck, 1993), remove the prop from the bag and pass it, or if the group's size and room layout permits, 'toss it' to someone in the group who you have pre-selected as a likely candidate to experience this phenomenon. Ask this client to comment on the first thing that comes to mind upon touching the prop (the more that can be done to make the prop real, the better, e.g., if a beer bottle, make sure the bottle has been chilled). Next, ask the group to follow-up with questions for this client. Typical client responses include statements like, "Man, that feels like it fits like a glove'" or "That's not what I drank, but it still feels good in my hand." It is not uncommon for the client to smell the mock "joint" made from oregano or the open baggie with ordinary lose green tea as a reflex action. These reactions to the unexpected prop often generate interesting comments about cues and their power to stimulate cravings. This, in turn, opens the group to discussion of cues they have experienced in the past and how those cues initiated binges or relapse. When the discussion reaches a point of closure, have the individual with the prop pass it on with the same instruction for the new recipient to comment on what thoughts come to mind or what feelings are experienced. Each member of the group does not have to receive the prop and comment for this group to be effective. As a matter of fact, the prop will usually lose its ability to prompt spontaneous and revealing comments shortly after the first client or two has received it. This is not a problem as this particular technique is designed to be an introduction to group process and get the group focused on the threat cues and triggers will represent in their recovery.

It should be noted that if this technique is used with an outpatient group, the counselor should be certain to adequately debrief the group regarding the experience. This is a particularly powerful group and can trigger many different client reactions. It is useful to close this group by having individual members review personal approaches to proactively using the period of time between the onset of craving and giving in to an urge to use (Beck, 1993). Such steps can include each member of the group mentioning a specific behavioral response to encountering a cue. Another effective closing when this technique is employed is to have the group make a verbal contract to keep a personal journal to record specific cues or triggers. This contract should include the understanding that this experience will be shared in the next group. Sharing the experience of having a craving to use, set-off by a specific cue, can enhance the client's sense of self-efficacy while demonstrating trust in the group. Employing an automatic thought record to record one's reaction to the cue can be an effective counter measure and provide a specific account of the experience for discussion when the next group meets.

The Grab Bag

Bring a paper bag with words/phrases related to addiction hand-written on slips of paper. These can be designed to probe a specific issue the counselor wishes to address in group. For example, slips with words or phrases like, "one day at a time," "easy does it," and "first things first" can generate discussion about 12-step meetings and the significance of self-help groups as an adjunct to therapy. Terms like, "risk taking," "letting go," "friendship," and "willingness to share" can direct the group's focus to issues of trust. It is easy to recognize that this particular technique presents limitless opportunities for the counselor to break the ice and create the potential for group discussion.

Make sure there is at least one slip for each member of the group. Inform the group that difficulty deciphering your handwriting can be expected and invite members to ask for help reading your writing. This announcement provides protection for those in the group who may be illiterate if such has not yet been shared with the group. Once the slip is read, ask the individual who made the selection to talk about what the word or phrase means and how it relates addiction, from a personal perspective. Once completed, have the individual pass the slip on to someone in the group. Rarely does this exercise result in all members of the group drawing from the grab-bag as discussion is stimulated by comments made in response to the first few selected items. Individuals will tend to pass the slip on to someone they either respect and look up to or someone they believe is less than serious or in a very early stage of change, e.g., precontemplative or contemplative. As this happens, it becomes easier for the counselor to segue the group into a discussion of personal perspectives of recovery or obstacles that preclude growth.

For example, Michael retrieves a slip of paper on which is printed, "honesty." He is asked to comment and says, "This is a tough one for me. Whenever I have been honest in the past, something terrible has always happened. Like just before I came to treatment, my girlfriend asked me if I wanted her to come see me while I was here. I told her I was afraid if she did, I would be tempted to leave so I wanted her to not visit for at least the first week. Well, she accused me of not caring about her and asked if I was gonna try and get rid of her and all kinda talk like that. It would have been better if I had just said nothing or told her to do what she wanted."

This remark might result in any number of comments from members of the group, but whatever follows Michael's disclosure, it can be assured that there will be material to be mined by the counselors. When it was time for the next person to comment, Michael might pass the slip with "honesty" on it to Raoul, his roommate, knowing that Raoul has been wrestling with a similar issue or perhaps that he has been "dis"honest with the group. However Michael chooses to discharge his obligation to pass the slip along, it is all but certain that the group will be presented with appropriate issues to consider as a counseling group.

Name that Tune

Create a specific audiocassette or bring pre-selected audio tapes or compact discs with songs having lyrics that relate to sobriety or some emotion/experience likely to be encountered by the addicted individual in treatment or recovery. After each song, stop the recording and ask the group for whom in the group the song was specifically written. When someone responds, either indicating him-/herself or a specific member of the group, ask why and then ask for group comment. This will often result in a discussion of emotions and opens the door for sharing as others either relate to the lyrics or the specific comments made by other members of the group. While the Country and Western genre of music is particularly rife with references to addictive disorders, most forms of music can provide ample songs to facilitate good discussion. As with other suggestions thus far, rarely will the counselor use all the recordings brought to group and should not feel obligated to do so. Examples of songs the author has used include, from the Country and Western genre, Larry Gatlin's "Prince Valium and the Daytime Heros," from pop music, Billy Joel's "Captain Jack," and from acoustic, David Wilcox's "Strong Chemistry." Again, there are literally thousands of lyrics that can present the group with opportunities to reflect on the progress they or a peer are making in treatment.

This technique stands to accomplish two results in addition to its goal of initiating discussion in a group. First, using elements of the popular culture as a vehicle for clinical work allows the clients to recognize the therapeutic potential of activities previously thought to be exclusively entertainment. In recognizing the therapeutic potential of employing music in a counseling group, it is just as important to consider the potential for films, literature, television or other forms of popular culture as well. These can be just as easily employed to accomplish the same end, essentially enabling the client to revisit themes raised in counseling on a regular basis outside a traditional therapeutic setting. A second potential benefit of this technique is its ability to reach individuals who are at a precontemplative/contemplative stage of change. While some clients with addictive disorders may be able to deny the logic presented in a more didactic presentation, using this technique presents the counselor with a somewhat unexpected vehicle for bringing one's addiction to consciousness. Whether moving a client from a position of denial of the appropriateness of change to a readiness to engage in treatment through traditional therapeutic techniques or recognizing the indirect potential of the popular culture to facilitate a similar insight, the result is the same; the client becomes more accepting of the importance of change.

Counseling Groups: Sharing or Bonding

This classification of technique is intended to assist the counselor in developing a sense of respect and cohesiveness between individual members of the group. While cohesion is a frequent result of the process of group counseling, it cannot be assumed that this will automatically occur simply because the group has met on a number of occasions.

These techniques are suggested as possible ways to facilitate a group's realization of the importance of each of its individual members and vice versa.

These groups are particularly effective when clients are motivated to change. Once clients have reached the action stage in their progression through Prochaska and DiClemente (1984) model of change and are prepared to act on their addictive disorders, they are ready to address the mitigating personal issues they believe have either excused their addicted behavior or caused it. When this work is to be pursued in the context of a counseling group, a necessary prerequisite of client growth is the willingness to interact with peers in the group. The techniques outlined in this section are designed to foster individual sharing in such a therapeutic setting and facilitate the bonding between members that is a prerequisite of the trust that permits self-disclosure and the acceptance of help from other recovering addicts.

The Golden Doorstop Award

This simple technique reinforces individual group members for their work during a particular period of time. Utilizing the power of symbols or allegory, a triangular doorstop is made from a simple piece of wood. The doorstop is then painted gold, representing an icon that is then awarded to a particular client in recognition for work completed in-group. Examples of such group accomplishments may include spontaneous self-disclosure in the group by a client who has been quiet, guarded, and withdrawn; an individual who shares a particularly traumatic experience that has been an excuse to drink or drug for years; or the client who has previously been overly talkative in the group, but has not been genuine in sharing. This last individual's willingness to listen and accept the comments and feedback from peers may mark a monumental change in attitude and perceived role in the group.

On a regular basis, weekly for inpatient or intensive outpatient groups, monthly for traditional outpatient groups, have the group nominate and vote on who has "opened the door the farthest," that is, demonstrated a serious investment in the therapeutic process of the group in the last week/month. If there is a unanimous nomination, this individual is then awarded the golden doorstop, recognizing previous achievement and symbolizing the need to "keep the door open" and foster continued participation. If two members of the group receive the majority of the votes, the award can be shared. If shared, the member with the most votes receives the award for the first part of the week/month, the other for the second. The initials of the recipient(s) and the award date are inscribed on the doorstop. Once the doorstop becomes covered with the initials of recipients, it can be "retired" and placed in a position of prominence in the group room or other public area of the treatment center for all to appreciate. This will add a sense of history to the group/treatment center and create a powerful ritual, fostering the efficacy of the group experience. It is surprising how fast the doorstop becomes both a coveted award and powerful incentive for people to participate and share in group.

Award recipients commonly respond tearfully. For such clients, it has been a very long time since they were recognized for their commitment to others and reinforced for sharing themselves, especially when to do so required that they make themselves vulnerable. Client comments range from the expected, "I don't know what to say...nobody has ever listened to me before like you guys," to the more revealing, "I've only ever been beaten or made fun of when I would talk about my feelings and you people tell me I'm doing good." Counselors should not use this technique if they are not prepared to allow themselves to share in the emotion that is frequently displayed in this group. It is also important not to over "therapize" the experience by processing the experience with the recipient or the group. While this technique can be used as a closing exercise at the end of a regular group or a free-standing group, the counselor needs to let the group end when the award has been accepted and the recipient has thanked the group, however short the group may have been. To move on to new business or other issues will tend to stifle the experience for all members of the group.

Gift Giving

This is another technique that can be used when the group is at the "action" stage of change (Prochaska, DiClemente, & Norcross, 1992) and members are committed to the process of working together. The counselor can use this technique to demonstrate the depth of commitment members share. A powerful group experience for such committed clients is to involve them in a "gift giving group." In this particular group, instruct all members of the group to return to their room, if in an inpatient treatment facility - outpatient group members can be instructed to bring a gift with them to the next group - something personal to give away in group. Clients should be told that this is a real gift and will be given away "for keeps," becoming the property of the individual in the group to whom it is given. Inform members that the gift can be something symbolic if they wish. For inpatient groups, it is recommended that the members not be given too much time to consider the directive, about five to ten minutes at best. For this reason, this group may not be particularly effective if clients have several days between group sessions to intellectualize their charge.

Once the clients return to group, someone is asked to begin the sharing. This is introduced by re-explaining to clients that each member of the group is to explain why s/he chose the particular gift selected, including an explanation of its personal meaning and significance. Once the gift has been explained and its significance outlined, the individual is instructed to give it to another group member, explaining why that particular person was chosen. This is another group that tends to produce lots of emotion and occasionally resentment on the part of those who receive no gifts. Even resentment, however, becomes grist for the counseling mill as processing how it feels to be unrecognized or reviewing the process used by gift-givers when selecting their recipients tends to foster bonding and growth.

Clients who receive no gifts, especially if they see themselves as "ideal" clients or "junior-counselors," tend to sulk, perhaps even withdraw from the group. It is important for the counselor to engage these clients and process what they are thinking/feeling. Just as it is an empowering experience to learn that one is a valued member of the group and to hear one's peers explain the rationale for proffering their gift(s), it is an equally powerful experience for the disingenuous client to receive feedback regarding her/his group behavior as well.

This exercise yields insight into the depth of a client's commitment to the group and, consequently, the degree of personal growth. Likewise, it is rewarding for the counselor to experience the range of client creativity and capacity to emote that this exercise can generate. Again, it is recommended that this exercise be used to move an already committed group to the next level of commitment. Likewise, it is NOT recommended that this exercise be attempted with a group of uncommitted clients or with individuals resistant to the process of counseling in general or group counseling specifically. To do so would invite an opportunity for such clients to sabotage the group in order to demonstrate resistance or undermine the authority or credibility of the counselor.

COUNSELING GROUPS: FEEDBACK

Based on the premise that awareness of a particular behavior is a prerequisite to even contemplating the need to change the behavior (Prochaska, DiClemente, & Norcross, 1992), these exercises are designed to confront clients with the reality of their personal situation. By receiving feedback on specific defense mechanisms or examples of resistance to treatment, addicted clients are presented with the opportunity to confront those personal characteristics that insulate them from the rest of the group and its proactive behaviors. This is particularly helpful when treating clients with addictive disorders (Doweiko, 1996; George, 1990). Often clients must not only change their drug consuming habits in order to successfully address an addiction, but must also change, to quote an oft used slogan in twelve-step programs, "the people they associate with, places they go, and things they do."

The Hot Seat

This technique is designed to place each member of the group in the position of delivering as well as receiving feedback. Too frequently, clients are unfamiliar with providing assertive feedback, opting instead to say nothing (while continuing to hold a resentment) or assume an aggressive "in-your-face" approach to confrontation. This exercise is designed to demonstrate how caring and specific feedback can be useful in affecting an individual's process of change.

Place a swivel chair in the center of group. Inform the group that each member will take a turn in the hot seat, including the group leader. The individual in the chair simply sits and listens, receiving feedback from the individual members of the group. Use of this technique by a counselor unwilling to sit in the hot seat will only serve to distance the counselor from the group and hinder the process of bonding with the group and sharing.

There are a few simple rules for this group: 1) Everyone is offered the opportunity to sit in the chair; 2) everyone must provide feedback; 3) feedback must include one positive statement about the individual's role in the group/treatment that indicates commitment to growth/change and one comment on an aspect of the individual's behavior that retards or prohibits growth; 4) the individual on the hot seat must swivel to face the person providing the feedback and *MAY NOT* respond. If someone refuses to participate in the group, the client can be offered the opportunity to skip her/his turn. When the last client has taken a place in the hot seat, the individual who refused to participate earlier is asked to take a place in the hot seat. Having seen how the feedback has been delivered and received by group members, resistant clients will usually accept the invitation to participate. If the client still refuses, this can be explored with the client in a one-on-one session later in the day.

This group tends to be long, perhaps as much as ten minutes per group member. A variation of this group is the "life story" group. In this technique, individuals will share their life story with the group and receive feedback according to similar guidelines mentioned above. It is usually a good idea to schedule a client's life story early in treatment, but not immediately upon admission to the group. The opportunity to sit through a peer's life story before delivering one's own, can be quite helpful because the expected behavior is modeled and because seeing the process often reduces anxiety about the process.

Dear Al

For individuals in a group who are certain that they will never drink/use again and/or are unaware of how difficult sobriety can be, have the over confident member write a letter to his/her addiction and name the addiction "Al," short for Al K. Hall - or Mary for Mary J. Wanna, or Harry for Harry O'Winn, etc. In this letter, have the member tell Al about what he has done to disrupt the client's life and how the client feels about that. Also, have the individual spell out the steps to be taken to never again use.

What follows is a sample letter presented to illustrate this technique:

Dear Al,

I have been asked by Robert to write you a letter, explaining how I feel about you and what you have done to me over the years. I must admit that, at first, I thought this was a silly suggestion. But as I thought about the assignment and, more specifically about you and what you have done to me, I began to look forward to this letter.

I have been learning that I am not a bad person - I am not a loser as you have tried to tell me for so many years. Ever since I first met you when I was 16, you have told me I was not good enough, not strong enough, to change my life. You told me that you would be my ONLY friend and that anyone who tried to get close to me was a fake and only interested in getting something for themselves and would use me in what ever way he or she could to get what they wanted.

But I am learning now that you have never cared for me. Your only interest in `being my friend' was so that you could use and control me. You played on my fears and only cared that I would turn to you for comfort.

Each time I would come to you, you would promise me that it would be OK that I would not have to worry about the problems in my life. But then you would take me to places and introduce me to people and have me do things that only embarrassed me and robbed what little self-respect I had left.

You are a liar and a cheat and the most deceitful being I have ever encountered. You promise strength, but have only delivered humiliating weakness. You promised peace and calm, but have only cast me headfirst into a turbulent sea that has pulled me under and snuffed the life from my soul. You promised to always be there for me, but every time I agreed to go with you, you would abandon me to deal with the horror you would create.

I know now that I am no match for you. The fight is over and you are the stronger. But while you are stronger than I am, you have not won. I know your powers and I know that you do not care for me. I know that I must avoid your charms and the temptation you bring to me each time I hear your name, or see your face, or smell your scent.

I have listened to and followed you for too long. Get out of my life and leave me alone. I no longer need you as I have found a new way to give my life meaning.

I resent you, I fear you, I hate you, but most of all I accept you as the curse of my life. So be gone, fore I have no more use for you or your empty promises. You are the bane of my existence and source of all my pain. Go back to hell from whence you came, fore I need you no longer!

Emphatically yours,

This is a particularly good assignment to use with an individual who the counselor treats in both individual and group counseling. Next, the individual is asked to read the letter aloud to the group. When finished, the individual will often be beaming as if to say, "I told him off, didn't I!" After reading the letter the members are asked to provide feedback regarding the letter. More often than not, group members respond positively and supportively, thereby fueling the individual's grandiosity and belief in triumph over the addiction.

Now, ask the individual to read the letter again. But this time, before the client begins, bring your chair up directly in front of the individual, knee to knee if possible, and then sit on the back of the chair or in some fashion so as to be above and looking down on the individual. Announce that you are going to role-play Al and then have the individual begin reading.

As the letter is being read a second time, interrupt, often and obnoxiously, with snide comments to the rest of the group about how you "love to hear such tripe" because it only serves to set the person up for a slip. Within reason, use information about the individual's life and background, especially information shared in the group, to challenge the reader's likelihood of maintaining sobriety. In short, make this a difficult experience for the reader.

Once the letter has been read, sit back down in your chair, and return it to the circle, and in your best counselor's empathetic tone, which signals you are no longer Al, ask the reader about feelings or reactions to the role play. Frequently, the client is surprised if not angry as a result of the number and intensity of the rejoinders presented by Al. Be this as it may, the client is no longer as confident and this shows in both demeanor and comments.

If the group did not attempt to interfere with your heckling of the reader, which they probably did not, chastise them sternly. Ask them if they could tell the reader was frustrated or in trouble. If they say yes, ask why they didn't do something to help. Remind them that group is designed to be both a sharing and supportive experience and each member must be prepared to come to the aid of another, often, and frequently without invitation.

Now ask the reader to read the letter to the group a third time. Place your chair knee-to-knee and again assume the role of Al on the back of the chair. As the reader reads, heckle. If the group does not come to the readers support, break from your role as Al and direct them to become involved and do whatever they think is called for to assist their peer. If the reader gets up and moves about the group room, follow. What you will likely find at this point is the group literally encircling the reader, shouting at Al and supporting the reader. When the letter has been read the third time, ask the reader about feelings, reactions and anything learned from this experience. Ask the group the same.

A point of closure for this group is often to: 1) Add your support to those aspects of the reader's letters that are sound and, 2) have the reader, in a safe place, perhaps outside if possible, burn the letter or otherwise symbolically let go of the resentment, thereby adding a ceremonial aspect to the group's support for one of its own.

This group may last between 30 min. and 1 hour, or longer. Even if it ends before the regular group dismissal, this group is over when it is over. *DO NOT* attempt to tack on other business to this group, as doing so will tend to diffuse the learning experience you have just created. In addition, this group tends to be yet another emotionally charged group experience. It is suggested that it be used when the counselor knows the majority of individuals in the group rather well. While confronting the reader with specifics about personal background is the backbone of this dynamic, it does not include sharing confidential information in the group. Be careful you do not get caught up in your role as Al and disclose information shared with you in confidence by the individual or significant others outside of the group.

CONCLUSION

Group can be a powerful vehicle for change (Lawson, Lawson, & Rivers, 1996; Yalom, 1995) and especially useful for treating addictive disorders (Lewis, et al., 1988). However, as useful as groups may appear, evidence to suggest that such an approach to addressing addictive disorders is preferable or superior to individual counseling does not exist (Holder et al., 1991).

To employ this approach in the treatment of addictive disorders with particular attention to the stages of change an individual passes through on the way to recovery and the processes of change that work best at each given stage (Prochaska et al.,1992), is to increase the likelihood that individuals with addictive disorders will benefit from their counseling experience.

The techniques presented in this chapter have been merely examples of what a counselor can do in group to better target individual members of that group to increase the likelihood of moving to the next stage of change. To use a military metaphor, this chapter has suggested using "smart bombs" to strategically target individuals with exactly the type of intervention most likely to motivate change.

We know that viewing "denial" as the undesirable pole in a dichotomous view of addiction treatment only serves to alienate clients and foster an adversarial relationship between that individual and the counselor. By combining the strengths of group counseling with an awareness of how individuals change, mental health professionals increase the likelihood of providing a treatment experience rife with promise. As is so often the case in this life, the confluence of two disparate ideas can result in the discovery of a new and more effective solution to a problem.

REFERENCES

Beck, A., (1993). *Cognitive therapy of substance abuse.* NY: Guilford Press.

Doweiko, H. E., (1996). *Concepts of chemical dependency.* Pacific Grove, CA.: Brooks/Cole Publishing.

George, R. L., (1990). *Counseling the chemically dependent: Theory and practice.* Englewood Cliffs, NJ :Prentice Hall.

Holder, H., Longabaugh, R., Miller, W. R., & Rubonis, A. V. (1991). The cost effectiveness of treatment for alcoholism: A first approximation. *Journal of studies on alcohol, 52,* 517-540.

Kelman, H. C. (1971). Compliance, identification, and internalization: Three processes of attitude change. In B. L. Hinton & H. J. Reitz (Eds.), *Groups and organizations: Integrated readings in the analysis of social behavior*, 201-209. Belmont, CA: Wadsworth.

Lawson, G. W., Lawson, A. W., & Rivers, P. C., (1996). *Essentials of chemical dependency counseling, second edition*. Gaithersburg, MD:Aspen Publishers, Inc.

Levy, M. (1997). Group therapy in addictive and psychiatric disorders. In: N.S. Miller, Ed. *Principles and Practice of Addictions in Psychiatry*, Philadelphia, PA: W.B. Saunders Company.

Miller, W. R., Genefield, G., & Tonigan, J. S. (1993). Enhancing motivation for change in problem drinking: A controlled comparison of two therapist styles. *Journal of Consulting and Clinical Psychology, 61,* 455-462.

Pedersen, P., (1994). *A Handbook for Developing Multicultural Awareness*. Alexandria, VA: American Counseling Association.

Prochaska, J., & DiClemente, C. (1984). *The transtheoretical approach: Crossing traditional Boundaries of therapy.* Homewood, Illinois: Dow-Jones Irwin.

Prochaska, J., DiClemente, C., & Norcross, (1992). In search of how people change: Applications to addictive behavior. *American Psychologist, 47*(9), 1102-1114.

Straussner, S.L.A. (1997). Group treatment with substance abusing clients: A model of treatment during the early phases of outpatient group therapy. *Journal of Chemical Dependency Treatment, 7*(1/2) 67-80.

White, W. L. (1998). *Slaying the dragon: The history of addiction treatment and recovery in America.* Chestnut Health Systems/Lighthouse Institute.

Yalom, I.D. (1995). *The theory and practice of group psychotherapy* (5th ed.). New York: Basic Books.

Chapter Eleven

ANGER MANAGEMENT TREATMENT FOR SUBSTANCE ABUSING PATIENTS

Robert M. Awalt and Deborah A. Miscoll

INTRODUCTION

Anyone can become angry, that is easy. But, to
become angry with the right person, to the right
degree, at the right time, for the right purpose, and
in the right way, this is not easy.
Aristotle, The Nicomachean Ethics

This chapter focuses on a multi-component approach for the treatment of anger control problems in patients whose clinical picture is further complicated by substance abuse or dependency. Emphasis is placed on the acquisition, practice, and implementation of specific skill sets designed to inhibit dysfunctional anger as well as maladaptive behavioral responses, such as drug abuse, thought to result from anger. Cognitive and behavioral coping skills are discussed in terms of their utility in managing anger and reducing the risk of relapse to psychoactive drugs.

DEFINITION OF ANGER

Prior to considering the development, experience, expression, and treatment of anger, and studying the relationship of anger to substance abuse, the construct of anger must be defined and understood. Unfortunately, numerous attempts have been made by researchers to define the construct of anger, but a review of the literature indicates that the field remains unresolved with regard to a simple, uniform definition of anger (Tsytsarev & Grodnitsky, 1995). All too often constructs such as anger, annoyance, aggression, or hostility are used interchangeably (Spielberger, 1988). This failure to distinguish between experiential and expressive components of anger have contributed to problems in the research of these constructs and the development of reliable and valid means of assessment and evaluation (Deffenbacher, Oetting, Thwaites, Lynch, Baker, Stark, Thacker, & Eiswerth-Cox, 1996).

In an effort to eliminate any conceptual confusion with regard to the construct under discussion, a clear definition of anger must be delineated. Kassinove and Sukhodolsky (1995) developed a comprehensive definition of anger that appears consistent with a cognitive-behavioral approach to the development and treatment of dysfunctional anger, and, therefore will be used as the definition of choice throughout the remainder of this chapter.

Anger is defined as a "negative, internal feeling state associated with specific cognitive and perceptional distortions and deficiencies (e.g. misappraisals, cognitive errors, and attributions of blame, injustice, preventability, and/or intentionality), subjective labeling, physiological changes, and action tendencies to engage in socially constructed and reinforced organized behavioral scripts" (Kassinove & Sukhodolsky, 1995, p. 7). Further, the anger response is known to vary in frequency, duration, and intensity and individuals experience and express anger in a myriad of ways. Although anger is known to occur frequently (Averill, 1983), extreme experiences or expressions of anger leading to disruptive negative consequences or other psychosocial problems causes the most concern.

A review of the literature into the effects of dysfunctional anger shows that individuals who experience frequent and intense episodes of anger are at risk for stressing the human system, both in terms of physical and emotional health. Research has shown, for example, that maladaptive anger responses have been implicated in a number of medical conditions including hypertension, coronary artery disease (Siegel, 1986), and cancer (Speilberger, 1992). Interpersonal relationships have been found to be affected profoundly by dysfunctional anger (McKay, Rogers, & McKay, 1989), thereby resulting in negative evaluations by others (Deffenbacher, 1992). The development of a negative self-concept and low self-esteem (Brooks, Walfish, Stenbmark, & Canger, 1982; Chaney, Rozell, & Cummings, 1985; Welte, 1988; Brownell, Marlatt, Lictenstein, & Wilson, 1986; Gould, Ball, Kapsi, Otto, Pollack, Shekhar, & Fava, 1996) as a result of dysfunctional anger are also common. Because negative mood states such as anger and interpersonal conflict are among the highest risk situations for relapse for the substance abusing patient, treatment implications with this type of patient would seem obvious (Marlatt & Gordon, 1985).

The benefit of resolving anger control problems in substance abuse patients are twofold. As stated above, anger management training may eliminate or reduce the risk of relapse to substance abuse. Consider the following scenario:

> Lynn frequently ingested alcohol whenever she experienced stress in her interpersonal relationship with her long-term partner. As a result of chronic conflict within the relationship, Lynn often became angry due to her belief that her partner attempted to humiliate and demean her deliberately. Lynn insisted she used alcohol in order to "get back" at her partner, whom she knew found her alcohol use unacceptable. When the symptom of dysfunctional anger was targeted for intervention by the treatment team,

> Lynn learned to reconstruct cognitive errors contributing to her inappropriate behavior, manage physiological symptoms of her anger response, and communicate appropriately and assertively with her partner during times of interpersonal conflict. As a result of anger management training, Lynn reduced her risk of relapse when she experienced negative mood states, such as high levels of anger.

Anger management training also may aid the substance abuse patient in his or her attempt to successfully complete a drug recovery program where anger episodes are known to complicate the treatment protocol. For example:

> Michael was enrolled in a substance abuse treatment program for cocaine dependency, but he experienced considerable interpersonal difficulty in his interactions with staff and fellow patients. He was frequently angry and belligerent with staff, and he expressed much resentment with regard to treatment rules and regulations. During therapy groups, Michael often was intimidating in his interactions with other patients, and he often attempted to monopolize the group at the expense of others. When the symptom of dysfunctional anger was targeted for intervention by the treatment team, Michael reconstructed cognitive errors contributing to his inappropriate behavior, and learned new interpersonal skills to communicate effectively with others and meet his needs in a more appropriate manner. As a result, Michael maintained his placement within the treatment group, eventually completing the program successfully.

Clearly, anger management training has important implications for clinicians who encounter individuals who suffer from anger control problems coupled with substance abuse issues. Successful resolution of anger control problems may assist the patient in reducing the risk of relapse due to the experience or consequence of this negative mood state, an important component of substance abuse treatment. Resolution of anger control problems also may foster a more collaborative treatment environment.

In order to develop a comprehensive treatment program that considers the interaction of anger and substance abuse problems, the issues must be understood in terms of a theoretical base. A review of the literature shows that the cognitive-behavioral perspective offers a solid framework for conceptualizing and treating dysfunctional anger in substance abuse patients.

Cognitive-Behavioral Perspective on the Development of Anger

The hallmark of the cognitive-behavioral perspective is the emphasis on cognitive appraisal or interpretation of stimulus events that harbor the potential to elicit anger responses comprised of internal cognitive, affective, or physiological components as well as overt displays of motor or verbal behavior. According to Eckhardt and Deffenbacher (1995), anger can be generated by one or more of three stimulus classes. A potentially angering stimulus event may be an actual identifiable event such as rude treatment by a sales clerk, or an angry memory or image triggered by an external cue or other cognitions or emotions. For example, an employee may react angrily to critical feedback from his or her supervisor because the incident was reminiscent of verbal abuse suffered during childhood. Alternatively, anger may occur secondary to another emotion, such as humiliation or rejection. Of course, certain concomitant conditions may predispose an individual to experience dysfunctional anger, such as immediate physical (i.e. hunger, fatigue, pain) or emotional states (i.e. stress) (Berkowitz, 1989; 1990) or the perceived violation of personal values or beliefs (Beck, 1976).

Once exposed to one of the three classes of stimuli, Deffenbacher (1993) contends that an individual then analyzes the stimulus event utilizing two specific appraisal processes, primary appraisal and secondary appraisal. With regard to primary appraisals, an individual initially evaluates a stimulus in terms of its relevance and threat or harm value. If a stimulus is judged to be irrelevant or non-threatening it is unlikely to provoke a maladaptive anger response. However, if a stimulus is judged to be relevant and/or threatening or harmful, the potential for the development of an anger response is increased (Lazarus, 1991). The increased potential for an anger response particularly is true if the stimulus is judged to be threatening with regard to an individual's concept of personal domain, expectations or freedoms, or pursuit of goal-directed behavior (Lazarus, 1991). Additionally, if an individual engages in certain collateral appraisals, anger may escalate even further.

Anger can be fueled by specific maladaptive cognitive patterns. Such distorted patterns of thinking can involve misattribution of cause, fairness, intentionality, preventability, or blameworthiness (Deffenbacher, 1993). Other forms of cognitive misappraisal contributing to dysfunctional anger can include overgeneralizing, dichotomous or "black and white" thinking, inflammatory or provocative labeling of self or others, and catastrophizing (Tsytsarev & Grodnitsky, 1995).

An individual also evaluates a stimulus using the process of secondary appraisals. Secondary appraisals refer to the tendency to evaluate stimulus events with regard to the individual's abilities to manage or cope with the event (Deffenbacher, 1993; Lazarus, 1991; Tsytsarev & Grodnitsky, 1995). An individual may appraise a stimulus event and determine that he or she maintains the capacity to manage or cope with the event effectively and, as a result, a maladaptive anger response is inhibited. If, however, an individual appraises the event as one that exceeds his or her ability to cope, an anger response is more likely to develop. This particularly is true when overt aggression has been the preferred manner in which an individual copes with potentially angering events, and when the individual maintains positive outcome expectancies with regard to the effectiveness of such behavior in resolving the event (Lazarus, 1991).

According to the cognitive-behavioral perspective, a maladaptive anger response develops as the result of an individual's propensity to engage in the cognitive *misappraisal* of neutral, stimulus events. The misappraisal of the stimulus event then activates other related response systems which then culminates in a maladaptive experience and expression of anger in the affective, physiological, and behavioral domains which is considered inappropriate for the situation.

The experience of anger may be conceptualized in terms of related, yet distinct response systems -- cognitive, affective, physiological, and behavioral (Kirk, 1988). The cognitive system refers to an individual's encoding and information processing style. As the result of an initial misappraisal of a stimulus, the cognitive response system, which is considered to be an extension of the appraisal systems mentioned earlier, is thought to continue to develop and elaborate on maladaptive/distorted cognitions. In other words, a sort of cognitive "vicious circle" is created, and this "vicious circle" becomes more and more distorted. The affective system is also activated and will be characterized by verbal references to the subjective experience of specific feelings that the individual identifies as anger. Changes in the physiological system will be noticed and characterized by, for example, muscular tension, autonomic arousal, and adrenal and endocrine alterations. Finally, specific action characteristics of the behavioral system can be observed in an individual's overt motor or verbal expression. These response systems are thought to interact and influence one another, often very rapidly, and the individual experiences them together as anger (Tsytsarev & Grodnitsky, 1995).

The expression of anger may occur in numerous ways. Anger may be expressed outwardly, (i.e., anger-out style) as when an individual physically assaults another person, or the experience of anger may be expressed inwardly (i.e. anger-in style) as when an individual suppresses anger despite experiencing significant internal distress or turmoil. Anger also may be controlled (i.e. anger-control style), as when an individual employs a variety of coping skills to manage their anger experience (Speilberger, 1988).

Now that the conceptualization of anger has been outlined according to the principles of cognitive-behavioral theory, assessment of dysfunctional anger now may take place consistent with the standards set forth by this perspective.

Cognitive-Behavioral Assessment of Anger

Cognitive-behavioral assessment is based on simple principles and works toward the achievement of clearly delineated goals. A central principle of cognitive-behavioral assessment is that behavior is determined by interpretations of neutral stimulus events. The detailed analysis of the patient's cognitive patterns thus becomes a major focus of the assessment process (Kirk, 1989). The goals of cognitive-behavioral assessment are "to have agreed on a formulation of the target problems with the patient, and to have sufficiently detailed information about factors maintaining the problem to be able to design and present a treatment plan. Providing the patient with education with regard to the basic principles of the model of intervention also is recommended" (Kirk, 1989, p. 13.).

The main principle of cognitive behavioral assessment is that behavior largely is determined by the patient's interpretation of immediate stimulus events. It is crucial that the patient and treating professional engage in a collaborative effort of guided discovery in which information about those situations, cognitions, physiological states, and overt behavior that relate to and maintain a target problem is acquired.

ASSESSMENT COMPONENTS

Several modes of assessment may be used to uncover those specific response systems that relate to and maintain dysfunctional anger. Various methods exist to address each response system, so it may be helpful to utilize a variety of approaches in order to fully assess the target problem, acquire collateral data, and obtain a clearer, more accurate picture of what is happening for the patient.

The major component of a comprehensive, cognitive-behavioral assessment involves a behavioral interview in which the patient describes the target problem so that the treating professional can obtain data on potential antecedent and maintenance features that are related to the problem.

When considering the development of the problem, it may be useful to inquire about and analyze information regarding onset, course, and factors that might predispose the patient to develop the problem (i.e. family history). The treating professional then can acquire detailed information with regard to the antecedents (i.e. internal or external cues), responses (i.e. cognitive, affective, physiological, and behavioral), and consequences of the responses involved with a target problem. An assessment of the patient's strengths and weaknesses with regard to their ability to cope with the target problem is then performed.

Knowledge of the patient's prior psychiatric and medical history may be useful in predicting response outcome, so a detailed description may be taken during the assessment interview, as well. Knowledge of the patient's specific beliefs about the problem and about treatment also should be acquired so as to determine if any beliefs incongruent with the treatment protocol exist. If such beliefs do exist, they may be managed by the treating professional so as to minimize the potential for blocked treatment progress. Self-monitoring procedures, self-report questionnaires, and assessment instruments (e.g., State-Trait Anger Expression Inventory; STAXI, Speilberger, 1988), collateral interviewing of others, direct observation, and physiological measurements may help to expand the behavioral interview and acquire more specific data with regard to the target problem.

It is important to note that this approach clearly emphasizes individualized assessment and treatment of the target problem. The choice to utilize the method of cognitive-behavioral assessment does not preclude its use in a group setting, however. The method remains the same, it merely is applied in the larger group context. Each patient in the group enjoys multiple opportunities to participate in and practice becoming proficient in the comprehensive analysis and planning sessions for target problems. As a result, each patient's skills in this area are enhanced.

Note that once such data is obtained, the application of the experimental method to problems of individual patients is performed. The use of the experimental method is central to the cognitive-behavioral approach to the assessment and, ultimately, the treatment of the patient (Kirk, 1989). Much like a single-subject experiment, a conceptualization of the problem is formulated, and assessments and measurements with regard to the problem are obtained. Treatment interventions then can be tailored to manage the specific features of the target problem, and then implemented. A detailed assessment drives the formulation of the specific treatment plan for each patient. However, assessment does not stop there. Following the implementation of a treatment intervention, patient progress or change can be monitored through repeated assessment and measurement and compared to those obtained in the initial behavioral interview and assessment process. In this manner, the patient's treatment can be continuously monitored and analyzed and the most effective treatment options may be determined and reinforced, while those deemed ineffective may be discarded.

Once a detailed assessment has taken place, the treating professional may select from a variety of interventions specifically designed to manage the particular response systems involved in the experience and expression of the target problem, such as anger, substance abuse, or both.

Cognitive-Behavioral Anger Management Group Interventions

Anger management groups primarily emphasize the development and application of specific behavioral and cognitive coping skills to reduce the likelihood of maladaptive anger experience or expression. Previous research supports the use of cognitive-behavioral therapy as an effective intervention for the reduction of anger (Awalt, Reilly, & Shopshire, 1997; Deffenbacher, Demm, & Brandon, 1986; Hazaleus & Deffenbacher, 1986; Moon & Eisler, 1983; Novaco, 1975). Although anger management interventions traditionally have been delivered in an individual setting, Hazaleus and Deffenbacher (1986) believe that anger management interventions utilizing a cognitive-behavioral approach may be applied effectively in group settings. Group application of anger management principles has many unique benefits that the treatment practitioner may consider when deciding on the best approach for his or her patient. For example, Beck et al. (1979) suggested that interpersonal interactions in a group setting yield greater demonstrations of dysfunctional cognitive appraisals which can then be addressed in this group context. However, it is important to realize that, within a group environment, treatment strategies must be tailored for each individual and those specific symptoms targeted for modification.

Designing an anger management/substance abuse group should consider the following (adapted from Malico, 1994):

Size

A group consisting of five to ten patients is recommended for anger management/substance abuse treatment. According to Rose (1990) and Yalom (1975), groups with fewer than five participants often fail to achieve therapeutic cohesiveness and interactions, considered to be special attributes of a group setting. Groups with more than ten participants often inhibit the full responding of each member, thereby limiting therapeutic effectiveness. Patient attrition should be considered when designing an anger management/substance abuse group, as well.

Model

It is recommended that group facilitators adhere to the principles of cognitive-behavioral theory and treatment when designing an anger management/substance abuse group. Such a recommendation is grounded in theory and research that supports the utility of this particular model for the reduction of anger and modification of maladaptive anger responses. Malico (1994) further recommended that facilitators adopt a co-therapy model of treatment, as the use of cognitive-behavioral methods demand much from the treating professional, and sharing the burden of treatment administration may increase the opportunities for effective therapeutic intervention.

Therapist Qualifications

It is essential that treating professionals demonstrate proficiency with regard to their theoretical knowledge and application of cognitive-behavioral treatment interventions. Knowledge of the principles of substance abuse and anger related problems and treatment also is essential.

Group Composition

According to Yalom (1975), the design of a group should consider fully homogeneous patient variables such as age, sex, cultural and social background, to increase the attractiveness of the group to its members. Alternatively, Malico (1994) suggested homogeneous anger groups may actually amplify the exhibition of destructive behavior, so constructing a group in which patients have been known to express their anger in a variety of ways may serve to minimize destructive or counter-therapeutic behavior. Heterogeneity of substance abused can also be utilized effectively within the group setting.

INTERVENTIONS

The effectiveness of anger management interventions based on established cognitive-behavioral techniques has been well documented. Tafrate (1995) performed an exhaustive review of the psychotherapy outcome literature on anger and discovered several, general classes of interventions which are considered to be most effective in treating anger problems. Note that, while a variety of general classes of interventions are reviewed here, it is not possible to provide detailed information on each approach due to space limitations. However, the information provided in this chapter may serve as a resource guide for practitioners unfamiliar with the interventions discussed. If needed, it is recommended that the practitioner consult the references provided for more specific and in-depth discussion of each treatment technique.

Cognitive Therapies

Cognitive interventions specifically are designed to assist the patient in understanding the relationship between cognitive appraisal processes and the related affective, physiological, and behavioral response systems influencing the experience and expression of anger (Beck, 1976; Ellis, 1973). The goal of cognitive approaches to anger management is to assist the patient in constructing a system of cognitive appraisal that is more utilitarian, resulting in reductions in the frequency, duration, and intensity of an anger experience and more adaptive anger expressions. Cognitive therapies teach the patient to monitor cognitive activity, recognize and identify distorted or dysfunctional thoughts, and reconstruct cognitions determined to be influencing a maladaptive anger response. Three cognitive models predominate and include: Meichenbaum and Cameron (1973) Self-Instructional Training, Beck's (1976) Cognitive Therapy, and Ellis' (1962) Rational-Emotive Therapy, now referred to as REBT. Strong empirical support exists for the use of Self-Instructional Training and Beck's Cognitive Therapy model, although no controlled outcome studies exist to clarify the effectiveness of Ellis' Rational-Emotive Behavior Therapy (Tafrate, 1995).

Relaxation Therapies

It is well established in the literature that the experience and expression of anger is accompanied by physiological arousal as measured by muscle tension, breathing rates, and adrenal and endocrine changes (Berkowitz, 1990; Novaco, 1979). Because the physiological response system is activated during an anger episode, a number of relaxation interventions are available to assist the patient in reducing symptoms of physiological arousal. The goal of relaxation interventions is to assist the patient in developing skills to inhibit sympathetic nervous system arousal in anger-provoking situations and acquiring more self-control. Examples of relaxation interventions include progressive muscle relaxation, breathing-cued relaxation, autogenics relaxation training, guided imagery, biofeedback, and meditation. The most common relaxation therapy used in the treatment of anger is a modified version of Jacobson's (1938) progressive muscle relaxation technique, which involves the systematic tensing and releasing of major muscle groups. The intervention often is used in desensitization programs, in which anger-provoking stimuli are paired with the relaxation intervention in an effort to extinguish the anger response. Much empirical support exists with regard to the use of relaxation therapies for the treatment of anger and the effectiveness of this class of interventions in modifying the anger response.

Skill Training Therapies

The major premise underlying skill-based approaches to the treatment of anger involves the relationship between interpersonal skill deficits and the experience and expression of this emotion. Poor interpersonal responding is thought to inhibit the patient's ability to manage difficult situations and achieve personal goals, resulting in negative mood states such as anger (Tafrate, 1995). The goal of skill-based therapies is to assist the patient in acquiring new behavioral responses that will likely enhance their ability to achieve more effective and adaptive outcomes. One common skill-based intervention is assertion training. Assertion training involves teaching patients to appropriately express their feelings and make or deny interpersonal requests (Masters et al., 1987). Social skills training teaches the patient socially acceptable methods of communicating and relating in interpersonal interactions. Note that assertion training is often subsumed under the more general category of social skills training. Modeling, coaching, behavioral rehearsal, and feedback are used to teach the patient new social skills, which he or she then would be expected to adopt and employ independently, outside of the therapeutic environment. Problem solving interventions emphasize the development of skills to assist the patient in identifying, evaluating, and implementing alternative strategies in response to potentially angering situations (D'Zurilla, 1988). The overall effectiveness of this general class of interventions has been studied and it has been determined that such interventions are useful in the treatment of anger problems (Tafrate, 1995).

Multi-Component Treatments

Multi-component treatments combine a variety of cognitive and behavioral strategies and use them together so that the intervention may yield superior effects over any single approach alone (Novaco, 1975). The multi-component approach is consistent with a cognitive-behavioral approach to the development and treatment of anger problems and is a perspective advocated in this chapter. Multi-component approaches to the treatment of anger have been widely studied since Novaco's initial study in 1975, and it has been determined that the multi-component method of stress inoculation does, indeed, yield large treatment effects. However, other combinations of cognitive and behavioral treatments have not yet been studied, so it is unclear which combinations of strategies are particularly effective for the treatment of anger problems at this time.

The emphasis of treatment up until this point has been focused on learning, practicing, and applying cognitive-behavioral coping skills. It is essential that the patient continue to utilize his or her skills when faced with anger-provoking events in the future so as to avoid a return to maladaptive responding. Anger control planning offers the patient the opportunity to develop a specific, comprehensive plan of action designed to reinforce change.

The Anger Control Plan: A Relapse Prevention Approach to the Maintenance of Behavior Change

When effective interventions have been acquired, the adaptive changes must be maintained so that the patient does not return to former patterns of maladaptive responding. An example of a treatment approach consistent with cognitive-behavioral theory has been developed by Marlatt and Gordon (1980). Known as *relapse prevention*, this approach is a self-management program specifically designed to reinforce the maintenance stage of the habit-change process. The goals of relapse prevention are to assist the patient in how to anticipate and prevent the problem of relapse, and assist the patient in developing a comprehensive plan of action to manage a lapse before it results in a return to the original pattern of maladaptive responding, such as anger or substance abuse. A more global goal of relapse prevention involves the development of a balanced lifestyle in which the patient learns to prevent the development of unhealthy habits. Relapse prevention utilizes behavioral skill training, cognitive interventions, and lifestyle change processes to accomplish its goals (Marlatt & Gordon, 1985). You will note that the relapse prevention approach is consistent with the cognitive-behavioral approach described elsewhere in this chapter.

Marlatt and Gordon (1985) outline several techniques that characterize this approach. One technique involves the identification of high-risk situations most likely to threaten an individual's sense of control and to increase the risk of returning to maladaptive responding. Although general categories of high risk situations have been identified as contributing to a significant proportion of relapse episodes, such as negative mood states or interpersonal conflict, an individualized approach must be adopted because the antecedent conditions of relapse and response systems involved may or may not be similar across individuals. The identification of high-risk situations most often is achieved through self-monitoring procedures and the analysis of prior events. The patient then participates in instruction and behavioral rehearsal of strategies to manage the high-risk situations identified by the patient. Such strategies often are those learned in the context of cognitive behavioral therapy, as discussed earlier, but the focus of attention is placed on the maintenance of habit-change as opposed to simple skill acquisition. Direct instruction, modeling, behavioral rehearsal, coaching, and feedback may be used effectively by the treating professional in order to reinforce skill acquisition.

Of course, it is not possible to identify and plan for all potential high-risk situations for relapse for any individual. Assisting the patient in developing and implementing a wide range of generalizable skills is the main task. In order to develop a more general and complete prevention plan, Marlatt and Gordon (1985) recommend that the treating professional attempt to assist the patient in developing lifestyle balance to increase the patient's overall ability to cope with stress, and to identify and manage any high risk situations. Techniques used to achieve lifestyle balance include many methods already discussed, stress management methods, relaxation and cognitive restructuring, and assertiveness training. For a more detailed discussion on the theoretical rationale and treatment approach from a relapse prevention perspective, refer to Marlatt and Gordon (1985).

It is suggested that a treatment program for individuals with substance abuse problems concurrent with dysfunctional anger incorporate the concepts and interventions detailed throughout this chapter. In addition, a model for this type of group practice is outlined below and may serve as a guide to assist the treatment professional in the design and implementation of a similar program.

A Model 12-Week Anger Management Group for Substance Abuse Patients:

Researchers at the University of California, San Francisco and the Veterans Administration Medical Center, San Francisco offer a promising treatment for substance abuse patients who experience difficulty controlling their anger (Reilly, Shopshire, & Clark, 1999). The manualized treatment protocol has undergone extensive study, and research results show that patients exhibit marked improvement with regard to their ability to manage anger and thus, reduce their risk of relapse to substance abuse (Reilly, Shopshire, & Clark, 1999).

This anger management treatment model utilizes a cognitive-behavioral approach with regard to conceptualization of anger, assessment, and treatment. The treatment protocol involves three phases: (1) development of a trusting and collaborative relationship with the patient; (2) skill acquisition, enhancement, and rehearsal; and (3) transfer and maintenance of learned skills to the client's natural world.

The goal of Phase 1 of the treatment protocol is to develop a working relationship with the patient and assist the patient in developing a comprehensive and personal understanding of anger. More specifically, the patients learn to analyze internal and external cues that comprise their anger response. The goal of Phase 2 of the treatment protocol is to acquire alternative behaviors that will assist the patient in reducing the frequency, duration, and intensity of anger. Patients learn various cognitive-behavioral methods to manage anger, such as cognitive restructuring and relaxation training. Note that emphasis is placed on the patient's ability to self-regulate behavior. The goal of Phase 3 of the treatment protocol is to generalize new learning to situations encountered in daily living, and maintain adaptive changes made by the patient.

Anger management groups meet once a week for 12-weeks, and treatment sessions are 90-minutes in length. The treatment protocol is designed to have a cumulative effect for patients. In other words, each session builds on the one that precedes it. Initial sessions provide patients with the cognitive-behavioral framework for understanding anger. Subsequent sessions are used to analyze patient accounts of anger episodes according to the cognitive-behavioral framework. Patients then learn, practice, and apply specific cognitive-behavioral interventions, such as cognitive restructuring and relaxation. Final sessions are devoted to skill generalization and maintenance issues. Throughout the group experience, the clinician heavily reinforces the use of cognitive-behavior strategies for anger management. Note that the use of anger measures such as the State-Trait Anger Expression Inventory (STAXI; Spielberger, 1988) may assist the treating professional in monitoring treatment effectiveness over time. The researchers suggest that assessments take place at baseline, and at four-week intervals thereafter.

An outline of each session is detailed below, which will be followed by a case vignette.

Session 1: Overview of Treatment and Anger Monitoring

In the first session, the rationale and assumptions of the anger management treatment program are presented. Group rules and issues pertaining to confidentiality are also discussed. Patients are taught to monitor and record the intensity of their anger using a Likert-type scale called an Anger Meter. A "1" on the Anger Meter represents a state of complete calm and relaxation, while a "10" represents a loss of control and the experience of negative consequences. It will be helpful to utilize audio-visual aids throughout the treatment.

Session 2: Cues to Anger and Anger as a Secondary Emotion

A cognitive-behavioral framework for understanding the experience of anger is presented in this session. Patients learn to identify the components of anger episodes such as the stimulus event, cues (i.e. behavioral, physiological, cognitive, and affective) and responses. The relationship between anger and other negative emotions is also discussed. Patients "check-in" on the Anger Meter and clarify any cues identified. The therapist may make use of modeling to demonstrate ways to identify anger cues.

Session 3: The Anger Control Plan and Relaxation Training

Patients are introduced to the concept of anger control planning for the reduction of anger and risk of relapse to substance abuse. Patients are instructed to anticipate high-risk situations for anger episodes and begin to develop an anger control plan for the resolution of these high-risk situations using cognitive-behavioral techniques. From the various techniques to be taught in subsequent sessions, patients are encouraged to select those techniques that have proven to be most effective in reducing anger for them. Patients are further introduced to the concept of relaxation training and participate in relaxation exercises. In implementing the personalized control plan, one takes responsibility for one's behavior, which adds to the experience of personal power.

Session 4: The Anger and Aggression Cycle

In this session, patients are presented information regarding the aggression cycle. The correspondence between the three phases of the aggression cycle (i.e. escalation, explosion, and post-explosion) and the anger meter rating is emphasized. It is important to comment here that individuals may *choose* to "get off" of the anger cycle at any point prior to hitting a 10.

Session 5: Cognitive Restructuring and the Self-Talk Model

In this session, patients are presented the A-B-C-D model introduced by Ellis (1973). Distorted cognitions thought to contribute to the anger response are discussed. Patients further learn, practice, and apply the method of cognitive restructuring to manage distorted cognitions and inhibit a dysfunctional anger response.

Session 6: Assertiveness Training and the Conflict Resolution Model

Patients are taught to distinguish between aggression, assertiveness, and passive-aggressive behavior in this session. The conflict resolution model is reviewed, and patients are taught to manage interpersonal conflict using this approach.

Session 7: Review Session

Patients review their progress and report on the status of their individualized anger control plan in this session. The clinician coaches patients with regard to the effectiveness of the anger control plan and facilitates further refinement of skill acquisition and application.

Session 8 and 9: Analysis of the Most Violent Incident

In these sessions, patients participate in a structured exercise designed to gather data regarding the most violent incident from the patient's past. Cognitive-behavioral assessment of the incident is performed in the group setting, and the patient is encouraged to discuss the manner in which he or she might have implemented specific strategies to manage the anger episode.

Session 10 and 11: Anger in the Family of Origin

In these sessions, patients participate in a structured exercise designed to highlight the relationship between the experience and expression of anger and the family of origin. Emphasis is placed on how anger was expressed within the family, how the patient was disciplined, the role the patient played in the family, messages the patient received about the role of men and women, and how these issues currently impact their adult lives and relationships. Patients further are asked to consider how they might behave differently now, in light of the issues discussed. Similarities between family legacies of anger and substance abuse are also explored.

Session 12: Review and Final Wrap-Up

In this session, patients are asked to review their anger control plans. The clinician coaches patients with regard to the effectiveness of the anger control plan and facilitates further refinement of skill acquisition and application. Patients also enjoy the opportunity to provide the clinician with feedback about the group process via written evaluations at this time.

Note: Although the researchers did not include aftercare groups as part of the research protocol, subsequent aftercare sessions may be necessary for ongoing patient support and the reinforcement of the individualized anger control plan.

Case Vignette

Shane was referred to treatment by his probation officer. Shane had an extensive history of alcohol abuse and assaultive behavior problems. When he first came to treatment, Shane consistently reported high levels of anger, and he indicated he frequently used alcohol to manage this affective state. Initial Anger Meter ratings fell in the 8-10 range, and Shane said he often felt "out of control." As a result, Shane often reacted to minor stressors with extreme fury and rage. Physical violence was not uncommon. Through participation in early group sessions, Shane learned to identify specific internal and external cues that triggered his anger. He learned, for example, that when he felt slighted or disrespected by others, he became quite angry and would act out inappropriately. Shane further identified physiological factors, such as increased heart rate and muscle tension, as components to his anger response. Cognitive misappraisals involving the concept of intentionality also escalated Shane's anger. Shane learned to employ deep breathing and progressive muscle relaxation exercises to counteract his state of hyper-arousal. Shane also learned to dispute maladaptive cognitions that contributed to his anger. His frequent practice of techniques during group role-plays and other in-session exercises, homework assignments, and his acceptance of critical feedback from the clinician and group members reinforced Shane until their use became second nature. During weekly check-ins, Shane rated his anger in the 3-4 range on the Anger Meter. He reported his feelings of anger were reduced, and he was able to handle his physical, behavioral, and cognitive symptoms as they occurred rather than letting them build up to an unmanageable level. Shane also reported that his urge to use alcohol to manage anger had decreased, as he was able to employ alternative coping skills to manage this negative mood state. During the final stages of treatment, Shane identified high-risk situations for anger, and refined his anger control plan. By the end of treatment, Shane reported that he felt more confident in his ability to manage anger because he had successfully employed his anger control plan on a number of occasions. As a result, his relationships with others improved, his substance use decreased, and he reported a significant ability to cope with potential anger provoking events in the future.

Post script: For further information about the treatment protocol, or to receive a copy of the detailed anger management treatment manual, please correspond with Drs. Awalt,

Miscoll, Reilly, or Shopshire in care of the Veterans Affairs Medical Center, Substance Abuse Outpatient Program, 4150 Clement Street (116E), San Francisco, CA 94121.

REFERENCES

Averill, J. R. (1983). *Anger and aggression: An essay on emotion.* New York: Springer-Verlag.

Awalt, R., Reilly, P., & Shopshire. M. (1997). The angry patient: An intervention for managing anger in substance abuse treatment. *Journal of Psychoactive Drugs, 29,* 353-358.

Beck, A. (1976). *Cognitive therapy and the emotional disorders*. New York: International Universities Press.

Beck, A., Rush, A., Shaw, B., & Emery, G. (1979). *Cognitive therapy of depression*. New York: Guilford Press.

Berkowitz, L. (1989). Frustration-aggression hypothesis: Examination and reformulation. *Psychological Bulletin, 106*, 59-73.

Berkowitz, L. (1990). On the formation and regulation of anger and aggression: a cognitive-neoassociationistic analysis. *American Psychologist, 45*, 494-503.

Brooks, M., Walfish, S., Stenmark, D., & Canger, J. (1982). Personality variables in alcohol abuse in college students. *Journal of Drug Education, 11*, 185.

Brownell, K., Marlatt, G.A., Lichtenstein, E., & Wilson, G.T. (1986). *American Psychologist, 41*, 765.

Chaney, E.F., Roszell, D.K., & Cummings, C. (1985). Coping in opiate addicts maintained on methadone. In S. Shiffman and T. Wills (Eds.), *Coping and Substance Abuse*. Academic Press: New York.

Deffenbacher, J., Demm, P., & Brandon, A. (1986). High general anger: Correlates and treatment. *Behavior Research and Therapy, 24*, 481-489.

Deffenbacher, J. L. (1992). Trait anger: Theory, findings, and implications. In C. D. Spielberger and J. N. Butcher (Eds.), *Advances in personality assessment* (Vol. 9, pp. 177-201). Hillsdale, NJ: Erlbaum.

Deffenbacher, J. (1993). General anger: Characteristics and clinical implications. *Psicologia Conductual,* 49-67.

Deffenbacher, J. L., Oetting, E. R., Thwaites, G. A., Lynch, R. S., Baker, D. A., Stark, R. S., Thacker, S., & Eiswerth-Cox, L. (1996). State-trait anger theory and the utility of the trait anger scale. *Journal of Counseling Psychology, 43*, 131-148.

D' Zurilla, T. (1988). Problem solving therapies. In K. Dobson (Ed.), *Handbook of cognitive behavioral therapies* (pp. 85-135). New York: The Guilford Press.

Eckhardt, C. & Deffenbacher, J. (1995). Diagnosis of anger disorders. In H. Kassinove (Ed.*), Anger disorders: Definition, diagnosis, and treatment* (27-47). Philadelphia, PA: Taylor and Francis.

Ellis, A. (1962). *Reason and emotion in psychotherapy*. New York: Lyle Stuart.

Ellis, A. (1973). *Humanistic Psychology: The Rational Emotive Approach*. New York: Julian Press.

Gould, R.A., Ball, S., Kapsi, S.P., Otto, M.W., Pollack, M.H., Shekhar, A., & Fava, M. (1996). Prevalence and correlates of anger attacks: A two site study. *Journal of Affective Disorders, 39*, 31-38.

Hazaleus, S., & Deffenbacher, J. (1986). Relaxation and cognitive treatments of anger. *Journal of Consulting and Clinical Psychology, 54*, 222-226.

Jacobson, E. (1938). *Progressive muscle relaxation.* Chicago: University of Chicago Press.

Kassinove, H., & Sukhodolsky, D. (1995). Anger disorders: Basic science and practice issues. In H. Kassinove (Ed.), *Anger disorders: Definition, diagnosis, and treatment* (1-26). Philadelphia, PA: Taylor and Francis.

Kirk, J. (1988). Cognitive-behavioural assessment (1988). In Hawton, K., Salkovskis, P., Kirk, J., & Clark, D. (Eds.), *Cognitive-behavior therapy for psychiatric problems.* Oxford University Press.

Lazarus, R. (1991). *Emotion and adaptation*. New York: Oxford.

Marlatt, G.A., & Gordon, J.R. (1980). Determinants of relapse: Implications for the maintenance of behavior change. In P.O. Davidson & S.M. Davidson (Eds.), *Behavioral medicine: Changing health lifestyles*. New York: Brunner-Mazel.

Marlatt, G. A., & Gordon, J. R. (1985). *Relapse prevention: Maintenance strategies in the treatment of addictive behaviors*. New York: The Guilford Press.

Malico, R. (1994). Anger management using cognitive group therapy: *Perspectives in Psychiatric Care, 30*, (3), 17-20.

Masters, J., Burish, T., Hollon, S., & Rimm, D. (1987). *Behavior therapy: Techniques and empirical findings* (3d ed.). New York: Harcourt, Brace, Jovanovich College Publishers.

McKay, M., Rogers, P., & McKay, J. (1989). *When anger hurts: Quieting the storm within.* Oakland, CA: New Harbinger Publications, Inc.

Meichenbaum, D., & Cameron, R. (1973). Training schizophrenics to talk to themselves. *Behavior Therapy, 4*, 515-535.

Moon, J., & Eisler, R. (1983). Anger control and experimental comparison of three behavioral treatments. *Behavior Therapy, 14*, 493-505.

Novaco, R. (1975). *Anger control: The development and evaluation of an experimental treatment.* Lexington, MA: D. C. Heath.

Novaco, R. (1979). The cognitive regulation of anger and stress. In P. Kendall and s. Hollan (Eds.), *Cognitive-behavioral interventions: Theory, research, and procedures.* New York: academic.

Rose, S. (1990). *Working with adults in groups*. San Francisco: Jossey-Bass.

Siegel, J. M. (1986). The multidimensional Anger inventory. *Journal of Personality and Social Psychology, 51*, 191-200.

Spielberger, C. D. (1988). *Manual for the State-Trait Anger Expression Inventory.* Odessa, FL: Psychological assessment Resources.

Spielberger, C. D. (1992). *Anger-hostility, heart disease and cancer*. Paper presented at the American Psychological association, Washington, D. C.

Tafrate, R. (1995). Evaluation of treatment strategies for adult anger disorders. In H. Kassinove (Ed.). *Anger disorders: Definition, diagnosis, and treatment*. Philadelphia, PA: Taylor and Francis.

Tsytsarev, S., & Grodnitzky, G. (1995). Anger and criminality. In H. Kassinove (Ed.), *Anger disorders: Definition, diagnosis, and treatment* (91-108). Philadelphia, PA: Taylor and Francis.

Welte, J., Abel, E., & Wieczorek, W. (1988). The role of alcohol in suicides in Erie County, NY, 1972-1984. *Public Health Report, 103*, 648-652.

Yalom, I. (1975). *The theory and practice of group psychotherapy*, (2d ed.). New York: Basic Books.

SECTION II: THEORY AND TRAINING

Chapter Twelve

INDIVIDUAL PSYCHOLOGY AND GROUP PSYCHOTHERAPY: TOWARD AN ADLERIAN GROUP PSYCHOTHERAPY ORIENTATION

Joshua M. Gross and Miller A. Garrison

INTRODUCTION

Over the past six decades group psychotherapy has steadily become embedded in the armamentarium of eclectic mental health practice. Since the earliest work of Burrow, Dreikurs, Pratt, Wender, and others, various theoretical applications and techniques have developed, progressed, and evolved into a generic interpersonal group approach which is common to most psychotherapy practice venues (MacKenzie, 1992). This chapter describes group psychotherapy from the orientation of Adler's Individual Psychology. It begins with an overview of Adler's Individual Psychology with the goal of giving the reader a historical, philosophical, and theoretical background. It then discusses group therapy practice presenting a set of six different and distinct populations demonstrating a range of psychological intervention from the Individual Psychology approach. These groups will serve as examples of how the theory is applied and what interventions are made in the context of the orientation. It is hoped that this chapter will give the interested reader an introduction to Individual Psychology and group psychotherapy with the goal of developing an Adlerian group psychotherapy orientation. This orientation is flexible and adaptive, much like human nature itself. This flexibility and adaptability allows for the improvement of the quality of life for a wide range of human conditions and situations.

ORIGINS OF THE PSYCHOLOGY OF ALFRED ADLER

Alfred Adler was born in Vienna in 1870. He studied medicine at the University of Vienna, graduating in 1895. During his student years he was active in the socialist movement, and met his wife, Raissa, at these meetings. Apparently Adler was drawn to the egalitarian and idealistic aspects of this movement more than he was committed to the political ideology (Hoffman, 1994). In 1898 he published *Health Book for the Tailoring Trade*, which connected many of the diseases experienced by tailors to the socioeconomic structure of the tailoring trade and declared that the economic plight of the trade produced a "hostility" toward health (Stepansky, 1983). He called for preventative efforts by physicians and society and insisted on an awareness of the context as a part of the diagnostic process.

In 1902 Sigmund Freud invited Adler and three other physicians to an informal discussion group, which became known as the Psychological Wednesday Society and later the Vienna Psychoanalytic Society. Adler was an active member and attended frequently. After 1906, when minutes of the proceedings began to be kept, his primary contributions were related to elaborating his theory of organ inferiority. This theory asserted that all neuroses were derived from a congenital weakness and the effort to overcome the congenital disability in a struggle for social adaptation. By 1909 Adler expressed some reservations about the "sexual factor," and he and Freud were periodically disagreeing openly in meetings. By the fall of 1910 Adler's views were generally recognized as being distinctive. "... Adler never accepted the etiological authenticity of sexual themes in his clinical work; he consistently maintained that sexual factors embodied a 'manifest content' not to be taken at etiological face value" (Stepansky, 1983, p. 54).

Early in 1911 the differences between Adler and Freud became so great that Adler resigned his membership as well as society chairperson and editor of the psychoanalytic journal. About 10 of the 25 active members left with him, and together they formed the Society for Free Psychoanalytic Study. In 1912 the group changed their name to the Society for Individual Psychology.

> The name Individual Psychology intends to express the conviction that psychological processes and their manifestations can be understood only from the individual context and that all psychological insight begins with the individual (Furtmuller, 1914).

Freud's increasing criticism of Adler and other dissenters has been attributed to his growing confidence that psychoanalysis had become established as an international movement. This as well as a "deepening frustration with the quality of his entire Vienna circle" caused him to believe that dissidents like Adler needed be tolerated no longer (Stepansky, 1983, p. 138).

Adler most likely met Carl Furtmuller through their Russian born wives, and they had a life-long collaboration (Hoffman, 1994). Furtmuller was bright, articulate, politically active, and by the beginning of the 20th century he had a national reputation as an educational reformer. Furtmuller joined the psychoanalytic circle in 1909, left that group with Adler in 1911, and was Associate Editor of *International Journal of Individual Psychology* for a number of years. His monograph *Psychoanalysis and Ethics*, which was written in 1912, was the first publication of the new Society for Free Psychoanalytic Research. He went on to co-edit *Healing and educating: Foundations of the art of education for physicians and educators* in 1914 with Adler as well. It is likely that Adler's thinking on educational innovation and social change was profoundly shaped during discussions with Furtmuller.

Another early influence on Adler's thought was Vaihinger's philosophy of "as if" published the same year as Adler withdrew from the Vienna Psychoanalytic Society (Vaihinger, 1924). The two carried on an active correspondence for a number of years, and Adler in 1916 wrote that he was "... considerably assisted and confirmed in my view by Vaihinger's work" (p. 77). Vaihinger's influence marks a shift for Adler to a phenomenological point of view in which causality is subjective and soft. "The three psychological meanings of the term fictional [which he adopted from Vaihinger], as subjective, created, and unconscious, remained the most essential components of Adler's goal concept" (Ansbacher & Ansbacher, 1956, p. 90). Drives are replaced by values, goals, and beliefs as the central motivational elements in the personality. Fictions are creations of the individual and not reducible to objective causes. The seemingly objective factors of environment, heredity, and developmental experience are utilized by the person in forming the goal, which is then acted upon "as if" it were truth.

After World War I Furtmuller used his political influence and his position as State Inspector for Vienna's experimental schools to get Adler an invitation to help create child guidance clinics attached to the State schools. This work is the beginning of group based interventions for Adler and despite the fact that they are not group therapy, they do indeed show a movement away from the private one to one format exemplified by the practice of psychoanalysis. Furthermore, they are a movement away from a medical and disease based model toward an idea of incorporating education and reorientation as a psychological intervention. Adler developed a creative and unique format in which a teacher described a difficult child to Adler in front of an audience of colleagues. After asking some questions, Adler would present his impressions, and then would interview the child and the parents. Once this was completed and the family left, he would lead a final discussion of the case. The procedure was extended from the schools to the community, serving parents at Centers for the Guidance of Parents (Dreikurs, et al, 1959). These clinics proliferated in schools and in the community, and were the primary method for interested persons to become acquainted with the principles of Individual Psychology. By 1935, when the Fascists shut them down, there were about 30 such clinics in operation in Austria as well as several in Germany. Adler also founded a school based upon his principles and lectured at adult education centers and local universities.

During this time Adler began speaking to audiences throughout Europe. He had a reputation as an inspiring and thought-provoking speaker, and was quite popular. His writings have been characterized as the original self-help books (Hoffman, 1994). He made his first trip to the United States in 1926 as a part of a lecture tour. In 1932 he became Chair of Medical Psychology at Long Island Medical School and moved to America. Adler's family, associates, and followers in Europe were forced to flee for their lives when the Fascists came to power. Adler died in 1937 while on a lecture tour in Scotland.

INDIVIDUAL PSYCHOLOGY AND GROUP APPROACHES

Rudolph Dreikurs, Adler's premier follower and a major theoretical contributor to Individual Psychology in his own regard, is credited with being among the first private practice group psychotherapists circa 1925 (Terner & Pew, 1978). The story goes that due to an overcrowded schedule he suggested that three of his patients come to share a single interview appointment. Given that they were all at an advanced stage of their work with Dr. Dreikurs it was assumed that they would be able to gain from each other's experience. This initial serendipitous event led to a longstanding interest in group psychotherapy that Dreikurs would practice in his remaining years in Vienna and then carry with him in his work in Chicago.

As group approaches became more widely accepted, Adlerian practitioners have participated actively in the theory and practice of group psychotherapy. Bierer (1951) applied the principles of Individual Psychology to the treatment of hospitalized psychiatric patients, emphasizing the encouragement of social interaction. Papanek (1954) wrote on the combined practice of group and individual therapy in private practice and the importance of the social setting in milieu therapy (1970). Kadis wrote on the use of family constellation (1956) and childhood recollection (1957) in group therapy. The Alfred Adler Clinic in New York utilized a social club to treat psychiatric patients (Mohr & Garlock, 1959). Kadis and Winick (1960) wrote on the importance of the role of the stranger in group psychotherapy. Shulman and Hoover (1964) describe democratic staffing patterns and interactions for a psychiatric hospital unit. Sonstegard and Dreikurs (1975) wrote a comprehensive chapter on group psychotherapy and counseling as part of a textbook on basic approaches to group psychotherapy. Dinkmeyer and Muro (1971) describe a set of methods and procedures for the practice of Adlerian group counseling. The theory and practice of group psychotherapy has been further described in chapters of texts by Dinkmeyer, Dinkmeyer, and Sperry (1987), Manaster and Corsini (1982) and Sweeney (1989). The literature on group psychotherapy and counseling from the perspective of Adler's Individual Psychology has been consistent and longstanding despite its unsung presence in the larger literature of theory and practice of group psychotherapy.

Individual Psychology is first and foremost a practical and adaptive theoretical approach. The psychological interventions described in the literature of Individual Psychology address the full range of human conditions from the normal difficulties of healthy people to the extreme needs of the chronically mentally ill. In developing an Adlerian group orientation it is essential to consider the varying circumstances in which group interventions are applied. Caplan (1970), in his classic work on mental health consultation, makes clear the distinctions between various assumptions in mental health relationships. In the application of psychotherapy there exists an assumption of pathology with the concomitant goal of treatment and rehabilitation. In the case of consultation, supervision, and or education the assumption is that of normal range functioning on the part of the client. Here the assumption is that the individual will adapt better with some help through education and encouragement. There is a wide range of normal human functioning and many people will do well to receive assistance for problems of daily living. Adlerian-based group techniques make this distinction clear with the goal of developing interventions that are facilitative, educational, or advisory in nature for conditions that fall short of diagnostic criteria that suggest mental illness or dysfunction.

In Individual Psychology the goal of education is to increase the individual's understanding and to develop specific skills. The teacher or trainer provides the student with information about interpersonal patterns, disease processes, self help approaches, and other objective data that can be of assistance in promoting adaptation and coping in the face of difficult life problems. In the area of parent education Soltz tells us that:

> "The goal of parent study groups is to understand the purpose of children's misbehavior, to become aware of the actual meaning of 'mutual respect', and to gain skill in democratic approaches for coping with the daily problems of living together as equals." (1967, p. 8)

In Individual Psychology the distinction between counseling and psychotherapy is related to the scale of the change being sought. Counseling is more concerned with acute situations while psychotherapy concerns itself with changing the totality of the person's life style--his or her view of themselves, others and the world. In counseling the client is encouraged to act differently; while in psychotherapy the client is helped to understand their basic beliefs. Both processes lead to a reorientation of the client's style of solving the tasks of life.

While avoiding the traditional stigma of medical diagnosis and classification, Individual Psychology counselors and psychotherapists generally conduct a rigorous evaluation at the beginning of treatment (Powers & Griffith, 1987; Shulman & Mosak, 1988). Dreikurs, Shulman and Mosak (1984) proposed an innovative use of the life style interview in which one therapist collects some initial information and then meets with the client and a second therapist for a review, interpretation, and summation of this information and treatment planning. The second therapist implements the agreed-to plan and continues the treatment of the client in individual counseling or psychotherapy, family therapy, psycho educational intervention, and or group psychotherapy. Powers and Griffith (1987) note that some clients choose to conclude treatment at the time of the interpretive interview, reporting that they feel ready to try out some new behaviors in meeting the life tasks. The initial inquiry process is educative in that the therapist provides the client with life style information. It also involves counseling in that the therapist encourages and points out alternative behaviors for coping with the present life task. And finally, it is psychotherapy in that the basic beliefs are interpreted to the client with the goal of helping them understand and have more adaptive control over their lifestyle.

Dreikurs, Grunwald and Pepper (1971) apply the concepts of life style analysis, encouragement, equality and group processes to the classroom. The teacher is advised to structure the classroom democratically, to encourage student participation in resolving conflicts with in the class and to utilize the relationships within the classroom group as learning tools.

There is a great deal of overlap in the processes of education, counseling, and psychotherapy and in any group it is likely that all three processes will occur to some degree. Relationship factors greatly influence the outcome for each, and for individual psychologists a collaborative relationship (mutual respect and alignment of goals between therapist and client) is central to the success of each process.

Mechanisms of Psychological Intervention

As a psychodynamic and interpersonal theory of personality, Individual Psychology is concerned with the process of helping the patient or client become aware of unconscious motivations for their behavior and lifestyle decisions. The premise is built upon the notion that the individual with psychopathology has problems in living and is discouraged rather than sick. These problems in living are seen as resulting from poor preparation for the tasks of life, and the therapeutic task is to encourage the person, to activate social interest, and to develop a new life-style through relationship, analysis, and action methods.

Dreikurs describes the process of Adlerian Psychotherapy as an uncovering and interpreting form of psychotherapy that is based upon the premise that man is an indivisible holistic social being whose every action has a purpose (Dreikurs, 1967). Dreikurs talks about the working process of counseling and psychotherapy following a four step series of interventions involving Relationship, Psychological Investigation, Interpretation, and Reorientation.

The idea that the therapeutic relationship is basic to the work of counseling and psychotherapy is central to all theories of psychological intervention. The relationship is the fundamental medium through which the work is conducted and is initiated with the first contact between the patient or client and the therapist. The ability to develop a trusting and cooperative relationship is primary to the initial tasks of information gathering, problem identification, diagnosis, and treatment planning. The theory of Individual Psychology has always promoted the ideas of collaboration, social equality, and reduction of emphasis on pathology as a means for developing a horizontal rather than vertical relationship between the client or patient and the therapist (Garrison, 1994; Grunwald & McAbee, 1985).

The process of psychological investigation involves a gathering of information and testing of hypotheses making use of the stochastic method (Manaster and Corsini, 1982). The Individual Psychology therapist considers the presenting problems in the context of the developmental history, family constellation, and lifestyle data and seeks to understand the purpose and psychological context of the behavior or symptoms in question.

The process of interpretation involves the use of language and behavior to assist the patient or client in understanding the underlying motivations for the lifestyle decisions involved in the behaviors or problems in question. The ability to communicate with the patient or client in a manner that reduces psychological defensiveness and increases the courage to understand the motivations for the actions is a fundamental skill set that each mental health professional needs to develop in the course of their training and professional work. At best the interpretation process assists the person in gaining additional understanding of the motivations and lifestyle decisions that underlie behavior with a minimum of shame, guilt, or anxiety response. Psychological insight is best obtained when one feels able to join in with the group or community at large and feels less stigmatized by symptoms, actions, or experiences.

The process of reintegration involves the patient or client working through the applications of the insight in the various components of developmental and social life experience. With a newfound understanding of the purpose of a behavior the individual is in the position to make increasingly adaptive decisions in the course of life and to have an increasing sense of control and mastery in daily living.

The process of group psychotherapy makes use of these same intervention methods. In the early stages of group, as the members are normalizing their relationships with each other, there is a process of developing a working alliance. This is a critical period in the life of a therapeutic group and the leadership must work to support the development of trust and support so the group will be able to work through the inevitable conflicts and confrontations that will be a part of future group interaction. As the group members are increasingly aware of each other's presenting problems, family and developmental history, as well as their presence in the group there is ample opportunity to better understand the context of the psychological problems or shortcomings that are brought forward for work in the therapy.

As group members become more able to explore and ask questions of each other, the process of investigation evolves between members of the group as well as on the part of the therapist leader. As groups develop, they are more able to tolerate conflict and disagreement, which allows the membership to better explore the relationships within the group in the context of the history and problems that are presented for work.

As the group matures to the point of accepting interpretations from each other, the process of exploration matures. The group at this point grows able to accept and tolerate varying levels of confrontation, disagreement, interpretation, and questioning. This is the time in the life of a group where a normalizing process occurs in the membership and participants cooperate in the course of their work. As members learn more about each other and are able to work together for the common goal of self-growth and exploration the process of interpretation and reorientation occur on an ongoing basis.

The Individual Psychology oriented group psychotherapist makes use of group process to form a collaborative corrective social construct that can be compared to and conferred with in the participant's exploration of his or her own external and developmental experience. The individual's relationship with the group serves as a teacher and corrective influence which reduces the stigma of having deficiencies and enhances the ability to experiment with and change values without the loss of dignity (Sonstegard, 1998a).

The social responsibility and community building philosophy of Alfred Adler is deeply embedded in this approach. This idea is not solely the domain of Individual Psychology. Frances, Clarkin, and Perry (1984) in their work on the selection and prescription of psychiatric treatment point out that much of what makes treatment successful is matching the problem to the therapeutic intervention. MacKenzie (1995) has written on the importance of developing different approaches to group work when serving diverse populations in managed care delivery systems (1995). Group therapy as a theoretical and practical discipline has always stressed the importance of individual differences, the importance of patient selection, group composition, and theoretical orientation as fundamental to quality care. These ideas are central to the practice of group therapy and can be found across the range of literature from the classic early works to the most recent practice development oriented publications (Fehr, 1999; MacKenzie, 1992, 1995; Price, Hescheles & Price, 1999; Rutan & Stone, 1993; Yalom, 1995) Adler himself tended to work in psycho-educational groups in the Child Guidance Clinics then popular Vienna. The process of these clinics evolved from Adler's emphasis on the social context as being central to understanding and treating the child and family. In the course of counseling Adler worked to promote an open, egalitarian, and encouraging environment for families and children with behavioral or school based problems. They would be interviewed and the problems would be discussed in the presence of teachers, families, and community members. The great emphasis on the importance of the leader being responsible to promote a constructive and educational environment was the foundation for the success of this public forum counseling approach.

Over the years the traditions of demonstration family counseling have persisted and there are communities where these strategies are still applied in the present day. As the techniques of group therapy were advanced with research and theoretical development in the areas of interpersonal theories, systems theories, and group-as-a-whole dynamics the applications of Individual Psychology in group psychotherapy have evolved to incorporate an interpersonal and interactive approach. The task of the work is to assist the individual in joining with the group to engage in understanding unconscious aspects of lifestyle through the use of relationship building, psychological investigation, interpretation, and reorientation.

Despite the fact that Individual psychology is not often credited as a widely popular theoretical orientation, its roots in psychodynamic psychology as well as its interpersonal, family, and community based premises make it a significant contributing theory that underlies contemporary eclectic psychological group approaches. The applications of group therapy are present in Individual Psychology from its earliest roots in its consistent use and application of group processes in counseling, educational, and training interventions.

Table 1: Individual Psychology Approaches to Group Work

	Time Limited Psycho-Educational Program	Demonstration Family Counseling	Psychiatric Chem Dep Inpt Ward	Outpatient Private Prac Group	Hospice Team Support	PTA Parenting Workshop
Population	Physician & self referred patients with a distinct med/psy problem	Self or other referred parents	Mixed psychiatric Dual diagnosis CD Voluntary admits& legal hold admits	Self motivated and invested pts who are working and self sufficient	RNs, LVNs, health care aids, MSWs, physical therapists.	Parents of a public school joining in an evening meeting
Intervention Parameters	Thurs @ 6 pm community clinic 8-12 person coed Various Topics Cost: $20.00	Saturday 9 am to noon Walk-in members Ongoing donation	9am Daily 60 minutes Coed mixed age 6 days per week Cost: $90.00	Tues @ 6 pm Private Office 8 person coed 2 yrs average Cost: $45.00	Alt Tues 9am Rotating Home 7-9 members Ongoing No fee to staff	Annual event school cafeteria 25 members Lead discussion No fee: Volunteer
Intervention Intensity	Minimal	Moderate	High	High	Moderate	Minimal
Psychotherapy	Low	Low	Medium	High	Low	Low
Counseling	Medium	High	High	Medium	Low	Low
Education	High	High	Medium	Low	Medium	High
Structural Issues	Education Normalization	Education Skill Building	Diagnose/Stabilize Improve and refer Out	Reconstruction Improve lifestyle quality	Team Building Stress Reduction	Education Normalization
	Self Choice Attend	Self Choice Attend	Mandated Care	Self Choice Care	Employer mandated	Self Choice Attend
	Psy/Ed Model	Demonstration Counseling Model	Med/Psy Model	Med/Psy Model	Psy/Ed Model	Education Model

Table 1: Individual Psychology Approaches to Group Work (Continued)

Group Member Issues	Motivation to improve condition Public discussion of private and personal problems	Interest in improving skills Public discussion of family issues	Dignity Motivation Self control	Investment in Rx Plan Motivation and Resistance	Mourning Connecting Team work and dissention	Interest in how to improve skills Public discussion of private and personal problems
Process Focus	Encouragement and support for self disclosure Information dissemination	Encouragement Goal disclosure	Encouragement Self assessment Information Skill acquisition Shared learning	Relationships within the group Parallels between history and group relationships	Relationships within the team Acknowledging similarities and differences	Encouragement and support for disclosure Information dissemination
Member Factors	Potential for resistance if sent by insurer Seeing self as similar to others	Self selected Guilt and regret about past mistakes Seeing self as similar to others	Mandatory vs. choice for care Less control of Rx Maintain dignity Confidentiality	Self choice for care Control over Rx Maintain dignity Confidentiality	Team based socialization Employer lead Maintain dignity Confidentiality	Self Selected Question of self disclosure Seeing self as similar to others

Clinical Examples

Six clinical examples are provided here to demonstrate the breadth of Individual psychology and group psychotherapeutic approaches. Table 1 presents and contrasts six different types of group intervention. The psycho educational group meets weekly in a clinic setting for a limited time with the same clients. The demonstration family-counseling group meets weekly in an educational setting with a walk-in clientele. The chemical dependency group meets daily on an inpatient psychiatric/chemical dependency unit and attendance is required of all persons on the unit. The outpatient psychotherapy group meets weekly in a psychologist's consulting room and has little turnover in-group members. The hospice team support group meets every other week and is required of all staff at the hospice. The PTA parenting workshop is a one-time annual meeting in the school cafeteria for all who choose to attend.

Teleology and Life Style

In Individual Psychology the analysis of the person is based upon an understanding of the goal of the psychic movement, at various times called the fictional goal, the guiding fiction, the guiding self-ideal, or the fictional final goal by Adler. A person's behavior is viewed as a consistent and purposive striving toward their unique fictional final goal. This goal is the central organizing principle of the personality, which is variously called the guiding line, life plan, life style, style of life, or unique law of movement in Individual Psychology. "The personality of the individual was seen by Adler as a unity and all drives, strivings, tendencies and aspirations were part of this unity and all inclined in the direction dictated by the unique law of movement" (Shulman, 1973, p. 16).

The goal is a self-created fiction or narrative world view formed early in life and is based originally on biological and environmental influences. As the infant develops, he or she organizes the world and formulates rules about their experience as a means of adapting and coping. These rules of thumb in turn begin to limit and define what is experienced. "It [the unique law of movement] cannot help but be reinforced by experience because it is the rule by which experience is perceived" (Shulman, 1973, p. 17). Through the course of early life the pattern elaborates and becomes the guiding principle for the person's movement through life.

> Personality is the result of training that is less stimulated by heredity and environmental influences than by the child's own interpretations, conclusions and decisions. The basic concept of himself and life, the guiding lines which he has set for himself for orientation toward social participation form a fixed pattern - the style of life (Dreikurs, 1967, p. 6).

The fictional final goal and the life style are believed to crystallize between the ages of 4 and 7, with change in the core beliefs or the goal being relatively rare. Various authors have discussed a variety of components of the life style and a hierarchical organization has been proposed (Kopp & Garrison, 1976). The components are always viewed as consistent with one another and as organized by the fictional final goal. There is typically a cognitive component made up of convictions, beliefs, expectations and/or ideals, and a behavioral component that includes emotion and mood. The cognitive component may include self-concept, belief or expectation about others, world image, image of the social world, gender guiding lines, private logic and/or hidden reasoning. The behavioral component is generally conceived of as expressing the methods utilized by the person to achieve their goal. Individual psychology is a cognitive psychology that views emotion as secondary to the beliefs and as an expression of the person's goal in the specific context and situation. Adler has been quoted as saying that to know where a person is going watch the tongue in their shoe rather than listen to the tongue in their mouth.

The life style organizes and simplifies experience for the person, and exerts a selective function on experience. "The world is seen through a stable schema of apperception: experiences are interpreted before they are accepted, and the interpretation is always in accord with the original meaning given to life" (Adler, 1958, p. 60). Events are perceived according to the logic of the life style leading to fulfillment of the expectations and reinforcement of the beliefs contained within it.

As Individual Psychology has evolved and developed, the concept of life style has been applied to a variety of family and social units. Ansbacher (1967) also proposed using the term life style "... in reference to the behavioral and cognitive aspects of a relatively permanent, small group, down to a dyad, where the members are interacting with one another" (p. 200). There have been discussions in the literature of marital life style (Hawes, 1983), family life style (Deutsch, 1967) and group life style (Kadis, 1959).The next section describes the use of time limited group psychotherapy as an example of how interventions that make teleological and lifestyle issues more obvious to the members of a group can promote significant psychological benefit and growth. The intensity level of intervention in a psycho educational time limited group is relatively minimal. The major emphasis is on education with the goal of increasing the member's understanding of their lifestyle, unconscious goals, and their ramifications on the quality of daily life. As a result of this understanding the counseling, or approach to specific life situations, is of a medium level. The psychotherapeutic, or depth understanding of lifestyle is low at best.

TIME LIMITED GROUP THERAPY

Time limited psychoeducational groups have become quite popular in the past 15 years. They generally run between 10 and 20 sessions, and are designed for a homogenous population. They can be composed of persons with a specific problem, life concern, diagnosis, or life developmental phase related difficulty. Participants may be self-referred or referral may be from a physician or mental health professional. These are usually closed groups, meaning that members are not added during the course of the group. Cost is generally considerably lower than that in individual or long-term group psychotherapy. Most time-limited groups have a curriculum or guide, and leader manuals are utilized in research and clinical practice.

Individual psychology has a long history of time-limited groups. Lott and Nelson (1988) provide outlines for eight different courses on parenting, utilizing eight different parenting books. There is also mention in the individual psychology literature of life style groups (Dinkmeyer, Dinkmeyer, & Sperry, 1979), marriage enrichment groups (Hawes, 1983), marital communication groups, (Hawes, 1983), encouragement groups (O'Connell, 1975), health care counseling groups (Dinkmeyer et al, 1979), and action therapy groups (O'Connell, 1975). The process of these groups is to have some content presented by the leader or by a book, and then group discussion of the content with an emphasis on self-disclosure and on resolving to act differently in specific situations. Education and counseling are the predominant therapeutic modalities, but there are frequently changes in a participant's life style that emerge from the new behavior patterns.

The four goals of a child's misbehavior are consistently presented and discussed in individual psychology parenting groups. These goals are attention, power, revenge, and display of inadequacy and are discussed as the purpose of a specific misbehavior and as a pattern of misbehavior. Thus the purpose of an act of misbehavior can be identified as attention seeking and a child can be identified as engaging in numerous attention-seeking behaviors. Various parenting strategies can be taught as appropriate for the different goals of misbehavior. The use of encouragement for more appropriate, high social interest alternative behaviors is typically a part of these strategies.

Clinical Illustration

Mike and Linda are 42 and 40 years old respectively, and enrolled in a time limited parenting group offered in a private practice setting. They married 3 years earlier, and each had children from prior marriages. Linda's son, David, is 10 and has lived with them since their marriage. Mike's daughters, Kate, 13, and Emily, 11, had visited on a regular basis. Two months prior to beginning the group Kate decided to move from her mother's home to her father's home and she was the focus of their concern. Kate was being noncompliant and verbally disrespectful to Linda and engaging Mike in long conversations about a variety of subjects. These conversations seemed to occur frequently at bedtime and were sufficiently long that Linda was frequently asleep when Mike came to bed.

At the first session, when families were asked to introduce themselves and their families, Mike and Linda noted that about one third of the families included stepchildren. This was discussed in the group as a subgroup that might have special concerns. As the goals of misbehavior were presented in the second session, Mike and Linda recognized Kate's goal with Mike as being attention, and her goal with Linda as being power. They were encouraged to hear that other parents were also experiencing similar difficulties. They collectively formulated a plan that included:

- Mike setting firmer limits about bedtime and clarifying appropriate times for conversations,
- Linda disengaging from power struggles and disrespectful interactions with Kate,
- Linda taking Kate to a movie, and
- Both parents noticing Kate's respectful interactions with them.

They also met with Kate together and clarified the consequences for noncompliance, emphasizing consistency between the two parents.

At the third session they reported that Kate' disrespect had increased with Linda and she had become more demanding with Mike, but the noncompliance had subsided. This was just as had been predicted in group as they presented their plan. They were encouraged to continue with the plan for another week and by the fourth week the presenting problems were resolved, and did not emerge through the course of the 12 week group.

During the fifth session the group was broken into small groups and Mike and Linda participated in the stepfamily small group. It was particularly important for them to hear about the struggles of other stepfamilies. This group requested that they have time to meet each week for the remainder of the class and the leader adjusted the curriculum and timetable of the course to allow this to occur.

SOCIAL INTEREST

Adler's term Gemeinschaftsgefuhl has been translated as social feeling, community feeling, fellow feeling, sense of solidarity, communal intuition, community interest, social sense and social interest (Ansbacher & Ansbacher, 1956). Ansbacher (1978) traces the development of this concept in Adler's writings. It is the most distinctive and valuable concept in individual psychology and one of the most difficult to understand comprehensively. Social interest has been called "... the cardinal personality trait" (Ansbacher, 1968, p. 131), which is "... the main characteristic of each person and is involved in all his actions" (Adler, 1937, p. 774)." It is the criterion for mental health and for well being, and thus represents a statement of the values of Individual Psychology. Social interest is assumed to be "... an innate potentiality which has to be consciously developed" (Adler, 1929, p. 31).

Human beings are portrayed as constantly moving in Individual Psychology, and in this portrayal, social interest serves as the compass. Social interest is based on the premise that human beings are socially embedded one with the other and the realization that human beings only exist within a society. Social interest is equated with an affirmative attitude toward life in general, manifested by a sense of connection and cohesion.

The innate social feeling is actually a community feeling, a reflection of the coherence of everything cosmic, which lives in us, which we cannot dismiss entirely, and which gives us the ability to empathize with things, which lie outside our body (Ansbacher, 1968). There is a unification of the interest for the well being of self and others, that promotes an essential harmony with mankind and the human community at large. In addition to this community aspect of social interest Ansbacher (1968) identifies a process dimension that is composed of three developmental steps.

- In Step 1, social interest is an assumed aptitude for cooperation and social living, which can be developed through training.
- In step 2, this aptitude has been developed into the objective abilities of cooperating and contributing, as well as understanding others and empathizing with them.
- In step 3, social interest is a subjective evaluative attitude determining choices and thus influencing the dynamics of the individual (p. 132, Italics in the original).

Dreikurs (1967) conceived of social interest as a feeling of belonging, a sense of having a place within the immediate group and the larger community, and based on a desire to be useful and to make a contribution to the group and community. He saw social interest as "movement on the horizontal plane" (p. 40), and emphasized the relationship between social interest, social equality, and democracy.

O'Connell (1965) proposed "humanistic identification" as a more appropriate translation for Gemeinschaftsgefuhl. He points out that this translation broadens the reference point (humanistic is broader than social) and energizes the activity (identification in contrast to interest). For him social interest is

> Demonstrated intellectually by 'outsight,' a commitment toward understanding the psychological needs of others and the tension generated by their lack of fulfillment; and by an active movement toward satisfying such needs and becoming a significant other (p. 44).

He combines the sense of cosmic connectedness with a behavioral expression. He also sees humanistic identification (social interest) as a precondition for authentic religious practice.

Different facets of social interest are manifested in the cognitive, affective, motivational, and behavioral processes of the person. Adler postulated three life tasks with which each person is confronted: friendship and community, work, and love. The manner in which these three tasks are pursued can be evaluated for the level of social interest present. Counseling, psychotherapy, parenting, and teaching are all opportunities to consciously develop social interest. The psychological movement of the person through life can be evaluated for the level of social interest and specific alternative behaviors can be formulated that are more socially interested and therefore likely to be healthier for the person and the other with whom they are interacting.

In the following example of a family education center the issues of social interest and family relationships are described. In this public forum counseling intervention the group format is utilized to normalize and reorient difficult behaviors in children and parents. The strategy of educational intervention, shared experience, and creative approaches to problem solving provides a moderate level of intervention intensity. The emphasis is on education and counseling with a comparative low level of psychotherapy in that the work is directed toward specific difficult behaviors and various approaches to eliminate them.

FAMILY EDUCATION CENTER

The family education center is a service delivery modality that is unique to Individual Psychology. There are typically one or more playrooms for children, with some centers offering different activity groups for various ages. The centers generally convene once a week in an on-going manner and are composed of walk-in members who may have been referred by a community caretaker or self-referred. Fees vary from donation to $5 per session. Some centers are freestanding; others work in conjunction with a community college or university, while others are affiliated with a public or private K-12 school. Staff are predominantly volunteers who have attended parenting groups (which are frequently offered in conjunction with a family education center).

When a family comes to the center the children go to the playroom while the parents convene in a group--generally between 15 and 50 people. First there is a brief presentation of a parenting principle from individual psychology by one of the volunteer staff. Then a family who has attended several previous sessions and who volunteered the previous week is interviewed in front of the group. First, the parent(s) are interviewed, then they are asked to leave the room and the child(ren) are interviewed. After this, the parent(s) are asked to return and the playroom worker and/or teacher (if the FEC is operating in conjunction with a school) is asked to report their observations of the child(ren) and how they relate to the other children and to the group. Then the counselor gives explanations of the dynamics of the child(ren)'s behavior and makes recommendations regarding parenting strategies. There is some discussion by the group of the principles being applied to the demonstration family and then the group concludes.

Educational Illustration

Don and Marta are both 21 years old and have been married for three years. They have a four year old daughter, Kirsty, who is having frequent tantrums with both parents and with their day care provider. The day care provider had attended a parenting class through the family education center and recommended to Don and Marta that they consider attending one as well. They attended a total of four demonstration family counseling sessions and did not serve as a demonstration family.

The first demonstration family they witnessed had an attention-seeking child, and did not seem particularly relevant to their situation. They enjoyed the supportive and nonjudgmental atmosphere at the family education center, and were pleasantly surprised by the manner in which the other, mostly older parents took an interest in their situation. They began having family meetings based on the short talk that had been given at the beginning or the session and a book they purchased at the center.

The second demonstration family worked with was about attention seeking, but also involved the recommendation to institute a weekly family meeting. During the discussion after the demonstration Don talked about their first family meeting and received encouragement from several other parents. Don, Marta, and Kirsty ran into the demonstration family at lunch after the meeting and Don and Marta shared their experience with family meetings and gave the family some tips on how to hold one.

The third demonstration family (the Smiths) they watched was about a power-seeking child and was very relevant to their situation. They felt a strong kinship with the parents in this family, partially because the family dynamics were similar, and partially because this family was one of the other younger families at the center. Marta sought out the mother from this family at the end of the session and they had dinner together later in the week. They shared techniques for withdrawing from the conflicts and enlisting the help and cooperation of the child.

Don and Marta did not attend the next several sessions, but they maintained some contact with the Smith family and were mutually supportive of the changes each parent was making in their parenting style. They continued to have weekly family meetings and supported one another in their new parenting strategies. Kirsty's tantrums gradually decreased in frequency and severity during this time.

Don and Marta attended one more session and watched another family with a power-seeking child. After this demonstration they agreed that they were happy with the way things were going in their family and decided to stop coming to the center. They continued a friendship with the Smith family. Marta volunteered to work in the young children's playroom and continued to do so for about six months. She participated in several demonstrations as the playroom reporter, and co-led a parenting group for young parents.

In the Family Education Center Example the development of social interest in the interaction of the family is the major underlying component of the educational intervention. In the next example it can be seen that a far more complex health problem, depression and chemical dependency, is addressed with a similar application of promoting social interest. In the following example there are marked differences in the intensity of the intervention with the use of psychotherapeutic verses educational interventions. Nonetheless, the use of the individual's relationship to the community at large is a central and underlying common ground across both interventions.

Psychiatric/Chemical Dependency Inpatient Ward

The population found on an inpatient psychiatry service is usually a combination of involuntary and voluntary admissions. Much of the initial work in a chemical dependency or psychiatric emergency involves the stabilization, diagnosis, and initiation of a longer term care plan. For the most part group psychological interventions are commonly practiced in this setting. The daily group therapy session involves a rotating membership as patients are admitted and discharged on a daily basis. The last decade has witnessed a significant change in the use of hospitalization in psychiatric care. The managed care emphasis has reduced length of stay to a small percentage of what was common over the previous five decades. Much of what occurs in the daily group involves orienting patients to their condition and helping them to develop a healthy attitude and a sense of responsibility for their own rehabilitation.

The daily inpatient group usually meets for 60 to 90 minutes and is best lead by the same leader on a regular basis. The level of intervention is considered high as a function of the regular daily meetings and the need for confrontation of the symptoms, history, and lifestyle components of the current condition. With this emphasis there is a basic educational component that is central to the intervention. The patient needs to better understand how his history, both developmental and recent, has lead to the current condition. Much of what the patient needs to do is make changes in the course of daily living. Here we can see the counseling emphasis. As the patient learns more about how they deteriorated into the present situation there follow concomitant actions to be taken to improve the condition. In the case of those patients who are uncooperative or unable to take responsibility for their actions and situation the treatment team frequently resorts to a more intensive level of care. Despite the fact that many useful psychotherapy care plans initiate in an inpatient setting there is rarely the opportunity for a length of stay of sufficient duration to develop a true psychotherapy care plan.

The intensity of the work in the inpatient setting requires that the therapeutic staff remain mindful of the dignity and levels of discouragement experienced by the patients in the group. While the group can be a very useful approach in confronting the difficult patient it can also promote therapeutic casualties. The professional staff needs to work together for the well being of the unit at large as well as the individual needs of the patients in admission.

Clinical Illustration

Joseph was a 56-year-old depressive with a long history of alcoholism and multiple treatment episodes. He was admitted to the emergency room with abdominal pain and referred to the inpatient psychiatric/chemical dependency ward for detoxification from alcohol and treatment of depression. After three days Joseph was placed in the daily group therapy and presented in a withdrawn and apathetic manner. He would make sarcastic utterances under his breath and often appeared to be bored and disinterested. The leader actively confronted him with regard to his motivation for changing his lifestyle and the dangerous consequences of continued drinking. Despite his initial resistance and passive aggressive response an older alcoholic woman in the group who was crying because of her diagnosis of liver cancer finally touched him in the fourth meeting. Joseph's primary therapist on the unit coordinated care with the group therapist and they both agreed to continue with the confrontation approach. On the seventh day Joseph began to cry himself, telling of his father's alcoholism and the abuse he received as a child. He began to express regret for the ways in which he raised his children and become open to the idea that the family therapist on the unit could help him to try to improve the rapport with his adult children. At the time of discharge Joseph was able to verbalize to the group how useful the process had been for him and said that he hoped he had been of some help to the younger members who were dealing with their own alcoholism.

HOLISM

Many of Adler's followers believe that "Holistic Psychology" would be the most appropriate name for their psychology. This basic concept was expressed in Adler's choice of Individual Psychology as a name for his psychology. "The term individual in German has the connotation and denotation of a unity, an indivisible whole. It refers to the unique individuality of individuals" (Manaster & Corsini, 1982 p. 3).

A holistic approach to psychology includes the idea that the whole is greater than the sum of its parts, and that the parts, unified, constitute a unique whole.

> ...One can never regard single manifestations of the mental life as separate entities, but that one can gain understanding of them only if one understands all manifestations of a mental life as parts of an indivisible whole and then attempts to uncover the line of movement, the schema of life (Ansbacher & Ansbacher, 1956, p. 190).

Here Adler was disagreeing with Freud's analytic process of dividing the personality into id, ego, and superego or conscious versus unconscious and forging a theory with new basic hypotheses. Adler's early emphasis on organ inferiority and the subsequent compensatory strivings helped his thinking to avoid a mind/body split and contributed to this holistic position. "For Adler, the question was neither 'how does mind affect body?' nor 'How does body affect mind?' but rather how does the individual use his body and mind in the pursuit of his goals? " (Mosak, 1979, p. 52) As his thinking matured, the early focus on organ inferiorities developed into a focus on perceptions, beliefs and convictions. "Thus, in latter day Adlerian theory, an organ inferiority becomes a possible stimulus for psychic compensation if it is subjectively perceived as a defect or obstacle" (Shulman, 1973, p. 93).

Adler was among the first to appreciate the work of Jan C. Smuts (1926) who coined the word holism. Adler carried on a correspondence with Smuts after his book, Holism and Evolution (1926) was published. He was so impressed by this work that he arranged for it to be translated into German, but the translation was never realized (Ansbacher, 1961). Adler did arrange for a translation of Smuts' presidential address to the British Association for the Advancement of Science (Smuts, 1932). This may be the only time a psychological journal has published a paper by Smuts (Ansbacher, 1961).

This emphasis on a holistic understanding of the person led Adler away from a mechanistic conception of the person and toward a probabilistic, field theory perspective. Human beings are seen as indivisible, creative organisms functioning in a current social context and within the context of an evolutionary past. The focus of attention is shifted from the study of part-functions to a study of the whole person and how he or she moves through life. This perspective also contributes to thinking of all aspects of psychic life as movement and to the teleological conception of behavior.

The holistic perspective challenges the clinician to see each element of study in the context of the other elements of the person and to focus on the interaction between these elements as much as the individual elements.

> We must never treat a symptom or single expression: we must discover the mistake made in the whole style of life, in the way the mind has interpreted its experiences, in the meaning it has given to life, and in the actions with which it has answered the impressions received from the body and from the environment (Adler, 1931, p. 47).

Dreikurs (1967) utilized the concepts of holism and movement to define the assessment strategy that he called "two points on a line." Determining the unifying concept in two apparently contradictory behaviors or beliefs is like joining two points, and the resulting line of movement will point to the purpose of the behaviors and to the individual's goal.

In the following case example of the outpatient private practice psychotherapy group the holistic factors of human nature are a central component of the psychological group based intervention. In this type of group the level of intervention is high. The emphasis is on psychotherapy, the understanding of the individuals basic, and often unconscious, beliefs and goals. The educational component is comparatively low in that we are less concerned with didactic instruction and provision of information in favor of experiential learning. The counseling component is medium because a side effect of understanding unconscious motivations is the enhancement of the experience of control over the problems of daily living.

Outpatient Private Practice Group

The population found in the outpatient private practice group therapy is a well selected heterogeneous group of individuals who are brought together by the therapist with the idea of creating a working therapeutic intervention setting. Much of the work in an outpatient open-ended group involves a focus on the relationships between the members of the group and the evolving psychological processes that develop therein. One major underlying assumption is that there is a significant parallel between the experience of the individual group members in the group and their families of origin. Not only does the group tend to become more familiar with the families of origin from which each and every member has evolved, but also the group process itself tends to replicate, and in a sense demonstrate, how each group member tends to join and fit in. The discussions of salient history, problematic symptoms, and the actual ongoing process of the group is usually very instructive and helpful in allowing members to better understand the families that they grew up on and the recurring patterns of difficulty they experience in their lives.

The group meets on a regular weekly basis and has a rather stable pattern of membership, that allows for a high level of intimacy in the interpersonal relationships. The level of intervention is considered to be high as a function of the regular meetings and the levels of interpersonal disclosure and sharing of opinions. One of the major factors in a group that has adequate time to explore the relationship between presenting problems, personal history, and present day behavior is the obvious variation in experience and difference of opinion. The levels of conflict and disagreement are a central component to the therapeutic intervention in that members have as a central task the need to work through differences of opinion, conflicts, and disagreements. Many group members remark that group is one of the few places other than the family of origin where they are as aware of the wide range of personal feelings and experiences, that require resolution when conflicts arise. For many people, the group is the first place where they are able to work through and understand their place in the family of origin and its impact on their daily living.

The average length of stay varies considerably from one practice setting to another but it is often the case that treatment plans require several years of group work. In order to sufficiently understand the complex interpersonal relationship factors that follow from the family of origin and to see their symbolic recapitulation in the group and other contemporary social settings group members need adequate experience analyzing and interpreting their own situation and that of their fellow group members. Over time, as mastery is gained, the process of termination for an individual member becomes self evident to that individual and the group at large. Under these circumstances the process of leaving the group allows for the development of safe and useful individuation processes and for moving on with the grace of the group. Much like the family of origin who supports the maturation of the child through adolescence and into adulthood, the process of the group is a reworking of deficiencies from the family of origin.

Clinical Illustration

Jennifer was a 38 year old professional who was married and had two children. A happy and satisfying marriage for close to twenty years was becoming increasingly conflicted due to disagreements between Jennifer and her husband. Issues of financial planning, sexuality, and parenting were beginning to promote significant marital conflict. Initial consultations with Jennifer and her husband suggested that her family of origin included a history of gambling and alcoholism, the experience of abandonment, inappropriate seductive behavior on the part of the father, and an overwhelming level of responsibility in the care for her younger brothers. The marriage process itself was well intact and after a series of meetings Jennifer agreed to join an ongoing group to better understand how her childhood experiences in her family of origin contributed to her feelings of anxiety and anger in the marriage.

Over a series of months Jennifer became very emotional in group and began to understand that she had been very much out of touch as to how scared she was as a child. When conflicts arose between members of the group she would frequently assume that a dangerous physical event would follow. Over the course of several years she became more comfortable with differences of opinion and actually began to enjoy the idea that she was allowed opinions that were different from those of the more dominant men in the group. As this process began to unfold conflicts at home initially increased but over time the climate at home began to become much more enjoyable and cooperative. As an added bonus the increased ability to articulate feelings in words allowed for a tremendous improvement in communication and intimacy in the marriage. As Jennifer became more comfortable over time newer group members began to use her as an example of how much progress one can make in group and as a benchmark of when to think about leaving.

FAMILY CONSTELLATION

The Individual Psychology concept of family constellation views the family as analogous to a constellation in astronomy, as a group of bodies, each connected to the others and each with a place (Griffith & Powers, 1984). Understanding the family constellation is a developmental and historical undertaking. Adler worked to understand the family of origin as a whole system in his assessment of a person, examining their relationship with each family member. The person's unique life style (personality) is seen as developing out of the relationships and interpersonal process of the early years of life. "It is a common fallacy to imagine that children of the same family are formed in the same environment" (Ansbacher & Ansbacher, 1956, p. 376). The search for a place, for status and for methods of achieving significance is conducted within the family constellation. The family constellation defines what places are available as well as what is valued as the person grows up.

The focus on the whole family and their interrelatedness led to a focus on sibling relationships and birth order as one personality determinant. Adler defined five prototypic birth order positions or "vantages" (Griffith & Powers, 1984) from which the child perceives, evaluates, and forms the basic convictions of their life style. These positions are the oldest child, the second child, the middle child, the youngest child, and the only child. These positions are not rigidly defined and not everyone will fit one category - individual psychology is interested in the experience the child has as he or she grows up.

> It is not ... the child's number in the order of successive births which influences his character, but the *situation* into which he is born and the way in which he interprets it (Ansbacher & Ansbacher, 1956, p. 377) (italics in original).

Shulman and Mosak (1988) list eight components of family constellation in addition to birth order: gender, constitution, models, parental care taking behavior, sibling behaviors and interaction, family values, family atmosphere and ambient culture.

In the following example of a hospice team support group we see the recapitulation of family dynamics in the work team. The opportunity for a team involved in such an inherently stressful and emotionally invoking occupation is very high. It is common for such a team to experience difficult interpersonal dynamics in the course of normal range work activity. The use of the support group format as a means to promote team efficiency and prevent the stress and burn out response helps to keep the team working in an efficient manner. When team members better understand the impact of their feelings they are better able to work together to achieve the desired goal.

HOSPICE TEAM SUPPORT GROUP

The staff of a hospice team is essentially a specialty nursing team with an R.N. nurse manager, infusion specialist RN's, LVN's, home health care aids, physical therapists, and social workers. The team is a highly structured work group with an exceptionally high turnover over of patients, as cases are not admitted to the service unless the death of the patient is immanent. Major stressors involve the intensity of the work, size of the caseload, administrative problems that are often idiosyncratic to each case, and the expression of stress in the relationships amongst team members.

The bi-weekly support group meeting occurs in a rotating calendar of team member's homes. As a home health care organization team, members are accustomed to driving to domestic residences to conduct their work. The weekly meeting consists of approximately three R.N.s, two L.V.N.S, two health care aids, one physical therapist, and one social worker. The teams remain relatively stable and are comprised of healthcare professionals who chose to be in this intense line of work. The major point of intervention is the transformation of mourning, loss, stress, and frustration emotions into a common team experience. The tendency to experience one's self as alone leads to conflict among team leaders and promotes conflict. Most difficulties between team members, or the team and the hospice administration, are commonly found to have at their root an experience of alienation and/or overwhelming emotion, which is so common in this line of work. As a result of this tendency the hospice service has prescribed regular support group meetings as a means for reducing conflict and increasing team efficiency.

Clinical Illustration

Louise is a single mother R.N. infusion specialist. She is good at the technical aspect of the nursing work and is an exceptionally caring and hardworking individual. She commonly takes on extra work and will schedule more visits each day than is expected of her by the hospice administration. Louise is very dedicated to her young daughter and often has to rely upon the help of her mother and other team members to cover her when she over schedules at work. For the most part this work pattern has sustained itself well over the past eighteen months until she became especially connected to one case in particular. This terminal case died while she was on a five day vacation break she felt tremendous responsibility. Over the next week she became very angry with the home health care workers whom she felt were not doing enough to keep the patients clean and comfortable. The day before the support group meeting the nurse manager called the consultant to describe what had been happening and that there were a lot of conflicts on the team in the past two weeks.

With this information the consultant initiated the following day's support group meeting with the standard procedures. It became immediately clear that there were increased tensions in the air. One of the home health care aids began to talk about feeling picked on and soon broke into tears. Louise was quite cold and indifferent as she watched the story unfold. As each member had some say in the matter the consultant avoided the intensity of the matter and inquired as to how Louise's time off had gone. Within a matter of moments she expressed grief at the passing of the case to which she felt so connected. Soon she too was crying and with some clarification and support was able to state that the gentleman had reminded her of the best attributes of her father who had been an intermittent presence in her life. As she became more expressive and was able to understand the personal intensity of her sadness the anger at her colleague became self evident to her. With minimal intervention Louise came around to understand the events that had come to pass and made apologies to the home health care aid. The team spent an especially self-disclosing session this meeting with a recollection of many past cases they had cared for who had special significance for them. They were able to recall several events when their personal feelings had promoted team conflict. When the meeting ended most members had cried and there was a refreshed desire to return to work.

In the following example of a PTA Workshop we see the educational aspects of Individual Psychology. Many clinicians have the opportunity to speak in public on mental health related topics and issues. It is generally seen as a way to generate referrals for counseling or psychotherapy. Individual Psychology views education and the dissemination of information as a therapeutic intervention and this awareness is utilized in the planning of such talks. In keeping with the democratic and egalitarian nature of Individual Psychology, education is not set up in a hierarchical fashion. Other students are viewed as potential sources of information as well as the instructor and experiential techniques of teaching are utilized extensively.

PTA Workshop

Educational interventions vary greatly depending upon the context in which they are provided. This example is an annual talk sponsored by the PTA and open to anyone who wishes to attend. There is no fee for participation. The intensity of this intervention is minimal and predominantly educational in nature. In this illustration we show how information about one aspect of the family constellation, sibling position, can lead to significant change in the functioning of a person and a family.

Educational Illustration

Mary came to the PTA meeting because the speaker was going to speak about sibling relationships. She had a 3 year old boy, Sam, and a 6 month old girl, Bethany, and was a stay-at-home mother whose husband had been working a great deal of overtime for the past two years. A neighbor with school age children had told her about the workshop while they were talking about Sam's increased clinging, whining, and misbehavior. Mary and her husband were both only children in their families of origin. The workshop leader had the group break into groups of oldest children, middle children, youngest children and only children, giving each group the task of discussing what it is like to grow up with this view of family life and then presenting a report to the whole group. The leader then used the process of the groups and the style in which each report was delivered to the group as illustrations of the typical characteristics of each birth order position.

The group of oldest children elected a spokesperson that described the experience of dethronement and invasion of territory the group had recalled when their sibling was born. He also talked about the pressure of parental expectations and the stress they had felt to stay ahead of their sibling. The group of middle children had a spokesperson that used the slogan, "We Try Harder" to illustrate their aggression and competitiveness. Their report was longer than the report of the oldest children. They acknowledged that they had it easier in the family because their parents were more relaxed and confident with them. The group of youngest-borns did not really put together a report for the group as they had spent most of their group time telling of the mischief they had done as kids and the ways in which they had gotten their older siblings in trouble. The only children insisted on each giving their own report to the group.

Mary developed a new understanding of the emotional turmoil that Sam was experiencing. She also recognized how she and her husband were not functioning as a team in their parenting or family life. She purchased a book on parenting that the speaker had recommended and she and her husband read it together and made changes in their parenting style. During the next two years they did not seek out any additional therapy services.

Concluding Remarks Regarding the Development of an Adlerian Group Psychotherapy Orientation

An Adlerian group orientation is an adaptive and accommodating approach to education, counseling, and psychotherapy. As shown in these six diverse examples of intervention, the group therapist is able to approach a wide range of commonly encountered human problems. In the course of intervention the group therapist is able to work with a range of levels of intensity appropriate to the membership of the group and the problems being treated. Each clinical or educational situation requires an appropriate level of intervention intensity to promote an effective outcome. The varying emphasis on education, counseling, and psychotherapy is in direct proportion to the problems at hand and the needs of the specific group.

As Sonstegard has stated (1998b) group work is highly structural in that the leader has the responsibility to have very specific goals and objectives with regard to the specific interventions utilized. This structure follows from a thorough understanding of the problems and goals for the specific intervention. In the development of a group therapeutic activity, regardless of the range of intensity or emphasis, the group therapist must have a clear idea of what the overall plan is and how it addresses the specific problem area at hand. The basic matters of timing, cost, membership, duration, and climate are central to the outcome of the project.

When implementing a group psychotherapy program the leader must have a clear understanding of the goals and objectives the work is to accomplish. There is much to be considered in terms of the population and setting in which the work is to occur. The intervention parameters need to be well thought through in terms of their ability to fit well with the overriding social and political ramifications in the setting at hand and the specific characteristics of the individuals being considered for treatment. The group therapist must be concerned with both the understanding of the individual and the society, the idiographic and the nomothetic, in the development of group therapeutic intervention.

The orientation is based upon a unified understanding of human nature as a central theme in the personality theory. The interventions are based upon the premise that human beings are socially embedded, holistic, goal oriented, and subjective. These characteristics of human nature allow the group therapist to structurally arrange the social construction of reality within the group culture to facilitate the therapeutic task. In the psychoeducational, counseling, and psychotherapeutic modes of intervention, the four step process of relationship, psychological investigation, interpretation, and reorientation is employed. The major distinctions between the three models involve assumptions on the part of the social context of the intervention, the characteristics of the individuals, and their specific problems being worked with.

REFERENCES

Adler, A. (1898). *Gesundheitsbuch fuer das Schneidergewerbe* [Health book for the tailor trade]. Berlin: Heymanns.

Adler, A. (1916). *The neurotic constitution: Outlines of a comparative individualistic psychology and psychotherapy* (B. Glueck and J. E.Lind, Trans.). New York: Moffat, Yard and Co. (original work published 1912).

Adler, A. (1927). *Understanding human nature*. Greenwich, CT: Premier Books.

Adler, A. (1929). *Problems of neurosis*. London: Kegan Paul.

Adler, A. (1931). *What life should mean to you*. New York: Capricorn Books.

Adler, A. (1937). Psychiatric aspects regarding individual and social disorganization. *American Journal of Sociology, 42*, 773-780. (Original work published 1924).

Adler, A. & Furtmuller, C. (Eds.). (1914). *Heilen und bilden*. [To heal and to educate]. Muenchen: Reinhardt.

Ansbacher, H. L.(1961). On the origin of holism. *Journal of Individual Psychology, 17,* 142-148.

Ansbacher, H. L.(1967). Life style: A historical and systematic review. *Journal of Individual Psychology, 23,* 191-231.

Ansbacher, H. L. (1968). The concept of social interest. *Journal of Individual Psychology, 24,* 131-149.

Ansbacher, H. L.(1978). The development of Adler's concept of social interest: A critical study. *Journal of Individual Psychology, 34,* 118-152.

Ansbacher, H. L. & Ansbacher, R. R. (Eds.). (1956). *The Individual Psychology of Alfred Adler: A systematic presentation in selections from his writings*. New York: Harper.

Bierer, J. (1951). *The day hospital, an experiment in social psychiatry and synthoanalytic psychotherapy*. London: M. Lewis.

Caplan, G. (1970). *The Theory and Practice of Mental Health Consultation*. New York: Basic Books.

Deutsch, D. (1967). Family therapy and lifestyle. *Journal of Individual Psychology, 23,* 217-223.

Dinkmeyer, D .C., Dinkmeyer, D. C. & Sperry, L. (1979). *Adlerian counseling and psychotherapy*. New York: Macmillan.

Dinkmeyer, D. & Muro, J. J. (1971). *Group counseling: Theory and practice*. Otasca, IL: Peacock.

Dreikurs, R. (1967). *Psychodynamics, psychotherapy and counseling*: Collected papers of Rudolf Dreikurs. Chicago: Alfred Adler Institute.

Dreikurs, R., Corsini, R., Lowe, R. & Sonstegard, M. (1959). *Adlerian family counseling: A manual for counseling centers*. Eugene, OR: University Press.

Dreikurs, R. R., B. B. Grunwald & Pepper, F. (1971). *Maintaining sanity in the classroom: Illustrated teaching techniques*. New York: Harper and Row.

Dreikurs, R., B. Shulman & H. Mosak. (1984). *Multiple psychotherapy: The use of two therapists with one patient*. Chicago: Alfred Adler Institute.

Ettin, M. F. (1992). *Foundations and applications of group psychotherapy*. Boston: Allyn and Bacon.

Fehr, S. S. (1999). *Introduction to Group Therapy*. New York: The Hayworth Press.

Frances, A., Clarkin, J. & Perry, S. (1984). *Differential Therapeutics in Psychiatry: The Art and Science of Treatment Selection*. New York: Brunner/Mazel

Furtmuller, C. (1914). Preface to Journal of Individual Psychology, quoted in Hoffman, E. 1994. *The drive for self: Alfred Adler and the founding of Individual Psychology*. New York: Addison-Wesley.

Garrison, M. A. (1994). Misalliance movements in psychotherapy. *Canadian Journal of Adlerian Psychology, 24,* 20-33.

Griffith, J. & R. L.Powers, (1984). *An Adlerian lexicon*. Chicago: The American Institutes of Adlerian Studies.

Grunwald, B. B. & McAbee, H. V. (1985). *Guiding the Family: Practical Counseling Techniques*. Muncie, IN: Accelerated Development.

Hawes, C. E. (1983). Marriage counseling and enrichment. In Christensen, O. C. & Schramski, T. G. (eds) *Adlerian family counseling*. Minneapolis: Educational Media Press.

Hoffman, E. (1994). *The drive for self: Alfred Adler and the founding of individual psychology*. New York: Addison-Wesley.

Kadis, A. L. (1957). Early childhood recollections in the therapy group. Journal of *Individual Psychology, 13,* 182-187.

Kadis, A .S. (1959). Re-experiencing the family constellation in group psychotherapy. In Adler, K. A. & Deutsch, D. *Essays in individual psychology: Contemporary applications of Alfred Adler's theories*. New York: Grove Press.

Kadis, A. L. & Winick, C. (1960). The role of the deviant in the therapy group. *International Journal of Social Psychiatry, 6,* 277-287.

Kopp, R. R. & M. A. Garrison. (1976, May). The life style: A systems perspective. Paper presented at the North American Society of Adlerian Psychology Annual Conference, Vancouver, B.C.

Lott, L & J. Nelson. (1988). *Teaching parenting: A step-by-step approach to starting and leading parenting classes*. Provo, UT: Sunrise Books.

MacKenzie, K. R. (1995) *Effective use of Group Therapy in Managed Care*. Washington, D.C.: American Psychiatric Press.

MacKenzie, K. R., ed. (1992) *Classics in Group Psychotherapy*. New York: Guilford Press.

Manaster, G. J. & R. J.Corsini.(1982). *Individual psychology: Theory and practice*. Chicago: Adler School of Professional Psychology.

Mohr, E. & R. Garlock. (1959). The social club as an adjunct to therapy. In K. A. Adler & Deutsch, D. (Eds.). *Essays in Individual Psychology: Contemporary applications of Alfred Adler's theories*. New York: Grove Press.

Mosak, *H. H. (1979). Adlerian Psychotherapy. in R. J. Corsini (Ed.). Current Psychotherapies* (2nd Edition). Itasca, NY: F .E. Peacock.

O'Connell, W. E. (1965). Humanistic identification: A new translation for Gemeinschaftsgefuhl. *Journal of Individual Psychology, 21,* 44-47.

O'Connell, W. E. (1975). *Action therapy and Adlerian theory*. Chicago: Alfred Adler Institute.

Papanek, H. (1954). Combined group and individual therapy in private practice. *American Journal of Psychotherapy, 8,* 679-686.

Papanek, H. (1970). Adler's psychology and group psychotherapy. *American Journal of Psychiatry, 127,* 83-86.

Powers, R.L. & Griffith, J. (1987). *Understanding life-style: The psycho-clarity process*. Chicago: The Americas Institute of Adlerian Studies.

Price, J. R., Hescheles, D. R. and Price, A. R. (1999). *A Guide to Starting Psychotherapy Groups*. San Diego: Academic Press

Rutan, J. S. & Stone, W. N. (1993) *Psychodynamic Psychotherapy*, 2nd Edition. New York: Guilford.

Shulman, B. (1973). *Contributions to individual psychology*. Chicago: Alfred Adler Institute.

Shulman, B. & K. K. Hoover. (1964). Therapeutic democracy: Some changes in staff-patient relationships. *International Journal of Social Psychiatry, 3, [Special Edition], 16-23.*

Shulman, B. and H. Mosak. (1988). Manual for life style assessment. Muncie, IN: Accelerated Development, Inc.

Smuts, J. C. (1926). *Holism and evolution*. New York: Macmillan.

Smuts, J. C. (1932). Das wissenschaftliche Weltbild der Gegenwart. *International Journal of Individual Psychology, 10,* 244-261.

Sonstegard, M. (1998a). Adlerian group counseling: Step by step. *Journal of Individual Psychology, 54,* 176-216.

Sonstegard, M. (1998b). A rationale for group counseling. *Journal of Individual Psychology, 54,* 164-175.

Sonstegard, M. & Dreikurs, R. (1975). The teleoanalytic group counseling approach. In G.M.Gazda (Ed.). *Basic approaches to group psychotherapy and group counseling.* (pp. 468-510). Springfield, IL: Charles C. Thomas.

Stepansky, P.E. (1983). *In Freud's shadow: Adler in context.* Hillsdale, NJ: The Analytic Press.

Stolz, V. (1967). *Study Group Leader's Manual.* Chicago: Alfred Adler Institute.

Sweeney, T. (1989). *Adlerian Counseling: A Practical Approach For A New Decade.* Muncie, IN: Accelerated Development.

Terner, J. & W. L. Pew.(1978). *The courage to be imperfect: The life and work of Rudolf Dreikurs.* New York: Hawthorn Books.

Vaihinger, H.(1924). *The philosophy of 'as if': A system of the theoretical, practical and religious fictions of mankind* [C. K. Ogden, Trans.]. London: Routledge & Kegan Paul, Ltd. (original work published in 1911).

Yalom, I. D. (1995). *The Theory and Practice of Group Psychotherapy*, 4th Edition. Basic Books.

Chapter Thirteen

MAKING MEANING IN GROUPS: A CONSTRUCTIVIST DEVELOPMENTAL APPROACH

Richard L. Hayes

A growing interest in alternative epistemologies is currently being merged with counseling's long-standing basis in developmental theory and its more recent advocacy of a multicultural approach to practice. One significant result has been the re-emergence of counseling and psychotherapy models based on a constructivist developmental psychology. Constructivism offers a distinctly different approach to the traditional relationship between knowledge and reality that accounts for individual cultural differences within a universal developmental scheme. Because constructivism focuses on how people make meaning in their lives, it has profound implications for understanding the relationship between human development and social behavior, especially applied to group work. The purpose of this chapter is to orient the reader to the assumptions that frame a constructivist approach and to set the stage for their application to group work practice. In particular, this chapter is intended to: (1) offer a comprehensive definition of constructivism; (2) elaborate the common principles of a constructivist approach and their implications for group work; and, (3) provide some examples of a constructivist approach to working with groups.

COMPETING EPISTEMOLOGIES

Theory and practice in counseling and psychotherapy have been dominated for more than a century by a faith in the person as an individuating and autonomous self. This modernist position is supported by the positivist's faith in the capacity of the individual to know, to understand, and to control nature as part of a grand and unifying master plan to liberate the individual. Modernism accepts a notion of the self as autonomous and bounded, as having an independent nature, and as sharing an open-ended, but perfectible relationship with others. Consequently, modernism encourages personal control, especially over nature and thus of a humanly-created order that permits individuals to pursue their own wants and interests in the quest for self-fulfillment.

From a group work perspective, this set of assumptions supports a view of the group as comprising "a collection of individuals who have relations to one another" (Cartwright & Zander, 1968, p. 46), in some "interaction" with one another (Hare, 1976, p. 4; McGrath, 1984, p. 1), "in such a manner that each person influences and is influenced by each other person" (Shaw, 1981, p. 454), who "communicate with one another ... face-to-face" (Homans, 1950, p. 1), and "who stand in (more or less) definite status and role relationships to one another and which possesses a set of values of its own, regulating the behavior of individual members" (Sherif & Sherif, 1956, p. 144). This representation of the group as comprised of interacting but autonomous individuals frames group counseling as an intervention focused on changing individual behavior through group interaction.

Postmodernism, on the other hand, is characterized by a general loss of faith in the modernist enterprise as leading to the rational planning of an ideal social order and the consequent standardization of knowledge and production. Instead, postmodernism (Conner, 1987; Derrida, 1981; Foucault, 1972; Hayes, 1994a; Jencks, 1986; Lyotard, 1983) favors "heterogeneity and difference as liberative forces in the redefinition of cultural discourse" (*PRECIS*, 1987). In particular, postmodernism rejects the pictorial (iconic) metaphor of knowledge in favor of a *constructivist* (architectural) metaphor (Hayes & Oppenheim, 1997; Lyddon, 1995; Lyotard, 1983; Mahoney, 1991; Rickey, 1967).

Constructivism asserts that representations are not accurate *copies* that correspond to a real world but are *constructions* of order that constrain but do not specify courses of action. Rather than viewing the mind and body as separate entities, the constructivist sees them as interdependent forms of the same large system. Rather than being separate human processes, thoughts, feelings, and behaviors are understood as convenient myths to describe inseparable functions. In short, the constructivist asserts that the truth is *un*knowable, that it cannot be *verified*, that experiments cannot be *controlled*, that technology is a *poor* substitute for theory, that change isn't necessarily *progress*, and that progress is neither *inevitable* nor *linear* but rather is *contextual*. Significantly, the constructivist accepts that truth is not reality and that reality is not *discovered* but rather it is *invented*. What we experience, and thus come to know, is necessarily built up of our own building blocks and can be explained in no other way than in terms of our own ways and means for building. In this sense, reality is what *you* make it (Hayes & Oppenheim, 1997).

Although constructivists are not of one mind, especially related to their assumptions about change and causation, a set of common principles can be articulated that provide a meaningful contrast with the positivist approach (Hayes & Oppenheim, 1977). In particular, these assumptions lead to a reconceptualization of the group as socially constructed and group work as providing a social context for enhancing human development.

COMMON PRINCIPLES FOR A CONSTRUCTIVIST APPROACH

Individuals are Producers of Their Own Development

Inherent in human nature are certain structuring tendencies by which people attempt to make sense of experiences within themselves and of the world in which they live. What one knows (or rather, how one is knowing it) emerges in the light of interactions between certain organismic structuring tendencies and the structure of the outside world (Kelly, 1955; Piaget, 1960).

As biological organisms, humans inherit two basic functions: *organization* and *adaptation* (Kelly, 1955; Mead, 11932; Piaget, 1936/1954, 1926/1955). Organization refers to the tendency for all living things to attempt to order their processes. Once the object has been experienced, it is brought into awareness as a part of the way we think. Reality is constructed from experience and represents a relationship between the self and the world. Relevant environmental events are modified so that they may be incorporated into existing organizational structures. Incompatible situations are either distorted to conform to prior expectations or they are ignored. In a complementary process, modifications are made in our mental organization in response to environmental demands. Existing mental structures tend to be modified to suit the demands of the environment. In the process of organizing one's experience, the individual must simultaneously *assimilate* novel experiences into pre-existing structures and *accommodate* pre-existing structures to meet the demands presented by new experiences (Baldwin, 1902; Piaget, 1960). Thus, learning is the outcome of organizing our experience with objects.

The second function is the tendency of living things to make modifications in response to changing environmental conditions *in anticipation of* desired outcomes. The test of truth, therefore, is not *correspondence* with an external reality, but rather its *viability* in accurately predicting an indeterminate future. Constructivists argue that truth and knowledge are constructions within the mind of the individual and that meaning making and valuing are based on those constructions. Because mental phenomena have a relation to a content that is intentional in nature, all behavior is anticipatory rather than reactive. Thus intentionality establishes a person's way of being conscious of something. Humans adapt in order to enhance their potential to reap positive outcomes from an anticipated environment and, as such, operate as self-organizing systems.

The central implication for counseling of this constructivist account is that clients construct reality through their experience. Thus the client's reality represents a relationship between the client and the world as the client understands that world. It is not so much that clients *have* problems as that they *experience* problems, for how one understands and makes meaning of experience betrays the underlying logic of how one makes sense of one's own existence.

Cognitions represent internally organized systems of relations, which comprise a set of rules for processing information or connecting events in personal experience. Cognitive thinking, therefore, is the active relating of events. Therefore, human development represents the course of our attempts to make sense of those changes going on around us—to understand what it means "to be me in a world like mine at a time like this." This notion of the self as a self-organizing system has profound implications for understanding human development and, in turn, for reconceptualizing counseling as something other than adjusting the client's reality to correspond more accurately to the *real world* (Carlsen, 1988; Feixas, 1990; Friedman, 1993; Goodman, 1984; Hayes, 1994a; Ivey, 1986; Kegan, 1982; Kvale, 1992; Mahoney, 1985; Neimeyer, 1985; Saari, 1991).

Development is Contextual

Humans are creatures living in a time and place with other creatures. Thus, development is neither wholly a consequence of events that have happened to us nor wholly the result of inner urgings. Instead, development takes place in a social context wherein human knowing is both encouraged and bounded by the social context in which such understanding arises. Thus person and world are not separate, nor even in interaction, but rather are inextricably linked in *trans*actions with one another (Basseches, 1984; Gibbs, 1979; Mead, 1934; Piaget, 1936/1954, 1926/1955; Riegel, 1979; Viney, 1990; Vygotsky, 1934/1986). Understood in this way, human development is fundamentally a social event that demands interaction with others. The process of knowing emerges in the light of rcciprocal transactions between ourselves and our personal surroundings. In other words, objects are defined (in part) by their relationship to each other.

Meaning-Making is Self-Evolution

The idea of transactions going on between people and their environments leads the constructivist to a particular notion of cognitive development. Each person's self-regulating system emerges as a consequence of new states of equilibrium that were created by the previous self-regulatory system. Therefore, disequilibration serves as a stimulus to development, while equilibration is its goal. Development can be seen from this view as the natural outcome of attempts to make stable sense of a changing world. As a result of this recurring cycle of equilibration-disequilibration-equilibration, development takes a path that may best be described by a spiral. The outer turns are analogous to the person's attempts at the integration of novel experiences to existing structures. In each evolutionary turn, the spiral moves to a new level of organization analogous to the movement to a higher stage of development (Langer, 1969, pp. 95-96).

Although constructivists are not of one mind about the notion of stages, specifically, any use of the term is reserved to refer to "*qualitative* [italics in original] differences in children's modes of thinking or of solving problems at different ages" (Kohlberg, 1969, p. 352). Where developmental stages are hypothesized, each of these stages is understood as providing a "structured whole" (Piaget, 1960, p. 14) that represents an individual world view or frame of reference for meaning-making. Each succeeding stage represents the capacity to make sense of a greater variety of experience in a more adequate way.

Thus, each stage is a more differentiated, comprehensive, and integrated structure than the one before it. The fundamental reason for movement from one stage to the next, therefore, is that a latter stage is more adequate in some universal sense than an earlier stage. The basic notion of this stage concept leads to the conceptualization of development as the movement toward greater adaptation, differentiation, and integration of distinct modes of thought in a universal, invariant, and hierarchical developmental sequence (Kohlberg, 1969; Piaget, 1960; Werner, 1940/1973). The implication of this structural model of cognitive development is that individuals within a particular stage of development view reality in ways that are similar with regard to structure but may be vastly different with regard to content. In this way, each level of cognitive development might be viewed as a culture of cognitive structure.

From a constructivist approach, development is understood as successively more complex attempts to make meaning of the facts of one's social experience. As Kohlberg (1969) put it: "Social development is, in essence, the restructuring of the (1) concept of the self, (2) in its relationship to concepts of other people, (3) conceived as being in a common social world with social standards" (p. 349). If personality development is essentially the universal, ongoing process of meaning making, then counseling should focus on development and the person's experience of this process (Rosen & Kuehlwein, 1996).

Reality is Multiform

Because truth lies within the set of truths that can be brought to bear upon a single event, the truth can never really be known. Seen in this way, problems represent unsuccessful attempts to resolve difficulties and point to potential limitations in one's current way of knowing. Because constructivism accepts the possibility of multiple realities, it is necessarily self-reflective. Faced with the recurring possibility of error, counselors, no less than clients, should engage in a process of continual self-reflection. Because the problems encountered by professional practitioners are frequently complex, Schon (1987) argued that professional education should be centered on enhancing the practitioner's ability for "reflection-in-action." The recognition of one's own failed expectations--that sense of surprise--indicates the necessity to re-examine one's own beliefs and to reconsider one's values.

Language Constitutes Reality

As has been argued, a postmodern world is characterized by changing perspectives, with no underlying frame of reference. To find one's place in such a world, therefore, requires the development of a reliable, consensual system for negotiation. Language, the postmodernists teach us, provides the system necessary for grounding our understanding of the self *in relation to* the other. The postmodernist argues that rather than take the position that "seeing is believing," one might say that "believing is seeing." Language does not permit the accurate *re*-presentation of a world "out there," but rather is a symbol system for expressing sets of assumptions about our understanding of that world. Language does not mimic reality, rather language constitutes reality, with each language constructing specific aspects of reality, each in its own way. Rorty (1983) argues that the various vocabularies we use or the particular perspectives we take are instruments for coping with things rather than ways of representing their intrinsic nature. Thus, one vocabulary is not inherently better than another because it corresponds more closely to "reality" but rather because a given vocabulary works better in a particular situation for a given purpose.

When we enter the process of description, however, we invariably rely on conventions, which both expand and constrain what can be communicated. In effect, the words we choose reveal the ontological presumptions of a culture. Because clients actively construct their social world, the client's history is not so much a record of one's life experience as it is a living representation of how one is experiencing life. Understanding the world is thus not a product of the world as it is, but of an historical text. The constructivist's recognition of the social construction of discourse on the world (Gergen, 1991) points to the problem inherent in negotiated understandings across the boundaries of race, gender, ethnicity, culture, or personal experience. Constructivism encourages the development of a language of difference that would permit one to understand the Other as the Self, recognizing the inseparability of our knowledge of one another.

GROUP COUNSELING AS SOCIAL RECONSTRUCTION

Constructivism does not create nor explain any outside reality--no objective world facing the subjective. Any apparent separation of the world into pairs of opposites is constructed by the subject, and that paradox opens the way into autonomy as the recognition of one's ownership of his or her particular reality (see Dewey, 1963). Significantly, that reality is constructed within a social context born of relationships with objects, especially other people, that make up one's environment. Despite the subjective nature of reality, therefore, one's understanding of the self lies embedded in and is defined by one's relationships with others.

Although a constructivist approach to the counselor's work can be taken with individual clients, the full benefits of such an approach are best realized within the context of group work. Acknowledging that reality as one knows it is socially constructed is to recognize the dual nature of the self as defined in relationship to the other. Such a shift in thinking leads to a reconceptualization of individual counseling as but a subset of group counseling. Although group counseling is not a substitute for the "real" world, it serves as a real world context for developing relationships. As a consequence, one might properly understand all counseling fundamentally to be group work. Drawing upon the constructivist principles and their implications for counseling outlined above, a set of directives are addressed to the counselor who would take a constructivist approach to group work.

Focus on Meaning Making

The central implication of taking the constructivist's view of reality as a self-constructive activity is that counselors should try to understand how clients make sense of personal experience, that is, how clients make meaning. Significantly, clients make meaning within a social context that is informed by their current understanding of the past and their vision for the future. Group work, therefore, can provide the proper social context for both the reconstruction of one's own personal history and the rehearsal of alternative futures.

Taking a constructivist perspective, members are accepted as operating out of their own internal maps and not out of sensory experience. It is not so much that members have problems as that they *experience* problems; how one understands and makes meaning of experience betrays the underlying logic of how one makes sense of one's own existence. By noting a member's surprise or attending to apparent disappointments, the leader can open the door to discovering the core of the member's meaning making.

Because people are self-organizing systems, members are considered to have considerable powers of spontaneous recuperation and are recognized as making the best choices available to them at any given time, whether in the past or in the present moment of the group. Because the past is reconstructed in the present, the resources the member needs lie within his or her own personal history. Thus, member strengths and resources should be emphasized and presenting problems accepted as "real" for the member. It is assumed that people do the best that they can at any moment given their situation and the constraints of their constructs. In effect, it is recognized that members are never not themselves. In attempting to understand members' actions in the group, therefore, leaders should ask themselves, "Given all the things that this person might have said or done, who would say or do a thing like that?"

It is not inconsequential that Piaget (1924) patterned his "methode clinique" after psychiatric questioning "with the aim of discovering something about the reasoning underlying their right, but especially their wrong answers" (p. 244). In a reversal of the logic, questioning intended to uncover the member's meaning construction can facilitate understanding. Recognizing that the member's understanding of the past is socially constructed in the present, especially in the presence of the counselor and other family or group members, the leader should be more concerned with *how* rather than *what* or *why* members believe as they do.

Because the member's reality represents a relationship between the member and the world as the member understands that world, true understanding combines knowledge with felt experience. To understand another, Kegan (1982) suggested, is to enter into that region "between an event and a reaction to it--the place where it actually becomes an event for that person" (p. 2). It is in this *zone of mediation* that leaders will help members to make meaning of their experience. Consequently, leaders should shift their attention from changing what clients believe, or from helping them to uncover the reasons why, to varying the process by which clients arrive at those beliefs. Questions directed at uncovering members' understanding of their own personal history will necessarily ask,

"How did you decide to take this or that course of action? How do you know this is true?"

Promote Cognitive Conflict

The most important aspect of a constructivist view of how we think is that experience is the necessary condition for development, although experience itself is not enough. Because we tend both to organize and adapt, we must necessarily interact with the environment. Thus, each person's experience must be of a kind that presents genuine cognitive conflict for him or her. This conflict should present a discrepancy to some optimal extent between the individual's existing mental structures and his or her present experience (an idea given philosophical import by Dewey (1916/1944) and psychological credence by Kohlberg (1981, 1984). Thus, problems represent discrepancies between challenges and capacities.

Because people actively construct their social world, their history is not so much a record of their life experience as it is a living representation of how they experience life. Viewing knowledge as invented and evolving, Kelly (1955) hypothesized that the construing efforts of individuals were socially embedded. Further, he believed that a client's stories and metaphors functioned to establish continuity of meaning in the client's lived experience. The goal of his therapy, therefore, was to assist the client in developing a perspective shift or conceptual reframing that could permit new courses of action. This constructivist view of development rests on the dialectical metaphor of cognitive development as "the progression of ideas in discourse and conversation" (Kohlberg & Mayer, 1972, p. 456). Accepting that the group leader is part of the social environment, group work from this perspective looks like a dialogue among the group members and the leader. The mind and the self emerge through language in a social process. As Mead (1934) explained, "the individual experiences himself as such, not directly, but only indirectly, from the particular standpoints of other individual members of the same social group, or from the generalized standpoint of the social group as a whole to which he belongs" (p. 138).

The suggestion is that the experience of social interaction in the group involves a simultaneous experience between the member and his or her environments and between the member as actor and as acted upon. The implication is that the personal experience of members in discussing and in hearing themselves in discussion will promote self development to the extent that the experience represents some perturbation. The experience of taking the role of others in a group in the presentation of one's own argument is causally related to development such that thinking is a conversation carried on by the individual and the generalized other (Mead, 1934). The general form and content of this conversation is determined by the experience of some sort of problem to be solved. Importantly, the extent to which perturbations arising from social experience are and can be made part of the self is a matter of individual cognitive regulation (Piaget, 1968). The task for the group leader, therefore, is to determine the nature and magnitude of requisite soluble problems that may arise from systematic, social experience in a group setting.

Kohlberg and his colleagues (Rest, Turiel, & Kohlberg, 1969) found that exposing individuals, through moral discussion, to the reasoning of those who were more developmentally advanced was most successful in stimulating the development of moral reasoning when the arguments were presented at a level just beyond the individual's current level of functioning. Because each level represents the capacity to make sense of a greater variety of experiences in a more adequate way, "there is a hierarchical preference within the individual, i.e., a disposition to prefer a solution of a problem at the highest level available to him" (Kohlberg, 1969, p. 353).

Translated to group work, these findings suggest that leaders should help members by clarifying arguments and by supporting or directing attention to arguments at cognitively more complex levels. Likewise, in hearing themselves struggle with the presentation of their own thoughts, members must attempt to clarify the meaning of their arguments for this or that alternative and, by doing so, enhance their capacity to solve their own problems. Using a model of "group pacing," D'Andrea and Daniels (1994) demonstrated some initial success in moving clients to more mature levels of psychological reasoning by structuring "the group process in such a way that clients are systematically engaged in interactions that act as catalysts for personal growth" (p. 587).

In proposing an integration of social and cognitive-developmental psychology, Feffer (1970) argued for a view of interpersonal behavior on the group level as conforming to the same dynamic explanation as that offered by Piaget on the individual level. For Feffer (1970), the interpersonal event "is composed of interacting participants who occupy such roles and reciprocals as giving-taking, asking-answering, and dominating-submitting. The greater complexity notwithstanding, a stable construction of the interpersonal event depends, as in the impersonal realm, on a reconciliation of these complimentary dimensions" (p. 208). Within the context of the group, these different positions include elements that may be potentially in conflict such as task and maintenance functions of the group, the ideas of self and other, and conflicting aspects of the self and social relationships, such as self-defeating behavior or the recognition by professionals-in-training that professionals make mistakes or that they may sometimes be compromised by institutional demands (see Jansen & Glinow, 1985; Wren, 1985).

The suggestion is that the individual in a group, in assuming one role as actor, will assume the complementary role as acted upon. As a consequence, he or she will construct the interpersonal event in polar dimensions that may potentially be in conflict. Anything less than ideal equilibrium provides opportunities for this conflict. The resolution lies in a more stable form of self-organization in the individual and a more stable equilibrium between the individual and the group.

The concept of equilibration views conflicts and problems as opportunities for growth and suggests that it is sometimes appropriate to challenge or disrupt a person's current understanding to promote change. Because reestablishment of equilibrium lessens the urgency toward change, this period requires different intervention styles than does the period prior to intervention. In effect, interventions intended to challenge current understandings will necessarily be different than interventions intended to consolidate new understandings. Group leaders should understand the fundamental differences between assimilation and accommodation and should know when to use each process most effectively.

Understanding that problems represent unsuccessful attempts to resolve difficulties helps point to potential limitations in one's current way of knowing. In exploring the means by which members create their experiential world, however, leaders can increase both their own and members' awareness of the limitations and opportunities that their present understandings provide. Recognizing that we cannot escape our own constructed reality, group work from a constructivist perspective is nothing less than an attempt to create the conditions for such exploration.

Promote Self-Reflection

Humans are meaning making creatures who rehearse encounters in anticipation, interpret the meaning of encounters in the moment, and reflect on the implications in retrospect. Thus, conduct and character derive from a conscious self, which becomes increasingly more stable through present reflection upon its own past conduct in the light of predicted future conditions within a social context. What is of value, therefore, is that which is thought of as making a difference in the "self." As Dewey (1960) explained: "In committing oneself to a particular coursc ... one is in reality choosing what kind of a person or self one is going to be" (p. 149). In making judgments about the people and events in one's life, therefore, one is making judgments about the kind of self one is and ought to become. By promoting self-reflection by group members about their own past behavior, leaders can provide opportunities for shaping a person as yet unrealized. Rather than focus on why the member has behaved in particular ways in the past, therefore, the leader shifts attention to a consideration of how the member will be different in the future, what the member will need to do to effect such a change, and what the member will ask of others in the process.

The implication of this perspective is that group work can provide a context for and a stimulant to development when group members are involved in the examination of their own and others behavior in the group. Yalom (1995) suggested that self-awareness, gained through self-observation and feedback about how one is perceived and experienced by others in the group, is the basic mechanism for therapeutic change. He explained that "the final common result of all our intellectual efforts in therapy is change; each clarifying, exploratory, or interpretative act of the therapist is ultimately designed to exert leverage on the patient's will to change" (1995, p. 95). Group work provides a context for such interaction among members who are encouraged to take risks with one another and to examine the consequences upon their relationships with other group members. What remains is for the educator to encourage a dialogue among group members, especially between those having different perspectives.

From a constructivist perspective, group work takes the form of a dialogue between the member's structures and the structures of the group environment, where the leader may be understood as one of many elements in that environment (Gergen, 1991; Kelly,

1955). What members learn in the course of the group, even if they are unable to articulate it fully, is how theory dependent their actions are. Yalom (1995) has theorized that when the group member "is fully aware of his responsibility for his interpersonal world, he may then begin to grapple with the corollary of this discovery: since he created his world, it is only he who can and must alter it" (p. 40). In taking the perspective of the group as an audience to the member, each member experiences him or herself in new and potentially more growthful ways.

Provide Role-Taking Opportunities

Acting in the context of a public decision-making process helps members to consider the opinions of others and places responsibility on members for the consequences of their actions (see Haan, 1977). As Kohlberg (1969) argued, "the more the individual is responsible for the decision of the group, and for his own actions in their consequences for the group, the more must he take the role of the others in it" (p. 399).

In a particularly relevant study, Carson (1969) observed that group members often evoke congruent responses from other group members through a process of reciprocal social influence by restricting their own behavior to certain safe interpersonal stances. As an antidote to reinforcing rigid and inappropriate interpersonal stances, Beier (1966) and Lewis (1987) have suggested that a major task of the group leader is to refuse to make the very response that the group member invokes in him or her, and to elicit more adaptive patterns from the member instead. Recognizing that deficiencies in the other are actually deficiencies in our construction of the other, helps us to become more tolerant of others. One goal of the leader, therefore, is to enhance the members' abilities to take the perspective of others and to help them examine their impact upon others in order to understand themselves better.

For the leader, the directive is to promote individual self-organization through the creation of group situations in which members are encouraged to take roles and then role-take. Group members are asked to act and then to examine the effects of such action from the perspective of those acted upon. Increasing stability in the development of the self will be evidenced in increased stability of the group's organization

Creating a Context for Reconstruction

People make meaning within the context of their own understanding. In this way, the member's present concerns can be described as the rooting of the subject of inquiry in its immediate historical context. The chief means toward this end, however, is the reenactment of the past in the member's own mind. In reconstructing the past, the member serves as his or her own historian by superimposing the present context over the past. This reenactment process taking place in the member qua historian's mind reflects present understanding and is not necessarily congruent with the former reality. Thus member narratives may be seen as more fabrication than recreation (Howard, 1986; Noam, 1988).

Because the sets of events from which one composes a life are experienced uniquely, each person's life can be viewed as its own grand narrative (Gergen & Gergen, 1988; Howard, 1990; Mair, 1988; Neimeyer, 1994; Polkinghorne, 1993; White & Epston, 1990). If we understand the member's history as the construction of a personal social narrative, then all actions are essentially incomplete, susceptible to limitless interpretations by ever-more imaginative interpreters. Therefore, the test of truth, as noted earlier, is pragmatic--it is the viability or practical utility of knowledge that makes it "true." As Botwinick (1993) argued: "the historian in a sense serves as a public therapist unblocking our relationship to the past so as to create a clear path for successful action in the present" (p.129). From a constructivist perspective, the member serves as his or her own historian in confronting the past either as menacing and unknown or as an organizing framework of thought and feeling that needs to be assimilated into present structures.

The implication of this perspective is that counseling should create a social context for reconstruction--an expansion across the life history of what Winnicott called the "holding environment" (Kegan, 1982, p. 256). As noted above, constructivist counselors will want to focus more on present understandings in the service of future actions than on past actions in the service of present understandings. In attempts to understand members' present efforts at making meaning, leaders should focus on the interaction between members and their present environments, recognizing themselves and the contents of the members' own narratives as objects in that social environment. In this way, the leader attempts to provide an environment for facilitating members' development that acknowledges their separate realities while providing a social context for the dialogic reconstruction of personal narratives.

Group work involves a reciprocal understanding of the other and should focus upon the form of the relationship between the leader, the group, and its members. A central feature of group work, therefore, involves negotiating multiple relationships over time in service of the development of all participants to the relationship. Rather than intervene in the lives of individual members as autonomous human beings, therefore, the leader should attend to relationships among members as humans who are beings in a developmental context. From such a perspective, the group leader no longer asks "How should I relate to group members?" or "What should be the appropriate (right) course of action (read as intervention)?" Rather, group leaders should recognize that they are already in relationships with the group members as other people. Consequently, leaders should ask of themselves: "Who am I in this relationship? How am I relating to the other? What can I do right now to effect a change that will encourage greater understanding between us?"

In building the proper context for change, the group should provide opportunities for members to be at their best in a supportive social setting while being challenged to work toward the realization of a preferred, but as yet unrealized, future. Rather than conceal members' genius and reveal their disabilities, group counseling should reveal their genius and minimize their disabilities. Understanding that "resistance" reflects natural self-protective processes that serve to guard the integrity of the individual's meaning making system, leaders should work to understand the member's experience rather than attempt to change or control it.

Because people socially construct their world, they are, in actuality, always cooperating with others. Through their efforts to maintain their integrity, they show us who they are and, by implication, how they think they can change. The sensitive group leader will use such opportunities to acknowledge the member's reality and seek to understand its significant in the member's life. Similarly, pathology can be seen as a condition under which the "natural facilitation of development has somehow and for some reason broken down" (Kegan, 1982, p. 256). In this context, group work represents an attempt to provide an environment that will facilitate the member's efforts to restore some balance to the world as the member knows it.

Because groups are social organizations, the leader is encouraged to move the members beyond those factors affecting them directly to a consideration of factors affecting the group as a whole. As noted earlier, "the self reveals itself in its choices." Thus if I choose the kind of person I want to be, I will not only know who I am, but the group will also know what I have to do to be the kind of person I would like to be. In encouraging each member to share in this process with one another, the group comes closer to creating a common vision toward which they can work. In realizing this vision, the leader must build a level of trust within the group that will allow the members to take responsibility collectively for what is happening and will happen. Effective dialogue must be developed so that effective communication patterns can be established (Habermas, 1981/1984; Tennyson & Strom, 1986). By definition, the members in a group are those who share a goal and state their desire to do something about making it happen (Walter & Peller, 1992). Within the context of group work, therefore, group members should be asked to commit themselves to help one another within the group to realize self-identified goals related to desired behavior outside the group. By successfully negotiating their place within the group in the pursuit of compatible goals, group members will enhance their own development in the process.

Finally, constructivism recognizes that people are fundamentally social beings. As such, nearly all clients will belong to a supportive social network. Recalling that people are never not themselves, the group leader recognizes that the group takes place for only a brief period of time in the member's life and that significant change is likely to take place away from the group, outside the view of the leader. As well, the leader recognizes that the goal of treatment is to return the member to the "real world" outside of the group. One's life in the group, therefore, is not necessarily accepted as having a timeless quality but is viewed rather as a window of opportunity for change along a life trajectory.

REFERENCES

Baldwin, J. M. (1902). *Social and ethical interpretations in mental development* New York: Macmillan. (Original work published 1897.)

Basseches, M. (1984). *Dialectical thinking and adult development*. Norwood, NJ: Ablex Publishing.

Beier, E. (1966). *The silent language of psychotherapy: Social reinforcement of unconscious processes*. Chicago: Aldine.

Botwinick, A. (1993). *Postmodernism and democratic theory*. Philadelphia: Temple University Press.

Carlsen, M. B. (1988). *Meaning-making: Therapeutic processes in adult development*. New York: W. W. Norton.

Carson, R. (1969). *Interaction concepts of personality*. Chicago: Aldine.

Cartwright, D., & Zander, A. (1968). *Group dynamics; Research and theory* (3rd ed.). New York: Harper & Row.

Conner, M. B. (1987). *Postmodern culture: An introduction of the contemporary*. Oxford: Blackwell.

D'Andrea, M., & Daniels, J. (1994). Group pacing" a developmental eclectic approach to group work. *Journal of Counseling & Development, 72,* 585-590.

Derrida, J. (1982). *Margins of philosophy*. Chicago: University of Chicago Press.

Dewey, J. (1910). *How we think*. Boston: D. C. Heath.

Dewey, J. (1944). *Democracy and education*. New York: Free Press. (Original work published 1916)

Dewey, J. (1960). Theory of the moral life. In J. Dewey & J. Tufts, *Ethics* (1932; rev. ed., Part II). New York: Holt & Co.

Dewey, J. (1963). *Experience and education*. New York: Collier.

Feffer, M. (1970). Developmental analysis of interpersonal behavior. *Psychological Review, 77,* 197-214.

Feixas, G. (1990). Personal construct theory and the systemic therapies: Parallel or convergent trends? *Journal of Marital and Family Therapy, 16,* 1-20.

Foucault, M. (1972). *The archaeology of knowledge*. New York: Harper Colophon.

Friedman, S. (Ed.). (1993). *The new language of change: Constructive collaboration in psychotherapy*. New York: Guilford.

Gergen, K. (1991). *The saturated self: Dilemma of identity in contemporary life* New York: Basic Books.

Gergen, K., & Gergen, M. (1988). Narrative and self as relationship. In L. Berkowitz (Ed.), *Advances in experimental social psychology*. New York: Academic Press.

Gibbs, J. (1979). The meaning of ecologically-oriented inquiry in contemporary psychology. *American Psychologist, 34,* 127-140.

Goodman, N. (1984). *Of mind and other matters*. Cambridge, MA: Harvard University Press.

Haan, N. (1977). Two moralities in action contexts: Relationships to thought, ego regulations, and development. *Journal of Personality and Social Psychology, 36,* 286-305.

Hare, A. P. (1976). *Handbook of small group research* (2nd. ed). New York: Free Press.
Hayes, R. L. (1986). Human growth and development. In M. Lewis, R. L. Hayes, & J. Lewis (Eds.), *An introduction to the counseling profession* (pp. 36-95). Itasca, IL: F. E. Peacock.
Hayes, R. L. (1991). Group work and the teaching of ethics. *Journal for Specialists in Group Work, 16,* 24-31.
Hayes, R. L. (1993). A facilitative role for counselors in restructuring schools. *Journal of Humanistic Education and Development, 31,* 156-162.
Hayes, R. L. (1994a). Counseling in the postmodern world: Origins and implications of a constructivist developmental approach. *Counseling and Human Development, 26*(6), 1-12.
Hayes, R. L. (1994b). The legacy of Lawrence Kohlberg: Implications for counseling and human development. *Journal of Counseling and Development, 72*, 261-267.
Hayes, R. L., & Oppenheim, R. (1997). Constructivism: Reality is what you make it. In T. Sexton & B. Griffin (Eds.), *Constructivist thinking in counseling practice, research, and training* (pp. 19-40). New York: Columbia University Press.
Homans, G. C. (1950). *The human group*. New York: Harcourt, Brace, & World.
Howard, G. S. (1986). *Dare we develop a human science?* Notre Dame, IN: Academic Publications.
Howard, G. S. (1990). Narrative psychotherapies. In J. K. Zeig & W.M. Munion (Eds.), *What is psychotherapy?* (pp. 199-201). San Francisco: Jossey-Bass.
Ivey, A. (1986). *Developmental therapy: Theory into practice.* San Francisco: Jossey-Bass.
Jansen, E., & Glinow, M. (1985). Ethical ambivalence and ethical reward systems. *Academy of Management Review, 10,* 814-822.
Jencks, C. (1986). *What is postmodernism?* New York: St. Martin's Press.
Kegan, R. (1982). *The evolving self.* Cambridge, MA: Harvard University Press.
Kelly, G. A. (1955). *The psychology of personal constructs.* New York: Norton.Kohlberg, L. (1969). Stage and sequence: The cognitive-developmental approach to socialization. In D. Goslin (Ed.)., *Handbook of socialization theory and research* (pp. 347-480). Chicago: Rand McNally.
Kohlberg, L. (1981). *Essays on moral development (Vol. I): The philosophy of moral development.* New York: Harper & Row.
Kohlberg, L., & Mayer, R. (1972). Development as the aim of education. *Harvard Educational Review, 43,* 449-496.
Kvale, S. (Ed.). (1992). *Psychology and postmodernism.* Newbury Park, CA: Sage.
Langer, J. (1969). *Theories of development.* New York: Holt, Rinehart and Winston.
Lewis, P. (1987). Therapeutic change in groups: An interactional perspective. *Small Group Behavior, 18,* 548-556.
Lyddon, W. J. (1995). Forms and facets of constructivist psychology. In R. Neimeyer & M. Mahoney (Eds.), *Constructivism in psychotherapy* (pp. 69-92). Washington, DC: American Psychological Association.
Lyotard, J. (1983). *The postmodern condition: A report on knowledge.* New York: Basic Books.

Mahoney, M. J. (1985). Psychotherapy and human change processes. In M. J. Mahoney & A. Freeman (Eds.), *Cognition and psychotherapy* (pp. 3-48). New York: Plenum.

Mahoney, M. J. (1991). *Human change processes: Notes on the facilitation of personal development*. New York: Basic Books.

Mair, M. (1988). Psychology as storytelling. *International Journal of Personal Construct Psychology, 1,* 125-138.

McGrath, J. E. (1984). *Groups: Interaction and performance.* Englewood Cliffs, NJ: Prentice-Hall.

Mead, G. H. (1934). *Mind, self, and society*. Chicago: University of Chicago Press.

Neimeyer, R. (1985). *The development of personal construct psychology*. Lincoln: University of Nebraska Press.

Neimeyer, R. (1994). The role of client-generated narratives in psychotherapy. *Journal of Consulting and Clinical Psychology, 7,* 229-242.

Noam, G. (1988, Spring). A constructivist approach to developmental psychopathology. In D. Nannis & P. Cowan (Eds.), Developmental psychopathology and its treatment [entire issue] (pp. 91-121). *New Directions for Child Development* (No. 39). San Francisco: Jossey-Bass.

Piaget, J. (1924). *Judgment and reasoning in the child.* New York: Harcourt Brace.

Piaget, J. (1954). *The origins of intelligence in children.* New York: International Universities Press. (Original work published 1936)

Piaget, J. (1955). *The language and thought of the child.* Cleveland: World Publishing. (Original work published 1926)

Piaget, J. (1960). The general problem of the psychological development of the child. In J. M. Tanner & B. Inhelder (Eds.), *Discussion on child development: A consideration of the biological, psychological, and cultural approaches to the understanding of human development and behavior* (Vol. 4). New York: International Universities Press.

Polkinghorne, D. (1993). Narrative configuration in qualitative analysis. Paper presented at the annual meeting of the Qualitative Research Interest Group, Athens, GA, January.

PRECIS. (1987). [Editorial], pp. 7-24.

Rest, J., Turiel, E., & Kohlberg, L. (1969). Relationships between level of moral judgment and preference and comprehension of the moral judgment of others. *Journal of Personality, 37,* 225-252.

Riegel, K. F. (1979). *Foundations of dialectical psychology.* San Diego, CA: Academic Press.

Rickey, G. (1967). *Constructivism: Origins and evolution*. New York: Braziller.

Rorty, R. (1983). Method and morality. In N. Haan, R. N. Bellah, & P. Robinson (Eds.), *Social science as moral inquiry* (pp. 155-176). New York: Columbia University Press.

Rosen, H., & Kuehlwein, K. (Eds.). (1996). *Constructing realities: Meaning-making perspectives for psychotherapists.* San Francisco: Jossey-Bass.

Saari, C. (1991). *The creation of meaning in clinical social work*. New York: Guilford.

Schon, D. *Educating the reflective practitioner*. San Francisco: Jossey-Bass.

Shaw, M. E. (1981). *Group dynamics: The psychology of small group behavior* (3rd ed.). New York: McGraw-Hill.

Sherif, M., & Sherif, C. W. (1956). *An outline of social psychology* (rev. ed.). New York: Harper & Row.

Tennyson, W., & Strom, S. (1986). Beyond professional standards: Developing responsibleness. *Journal of Counseling & Development, 64,* 298-302.

Viney, L. (1990). Psychotherapy as shared reconstruction. *International Journal of Personal Construct Psychology, 3,* 437-456.

Vygotsky, L. S. (1986). *Thought and language* (Kozulin, Trans.). Cambridge, MA: M. I. T. Press. (Original work published 1934)

Werner, H. (1973). *The comparative psychology of mental development.* (2nd ed.). New York: International Universities Press. (Original work published 1940)

White, M., & Epston, D. (1990). *Narrative means to therapeutic ends.* New York: W. W. Norton.

Wren, T. (1985). Whistle-blowing and loyalty to one's friends. In W. Heffernan & T. Stroup (Eds.), *Police ethics: Hard choices in law enforcement* (pp. 25-43). New York: The John Jay Press.

Yalom, I. (1995). *The theory and practice of group psychotherapy* (4th ed.). New York: Basic Books.

Chapter Fourteen

THERAPIST USES OF SELF IN GROUP PSYCHOTHERAPY

Judith Simon

Since the beginnings of psychotherapy the role of the therapist has been discussed, studied, deliberated and evaluated. As the field evolved, questions of therapists' self-revelations or personal involvement were pondered. From the early years of Freud's work, with his adherence to a non-disclosing stance, to the 60's emphasis on therapist genuineness, clinicians have come and gone full circle on this issue. Therapists continue to grapple with questions regarding how they use themselves in their work.

The issues of countertransference, self-disclosure, therapist activity and therapist "realness" are as relevant to the group therapist as they are to the individual therapist. Therapist use of self in groups, however, is a more complicated matter. With numerous patients, transferences, diverse needs and concurrent dynamics, therapist intentional use of self in group psychotherapy becomes a delicate art.

The literature on this subject is sparse in contrast to other treatment and therapist-patient relationship issues. Within the context of individual psychotherapy, there are many professional writings on transference and countertransference (Freud, 1933; Little, 1951; Racker, 1968), some writings on the real relationship (Greenson, 1978), much about clinical interventions with various patient populations (Gunderson, 1984; Masterson, 1976; Spotnitz, 1976), and few writings on therapist self-disclosure, (Simon, 1988; Weiner, Cody, & Rosson, 1974). Most of the work addressing therapist self-disclosure is presented within the context of specific situations, e.g., the therapist's illness, (Abend, 1982,) or marriage (Flaherty, 1979). In an attempt to fill this gap, this chapter discusses four aspects of therapist use of self in group therapy: the leader's role, the "real" relationship between therapist and patient, countertransference, and therapist self- disclosure (transparency). Clearly, these categories overlap.

The Modern Analytic theoretical orientation is founded on the premise that resolution of resistances and maturation experiences are the crux of the therapeutic process (Ormont, 1990). Stemming from the assumption that the patient's ego development has been arrested early in life, ego boundaries ebb and flow. Resultant anger and aggression is often turned against the self, undermining self-satisfaction and actualization. Enabling patients to verbally express this aggression is central to the work. All emotions, especially strong feelings that have been repressed, are encouraged.

There is common resistance to these expressions. Many families teach children that intense emotions are unwelcome or simply bad. It is not unusual for an adult to have experienced negative reactions from ardent and/or violent manifestations of emotions. It is typically uncomfortable to be a participant or witness to strong emotions. To counteract this resistance and discomfort, the group encourages verbal expression of all emotions and, therefore, aspects of the group process increase the likelihood that resistances will surface. Leaders understand that they themselves experience emotions and sometimes utilize these induced feelings as tools for group facilitation. The Modern Analytic group leader assumes an active role in enhancing communications, highlighting resistances and encouraging members' verbal participation.

A brief presentation of the author's concept of a well functioning psychodynamic psychotherapy group provides the context for this paper. Such a group is characterized by evolving trust, safety, cohesion and dynamic interpersonal interactions among its members. Group members are asked to freely discuss all feelings and reactions, i.e., to allow other members to have an effect on them and to discuss these effects. All members are expected to participate in the group process and members agree to take their share of the total talking time. The usual goal for a group member is increased capacity for intimacy in interpersonal relationships. The grouping of several patients affords opportunity for positive and negative transference, modeling, honest feedback, mirroring and support for growth.

Leader's Role

While most of the value and growth stems from interactions among and between the group members, the leader's role as facilitator is critical. The leader is ultimately responsible for the success of the group and for each member obtaining therapeutic value. Clinicians function in multiple capacities when leading groups; they must pay attention to the individuals and their personal issues concurrently with attending to the entire group's viability. In the Modern Analytic model, the leader must be active to guide discussion, to protect members from emotional hurt, to highlight important occurrences and intra-group connections, and to ensure that each member participates and maintain the boundaries. Some groups, and oftentimes a particular group, function well without the leader's active involvement. Nonetheless, the leader must be attentively present to encourage meaningful interaction.

The level of leader activity is greatest in the early stages of the group's life. During the early meetings the leader functions in an educative capacity enabling the participants to learn how to be group members. The stage is being set for interpersonal connections and honesty where members are taught the value of verbally expressing feelings and reactions as they are experienced. The leader educates about the concept of transference in a language that communicates the importance of unconscious projections onto others. Attention is paid to members' anxieties regarding inclusion and exclusion and evolving group cohesion. For example, commenting on these similarities when they occur enhances identifications with other members. Leaders communicate tolerance for all feelings by welcoming any and all reactions directed their way, and repeated receptivity to a broad spectrum of emotions is expressed. Anger and aggression are especially invited towards the leader. First, verbal expression of anger is regarded as maturational. Second, expressing these difficult emotions towards the leader protects individual members from directly experiencing the emotion.

While leaders are often aware of unexpressed anger and aggression in their groups, it may require their own initiative to enable the group to verbalize these emotions. A leader's willingness to be a lightening rod for aggression is crucial because often such anger or hostility is expressed through displacement on some disliked there-and-then authority figure or acted out behaviorally. In one example, Rose, the group leader, had to cancel an excessive number of group sessions over a six-month period. The group members appeared to act out their reactions by coming late, canceling and not showing up. Additionally, the sessions lacked energy for several weeks. The leader suspected that there was unexpressed anger and resistance but was unable to elicit the material. Following consultation and encouragement to directly invite the aggression towards her, the group moved past its impasse.

The leader establishes and maintains the group contract, which is important for creating the context for the group's trust and boundaries and also for ensuring that resistances come to the fore (Ormont, 1988). Lateness is a common resistance manifestation. In one case, Barbara was consistently late. Typically she sat down, mumbled apologies for her tardiness, and joined the group discussion. Given that she was never present at the opening, she never contributed to the tone or early flow of the session. After many weeks, the leader inquired of Barbara, "How should we understand your lateness? Since you know about the group contract, including being on time, it probably has some meaning for you." Barbara dismissed it: "I am late every place!" Weeks later she was on time and disclosed that she now had some insight into her lateness.

The source of resistance can also be the leader. In the following vignette, the leader colluded with the group's resistance by allowing the monopolization and not assisting the members to participate. Jay, a novice group leader, presented his new group for consultation. One woman had monopolized the time for six sessions: others offered suggestions but Bob complained that only Nancy was "getting into it." Although Jay said that he was growing impatient, he wanted to let the group unfold. He was waiting for the members to take Nancy on. Jay was questioning his role as leader, struggling between adhering to psychoanalytic tenets of free-association and the realization that the group was not functioning well. It became clear to Jay that his inactivity was collusion with the group's resistance. He returned to the group and observed that the group was allowing Nancy to do all the work. Thus, he began to take charge of his group.

Management of silences also comes under the purview of the leader's responsibility. Silences are less well tolerated, less productive, and usually expressions of resistance by the group in the early stages of the group process. The leader's role is to titrate the length of the silence with respect to its productivity and to break the silence if it progresses to impasse. Exploration of members' withheld communications is productive. The leader can break the silence with a question and an instruction. For example, "What is this silence about?", followed by "a group is often silent when members are reluctant to speak about something. What is not being said?"

The level of leader activity is ideally calibrated by the group's functioning. It is the leader's task to be sufficiently active to ensure that meaningful interactions are occurring and that all members are involved. Sometimes a direct intervention is required, e.g., "Are you getting what you need in here?" or a reminder that members must take their share of the group's time, while keeping in mind that a well functioning mature group may be most benefitted by a less verbally active leader.

The Real Relationship

As the multiple dynamics and relationships unfold in the therapy group, so too does the therapist's relationship with each member and with the group as a whole. Although the therapist is not personally transparent, he/she is very present and this realness constitutes a facet of the therapist's contribution to the process. The following case example helps point out the important distinction between therapist authenticity and therapist transparency. Carolee was a particularly feisty and contentious long-term group member. She consistently questioned authority figures in her family, at work as well as in the group. The leader actually liked and admired her for her wit, intelligence, and perseverance in her personal growth. At the same time, she was difficult to contain and frequently challenged the leader's clinical capacity. One of several instances involved group discussion about money and equality, and Carolee verbally attacked the leader for not being fair and making mistakes. Having thought and observed that Carolee is often unaware of her impact on the people she confronts, the leader disclosed how he was feeling. He said, with a tone congruent with the intensity of her demeanor, "I am feeling attacked and upset and I would like you to know that that is how you are impacting me right now." Carolee fell silent. She then said, "Oh my God, I didn't mean to do that. I really like you." The therapist's authentic sharing helped facilitate Carolee's insight.

The therapist's personal openness is not necessarily fundamental to genuineness, empathy and warmth. However, the therapist's presence and personal authenticity is critical to the relationship. The real relationship is a component of the total object relationship between therapist and patient. It has been variously referred to as the non-transference relationship or extra-transference relationship. This was first alluded to by Anna Freud (1954, p. 357) when she said, "There is, even with the strictness of the analytic setting, a varying amount of ease felt by the analyst and patient." Greenson (1978) further defines the real relationship as the sense of being genuine but not synthetic or artificial, and realistic but not inappropriate or fantastic.

In the group context, the therapist's realness communicates respect and empathy, expresses emotions, e.g., tears, laughter, anger, and acknowledges errors, thereby modeling human imperfection and communicating respect. A common therapist mistake is an empathic failure to explore reactions and anger when the therapist errs. Therapist acknowledgment of an error moves patients towards increased individuation (Epstein, 1990.) This vignette illustrates the co-therapists' realness as they shared an error. Whether or not the group would meet over the Christmas holidays was being discussed in the group. The therapists made the decision not to meet given the small anticipated attendance. One member, Charles, expressed anger and disappointment. Over the following months the therapists came to feel that they had erred in canceling the group sessions, understanding that their action communicated low commitment to the group and especially to these two members. The same question arose the next year and Charles recalled his upset. The therapists acknowledged their error to the group and found that it furthered trust. This time the therapists maintained the group's schedule.

An example of therapist realness enhanced Sally's departure from group. Good-byes were being said in her last session. The leader was very fond of Sally, personally identified with her struggles, and was sorry to have her leave the group. While it was clear that Sally had grown, the leader's assessment was that she could continue to benefit from group. This therapist wanted to say something supportive and acknowledging without burdening Sally with his positive subjective countertransference. He felt and said with apparent warmth, "it has been very satisfying for me to have been a partner in your maturation." This example also demonstrates a positive termination in the transference relationship, freeing Sally to work with an alternate therapist in the future and also exemplifies the power of being authentic within the real relationship.

Occasionally the content of a session is emotionally powerful. In this vignette, the leaders felt that it would have been impossible not to react. And indeed, the absence of a reaction would have been inappropriate and possibly injurious. In a long-term relatively stable group, one of the well-liked men said that he wanted to share something that was difficult and important to share. He had the group's attention and, with emotion building in his voice, informed the group that his 20-year-old daughter just tested HIV positive. Everyone in the room–the two therapists included–teared. The ability to share in intense emotions, when they occur within the group, is a vital aspect of the real relationship.

Sometimes a real occurrence in the life of the therapist demands attention to the real relationship. The following vignette addresses the therapist's likely need for surgery, which raised questions regarding management. Dr. B., a solo group leader, learned that it was likely that she would have to undergo serious surgery in about one month. As a psychodynamic therapist, she was very reluctant to disclose personal information. She struggled with balancing the needs and possible right of the group members to know what might lie ahead with her commitment to personal privacy. It was the acknowledgment of the real relationship between her and the group members that clarified the correct intervention; they needed to know about the probable disruption and basic details of her medical crisis. Sharing with them the probability of surgery, her plan for a substitute therapist and reassurance that a complete recovery was anticipated communicated respect and humanity. In all of the aspects mentioned, the real relationship is distinct from the transference relationship. It is, basically, the human-to-human connection that is vital to the therapeutic work.

Countertransference

Countertransference has evolved from being regarded solely as an impediment in psychotherapy to being a potentially useful tool, which can enhance the work. Freud's earliest comments on the subject admonished the physician to recognize this countertransference in himself and overcome it (1912). He later stated that "Every analyst's achievement is limited by what his own complexes and resistances permit" (Freud, 1933). Heimann (1950) wrote, "My thesis is the analyst's emotional response to the patient within the analytic situation represents one of the most important tools for his work. The analyst's countertransference is an instrument of research into the patient's unconscious." Winnicott (1949), Heimann (1950), Little (1951), and Racker (1968), among others, have marked the shift from the "countertransference is bad" to the "countertransference can be useful" point of view. Spotnitz (1976) further modified the conceptualization of countertransference by suggesting that it consists of objective and subjective components.

Reactions that originate in therapists' own psyche and allow their own complexes and resistances to intervene is termed subjective countertransference. These include feelings towards a patient which are reflective of his/her own life and are equivalent to Freud's description of countertransference. In contrast, objective countertransference is what the therapist experiences toward a patient as a result of the emotional contagion from the patient or group, i.e., a reaction that most anyone would have to a given person, situation or behavior. Such feelings would be induced in most therapists and in most group members. The following vignette describes a use of objective countertransference. Tom, one of the oldest group members, was sharing with the group that he and his family finally went to a family therapist, something the group had been urging for a long time. Understandably, there was much interest and much support. But it went on and on: the therapist observed that the members were inquiring about numerous details and she recognized that she was growing uncomfortable. She mentally scanned her reactions and ascertained that the reactions were not reflective of her personal psychology but rather an objective reaction to what was transpiring in the group. She then, again internally, groped for the accurate label for her feelings and then said to the group, "I am feeling puzzled by what's happening: people seem very interested in the details of Tom's experience but I am left feeling puzzled. I'm not sure what's going on." She suspected group resistance. Michael responded, with more affect than had been in the room for several minutes, that he wished his family had sought family therapy when he was a teenager. Jackie then talked about her acting-out older sister who got all the attention and how resentful she was and continues to be. Bert, a single parent who has worked very hard to improve his parenting skills, acknowledged how much better he and his son were relating. Tom added that he had been feeling grilled but felt that he couldn't rebuff people's interest.

Group resistance, in the form of several withheld reactions, can undermine connections and experiences of intimacy among members of the group. This following vignette describes subjective countertransference and demonstrates its detrimental effect. Mary, a long term group member, opened group with expressions of anger towards the therapists for an occurrence from several months' back. She recalled that she had expressed anger at member Bill for frequently being late and that neither of the therapists had validated her feelings. She described in detail what she recalled and felt in that earlier session addressing her remarks directly to the two therapists for several minutes. One of the therapists, Karl, then responded, "I don't think I was here that day." That remark closed off further expressions of anger towards Karl and, although Mary then re-directed her remarks to the female therapist, an opportunity was lost for her. Not until the therapists' wrap-up discussion did Karl realize that his remark stifled Mary and that it reflected some of his personal issues regarding culpability for his adolescent misbehaviors and his frequent excuse "I wasn't there!"

Therapist self-awareness is the basic underpinning of a clinician's ability to understand and use countertransference. (On the other hand, therapist absence of self-awareness is an open-door to countertransferential errors.) Therapist's induced feelings are a potentially helpful tool for deepening understanding of a patient.

Therapist Self Disclosure and Transparency

Therapist self-disclosure can be therapeutic, irrelevant, or counterproductive to the work. When used well, it can foster the therapeutic alliance, model mature behavior, validate patients and their reality, enhance patients' autonomy, boost the observing ego or break an impasse (Simon, 1988). When used poorly, it can injure, distract or collude with the patient's or group's resistance. In its benign form, it is simply a waste of time. This is true for individual and group psychotherapy.

There are fewer occurrences of disclosure of the leader's personal thoughts or information in group than in individual therapy. The therapist as person is less significant in a context in which there are numerous self-objects available to each member. Therapists of varying theoretical persuasions view therapist self-disclosure differently. For example, psychodynamic therapists who readily utilize transference in their work will generally self-disclose less readily that existential and Gestalt therapists. Additionally, professional thinking about self-disclosure and transparency changes over time.

Yalom (1975) expressed caution regarding "unchecked enthusiasm for leader transparency ... demonstrated by champions of the human potential movement." In 1990, Yalom encouraged therapist transparency in groups, stating that "it counteracts the effect of transference, or irrational responses to the group leader. In the face of ever-increasing reality-based data revealed by the therapist, members find it more and more difficult to maintain their fictitious beliefs about the group leader." Yalom continues to say that he regards factors other than transference as being more important in group therapy. He specifies altruism, vicarious learning, and cohesiveness. Clearly these are important factors: they can be successfully encouraged without therapist self-disclosures.

This writer disagrees with Yalom, finding it more productive to encourage rather than discourage patients' projections onto the therapist and the group's members. Their projections are entrees into personal dynamics and provide information about obstacles to interpersonal relationships. Patients' specific requests for information often constitute defenses against their fears and wishes. By directly answering personal questions, a potential affective connection may be precluded; answers can serve as a collusion to "protect" patients from their feelings. To deny the opportunity to learn more about oneself contradicts the purpose of psychotherapy.

Yalom also endorses therapists' disclosing ordinarily private personal information and personal reactions to model interpersonal sharing and honesty for the group members. While not disagreeing, this author believes that greater personal learning can be achieved by enabling patients to manifest this kind of sharing in the group. Encouraging them to be models for each other advances their experience of the satisfaction from contributing and connecting. However, if the therapist's reaction is thought to be valuable information for a patient and no group member expresses a similar one, therapist disclosure of this reaction is appropriate.

By being relatively non-disclosing, the leader allows transferential projections and individual's judgments. Knowing the leader's attitudes and preferences precludes a type of neutrality which, when present, facilitates free affective expression. Leader transparency dilutes the leadership role and undermines safety for some members. The author believes that the more the therapist is known the less free the patient feels to speak openly.

Research does not affirm that therapist self-disclosure enhances patient disclosure in group therapy (Weiner, Cody, & Rosson, 1974). The group leader who shares personal feelings or experiences in a group is not engaged in a simple therapeutic intervention because several variables affect the impact of therapist self-disclosure, e.g., timing, context, individuals' perceptions, and content. What some patients experience as modeling and validation may be experienced by others as undermining confidence in the therapist or as a distraction from the work. Concurrent evaluation of multiple patients' reactions requires careful consideration on behalf of group therapists. Despite the possible pitfalls, carefully and deliberately thought-out self-disclosure can be a potent intervention.

Therapist neutrality is not synonymous with therapist secretiveness and withholding. There is often more therapeutic mileage to be gained from the patient's own explorations of their inquiries than from prompt gratification of the request. Following exploration, further information is often no longer requested. The example demonstrates this point. Jim, a long-term group member, himself a spiritual man, wanted to know if the co-therapists were spiritual people. Rather than answering directly, the therapist inquired as to what he thought. He thought that they were not. She then inquired what might be behind the question. He insisted that he was simply curious. She gently said that she was skeptical about "simple curiosity" and asked another group member what she thought Jim might be struggling with. The member suggested that since Jim always ended up feeling abandoned by people he cared about, he was looking for an excuse to fend off his positive feelings towards the co-leaders. Jim sobbed. Later he said that he really didn't give a damn if the leaders were spiritual or not.

As in individual therapy, the patient's diagnosis may be a criterion for therapist self-disclosure. For example, neurotic patients who can tolerate the frustration of non-gratification and understand that the therapists' stance is therapeutic will be able to stretch and grow. Borderline patients who need their therapist to assist them in graining a sense of predictability often require a therapist self-disclosure to proceed. The group leader was preparing for a one-week vacation which included arranging for a substitute leader for a post- hospitalization group (Simon, 1992). The arrangement was fully discussed with the group over the course of the month preceding the absence. In the week before the vacation, one member, Maria, a bright woman with a borderline diagnosis, was direct in expressing her fear regarding the separation. The leader was prepared to disclose her plans and asked Maria if she wanted to know where she was going. Maria was clear that she did not want to know. As the members were leaving at the end of the session another member, Elaine, inquired of the leader, "So where are your going?" Maria quickly and emphatically said, "I don't want to know where she's going!" The therapist heard and understood Elaine's inquiry as a desire to connect but felt that a response was not mandatory. At the same time it was vital that Maria's stated need not to know be respected, at least until further exploration. In this example, the therapist's task was to evaluate and behave therapeutically for as many of the members as possible. The member in the most acute need at the time determines the therapist's disclosing or non-disclosing intervention.

Group patients sometimes push therapists for explanations of their clinical actions, for example, "Why are we adding a new member now?" As therapists grow and redefine their own clinical work, changes are apparent in their behavior and become the object of questions. Examples include altering the maximum number of group members, changing billing procedures, lengthening the time period between announcing a new member and the member's actually joining, and intervention changes which may be generally more or less gratifying. Often the most therapeutic response is not a direct answer.

Inviting the patients' projections, fantasies and exploration can foster insights. A quick direct answer denies this opportunity. The leaders had changed the method of distribution of bills following one of the therapist's reading a paper on management of money in group therapy. She convinced her co-therapist that this was, indeed, a superior method. He agreed while acknowledging his discomfort. (This was not discussed in the group.) Considerable reaction by the group members persisted over months and evolved into questions about the co-therapists consensus regarding the change. When the therapists did not directly respond, the members were able to experience their issues of fairness, male-female power and aggressive feelings. Private discussion between the therapists amplified the difficulty clinicians have in balancing maximum therapeutic benefit with being genuine and empathic. Therapist resistance to the group's displeasure and aggression often impacts the ability to manage these kinds of questions. By rising to the challenge to not gratify, the therapists were able to foster discussion of these important issues, including allowing expression of anger.

When able to withhold gratification and explore the material underlying questions, therapeutic gain is probable. At the same time, it must be noted that gratification (therapist self-disclosure) is sometimes the preferred therapeutic stance. Occasionally, thoughtful gratifying interventions may be the more therapeutically potent intervention.

Therapist self-disclosure and transparency is one of the aspects of the therapist's self that can be utilized in the work. Clinicians' own self-awareness increases the ability to use this facet of oneself skillfully.

Summary

Therapist use of self covers a broad range of therapist behaviors. Attention has been paid to these issues in individual therapy for many years; only recently have these concerns been addressed in group psychotherapy. Uses of countertransference, self-disclosure, the "real" relationship, and how active or inactive the therapist is are all aspects of this complex question. Although this chapter discusses these major aspects of the therapist's self, in reality they cannot be easily delineated. For example, the line between therapist transparency and the real relationship is difficult to discern, let alone discuss. Nonetheless, therapists' cognizance of these components of the therapeutic relationship enhances therapeutic skill. Appropriately utilized, these uses of self can enhance the work. Inappropriate use can derail the group's work, consume valuable time or heighten group resistance and undermine the development of the group.

The author wishes to thank Jerome Gans, M.D., for his valuable contributions to this paper.

References

Abend, S. M. (1982). Serious illness in the analyst: Countertransference considerations. *Journal of the American Psychoanalytic Association*, *30 (2)*, 365-379.

Epstein, L. (1990). Some reflections on the therapeutic use of self. *Group*, *14(3)*, 151-156.

Flaherty, J. A. (1979). Self-disclosure in therapy: Marriage of the therapist. *American Journal of Psychotherapy*, *33(3)*, 442-452.

Freud, A. (1954). The widening scope of indications for psychoanalysis: Discussion. *Writings*, *4*, 356-376.

Freud, S. (1912). Recommendations to physicians practicing psycho-analysis. *The standard edition of the complete psychological works of Sigmund Freud, vol. 12*. London: Hogarth Press.

Freud, S. (1933). *The future prospects of psychoanalytic therapy. Collected papers vol. II.* London: Hogarth Press.

Greenson, R. (1978). The real relationship between the patient and the psychoanalyst. In *Explorations in Psychoanalysis*, New York: International Universities Press.

Gunderson, J. G. (1984). *Borderline personality disorder*. Washington DC: American Psychiatric Press.

Heimann, P. (1950). On countertransference. *International Journal of Psychoanalysis*, *31*, 81-84.

Little, M. (1951). Countertransference and the patient's response to it. *International Journal of Psychoanalysis*, *32*, 32-40.

Masterson, J. F. (1976). *Psychotherapy of the borderline adult*. Washington DC: Bruner Mazel.

Ormont, L. (1988). The leader's role in resolving resistances to intimacy in the group setting. *International Journal of Group Psychotherapy*, *38*, 29-45.

Ormont, L. (1990). The craft of bridging. *International Journal of Group Psychotherapy*, *40(1)*, 3-17.

Racker, H. (1968). *Transference and countertransference*. New York: International University Press.

Simon, J. C. (1988). Criteria for therapist self-disclosure. *American Journal of Psychotherapy*, *XLII(3)*, 404-415.

Simon, J. C. (1992). The group therapist's absence and the substitute leader. *International Journal of Group Psychotherapy*, *42(2)*, 287-291.

Spotnitz, H. (1976). *Psychotherapy of preoedipal conditions*. New York: Jason Aronson.

Weiner, M. F., Cody, V.F., & Rosson, B. (1974). Studies of therapist and patient affective self-disclosure. *Group Process*, *6*, 27-42.

Winnicott, D. W. (1949). Hate in the countertransference. *International Journal of Psychoanalysis*, *30*, 69-74.

Yalom, I. (1975). Theory and practice of group psychotherapy. New York: Basic Books.

Chapter Fifteen

ADDRESSING "GROUP SCLEROSIS" THROUGH FISHBOWL SUPERVISION

Rendueles Villalba, Keri Lemmond and Scott Baymiller

INTRODUCTION

In this chapter we discuss a fishbowl technique of supervision that was developed to address "group sclerosis"--a state of fortified inertia in which group members collaboratively resist change. A fishbowl is a subgroup arrangement in which a group within a group is formed. The activity of the inner group is observed by the outer. Various permutations of this structure have been utilized in group psychotherapy. A search of the Medline (1966 to June 1998) and PsycLIT (1887 to June 1998) databases revealed a very small and outdated literature on fishbowl practices. We found three studies of the clinical use of fishbowls in psychotherapy (Berkovitz & Sugar, 1976; Fluet, Holmes & Gordon, 1980; Ho, 1976), two articles on the use of fishbowl techniques in the experiential training of psychotherapists (Cooper, 1972; Kane 1995) and one experimental study of a fishbowl variant of T-group experience (White, 1974). From this minimal literature, one might conclude that fishbowl techniques are rarely used clinically, and their use has essentially been confined to intractable populations (adolescents and prisoners) inspiring "extreme measures."

We offer the following discussion to raise awareness of the relatively neglected therapeutic option of the fishbowl, and describe a variation of the practice that facilitates both the therapy of group members and the supervision of co-therapists trainees.

The Problem of "Group Sclerosis"

Establishing and maintaining safety is such a first principle of any psychotherapeutic situation that it may seem paradoxical to suggest that a therapist should ever strive to actually evoke anxiety in his/her patient. From an Ericksonian purview of group development, the first developmental task will be the attainment of trust versus mistrust. Success will largely depend on a psychologically safe environment that will permit patients to relax maladaptive defenses, traverse a vulnerable transitional stage, and ultimately discover and practice adaptive coping styles. A sufficiently large number of factors threaten safety within group therapy that a therapist may assume a sentinel-like role, vigilantly safeguarding the group from elements that appear to subvert the "holding environment" they are attempting to create. This is a standard starting position for most, if not all, effective therapists. Yet this view has its problems.

The assumption that patients will naturally seek a path towards health if the therapist simply clears the way of threatening obstacles likely underestimates the static forces that keep a patient locked within their maladaptive coping styles. The desire or motivation for real change may be so atrophied by years of discouragement and demoralization that a patient may lack the initiative for a genuinely therapeutic venture. Many patients have the desire for change, but lack an internal locus of control. They passively wait for something to happen to them. Consequently, their therapy merely reifies their pathologic dependency. Other patients may not know what they want from therapy. Though unhappy and seeking relief, they are ignorant of their options for growth. As a result, they wander aimlessly for a goal that forever eludes them. Finally, resistance to change may be sufficiently fortified by secondary gain that its inertia overwhelms the comparatively diminutive impulse to move.

Groups composed of such individuals are at great risk of *group sclerosis*--that is, a state of static equilibrium in which the group compromises work for the comfort of only safe (familiar, well-rehearsed) topics or coping styles. In a functional work group, safety is *instrumental*. It is a *means* by which members gather strength to ultimately face a challenge. In the sclerotic group, safety is a not a means but an *end*, and supplants the desire to meet a therapeutic challenge.

One telltale sign of group sclerosis is a primary focus on there-and-then material. Any use of here-and-now material is largely of limited significance. In fact, a group may placate a therapist by complying with a here-and-now line of questions only to demonstrate the "ineptitude" of the approach--thereby disarming the therapist of his/her most powerful tool. The more the therapist pursues a here and now focus, the more the group begins to see the therapist as irrelevant or hostile. Rather than the sentinel of safety, the therapist is perceived as a threat. The antagonism may lead to group dropouts or revolts. A novice therapist may begin to feel inadequate, insufficiently empathic, or even sadistic. Consequently, they may return to a "polite," non-challenging, permissive position in an effort to regain favor with the group. Having effectively censored the therapist, the group re-establishes its default equilibrium, adding another layer of sclerosis from this "victory" over the threat of change. Repetitions of this cycle set in motion a feedforward effect, progressively strengthening the group's resistance and weakening the therapist's credibility.

Group sclerosis is perhaps most fruitfully viewed by combining the insights of Bion's Basic Assumptions with the dynamics of a "complex adaptive system" (Waldrop, 1992). Viewing a group as a complex adaptive system predicts that members will continuously attempt to maintain or increase their status within a group by adapting to the behavior of the other members and the group-as-a-whole. As the members engage in reciprocal adaptation, a perpetual flux is put into motion, since each member is adapting to a set of moving targets. The composite behavior of group members coalesces to produce an emergent property Bion described as a Basic Assumption. Bion (1961) identified three basic assumptions that may operate within groups--dependency, fight-flight, and pairing.

As group members struggle to adapt to (gain control over) a basic assumption operating within their group, the assumption rises to a conscious level and is scrutinized. Once the assumption is called into question it usually loses its operative status. The group is now freed of its control and consequently moves on to establishing a new basic assumption. Bion identified the presence of a "dual" (antithetical concern) within each basic assumption. This dual is the substrate from which the next developmental stage (basic assumption) germinates. When the dual is given due consideration by the group, it opens the most probable adaptive path away from the conflict at hand. If the dual is suppressed (for example out of irrational fear), the "adaptive" impetus becomes recursive, reifying the group's operating basic assumption--thereby locking it into the state of group sclerosis. Consider the following example:

Two groups, A and B, begin their activity from a position of dependency. As members of group A attempt to adapt to their group's passivity, they may develop a wish (the dual) to break free of the suffocating inactivity. As a result, the fight-flight assumption takes hold. Soon the open conflict achieves a critical point in which individuals feel vulnerable as separate agents (a new dual). The adaptive impulse consequently leads them to form alliances, to better weather the storm of conflict. Consequently, the pairing assumption ascends to prominence. Once pairing is underway, trust within these alliances set the stage for cooperation and shared identification with a common goal. At this point, group A has achieved the status of a "work group."

Group B also begins with the basic assumption of dependency. The same "dual" desire to free themselves of the tyranny of their passivity emerges. However, unlike group A, group B is unable or unwilling to explore their dual concerns. The dual is inaccessible or taboo. The feedforward adaptive process is denied its natural path to a new basic assumption. Consequently, group B "adapts" to its dependency by reifying the dependency, making it more subtle, more ego syntonic, more unconscious. At each turn the group's attempt to adapt to itself ratchets its behavior deeper into the dependency assumption in an effort to cope with the lack of developmental movement. At this point, group B has developed group sclerosis within the dependency assumption.

Group sclerosis should be distinguished from a growth-enhancing stasis that Lacan called *formal stagnation.* [While Lacan developed this idea to describe a development stage in an individual psyche (see Boothby, 1991), we believe it may be fruitfully applied to group development.] Formal stagnation is a process by which an immature group holds itself still in order to gaze upon itself and establish a gestalt image of "groupness" from a flurry of otherwise confusing chaos. One may see this as a group's process of achieving *object constancy.* Unlike group sclerosis, formal stagnation is a relatively brief hiatus from change or movement that ultimately expands the group's understanding of itself. Formal stagnation facilitates eventual change and reality-oriented adaptation.

Certain highly homogeneous populations may be predisposed to group sclerosis. We observed this in two groups, one exclusively composed of male USA military veterans (see the appended transcript for a discussion about this group), and another exclusively composed of homosexual men infected with HIV. This second group illustrates the dynamics at play in an extreme form of group sclerosis.

A group of HIV positive gay men were seeking a new therapist. The authors were consulted by one of the group members who arranged for the group to meet with us and discuss a potential transfer of their therapy to our leadership. The group had met weekly for six years. Their previous therapist confided to us that she felt she had come to a dead end. Although the group agreed that little work was being accomplished, they resisted termination. After two years of unrelenting resistance to termination, the therapist suggested a change in leadership.

We met with the group for three orientation sessions and offered to take up their therapy. Although they were initially appreciative of the offer, they opposed every treatment guideline we proposed. As they routinely saw each other casually (outside of sessions), they refused the recommendation that they discontinue these contacts. They objected to time limitations--if the group needed extra time for a session they intended to have it. They also refused the suggestion that the treatment course be limited to 6 months. Many members expected to receive treatment free of charge.

It was readily apparent that each member had settled into a fixed role within the group. Perhaps because of a clearly hypertrophied mutual dependence, they were constantly bickering. They repeatedly stated that the group's discussion should be limited to the challenges of living with their HIV infection. We suggested that occasionally a here-and-now approach would bring their interpersonal relationships to the fore. The group vociferously resisted this suggestion. After the third session, a chosen spokesperson for the group telephoned to tell us that they had decided not to continue seeing us as therapists. They would instead meet on their own.

While there may be some debate about the specific needs of this particular population, we believe this vignette illustrates the phenomenon of group sclerosis. We came to believe that the group had unconsciously equated its termination with death itself. Many of the members had stated that they felt they were alive largely because of the support they received from the group. Their prior therapist may have initiated this belief when she suggested, in a case report (about this group), that their immune function was positively affected by the group therapy. The irony is that the group had outlived the therapy. There was little novel work being done. The members lamented that they were bored, that they wanted a fresh outlook from a "more directive therapist." Their dependency was partly expressed as a desire for a therapist that would limitlessly hold the group in a state that would magically protect them from their illness. This ideal therapist would also entertain them out of their boredom, yet not challenge their immune enhancement fantasy with here-and-now processing. Resistance to an interpersonal focus possibly served to avoid a fear that examination of their bickering might lead to disintegration of the group. The *dual* desire of autonomy in the face of this overwhelming dependency was blocked by an unconscious taboo that equated autonomy with eventual death. Trivial bickering was the only tolerated expression of the dual. To prevent the bickering from developing into an actual fight or flight, more and more effort was expended to draw the members into a tighter circle of interdependency. Consequently, the group members came to rely on each other for almost daily contact (outside of sessions) for support and reassurance of the group's integrity. Growth beyond this dependency assumption appeared to be stifled by an unconscious fear that every step forward was a step closer to the dreaded termination.

What generally prevents the formation of group sclerosis? One might argue that naturally occurring factors will perturb the group's stasis, preventing it from hardening into the stalemate of sclerosis. "Accidents" will occur. This truism may buoy the confidence of the therapist who has learned to scan for, and capitalize on these "unpredictable" events-- the kernels of here-and-now material. This improvisational skill, however, is rarely intuitive. It is usually only attained from considerable therapeutic experience and tolerance of ambiguity. In the hands of an experienced therapist, group "accidents" may become a primary engine of therapeutic change. However, in the hands of an inexperienced or non-confident therapist, these accidents may go unnoticed or unattended, thereby potentially contributing to countertherapeutic processes. Here is where the value of a good supervisor becomes most evident. Drawing on the experience of the supervisor, a novice therapist may receive mentoring to develop an eye for the here-and-now, and build confidence to improvise productively in the face of uncertainty.

Returning to the paradox of safety, the cost of group sclerosis should be fairly evident at this point. Clearly, safety has its cons as well as its pros--hence, the standard affirmation that therapists offer patients when they "take a risk" toward the direction of change. Risks cannot occur in a completely safe environment. By definition they are mutually exclusive. Therefore, instead of striving for an Eden of safety, many modern schools of psychotherapy have integrated a beneficial role of anxiety within treatment. It is generally recognized that avoidance of anxiety-provoking stimuli usually makes the anxiety worse. Conversely, anxiety-evoking techniques (implosion, flooding, desensitization or stress inoculation) have achieved reputable success (Law, Logan & Baron; Meichenbaum & Deffenbacher, 1988; 1994; Skolnick, et al. 1982). Therapeutic mastery comes from the correct titration of safety and anxiety simultaneously.

This dynamic resembles the Yerkes-Dodson law--the classical contingency of optimal performance on a sufficient but tolerable level of arousal. When anxiety is too high, performance is impaired by excessive inhibitory processes - e.g. thought blocking, confusion, stuttering, etc. When anxiety is too low, insufficient stimulatory processes impair performance, e.g. apathy, false confidence. This basic tenet of anxiety and performance may be applied to group behavior. Bion (1961) observed that the best group performance occurred when a group felt threatened by an enemy. Members united and organized to mount their attack. Bion exploited this combat paradigm by calling upon the therapeutic group to organize its attack on the "enemy of neurosis" (Bion, 1961;

Symington & Symington 1996). Bion's legacy has included a variety of *hot seat* approaches--some with disastrous results (Malan, et al. 1974; Scheidlinger, 1993). It therefore stands reiterating that good therapy is both safe and challenging. Striking this balance to prevent or treat group sclerosis is the goal of the fishbowl technique of supervision we are developing.

In this chapter we will outline specific goals, strategies, and outcomes we have discovered from experimenting with this technique. At the time of this writing, Keri Lemmond and Scott Baymiller are Brown University residents in Psychiatry under the supervision of Rendueles Villalba, an attending psychiatrist at Rhode Island Hospital and a Brown University instructor in the Department of Psychiatry and Human Behavior. This biographical information is included because we will discuss the above outlined items from both sides of the supervisory experience.

Fishbowl Supervision

Fishbowl Supervision gets its name from the structural arrangement of the technique. Immediately following a one-hour group therapy session, the group members move their chairs to the periphery of the room while the co-therapists and supervisor meet in the center of the circle. The patients observe a twenty-minute segment of supervision as if viewing through a transparent barrier--hence the name fishbowl. Ideally, the supervisor is familiar with the group and has observed the session via a two-way mirror or closed circuit TV. The trainees are instructed to imagine they are in private supervision and try to ignore the patients' presence in the room. The patients are asked, in advance, not to speak during the supervision. Comments and questions that arise among the group members may be discussed in the ten-minute period following the supervision, as well as in subsequent therapy sessions.

The supervisor guides the co-therapists through a discussion of the important actions of the session that has just occurred. Trainees are asked to do two types of analyses. First, the trainees chronologically detail the events of the session, explicating the indigenous meanings they have concluded. This is analogous to the work of an ethnographer reporting their field observations after immersing themselves in the culture of a specific group. It is best (less threatening to the on-looking group members) if the trainees start with a group-as-a-whole perspective, then move to specific interpersonal interactions, and then finally individual disclosures. The supervisor will encourage the co-therapists to discuss their role within the group, e.g., their rationale for specific interventions, their understanding of their successes and failures within the group, how they would like to move in new directions, etc. With careful guidance to preserve therapeutic boundaries, some aspects of transference and countertransference may be discussed in the fishbowl. This discussion will offer the group not only an opportunity to hear about the here-and-now, but to see it in action as well.

The second type of analysis involves viewing the group from an outside, *big picture* perspective. How is the group enacting basic group processes or employing basic assumptions, e.g., dependency, fight/flight, pairing, etc.? Trainees are asked to describe the *lawfulness* of the group's actions, its movement through developmental stages, and its management of existential anxieties.

These two types of analyses are separated here for the purpose of description. In practice, fishbowl observations, free associations, interpretations, and questions flow spontaneously back and forth between both types of analyses. The supervisor must listen for neglected areas and maintain a balance of viewpoints. In the end, the here-and-now activity of the group is thoroughly discussed. Single dogmatic statements are avoided. Truth is seen as *plural* and contingent on subjective as well as objective perspectives. If elements of group sclerosis are identified, trainees are encouraged to explore the possible determinants fostering them.

At the close of the twenty-minute fishbowl, the supervisor leaves the therapy room (to resume remote observation), and the co-therapists take their places within the circle. During the final ten minutes, the group is queried about their thoughts and here-and-now experience of the fishbowl. All group members are encouraged to voice their reactions.

The fishbowl technique is most indicated when the group appears stuck in a unproductive pattern of relating, e.g., they are avoiding work in the here-and-now or complacently resting on the accomplishments of previous work. The fishbowl seems to be ideal for stimulating transitions through developmental stages of the group-as-a-whole. The entire group should participate in deciding (1) whether to incorporate fishbowls into the treatment, and (2) how often the fishbowls should be conducted. How the group goes about making these decisions is "grist for the mill." (Refer to Law, Logan, and Baron (1994) for a interesting discussion regarding patients' range of desire for control of their treatment.).

Before using the fishbowl technique, it is crucial to have a stable group formed, which is closed to new members and interested in utilizing this therapeutic intervention. If these key elements are not in place, the fishbowl could produce several untoward effects. Initiating fishbowl sessions too early in the course of a group's development may trigger dropouts or "paralysis through analysis." Comments made by the co-therapists and supervisor should be delivered in such a way that the group members are able to absorb and use them. The fishbowl experience can run the risk of alienating individual group members who do not receive equal time in the fishbowl discussion. However, by no means is it mandatory or necessarily therapeutic to discuss each group member's actions in every fishbowl. The fishbowl should not become an outlet for the co-therapists to do the majority of their work or to direct future sessions. Lastly, careful attention should be paid to the possibility of becoming too intellectualized in the fishbowl and miss the point of experiencing and exploring the here-and-now.

Knowing when, and how often, to enlist the fishbowl technique is crucial to the stability of the group. Fishbowls that occur too frequently may begin to interrupt productive group work or create excessive concerns among group members about being evaluated. A large part of the value of fishbowl sessions for the group, is the "outsider's perspective" it offers. Conducting the fishbowl too frequently would begin to blur the boundary between the therapy and supervision, thereby decreasing the group's ability to hear the fishbowl material as an objective outsider's analysis of the group's behavior. Finally, to the extent that each fishbowl session reminds the group that their co-therapists are *trainees*, it may reduce some the trainees' credibility and autonomy. We found that a frequency of one fishbowl per 6 to 8 sessions is reasonable in a 16 to 20 session course of time-limited treatment.

The fishbowl experience seems to have its greatest benefit if the supervision is carried out as though group members are not present. There is a tendency to fall into the trap of "talking at" the group members to promote change. This is not likely to be productive. Fishbowl sessions likely evoke a lot of anxiety in group members, biasing the way they may hear the discussion. Care should be taken to speak simply and slowly, and to avoid comments that may be misconstrued as a personal attack of an individual. Fishbowl sessions should not be used as a crutch or sanction to confront group members. It is not primarily intended to be indirect therapy. The goal is to dismantle the impasse of a sclerotic group.

A decision to do a fishbowl should not be entertained lightly. Getting started can be quite anxiety evoking for trainees *and* supervisors who do not have prior experience with fishbowl techniques. A rehearsal of the range of possible questions to be discussed in the first fishbowl may alleviate some of the initial anxiety. This is less necessary in proceeding fishbowl sessions, as anxiety naturally decreases with experience.

The Rationale of Fishbowl Supervision

Fishbowl supervision is a technique used to promote work and help a therapy group concentrate on the here-and-now. The physical arrangement creates a parallel group within a group. The fishbowl *turns the table* so to speak to allow the group members to observe the co-therapist during their mentoring. It offers psychoeducation and immediate feedback to the group to facilitate their understanding of what is going on in the therapy. It also models productive use of the here-and-now. Conversely, the trainees are given a unique learning challenge: that is, to process their understanding of the group activities while preserving a mindfulness of how these thoughts may be heard by the group. It is far easier to criticize the group behind a closed door. Whether this critique translates into effective therapeutic interventions, however, remains to be seen. In fishbowl supervision, the actual presence of the patients in the room challenges the trainees to phrase their questions and comments in neutral, jargon-free terms. In so doing, the trainees learn how to engage the group while tackling sensitive issues. The trainees may practice the art of disagreeing without being disagreeable. Yalom (1995) set a precedent for including patients in the processing of the group material. Following his sessions, he dictated process notes that were mailed to the group members. He found this greatly facilitated the therapy. Fishbowl supervision simply takes the process one step further to maximize here-and-now activity within the group.

Agazzarian (1997) has observed from her systems centered perspective, that complex group behavior commonly exists within nestled hierarchies. As a consequence of hierarchical structure, isomorphy emerges--that is the tendency for parallel relationships to appear between various subset tiers of the hierarchy. Fishbowl supervision concretely exploits this phenomenon. For example, a training therapist receives mentoring from a supervisor. This experiential form of learning in many ways approximates the therapeutic "mentoring" the trainee provides to the patients within the group. Likewise, a patient within the group may ascend to a work leader position (perhaps by identifying with the therapist) and "mentor" another less socially skilled group member. An economy of insight may be derived from appreciating these isomorphic relationships.

Insight acquired through analyzing one set of relationships may be utilized to interpret parallel processes in the counterpart isomorphic relationships. For example, through introspection a trainee may become aware of certain issues they wish to discuss with their supervisor but avoid out of fear their ignorance will be judged or interpreted in a non-flattering light. The trainee who has had this ambivalence has acquired first-hand knowledge of the parallel ambivalence his patients are likely experiencing. Using this experiential knowledge derived from supervision, the trainee will be attuned to group events that may indicate ambivalence. When the trainee recalls what factors lead to the resolution of avoidance, an empathic compass is created that may guide the wording, timing, and overall approach of therapeutic interventions within the group. Often the trainee will inadvertently duplicate, in therapeutic interventions, actions observed in a supervisor--consciously or unconsciously exploiting the swing position between two isomorphic relationships.

One challenge for trainees is to simultaneously attend to a multitude of relationships. Every comment or question will have direct and indirect effects. Given that usually only one, rarely two, relationships can be fully maintained in awareness at any one time, the side effects of an intervention will outnumber the explicitly intended direct effect. A trainee must develop comfort with this fact and learn not to become paralyzed. An aesthetic must develop that allows action without a need to predict all possible outcomes. Fishbowl supervision may help trainees cross an impasse toward acquiring this aesthetic. The unpredictable transience of the moment can become a source of exhilaration. As the trainee enjoys this quality of the here-and-now, pleasure in, and mastery of uncertainty may be a source of isomorphic encouragement to the patients. The chosen interventions will reflect this confidence. In turn, confidence may serve as a reservoir that patients may draw from (model).

It has been our experience that a group's motivation to work is greatest around the initiation and termination of treatment. Group sclerosis usually develops insidiously during the middle phase of treatment. Fishbowl sessions may break up the long expanse of the middle phase of treatment into segments that help a group to experience the march of time. As periodic fishbowls act to mark time, they make it much more difficult for a group to procrastinate and helps them to anticipate the eventual termination of the group. Each fishbowl session creates a milestone of group activity. A group will usually show a burst of work in anticipation of a fishbowl, as their anxiety about what will be discussed in the fishbowl mounts. Likewise, for a few sessions following a fishbowl, the group will show a heightened amount of work as they process the material raised in the fishbowl.

Fishbowl supervision has the potential to open an entirely new flow or discovery of subconscious material among the group members and/or co-therapists. To a certain extent, trainees may use the supervisor as a conduit to communicate with the group. In posing and answering questions in fishbowl supervision, trainees indirectly disclose their clinical observations one step removed from the actual experience. For the novice therapist, it is something of a hurdle to simultaneously observe and participate in the group process. The fishbowl offers an opportunity to make an intervention, albeit indirectly, without having to be immediately concerned with (and likely inhibited by) the group's reaction. We found that after practicing free-association and interpretive skills in the fishbowl, trainees generalized these competencies to their work with the group outside of the fishbowl. This in turn produced a greater degree of therapeutic engagement and flexibility among the trainees and group members. Fishbowl supervision may impact the working relationships among the co-therapists and supervisor. In our experience, the fishbowl contributed to the development of a greater degree of cohesiveness and complementarity between the co-therapist trainees. The fishbowl has the additional feature of involving the supervisor more actively in the actual therapy of the group. In the traditional arrangement of group therapy supervision, the supervisor may never meet the group members, much less take part in the actual therapy. The fishbowl draws the supervisor into the therapy room. This 'rubbing of shoulders" with the group members enriches the supervisor's capacity to identify salient issues quickly, as well as capture subtleties of group process that might otherwise go unattended.

Conclusion

Clinical experience has demonstrated that fishbowl arrangements in group psychotherapy can increase spontaneity, reduce defensiveness, and facilitate the acquisition of a productive attitude toward therapy in otherwise difficult clinical populations (Berkovitz & Sugar, 1976; Fluet, et. al 1980; Ho, 1976). Despite this success, research on the clinical use of fishbowls has been largely neglected in the literature. We have described a fishbowl variant in which supervision of co-therapist trainees is conducted in the presence of the group members. The beneficial, and potentially untoward, effects on trainee development and group process have been discussed--especially in relation to the phenomenon of "group sclerosis" (a special form of resistance to here-and-now work). We hope to inspire further exploration of the clinical and training potential of this robust tool.

References

Agazarian, Y. M. (1997). *Systems-centered therapy for groups*, New York: Guilford Publications, Inc.

Berkovitz, I. H., & Sugar, M. (1976). An experience in teaching adolescent group psychotherapy: Observers become participants. *The International Journal of Psychotherapy 26*, 441-453.

Bion, W. (1961). *Experiences in group*, London: Tavistock Publications.

Boothby, R. (1991). *Death and desire: Psychoanalytic theory in Lacan's return to Freud*, New York: Routledge.

Cooper, C. L. (1972). Group training for the helping professions: The Hampshire experience, *Interpersonal Development 3(1-4)*,152-158.

Fluet, N. R., Holmes, G. R., & Gordon, L.C. (1980). Adolescent group psychotherapy: A modified fishbowl format. *Adolescence 15(57)*. 75-82.

Ho, M. K. (1976). Fishbowl therapy with prison inmates. *Social Work, 21(3)*. 235-7.

Kane, C. M. (1995). Fishbowl training in group process. *Journal for Specialist in Group Work 20(3)*, 183-188.

Law, A., Logan, H., & Baron, R.S. (1994). Desire for control, felt control, and stress inoculation training during dental treatment. *Journal of Personality and Social Psychology 67(5)*,926-936.

Malan, D. H., Balfour. E. H. G., Hood, V.G., & Shooter, A. (1974) Group psychotherapy: A long-term follow-up study. *Archive of General Psychiatry 33*,1303.

Meichenbaum, D., & Deffenbacher, J. (1988). Stress inoculation training. *The Counseling Psychologist 16(1)*,69-70.

Scheidlinger, S., ed. Kaplan, H. I., & Sadock, B. J (1993). "History of group psychotherapy." *Comprehensive Group Psychotherapy*, pp. 2-10. MD: Williams & Wilkins.

Skolnick, P., & Paul, S. M., ed. Gatchel, R. et al. (1982). Anxiety: Mechanisms and Management. *Handbook of psychology and health, Vol. 1: Clinical psychology and behavioral medicine: Overlapping disciplines*, NJ: Lawrence Erlbaum Associates, Inc.

Sober, E., & Wilson, D. C. (1998). *Unto others: The evolution and psychology of unselfish behavior*, MA: Harvard University Press.

Symington, J., & Symington, N. (1996). *The Clinical thinking of Wilfred Bion*. New York: Routledge.

Waldrop, M., (1992). *Complexity: The emerging science at the edge of order and chaos*, New York: Simon & Schuster.

White, K. R., (1974). T-groups revisited: Self-concept change and the "fish-bowling" technique. *Small Group Behavior 5(4)*, 473-485.

Yalom, I., (1995). *The theory and practice of group psychotherapy*, 4th ed., New York: Basic Books.

APPENDIX A:

Fishbowl Transcript

The following is a paraphrased transcript of an actual fishbowl supervision session conducted by the authors. The majority of the actual discussion has been preserved. We edited the text only to correct speech dysfluencies or poor grammar. The names of the group members have been changed to preserve confidentiality.

Six group members were present for this session: Daniel, Richard, Jim, George, Jack, and Henry. Ronald had dropped out a few weeks earlier.

This particular fishbowl session was typical of the supervision the authors did over the course of a yearlong collaboration. The fishbowl occurred on the twelfth therapy session of a course of nineteen. All group members were USA military veterans receiving treatment at a Veteran's Affairs Medical Center.

The fishbowl technique was initiated on the seventh session after the trainees and supervisor observed the group to be stuck in a fight-flight mode of engagement. This was manifested by perpetual challenges of the co-therapists' status/authority, an "us against them" attitude regarding the group members' place in society at large, and extreme avoidance of here-and-now work.

We would like to highlight the discussion regarding various countertransference issues that were raised. In the fishbowl, the supervisor (RV) commends the trainees (KL and SB) for openly discussing their experience of being rejected by the group. This recognition was made for many reasons, and illustrates the multi-dimensional benefits of fishbowl supervision. First, the trainees correctly addressed the key issue of group sclerosis within the fight-flight basic assumption. Second, they displayed courage in actually exploring their reactions to the group's negative transference, and opened communication for the group to address their transference explicitly in following sessions. Third, their frank discussion of the here-and-now modeled an ideal norm of communication for group members. Not only did the trainees *and* group members benefit from this session, everyone benefited synergistically in ways that could not be replicated in traditional supervision.

RV: I'm going to follow your lead, but to get us started why don't you run through a chronology of the session?

SB: During the opening few minutes, everyone was explaining their feelings about Ronald leaving. There was a lack of energy among the group members with a lot of focus in the there-and-then. They expressed some final hope that Ronald would return. This discussion led to multiple different issues. George became more involved in here-and-now events, than he had in the past.

RV: Any thoughts about why George's participation was different today?

SB: It could be due to a few reasons. First, termination was brought up today. Maybe George wanted to get more out of the group before it ended, as though his time were limited. Second, the group seemed depressed and his input could be viewed as motivational to the group. Finally, George's increased participation could reflect that George has taken over Ronald's role in the group--that is, the experienced leader.

RV: (to KL) Any other thoughts?

KL: I see George's role as something like a grandfather; uh, I mean an experienced leader, especially when he shares stories from his past.

RV: I'm curious. Why do you want to take back the grandfather metaphor?

KL: ... I see him as a grandfather; this is a good thing, but he may be offended by the attention to his age.

RV: Do you think the group sees him in that light?

KL: They may. We haven't asked the group members. They haven't said anything about it.

RV: Getting back to your initial comment, Scott, about the role of elders in the group, now that Ronald may have left--Ronald was the other elder of the group. George steps in to provide where Ronald left open. I agree with your take on this. I had a similar impression ... George made a number of comments to other members that were hope instilling, very generative. It's the sort of thing that older individuals do to leave their mark. They leave something behind for the younger generation ... This suggests there's an ongoing feeling of termination, a death in essence, that the group is preparing for. The group wants to leave hope behind and it comes from the older member. Any thoughts about that?

SB: The termination of the group is a death?

RV: It may feel that way, yes.

KL: I felt like the group was grieving today. They seemed solemn and quiet. It felt like something definitely had happened.

RV: What do people do when they grieve?

KL: Sometimes they regress, talk about old things, people leaving, they relive memories, sometimes show anger that someone has left. Not everyone is convinced that Ronald has left the group. The group keeps hoping Ronald will come back.

RV: So, you see hope in the group about Ronald's possible return, but potentially there is denial as well. I thought it was pretty clear that Ronald said he wasn't getting anything out of the group. And yet I heard the group say that "that's not what I heard. I heard that Ronald really felt that he was getting something." There seems to be an effort to rewrite history.

KL: Right. I'm confused about that. Because when he was in the group, Ronald clearly stated he had not gotten anything from group, but maybe he said something outside the group ... sending a different message outside the group.

SB: It would be tough for the group to accept that one of their members wasn't benefiting from the group. Many group members have expressed the benefits that the group has had on them, while Ronald maintained that the group wasn't helping him. It is difficult to think that Ronald gave the group a chance and then decided that it was not worth it.

RV: So it sounds that you think that the group is reacting to a feeling of rejection?

SB: Sure!

RV: ... like saying, "look Ronald wasn't getting anything out of the group, but I'll show you - everyone else, that I am." Consequently, there were a series of testimonials of how the group had helped these members.

KL: We were also trying to get them to say that, too. I noticed that myself.

RV: I noticed that as well. What did you make of that?

KL: I don't know. We, I, may feel rejected. I posed my question to get a positive response to, "Are you getting something out of the group?"

RV: So, a little damage control?

SB: Yes, I think you did do that, Keri. ... I think I was trying to get someone to identify with me to say that they felt rejected. This ploy of mine likely corresponded to how I felt regarding Ronald's absence.

RV: In fact, I want to comment on the timing of your questions - both of you did this. There were moments where a few members had spoken ... I think Jim at one point was telling a very poignant story about how he felt that his communication with his wife had markedly improved and he seemed very genuine about this. There was essentially no lag time before you stepped in to direct this into a line of questions to get the result, "See how useful the group is." I thought there was a little bit of leading the witness in this. I would be careful of that. I'm glad though to hear that you are willing to scrutinize your motives here. ... other thoughts that come to mind?

KL: When Henry spoke today, he talked about past experiences of not getting much out of group. He accepted that he had put a wall between himself and the rest of the group. I disagree with that last part a little bit. He did speak and engaged others today. He is accurate though when he says the wall is up. I feel resistance from him each week. Maybe he doesn't want people in, or he is testing the group. He may want people in, but is afraid of rejection.

SB: I agree. I think Henry's participation today was a big step forward and something of an accomplishment. When it was pointed out to Henry that he seemed to be more involved though, there seemed to be some retraction--drifting back into passivity.

KL: I'm also worried about us talking about this in the fishbowl--how it will affect future sessions by talking in the fishbowl.

RV: So you are finding that you're much more self-conscious of your interactions and that there are times when it is difficult for you to engage with Henry because you don't know how to negotiate it.

KL: All the time.

RV: Because you're not sure how he's going to take it?

KL: So I thought George did an excellent job ... George talked to Scott and myself, he is saying great things ... compassionate things ... maybe George has the ability to connect with Henry.

SB: There was a lot of work done during that particular four minutes. George was talking directly to Henry about very delicate subject matter without "cutting any corners" or going around the issue.

KL: I think Henry actually heard him.

RV: It sounds, in a way, that you are "cashing in" on George's grandfatherly image potentially.
... You felt that Henry would be more accepting of feedback from George because of his elder position in the group.

SB: Out of all of the group members, George is the one most suited to give feedback to Henry. He is the eldest. Henry would accept criticism least of all from Keri and myself.

RV: Why is that?

SB: Because we are much younger.

KL: We are also doctors.

RV: Why is that important?

KL: He doesn't trust doctors. Every time he speaks, this is one of his statements. Why would he trust us? We are part of the establishment; he has been "screwed" by the establishment.

RV: So you're trying to tailor the message, or deliver it, in a way he can hear it. And part of the way you do that is to call upon other members in the group that can deliver it in a way that he can hear it. And hopefully also, he is hearing it now.

KL: I didn't know that was going to happen. It just happened that way. It wasn't planned. I had no idea George would take over that role. He was able to do it--and we went with it.

RV: In fact, that's part of the excitement of group therapy. It's live, it's not pre-recorded or taped. And you never know what's going to happen. I think there's a message behind that--that's the way life is; it's very unpredictable. That's what makes it interesting. Hopefully that's true within the life of group, too-- that people don't become so routinized in their patterns of talking with one another that they are not surprised occasionally by each other ... We still have two minutes. ... Anything else?

KL: Jack is doing well ... He is speaking spontaneously to other members, making eye contact, engaging people in conversations, listening to people. I think that is good.

SB: Today he was more spontaneous. He usually only responds when called upon or occasionally asks what seem to be "programmed" by us. It seems that he rarely asks questions out of his own curiosity.

RV: It's kind of a tall order to be spontaneous by design, and I think that's been something that Jack has tried to do in the past. I think he is painfully aware that at times he is very silent. And so he makes an effort to be spontaneous and that undermines the whole idea.

SB: That happened a couple of weeks ago. Richard mentioned that Jack didn't speak very much. The next week Jack asked "pre-planned questions," which I thought were in response to Richard 's comments.

KL: I find it interesting, other group members rarely give direct feedback to Henry or Jack.

Richard did it once ... I wonder what is going though the group members' minds and their response to all that we brought up.

RV: Well there's a good place to pick up.

INDEX

S

T

U

V

W

Y